The Canadian General Election of 2000

The Canadian General Election of 2000

Edited by Jon H. Pammett
and Christopher Dornan

THE DUNDURN GROUP

TORONTO · OXFORD

Design: Jennifer Scott
Printer: Webcom

Canadian Cataloguing in Publication Data

The Canadian general election of 2000

Includes bibliographical references.
ISBN 1-55002-356-X

1. Canada. Parliament — Elections, 2000. I. Pammett, Jon H., 1944– . II. Dornan, Christopher.

FC635.C366 2001   324.971'0648   C2001-930646-6   F1034.2.C366 2001

1   2   3   4   5   05   04   03   02   01

THE CANADA COUNCIL | LE CONSEIL DES ARTS
FOR THE ARTS | DU CANADA
SINCE 1957 | DEPUIS 1957

ONTARIO ARTS COUNCIL
CONSEIL DES ARTS DE L'ONTARIO

We acknowledge the support of the *Canada Council for the Arts* and the *Ontario Arts Council* for our publishing program. We also acknowledge the financial support of the *Government of Canada* through the *Book Publishing Industry Development Program* and *The Association for the Export of Canadian Books,* and the *Government of Ontario* through the *Ontario Book Publishers Tax Credit* program.

Care has been taken to trace the ownership of copyright material used in this book. The author and the publisher welcome any information enabling them to rectify any references or credit in subsequent editions.

J. Kirk Howard, President

Printed and bound in Canada.⊛
Printed on recycled paper.

www.dundurn.com

Dundurn Press
8 Market Street
Suite 200
Toronto, Ontario, Canada
M5E 1M6

Dundurn Press
73 Lime Walk
Headington, Oxford,
England
OX3 7AD

Dundurn Press
2250 Military Road
Tonawanda NY
U.S.A. 14150

Table of Contents

Introduction

If there is no comeback by the Conservatives, and no breakthrough by Reform, the Liberals will be left as the only national party in Canada. Under this possibility, the party may establish itself in a hegemonic governmental position well into the next century.
— Introduction, THE CANADIAN GENERAL ELECTION OF 1993

In some ways, the 1997 election was a logical extension of the results of the 1993 election.
— Introduction, THE CANADIAN GENERAL ELECTION OF 1997

The Canadian General Election of 2000 presents a puzzle of interpretation. In one sense, it resembles closely its predecessors of 1993 and 1997, which resulted in two majority Liberal governments. The Liberal victory in 2000 means the continuation of the dominance of that party, reasserting its control of the Federal Government for a third straight term in office. It appears unassailable, free to enact as much or as little legislation as it wishes, free to brush off opposition criticisms and ignore minor scandals, free to even now position itself to win a 2003/4 election by selecting the agenda for public discussion in the intervening years.

In another sense, however, it is easy to believe that Canadian federal politics is in a state of transition. A plurality of the public may not have seen an urgent reason to vote for change in 2000, but such a state of mild satisfaction will not last forever. The seeds of discontent are there: a faltering economy in 2001, continuing public disquiet with the state of social programmes, persistent feelings of regional grievance underlying the seeming acceptance of the *status quo*. There is a general expectation that something is going to happen — the question is, "What?"

The arguments that 2000 was a transitional election may appear a bit nebulous. They centre around the increase of support for the Canadian Alliance party, which achieved a growth of 7 percent in its popular vote over its predecessor, the Reform Party. Despite such an improvement in votes, particularly in the province of Ontario which had been a key element in the Alliance strategy, and despite an increase of six seats in Parliament, the Alliance campaign has been generally termed a failure. Expectations were for much higher than these incremental gains, and the measurement of performance against expectations rather than actual results often sets the tone for discussion, and indeed action.

The problems for the Alliance in the 2000 election were greatly exacerbated by the election timing. The personal decision by Prime Minister Jean Chrétien to call an election in the fall of 2000 rather than the spring of 2001 appears in retrospect to have been a masterstroke of political strategy. The economic downturn that struck Canada and other nations in the winter of 2001 would have provided a very different context for a spring 2001 election than prevailed in the fall of 2000. An election campaign that avoided prominent economic "problem" type issues would not have been possible; calls for action would have resounded from all sides. The Alliance platform proposing more extensive tax cuts than the Liberals had already announced could have been placed in the context of providing stimulation for an economic recovery, rather than the context of irresponsible cuts at the expense of social services. The Liberal attacks on the Alliance for its ruminations about reforming the health care system with more participation of the private sector, and on the Alliance proposals to hold referendums on moral issues like abortion, would likely have been less effective in establishing a public image for the party as a right-wing extremist group if the Alliance could have maintained a steady insistence on talking about a faltering economy.

As it was, the sudden call of a fall election caught the Alliance and other parties off-guard. Only a minority of candidates had even been nominated. Fund-raising for the campaign was not completed. Party platforms were not prepared and published in final form. Nobody was ready. Of course, the Liberal Party was not ready either — it had not nominated the majority of its candidates, raised its total campaign warchest, or written its campaign manifesto. But it was a bigger, more established operation; these things could be done on short notice. Most important, its leadership was well-established and well-known. Prime

Minister Chrétien may not have been especially popular with the public, but he wasn't unpopular either, and above all, he was a known quantity. The Alliance had, but a few months earlier, selected a new untried leader, Stockwell Day, who had to establish himself at the helm of a party that was itself supposed to be "new." If he had had six or eight months to create an election agenda, define a public profile for himself and the party, find better candidates in the Centre and East of the country, and above all, if he had been able to attack the Liberals over a broken economy, the result might have been better for the party. With stronger results for the Alliance, the 2000 election would have looked much more like a transition to a new pattern of party competition than a continuation of a one-party-dominant system.

In the 1997 election, the Progressive Conservative Party and the New Democratic Party could claim that things were looking up for them. They both improved their showing from the 1993 disasters that had befallen them. They both had reasonably popular new leaders, and could claim that, despite their distressingly regional bases of support, they had some national appeal and some prospects. The 2000 election dashed these hopes once again. The Conservatives asserted that the Alliance was a party limited by its regional base of support in the West from being successful in the rest of the country, and put itself forward as the party that was the "real national alternative" to the Liberals. The results, however, showed otherwise. The NDP, a party closely identified for ideological reasons with a commitment to preserving and strengthening the nation's social programmes, lost support in an election in which those programmes were the main national issues. Both of these parties faced the disappointing consequences of their electoral showings by launching soul-searching efforts to find their true role in the party system, but it became increasingly difficult to determine what that role might be. A person looking for evidence of transition might well write them off for the future.

Another indication of potential transitional status for Canadian politics comes with an examination of the voter participation rate. For the third election in a row, voter turnout declined, this time to a position in which just over six of ten registered voters, and less than six of ten eligible citizens, decided to exercise their franchise. As further examination of this phenomenon in Chapter 13 makes clear, there are multiple explanations for the turnout decline. Some part of it is due to the switch to a

Permanent Register of Electors, which requires constant updating. Newly eligible voters, whether through age or citizenship status, needed to take the initiative in placing themselves on the voter's list, or confirming their desire to be registered. There is evidence that as a result, turnout was particularly low among the youngest cohort of Canadians.

There is no doubt, however, that lack of interest in the election played the major role in the turnout decline. Part of this stemmed from the regionalized nature of party support, meaning that competition, a spur to interest and involvement, was lacking in many places. In the West, the Alliance was often in a dominant position; in Ontario, the Liberals. In parts of Quebec, the Liberals and Bloc Québécois were solidly in control. Only in the Atlantic region, where three parties were fighting each other, could it be said that the outcome was in doubt, and even here many MPs were re-elected. Another reason for public apathy about the election stems from the nature of the issues about which the election was fought. We have already mentioned the early timing of the election. There appeared to many to be no particular reason for holding the election in November, and no pressing economic problems to be discussed. The issue that did emerge as foremost in public concern was the preservation of the health-care system, but it was not clear that any of the politicians had much in the way of creative solutions to its agreed-upon deficiencies.

The 2000 election will not be remembered, then, as one in which serious issues were vigorously debated, or in which the country made a momentous decision between clearly argued alternatives. If it is remembered in its specifics at all, it likely will be as the final campaign of Jean Chrétien, who led his party to three consecutive election majorities. It will be examined as a contest of political craft, a case study in electioneering. On that score, the Liberals simply out-spent, out-organized and out-manoeuvred their opponents. They adopted the same strategy they had deployed in 1997, and a grudging electorate returned them to power.

There is a long-term cost to such a strategy, however. The problem of "governance" is much on the minds of senior federal officials, and has been for some years. The public is supposedly increasingly sceptical of political authority; citizens do not see their government as the champion of common best interests, and so disengage from national political affairs. For a governing party to so nakedly use its advantages to engineer its re-election — for the second time in a row — only contributes to disenchantment with the entire process. To political machines, elections may be about nothing but winning. Voters, however, have other legitimate expectations. When these are not met, another blow is dealt to the ideals of the democratic project, and animosity toward the manipulative governing party continues to calcify.

For students of federal politics circa 2001, the question that emerges from the 2000 election is obvious: How long can the Liberals keep this up? The party will have the luxury of calling the timing of the next election, but then its campaign will have to be run according to a different script, if only because there will likely be a new leader. He or she will have to have a platform to put to the people. The political professionals have learned the lessons of the disastrous campaigns headed by John Turner in 1984 and Kim Campbell in 1993, both new leaders of tired governing parties with nothing to offer the electorate but their "fresh" personalities. But in the next election, if the Liberals actually present an issue to the country and stake the outcome on the verdict of the public, they will draw their opponents onto the field of debate in a way they artfully avoided in the 1997 and 2000 campaigns. And if they lose, what then? As the editors of *The Canadian General Election of 1993* pointed out, "If the Liberals fall victim to the same forces which destroyed the Conservative government, the future may hold a splintered party system...."

Continuity does not necessarily mean stability. Though the Liberals won three consecutive elections — guaranteeing them power for at least a decade — there are persistent underlying political tensions abroad in the land, any one of which, or all of which together, could unseat the governing party. The issue of Quebec nationalism, which slumbered in the 2000 campaign, can always troublesomely reignite. In an economic downturn, the message of the NDP might strike a chord in a sufficient number of constituencies. The Canadian Alliance might either finally join forces with the Progressive Conservatives or one party might sweep the other out of existence. Or none of these things could happen.

That, however, is for a future election. The 2000 election deserves to be considered in its own right, as a moment when the nation committed itself to another stretch of government by the Liberal administration. How that happened and what it means is the subject of this anthology. Though it may have reproduced the contours and outcome

11

of the 1997 election, a good deal was new about this campaign, from the presence of a new political party and a new national leader to a new national newspaper with political designs. The chapters that follow examine and assess how the federal election of 2000 unfolded.

— *The Editors*

Chapter 1

The Liberal Threepeat:
The Multi-System Party in the Multi-Party System[1]

by Stephen Clarkson

For both observers and participants, the first federal election campaign of the new millennium was a dispiriting affair, an intellectually barren contest in which the four challengers were as uninspiring as the aging defender, who precipitated the premature contest and posed its only significant issue — whether, in his arrogance, he had overreached himself and would self-destruct. However uninteresting this phoney war may have been in its own terms, Election 2000 had real meta-analytical value for students of the Canadian polity. On the one hand, the restoration of the same constellation of players to the federal stage provided important material for analysts of the Canadian state. The Liberal Party's "threepeat" guaranteed the political economy would continue to be guided by a hybrid paradigm that could be labeled "Jean Mulroneyism" (to signal its commitment since the mid-1980s to trade liberalization) or "Brian Chrétienism" (to emphasize its balancing of fiscal prudence with social liberalism).

On the other hand — and this will be this chapter's main concern — analysis of the campaign can illuminate developments in Canada's electoral politics and party system. Although these related issues used to be studied separately, they must now be linked in the context of an ambitious study by Kenneth Carty, William Cross, and Lisa Young that reconceptualizes the current phase of federal party and electoral politics. *Rebuilding Canadian Party Politics*[2] may not provide the final word on the nature of the party system at the turn of the twenty-first century — indeed, this chapter takes issue with a number of its principal tenets — but it is heuristically indispensable, since it presents a number of analytical categories and challenging hypotheses through which to scrutinize the changes (or lack of them) experienced in the recent past.

Carty et al. build their study on top of a powerful historical proposition: Canadian party politics "collapsed" in the early 1990s. (page 3) Specifically, the 1993 federal election — "the greatest democratic earthquake yet recorded" (32) — marked both the eclipse of the previous, "third" party system that had governed Canada's national politics for several decades and the dawn of a decisively different, "fourth" party system. (3) Their argument has several components, starting with the number and nature of the parties (old as well as new), proceeding to their manner of electioneering and the character of the electorate, and ending with the technology of electoral communications.

They proceed to make strong claims about the three "old" parties, which had played a nation-consolidating role in the third party system but had failed in the early 1990s "to accommodate the forces of political, social and governmental change." (6) They felt these traditional parties, which voters in three of Canada's five regions "abandoned ... in large numbers" in November 1993, would not likely "dominate party competition" in the new system. (6) The Progressive Conservatives and the New Democratic Party lost so many seats in that election, they were deprived of official party status (defined as having a minimum of twelve seats in the House of Commons). As for the Liberals, their legitimacy as a national party was "not unscathed" either. In that election and the subsequent encounter in 1997, they won their two majorities with but 41 and 39 percent of the vote, or about one quarter of the population of voting age. (31) Just as the other parties had been reduced to regional bases, the Liberal Party of Canada (LPC)'s reliance for their parliamentary majority on one hundred seats from one province suggested it was "a party of Ontario with small pockets of support tacked on across the country." (7) Although it was attempting to reposition itself as the core of a new national party system, it had yet to demonstrate it would re-emerge as a national player. (82)

Besides addressing the changing nature of Canada's political parties, Carty, Cross, and Young make important contributions to our understanding of federal electoral politics, whose marked regionalization has become for them the emerging system's defining characteristic. In addition to all parties having regional bases, technological and demographic changes have altered the way that all these parties conduct their campaigns. New means of communicating their political messages enable parties to target their sectional voter bases. (178) In fragmenting their electoral appeal, the parties were responding to an increasingly informed and democratically demanding electorate whose identities were constructed more around special interests than national themes.

14

Regionalized parties exploiting technologies of fragmentation combine unwittingly to wage elections in which there is "no national political debate" any more. (224)

Stimulated by this arresting analysis, I will maintain that the Liberal Party's behavior in 2000 shows there is much less evidence of change than our scholarly trio maintains — whether this be change in the party system, change in the nature of the parties themselves, or change in the manner in which they wage their campaigns. My argument will develop along the following trajectory:

I   The behaviour of the Liberal Party in office has remained a mix of managing regional issues and declaring national objectives.

II   The regionalism demonstrated in the party's electoral activity was more reminiscent of its traditional behaviour than prophetic of systemic change.

III Issues of leadership, while peripheral to the Carty, Cross, and Young argument, detract from its persuasive power.

IV   The use of policy programs by the Liberal Party (and its opponents) suggests that the fourth party system is more similar to than different from the third.

V   Far from regionalizing the campaign, the communications media helped foster some national political debate, albeit of distressingly superficial quality.

VI   Even the new technologies of individualized communication failed to denationalize the campaign. At least as far as the Liberal Party's use of them was concerned, the new media actually worked to support the diffusion of its pan-Canadian message.

I The Liberal Party in Office

Come election time, the party in office occupies a position decisively different from that of its opponents. It has enjoyed the opportunity to wield the levers of power by passing legislation, appointing officials, making decisions, responding to crises, and representing the country in international affairs. Whether its record as a government plays to its advantage or disadvantage becomes evident at election time, when the media give its opponents' attacks full exposure for several weeks.

While the Carty team is concerned with *electoral* politics, the LPC's use of its power when in *government* has a direct impact on its behaviour when preparing for or fighting campaigns, so cannot be excluded from the analysis. What distinguishes the Liberal Party from its rivals is the extent to which it has found itself in this coveted position. The year 2000 marked the eighteenth out of twenty-seven elections since 1900 in which the Liberal Party was seeking re-election. Having recaptured power in 1993 and renewed his mandate in 1997, Jean Chrétien had given his supporters reason once again to be known as the "government party."

In the third party system (1963-93), the parties' focus shifted from the brokerage of regional interests that had characterized the second party system (1919-57) to a politics that was elite-driven (37) and national. (87) Having lost to the rise of federal-provincial diplomacy their function of inter-regional accommodation, parties in the third system engaged with pan-Canadian issues aimed at consolidating the nation from coast to coast to coast. For Carty, Cross, and Young, the fourth party system has lost this focus on bold nation-enhancing projects. Key to this part of their argument is the LPC, which, having "lost credibility as a national party" (82) because of its dependence on one hundred Ontario seats, was no longer offering pan-Canadian governance.

There is considerable substance to this view. Coming to power during a phase of retrenchment, the Chrétien government had completed the fiscal self-disciplining that Brian Mulroney had initiated. Cutting federal spending, privatizing Crown corporations such as Canadian National Railways and the St. Lawrence Seaway Authority, shrinking the size of the civil service, deregulating the application of environmental controls, devolving federal programs to provinces, and uploading federal powers to continental and global governance combined to reduce the size, visibility, and functions of the federal state.

Despite these actions, a year into its 1997 mandate the government was described as having "no discernible agenda".[3] Beyond managing the various files that crossed his desk — replacing the Navy's ancient helicopters, dealing with the victims of Hepatitis C, addressing the exhaustion of the fish stocks on the east coast and their predation by American fishermen on the west coast — Jean Chrétien's governing style seemed inspired less by the big vision model of Pierre Trudeau than by the cautious formula practised with even greater success by William Lyon Mackenzie King: all in good time. Chrétien had taken great pride in providing scandal-free, rather than inspiring, government, so when a public uproar greeted the government's proposal to offer a bailout package to the National Hockey League, he quickly axed the plan.

For all his blandness, Chrétien had never repudiated the activist role for government, which had typified the third party system. When under attack for irregularities in the administration of Human Resources Development Canada's billion-dollar Transition Jobs Fund, he defended himself without embarrassment. Mistakes are made in any big organization, he insisted. The important point was that his government was trying to help create jobs in areas with unacceptably high levels of unemployment and poverty. Government activism became even more attractive to the Liberals when they found themselves with cash on their hands. By 1997, when Paul Martin's earlier budget cuts and an unexpectedly buoyant economy had replaced the prospect of deficit cutting with the prospect of surplus spending, the Liberal Party quietly revealed its proclivity for positive pan-Canadianism again. While the Social Union Framework Agreement of February 1998 committed it *not* to initiate programs in areas of provincial jurisdiction without substantial agreement by the provinces, Ottawa used this affirmation of co-operative federalism to develop the National Child Benefit, which had been announced in the 1997 Speech from the Throne. Emboldened by the Supreme Court's debatable statements that appeared to legitimize the federal spending power, Ottawa spawned other pan-Canadian programs such as the Millennium Fund to give one hundred thousand students scholarships for post-secondary education, the Canadian Foundation for Innovation to encourage R&D in the high-tech side of the new economy, and the Canada Research Chairs to establish 2000 professorships in Canadian universities.

There is no question that the "selective activism"[4] of Paul Martin's fiscal policy was different from the blithely deficit-growing approach of Pierre Trudeau's finance ministers. Nevertheless, the Chrétien Liberals practised fiscal prudence with both a pan-Canadian and a regional face. On the nation-building front, the 1999 Speech from the Throne undertook to double parental leave offered under Employment Insurance. The 2000 budget re-indexed the tax system and enriched the Child Tax Credit, confirming that the government party was firmly wedded to pan-Canadian policy initiatives. The run-up to the election also showed the Liberals to be as adept as ever at responding to regional interests, as we will see in Part II.

Its record in office since re-election showed that the "government party" had lost neither its proclivity for pan-Canadian programs nor its capacity to respond to localized electoral demands. Since the de-nationalizing regionalization of Canadian electoral politics is central to Carty, Cross, and Young's depiction of the fourth party system, we will now turn to the regional quality of the Liberals' actual campaign.

II Regionalism, Liberal Style:
New Politics or Traditional Behaviour?

The Carty group appears on solid ground when pointing out the decisive difference between the national character of electoral politics waged under the third party system and its regional nature in the 1990s. In the 1960s, 1970s, and 1980s, federal politics consisted of a battle between the Liberals and the Progressive Conservatives, the two parties that could credibly vie for power. As a lesser factor, the New Democratic Party campaigned from coast to coast in the hope of wielding influence, particularly when neither of the other parties had a majority in the House of Commons. Competitive and antagonistic though it was, this two-and-a-half party system operated under a general consensus that accepted the legitimacy of official bilingualism, a generous welfare state provided by an activist government, and the integration of the regional components of the country into a national entity.

The 1993 debacle shattered this national consensus, with "regionally based parties increasingly acting as representatives of regional interests within the national political arena." (224) The PCs and the NDP were reduced to rump parties only retaining official party status because of support in the Atlantic provinces. Even the Liberal Party had to invent a different campaign strategy to deal with the different electoral permutation it faced in each area of the country. In the Atlantic, it had the familiar challenge of facing the Conservatives and the NDP. In Quebec, it had the novel problem posed by an avowedly separatist Bloc holding a majority of the province's seats. In Ontario it faced a disappearing left and a right split equally between the PCs and Reform. To the west of Ontario it had to face a resurgent regional hegemon in the shape of Reform, which had marginalized the PCs and was even eroding the NDP's prairie populist appeal. Important evidence for Carty,

Cross, and Young's regionalization hypothesis was the LPC's campaign in 1997. Although it was the only party to compete aggressively in all parts of the country, it "prepared different strategies and messages for each campaign," (223) going so far as to air commercials targeting separate regions with distinct appeals. (181, 198)

Because the basic partisan challenge the Liberal Party faced in each region in 2000 was essentially the same as it had been three years earlier, its regional strategy and tactics should have validated the Carty, et al. thesis. On the eve of the election, the *Globe and Mail* confirmed that the Liberal Party had developed a regional *strategy* for the campaign: "The Liberals are pinning their hopes for a majority on capturing virtually every seat in Ontario, picking up seats in Atlantic Canada and Quebec, and keeping their losses [in the West] to a minimum."[5] In other words, the Liberals did their electoral calculus region by region. But this was a practice as old as Canada.

As for their regional *tactics,* the Liberals certainly deployed their leader with a careful eye on the regional payoff that would accrue from his appearances. In a five-week campaign, Mr. Chrétien spent only parts of nine days campaigning west of the Ontario-Manitoba border. On each of the two days Chrétien visited Alberta (restricting himself to the city of Edmonton, where two Liberal MPs were in tough re-election battles) he visited two other provinces. He visited British Columbia, Canada's third largest province, just three times, sticking to the cities of Vancouver and Victoria.

Calculating how to get the best return for the leader's time is not, of course, new to the fourth party system. What differentiates Carty, Cross, and Young's thesis is their insistence on the parties — including the Liberal Party — tailoring different messages for specifically targeted regions. The Grits' 2000 campaign provides ample evidence for testing this proposition.

The Atlantic Provinces

The Liberals entered the campaign in Atlantic Canada with problems on their left. In 1997 they had lost twenty of the thirty-one seats won in 1993 to both the NDP and the PCs. In that election Jean Charest (who had adopted, as the PC leader, a neo-conservative position in Ontario) had attacked the government in the East for its deficit-cutting retraction of the benefits provided by the unemployment insurance system, which for years had topped up the earnings of seasonal workers in the Atlantic fishery. Even those in the fish industry who did not depend on this guaranteed-annual-income-by-another-name had been angered by the draconian quotas that a Liberal Ottawa had imposed on the cod catch in a belated effort to save that exhausted natural resource. Resentment remained strong in 2000, so Jean Chrétien took the action his long experience and his Atlantic counselors suggested.

First he sought strong lieutenants with provincial power bases to lead the campaign on the ground. He courted without success the former premier of New Brunswick, Frank McKenna, but had more luck with the then current premier of Newfoundland, who commanded the only provincial Liberal government in the four Atlantic Provinces. Seizing the chance to reactivate his federal leadership ambitions, Brian Tobin made a much-publicized return to Chrétien's cabinet as Minister of Industry just days before the election was announced. A second star for his Atlantic team was the former Nova Scotia finance minister, Bernie Boudreau, whom he had first appointed to the Senate as government leader there and who gave up his tenured safety to run for parliament in Dartmouth.

Next Chrétien backtracked on Employment Insurance (EI) reform both symbolically and substantively. Having learned the psychology of voter disaffection, Chrétien took it on himself to address the public's deepseated anguish over the loss of its federal support by personally apologizing for the hardships people of the region had been forced to endure as a result of Liberal Ottawa's efforts to get the Canadian economy back on track. While in Nova Scotia, Prime Minister Chrétien said, "I want to say thank you to the people of Atlantic Canada because it was probably tougher on you than the others."[6] He went on to explain: "But we were bankrupt. You all know that." When Chrétien returned to Atlantic Canada later in the campaign he made similar recantations in New Brunswick and PEI for the hardships his government's cuts had caused voters in these provinces. In New Brunswick he said, "We have realized it was not a good move that we made, in a sense. We should not [have done it] in retrospect. We had a huge problem and everybody had to pay a price to help us."[7]

Beyond the psychic cleansing offered by these *mea culpas* for his past sins of commission, Chrétien responded to the actual policy grievance. His chastened Atlantic MPs had been lobbying in the Liberal caucus since 1997 for restitution of the seasonal workers' benefits, and the

Party's March 2000 convention had adopted their position. Overcoming resistance in the finance department, Chrétien prevailed on Paul Martin to announce in his October 18 mini-budget that EI benefits would be reinstated for seasonal workers. Later in the campaign, when they came under attack for this policy's absence from the party's election platform, Boudreau and Tobin both promised it would be introduced as legislation and made retroactive to October 1st.

Atlantic Canadians were fully aware that the Liberals went on to promise goodies such as money for economic development to save their majority status. An opinion piece in the *Halifax Herald* made the following observation: "Truth is, the Liberals will perhaps need us, like never before, to return to power with a majority government for the third election in a row."[8] Maritimers understood the courting relationship being pursued by the Liberals and expressed it as a delicate twist of irony that the Atlantic Provinces seemed better treated by Ottawa when they shunned the Liberals than when they embraced them.

Quebec

Jean Charest had rallied both soft federalists and soft sovereigntists to capture 22 percent of the votes and five seats in 1997, but this revival did not outlast his departure from federal politics to lead the Quebec Liberal Party. Since Joe Clark had resumed the federal party's leadership, Conservative support in the province had collapsed, leaving the Liberals optimistic that they could make gains in a polarized, two-party fight with the sovereigntists. They proceeded along the double track of head hunting and policy-making. On the recruiting rail, the Liberals managed to bring out of political retirement Serge Marcil, one of two former provincial Liberal ministers to run, and seduce three Progressive Conservative MPs, who had won seats in parliament in 1997, to switch sides.

The Liberals' chief personnel problem could not be resolved by their long-practised art of elite co-optation among francophones, because it resided in the boss himself. Jean Chrétien was perhaps more unpopular than ever among vast reaches of Quebec francophones, who were ashamed of his coarse manner and embarrassed by his frequent demonstrations of linguistic ineptitude.[9] They were regularly reminded by overt sovereigntists and by a congenitally nasty pack of reporters in the media that he had "betrayed" Quebec by supporting Pierre Trudeau's constitutional reforms in the early 1980s and by opposing Brian Mulroney's attempt to reconcile a disaffected Quebec with the Meech Lake Accord at the end of that decade.

Deeply hurt by the antipathy of his own people, Chrétien as prime minister had taken the policy battle into his enemies' camp. Defying the timorous warnings of both his caucus and his cabinet, he had presented the Supreme Court with a request to rule on the constitutionality of Quebec's right to secede following a successful referendum on sovereignty. The Court avoided falling into the trap of supporting the federalists' position unequivocally, and pronounced Quebec would have the right to negotiate its secession from Canada should it receive a "clear majority" answer to a "clear question." Since it left the politicians to decide what would constitute a clear majority and question, Chrétien proceeded to initiate a "Clarity Act," which spelled out under what referendum conditions the government of Canada would envisage such negotiations. Far from provoking a political backlash, Chrétien's aggression had put the province's sovereigntist forces on the defensive by the time the writs were issued.

Parti Québécois Premier Lucien Bouchard made some *pro forma* gestures of support for Bloc candidates and railed for the record against his political nemesis, Jean Chrétien, as Quebec's number one enemy. In response, Chrétien challenged Bouchard to hold another referendum, indicating that he would have to follow the rules now put in place by the Clarity Act. Bloc Québécois leader Gilles Duceppe avoided sovereignty issues, saying there would be no referendum soon and Quebeckers should concentrate on this election. Sensing that he should not push his luck, Chrétien also backed away from his referendum challenge saying, "The people of Quebec don't want to visit the dentist one more time."[10]

Knowing they would prefer Santa Claus to root canals, the Liberals courted various ridings with specific promises, challenging BQ MP Daniel Turp by undertaking to build not one but two bridges and 14 kilometres of freeway in his suburban constituency of Beauharnois-Salaberry at a projected cost of $357 million.[11] Beyond confronting the sovereigntists and tempting winnable ridings with traditional-style goodies, the Liberals' policy message in Quebec repeated its pan-Canadian theme about the right-wing menace presented by the Canadian Alliance despite its not being a significant electoral force in the province. Liberal international trade minister Pierre Pettigrew said blatantly that the Alliance "doesn't like francophone Quebeckers."[12] This move to shift the agenda's main focus from sovereignty to social values was reckoned to be effective with a largely social democratic electorate that could be frightened by the spectre of a federal government unfriendly towards Quebec.

The contrast between a small-state, neo-conservative approach and their traditional large-state kind of federal governance was inadvertently made for the Liberals by the media which kept the question of political corruption in Chrétien's own riding of Saint-Maurice on the front page. Allegations of improper dealings involving the Prime Minister's Office (PMO) in feeding federal funds to cronies' projects in Shawinigan made the point loud and clear that the way to get goodies from Ottawa was to elect a Liberal. No targeted advertising was needed when the media could much more credibly make the case that this was an old-fashioned, pork barrel kind of government party. Chrétien himself was unapologetic. While denying any criminal involvement, he took advantage of the chance to be reported on the issue by repeating his standard line that the occasional mistake in a very big organization was not surprising, but insisting that government should help create jobs. The message for Quebeckers was clear: If you want to maintain the *status flow*, you know how to vote.

Ontario

The Liberals' golden goose certainly presented them with a delightful challenge: to hold on to their 101 seats and even regain the other two. The principal reason for their all-but-clean sweep in 1997 had been the even split on the right, with the PCs and Reform each taking 19 percent of the vote. This self-defeating situation had been at least temporarily rectified by Reform's partly successful effort to "unite the right" by transmogrifying itself into the Canadian Alliance and choosing in Stockwell Day a younger, more telegenic leader than Preston Manning. Aided by a press corps excited by the prospect of having a more confrontational politics to report and boosted by the *National Post*, a newspaper created by the media mogul Conrad Black to further his right-wing agenda, the Alliance had managed to raise its popularity in Ontario by October 1st to 25 percent, while the PCs had sunk to a bare 9 percent.[13]

Not only was the non-Liberal vote unlikely to split so self-destructively again in Ontario, it was about to be courted by a revitalized party with a brand new leader whose political future depended on making a significant breakthrough in central Canada. Faced with this threat to its main power base, the government party did what only a party in power can do. Before calling the election, it moved to address its Ontario problem through public policy. On September 11 the Prime Minister made a Health Accord with the premiers in which he promised to increase federal transfers from $15.5 to $21 billion by 2005-6, a deal that included $2.2 billion for early childhood programs, $1 billion for medical equipment over two years, $800 million for primary care over five years, and $500 million for health data technology. Shortly afterwards, Finance Minister Paul Martin pre-empted the Alliance's major policy appeal by issuing a mini-budget that promised sweeping tax reductions and undertook to allocate $10 billion to pay off the national debt — outclassing by $4 billion the Alliance platform's plank on this issue.[14] Just two days before he precipitated the election, Jean Chrétien appeared for a photo-op in front of the Toronto skyline with the premier of Ontario and the mayor of Toronto to announce a half billion dollar contribution to a three-level infrastructure project to enhance the city's bid for the 2008 Summer Olympics. Whatever the private understanding may have been between the normally Liberal-bashing Mike Harris and the Prime Minister, the fact is that the Ontario premier did not provide the Canadian Alliance with the subsequent electoral support on which it had counted.

On the personnel track, the Liberals recruited star candidates to take on their two upstart adversaries. Although former NDP premier Bob Rae resisted the Liberals' blandishments, the former mayor of the tiny Toronto municipality of York and the ex-chairman of the giant Metro government, Alan Tonks, agreed to run in York South-Weston to take on the former backbencher and now renegade Independent, John Nunziata. John McCallum, the media-adept chief economist and vice-president at the Royal Bank, was parachuted into the PCs' riding of Markham. Tonks and McCallum were additions to an already powerful cast of candidates in the province including fourteen cabinet ministers.

One issue with which the Liberals were unexpectedly forced to deal in Ontario was the repercussions from Canada's vote at the United Nations to condemn Israel's actions in the Palestinian Territories. In metropolitan Toronto there are several ridings with a concentrated Jewish population. In Eglinton-Lawrence, Liberal MP Joe Volpe broke ranks with the government vote from the beginning. Elinor Caplan was thought to be in the fight of her life in her Thornhill riding.[15] Thirty-five percent of this riding is Jewish and local leaders threatened to switch support to the Alliance because Caplan, who is Jewish herself, did not openly voice concerns with the government's stance in the Middle East. In the wake of a storm of criticism from Canadian Jews, Chrétien took it upon himself to deal with the anger through personal diplomacy. He issued a letter of apology to the Jewish community at large. Caplan, Art Eggleton (York Centre), Jim Peterson (Willowdale), and even John Manley in Ottawa South held meetings with prominent Jewish leaders to smooth ruffled feathers.

The Social Democratic West

However undifferentiated "the West" may seem to Canadians east of the Manitoba border, the four provinces could be grouped more appropriately for Liberal strategists into two pairs. In Manitoba and Saskatchewan the NDP controlled the provincial governments and still accounted for a quarter of the federal vote. On the right, the PCs attracted enough votes in Manitoba to prevent Reform from dominating the stage but had fallen below the 10 percent mark in Saskatchewan.

In Manitoba in 1997 the Liberals had lost half of the dozen seats that they had carried in 1993. But with six seats and 34 percent of the vote, they had edged out the NDP (four seats and 23 percent), Reform (three seats and 24 percent), and the PCs (one seat and 18 percent). In 2000 they failed to persuade Glen Murray, the mayor of Winnipeg, to fill the giant hole left by the left-liberal Lloyd Axworthy, the only member of Chrétien's cabinet to retire from politics before the campaign. Counting on attracting NDP voters, the Liberals conducted an urban campaign and hoped for the best.

Saskatchewan had been barren territory for the Liberals since 1958 when John Diefenbaker swept into power as a prairie populist. Exceptionally in 1993, they had taken five seats and 32 percent of the vote in a three-way split with the NDP and the new Reform Party, but they had fallen back to their more normal quarter of the vote in 1997, only keeping the urban seat in Regina held by Ralph Goodale, Chrétien's Minister of Agriculture. In a bid to appeal to the supporters of the NDP provincial government, Chrétien was thought to have solicited Roy Romanow, the retiring NDP premier, to run for his

25

team, but these rumours never translated into reality.[16] The party did manage to persuade a sitting Saskatchewan NDP member of parliament, Rick Laliberté, to change uniforms and join the Liberal team.

The Socially Conservative West

With Alberta and British Columbia, where Reform had already become hegemonic in 1993, the Liberals were in an even more unpromising situation. Their gun control law was widely unpopular in rural areas, where it had become a symbol of how disconnected the Ontario-dominated Grits were from Western sensibilities. Agriculture was another losing issue. The mini-budget's promises of tax cuts did little to change the mood in Western Canada, where many accused Martin of simply trying to steal the Alliance platform on taxes. The issue of health care remained particularly contentious in the region as the Alberta government continued to attack the federal Liberals on the topic. The provincial health minister, Gary Mar, accused Chrétien of posing as the saviour of medicare despite his transfer cuts being the reason for Alberta's Bill 11, the health care privatization bill.[17] The message that federal funding cuts had led to the parlous state of Canadian health care resonated strongly throughout the West.

Many journalists in the region argued that the Liberals had written off Western Canada in their pre-election manoeuvres in order to focus on ridings where they had a better chance to augment their seat total. Political scientist Roger Gibbins pointed out that they had gone to great lengths to recruit Brian Tobin to captain the campaign in Atlantic Canada, but had not found a similar leader in the West. "A good election outcome for the Liberals would be to have roughly the same number of seats, perhaps a few less than they have right now," he said.[18]

Early expectations of expanding their six-seat caucus of British Columbian MPs proved vain. It was not just that in 1997 Reform's 43 percent share of the vote had allotted them twenty-five of the province's thirty-four seats. Stockwell Day's by-election campaign had increased the Alliance's popularity in the province to the point that several B.C. provincial Liberals, including the MLA in Day's riding, had endorsed the new party. In an attempt to control friction between the right and left within the local Liberal Party on the eve of a provincial election call, its leader, Gordon Campbell, forbade all members of his caucus and staff from involving themselves in any way in the federal election. Campbell advised darkly just days before the writ was issued that "if someone has time to work federally they should probably think about working federally — full time, and get out of provincial politics."[19]

The Liberals' strategy was to focus on the metropolitan areas of Vancouver and Victoria whose multi-ethnic composition made their party more attractive than the Canadian Alliance and whose traditional NDP voters might be persuaded to abandon ship out of fear of Stockwell Day's social values. In the first week of the campaign, the Prime Minister announced a grant to be matched by funds from the other levels of government for rebuilding Vancouver's public transit system, Translink.[20]

On the personnel side, the Liberals had trouble finding solid candidates to run in many of the Canadian Alliance's strong seats. As late as October 30, only twenty-six had been nominated, compared to the thirty-two candidates already in place for the Canadian Alliance.[21] Chrétien visited Vancouver on the second day of the campaign to support the former provincial ombudsman, Stephen Owen, in Quadra, the winnable seat of former party leader John Turner and retiring MP Ted McWhinney, but efforts to recruit further star talent were stymied by an inability to coordinate the nomination process effectively. In the nomination meeting for Kamloops, a former federal Liberal operative beat out by just three votes the party elite's favoured candidate, Kathy Ferguson, the charismatic former president of the BC nurses union.

Whether the LPC tried to tailor its promises to specific electoral clients or tried not to do so, it ran into trouble. Minister of the Environment David Anderson seemed confused about his role as the Liberals' regional minister. On the one hand he said, "I have absolutely no expectation of announcements during the campaign. If anyone is voting Liberal to get largesse I think they should reconsider their reasons for voting." On the other hand he insisted that, "If re-elected, I look forward to fighting for Victorians to make sure our national plan pays local dividends."[22] This mixed message of disavowals and promises did not sit well with reporters. Journalist Barbara Yaffe interviewed the six B.C. Liberal MPs seeking re-election and asked them what they thought of the Liberals' munificence for Toronto's waterfront compared to their failure to back Vancouver's convention centre and a potential SkyTrain to the airport. After each one defended the decision, Yaffe reached the conclusion that "survival in

Chrétien's caucus means staying loyal to the team — even if it's pre-occupied with Eastern priorities."[23]

In this atmosphere the Liberals were damned if they did and damned if they didn't. To demonstrate Ottawa's responsiveness to BC's priorities, Paul Martin had flown to the province before the election to announce a $75 million contribution to help mend leaky condos, which had become a hot issue in Anderson's own riding in Victoria. This old-politics gesture had led the *Vancouver Sun* to dismiss the Liberal campaign in the province as "Vote Liberal — it's the only way we'll get any good stuff for this riding."[24]

Advertising for the Regional Vote

For the government party to lard its national campaign policies with specific promises responding to local demands is neither new nor claimed by Carty, Cross, and Young as a defining characteristic of the fourth party system. What distinguishes the new system from its predecessors, according to them, is the parties' use of the mass media to send *different* messages to different parts of the country. "Campaign communication at the outset of the fourth party system is no longer national in scope, but rather is targeted by region and a host of socio-economic factors." (181)

Evidence for this proposition was provided by the Liberal Party itself in 1997 when "for the first time" it "used regionally targeted advertisements" that responded to "different opponents attacking them on different issues, and from different directions, in each region." (198) Given the need to wage war on separate electoral fronts, "it quickly became apparent to the campaign's leadership that one set of national advertisements would not suffice. The party needed to tailor its advertisements to an electoral context of different opponents and different salient issues in each region." (198)

Although the Liberal Party faced the same variety of partisan battles in the 2000 campaign's different regions, its advertising was almost entirely pan-Canadian in content, even when its delivery was in regional markets or specialized media. (In Quebec, as Carty, Cross, and Young acknowledge, "the parties have always" treated their voters differently. (198) As has long been the custom, Liberal advertisements were designed for the province by an agency within Quebec. French language advertisements in the 2000 campaign played to Finance Minister Paul Martin's popularity, featuring him walking side by side with the Prime Minister.)

For the rest of Canada, advertising was created by Red Leaf Communications, the Liberals' consortium led by Vickers and Benson, a Toronto firm that had just been acquired by a French conglomerate. In contrast with the other parties, which bought commercial time in selected regions, most of the LPC's advertising, all of which was paid for by the national campaign, was purchased for showing nationally. A health care advertisement released on the third day of the campaign featured the prime minister saying: "Someone in Newfoundland, if he gets sick should not worry if he would be better off in Ontario or British Columbia."[25] The advertisement stressed that, irrespective of what province or region they lived in, Canadians should be granted the same rights. Aside from health care as an issue, its message was pan-Canadian.

Two variations of a "feel good" ad were produced to inform the public about the Liberal Party's accomplishments. One boasted about Canada's economic growth during the previous three years. It showed multi-ethnic Canadians of all ages interacting in happy places such as a park while calm, uplifting music played and included endearing scenes with a naked baby tottering along a pristine beach and an older couple sharing an apparently worry-free laugh. Statistics declaring Liberal achievements scrolled across the bottom of the screen. Ending with the words, "All this because of your hard work," the commercial suggested that the governing party respected Canadians, understood their desire for tax reduction, and would manage the budgetary surplus responsibly. The longer variation, intended for free time slots, added a scene — with breathtaking chutzpah for a government that had savaged funding for environmental regulations and transfers for universities — displaying the beauty of the Canadian wilderness and one with a boy in a library extolling the virtues of the Canadian education system.

The Liberals' last ad, which aired just before and just after Stockwell Day's eleventh-hour infomercial, emphasized the contrast between the two parties while warning voters about Joe Clark's claim that he would form a coalition with the Bloc Québécois in a minority government. Showing a number of Canadians in a variety of settings, the ad told Canadians not to take risks with other parties but to choose a strong, proven team.

Liberal advertising was "regional" in two restricted ways. The province of Alberta was the prime target of Liberal attacks in their national commercials on health care. Advertisements across the country highlighted the role Stockwell Day had played in introducing legislation allowing for a form of private health care in Alberta. One Liberal ad featured ordinary citizens-in-the-street in Alberta expressing apprehension about health care and the provincial government's controversial Bill 11, which was passed when Day was a member of the Alberta legislature. The ad ends by asking Canadians; "Does Stockwell Day's Reform Alliance speak for you?"

In the more normal sense, the one that supports the Carty, Cross, and Young thesis, the party produced and aired a few commercials for audiences in some provinces. Two ads aired exclusively in British Columbia. One attacked specific BC Alliance candidates such as Keith Martin and his stance in favour of "profit driven health care," concluding with a provincial variant of Red Leaf's mantra: "Does Stockwell Day's Reform Alliance speak for BC?"[26] The other attacked Day's belief that abortions, even in cases where women had been victims of rape or incest, should not be funded unless the pregnancy is life-threatening to the mother.[27] It was designed to appeal to voters in urban areas, where incumbent Liberal MPs were fighting tough re-election battles. This ad was also used in Alberta, for which the national campaign also designed a separate commercial featuring Justice Minister Anne McLellan and other Liberal candidates. For Saskatchewan, there was a commercial featuring Ralph Goodale on the need for the province to have strong representation in the federal government. Regional radio commercials stressing the importance of being represented in the government were produced for the Atlantic provinces.

The Liberals did prepare some ethnically separate communications that were mainly translations into Italian, Filipino, or Chinese of one of the national commercials with the final panel changed. In addition, a response ad in Chinese was aired in Vancouver, Calgary, Edmonton, and Winnipeg to exploit Alliance candidate Betty Granger's allegedly racist outburst in Winnipeg about an "Asian invasion" of Canadian universities.[28]

With the exception of these few provincial and ethnic ads, the LPC made no systematic effort to produce ads with messages specially tailored to appeal to voters in one part of the country or another. (One Liberal candidate in Ontario, Allan Tonks, purchased $10,000 worth of television advertisements, mainly on CFMT's Italian programming, to explain that he was the "real" Liberal in the riding where he was challenging the ex-Liberal MP, John Nunziata.[29]) In short, while the Liberals in 2000 did not contradict the Carty team's claim that parties are using television "as a primary tool in their efforts to send targeted messages to particular voting groups," (197) the extent — and therefore the significance — of this phenomenon seems relatively minor.

While broadcasting can target viewers in one geographic area, narrowcasting allows communications with specialized groups regardless of where they live. The specialty TV channels allow parties to appeal to "discrete groups of voters with campaign messages designed specifically for the targeted group." (178) Carty, Cross, and Young report that parties see specialty TV as the "wave of the future, and foresee producing a much larger number of advertisements, with each one tailored to a particular audience targeted through the television specialty channels." (199) While the Liberal Party did play some advertising on specialty channels during the 2000 campaign, it did not produce special ads with different messages aimed at these viewers. Instead, it simply aired the same ads produced for broadcast television. This may have represented a missed opportunity for appealing to certain demographics, but, given the resources necessary to make special ads for the minuscule audiences that most specialty TV channels attract, the party figured that its time and money would be better spent on pan-Canadian commercials.

Looking at the LPC's use of advertising in the 2000 campaign, it seems that nothing much has changed since the halcyon days of pan-Canadian politics. Canadians from coast to coast watched the same messages from the Liberals, who showed little inclination "to deliver substantially different targeted messages to particular subgroups of voters." (200) Pan-Canadian appeals were implicitly judged just as effective in the regions as any regional message might be. In sum, national messages prevailed over regional targeting in the Liberal campaign.

III Leadership and the Fourth Party System

Apart from noting that the fourth party system's new parties had charismatic leaders, (51) Carty, Cross, and Young do not pay much attention to political leadership as a factor differentiating the new system from the old. This is curious, since André Siegfried declared as long ago as 1907, Canadians "vote as much for the man who symbolizes the policy as the policy itself."[30] Almost a hundred years later, leaders remain the central elements in political parties, symbolizing their political history, policy, goals, and even character. It follows that the Liberal Party's position in the emerging party system can hardly be analysed without considering the nature of its leadership, whether in personal or systemic terms.

Appraising the leadership persona of Jean Chrétien is a difficult task for analysts. His performance in public view has been uneven, varying from dismayingly inept, particularly when he was leader of the opposition (1990-1993), to unapologetically insensitive, when he responded to the human rights abuse by police at the 1997 Asia Pacific Economic Co-operation conference in Vancouver. Beyond being generally difficult to understand in either official language because of his neurological speech problems, he often appeared disoriented and confused.

However disconcerting his verbal deficiencies, analysts resist taking him seriously at their peril. On his watch, the Prime Minister's Office has become a more exclusive centre of government power than ever.[31] Within the caucus, Chrétien is seen as more autocratic than his predecessors. Whereas Pierre Trudeau respected a backbencher's right to dissent even on so fundamental an issue as his beloved Charter of Rights and Freedoms, Chrétien has severely punished disloyalty even if trivial. Within the extra-parliamentary party, his power of appointment in constituency nominations has been enhanced by amendments made in 1990 to the party's own constitution.

While adamantly insisting on his prerogatives as leader, Chrétien has also shown great political shrewdness. He has refrained from excessive patronage, recently placing career diplomats, rather than partisans, as ambassadors in the key Canadian embassies in the USA, France, Italy, and the United Kingdom. Surprisingly, for a politician known to be vindictive towards the disloyal and particularly resentful of those who challenged him for the party leadership in 1990, he has been able to co-exist with an avowed rival for his job who is more popular with both party and public. But when Paul Martin's supporters met to strategize before the party's March 2000 convention in anticipation of the leader's imminent retirement, Chrétien defiantly fought off his lame duck label. He rallied party militants, insisting he would lead them on a populist campaign to stop the country's Americanization, preserve medicare, and build a compassionate society.[32] Following Martin's failed palace coup, journalists reported the two men did not speak, except at formal events. Nevertheless, these "two scorpions in a bottle" continued to run the government as a businesslike, bicephalous team.[33] Martin, who has been described as the most powerful minister of the century, was given a largely free rein to bring in his pre-campaign mini-budget and went on to play a major role in the campaign itself, making many appearances in Quebec and the West to compensate for Chrétien's personal electoral deficiencies.

Emblematic of the leader's omnipotence in relation to his party was his decision in the face of his caucus's nervousness to call an election after just three years and four months of his 1997 mandate had elapsed. Not only was Chrétien unchallengeable in power, he was secretive in his exercise of it. Even in the Liberal Party's Ontario office in Toronto, where the crucial part of the campaign would be run, the staff was completely in the dark as late as mid-October about whether and when the writs would be issued. These indications of Chrétien's omnipotence show the Liberal Party to be a significant exception to the trend identified by Carty, Cross, and Young that, in the fourth party system, parties are becoming more member-driven in response to the public's demands for a more democratic and participatory politics.

The Campaign

Chrétien may have clung to his leadership to stave off a challenge from inside the party, but what energized him into fighting form was the challenge from outside that came from the refashioned Reform Party and its new, socially conservative leader. The prospect of polarizing the election's discourse around the question of values led Chrétien on the 2nd and 3rd of June, 2000 to a meeting of centrist and social democratic NATO leaders in Berlin where he articulated his claim to be offering Canada its version of a "third way" government, "The Canadian Way in the 21st Century." Referring obliquely to the "forces of darkness" in an obviously intended, if quickly denied, reference to the Alliance, he repositioned himself as the defender of the generous state, apparently relishing the prospect of doing battle with Stockwell Day. Minutes after the writs were dropped in October, Chrétien declared outside Government House, "This election offers two very different visions of Canada, two crystal clear alternatives."[34] On October 31st in Week 2 of the campaign, the *Globe and Mail's* headline — "Alliance supports two-tier health care" — was manna from heaven for the reborn crusader. Chrétien immediately responded to the headline by asserting, "Never, never, never we will let the Alliance destroy [health care]."

Chrétien seemed to have luck on his side again when *The Globe and Mail* published information obtained from a Canadian Alliance "secret document." The "Policy Overview" was intended to be used by Alliance candidates to help them answer questions and debate issues. It stated that the Alliance would hold a referendum on an issue if 3 percent of voters signed a petition, that it would consider bids for the sale of CBC Television, and would make natives on reserves pay sales taxes.[35] This document seemed to give substance to Chrétien's claim that the Alliance, under Day's leadership, harboured a secret agenda, which contained views diametrically opposed to those of most Canadians

To offset the erosion of Chrétien's popularity with an unforgiving media, Red Leaf made him the subject of three commercials. Shown for the first three days of the campaign, one had him in a suit talking about tax relief and the Liberals' economic success. The second, which aired on Day 3, displayed a more casual prime minister, his sleeves rolled up, his tie loosened, and his shirt collar undone. Relaxed and calm, Chrétien used the ad as a vehicle to discuss health care as a pan-Canadian concern. Aired only during free time spots beginning midway through the campaign, the third ad had Chrétien in a casual jacket sitting on the steps to the porch of his official cottage at Harrington Lake, invoking Canadian values that included justice and equality and proclaiming, "In our Canada everybody must win." Like the ten other Liberal commercials, the ad ended with the Canadian flag blowing proudly in the autumn wind to identify the Liberal Party with a strong, united Canada.

The Liberal platform, entitled *Opportunity for All*, was also used to burnish the leader's image as an empathetic politician who looks out for every citizen's future in Canada and ensures that "values" have a place in that future. The platform was released in Week 2 with a personal message from "the Right Honourable Jean Chrétien" alluding to a "new era," "globalization," and "the future." It was an attempt to show him with a "plan for the future of Canada" based on "values" and "vision," in short the "Canadian way," a.k.a. the Liberals' "balanced approach."[36]

The commercials and the platform were tightly controlled means of portraying the leader in his best light. But they could do little to defend him on the hustings from four opposition parties hoping to draw blood. Chrétien's vulnerability was painfully evident in the televison debates, when the Prime Minister was reduced to a new kind of *primus inter pares*: he was the prime target for each of the other party leaders. During the French language debate in Week 3 of the campaign, with Alexa McDonough and Stockwell Day too inarticulate in French to be effective and Joe Clark punching only slightly harder, Gilles Duceppe led the assault, attacking Chrétien for cuts to health care, mismanaged funds, and even his commitment to Quebec.

Chrétien had the difficult task of responding to the other leaders' criticism without appearing too defensive. He adopted a dignified, prime ministerial pose and stressed the Liberal Party's vision of balance between social spending and tax cuts. He conceded that his government had made some deep cuts, but argued that they were necessary to repair the economic damage he inherited from the Conservatives under Mulroney. Chrétien also emphasized the Liberals' past experience in government, in contrast to the PCs' and NDP's weak federal standing, the Alliance's newness, and the BQ's sovereigntist irrelevance.

The next day's debate in English was harsher, because all four opposition leaders joined in the attack. Accusations of arrogance and corruption were not the worst of the personal opprobrium heaped on the Prime Minister. He was also "accused of lying, of being a hypocrite, gutting health care, misrepresenting his opponents' policies and calling an election to prevent Liberal rival Paul Martin from ousting him."[37] Chrétien's strategy was to ensure that he did not make any gaffes while remaining prime ministerial. Although he did not "win" the debate, he was able to avoid major errors. Stockwell Day's attempt to appear prime ministerial failed, but his energy and confidence succeeded in making Chrétien seem tired and worn out. On the defensive during most of the debate, Chrétien's one-liners were flat at best and he was unable to launch a successful offensive. As Edward Greenspon put it, his "inability to defend the very defensible must drive Liberals to total distraction."[38]

Given the five parties' needs to direct their appeals to their regional bases, the Carty group's thesis would lead one to expect that this climactic moment of the campaign would reveal the fourth party system's new dynamic. While the nature of the French language debate necessarily geared itself to the regional interests of Quebec, the English language debate paid almost no attention to regional divides within Canada. In part the structure of the debates frustrated any appeal that the Liberal — or any other — leader might have wanted to make to particular regions.

The English debate was particularly unstructured, and the journalists' five question topics — justice, public finance, health care, federalism and leadership — did not specifically raise the problems of different regions in the country. Had it been Chrétien's desire to speak to different regions, he could have reached out to them by making promises and slipping in references to local Liberal accomplishments in his answers. He did not. The only times that the regions entered the debate were when the province of Alberta was invoked in relation to health care and when Stockwell Day attacked the Liberal leader for having dared Quebec to hold a referendum. If Canada had truly entered a new party system in which regions take precedence over national messages, this would have been reflected in the debate. It was not. As a result, this pre-eminent moment of the campaign's communication with the electorate was more nationalizing than fragmenting.

Back on the hustings, Chrétien downplayed concerns about his leadership by emphasizing the experience and competence of his team. He urged voters to ask which team was best suited to lead the country: "As you all know a government is not a one man show," he said, adding, "History shows that the best governments are those with the best teams."[39] With the media digging deeper into the allegations of corruption concerning the Prime Minister's own riding, Chrétien attempted to relieve concerns about his long stay at the head of the party. Raising the possibility of retirement — "In the third year, or something like that, I will decide if I still want to do it or not" — he immediately cast doubt on this hypothetical scenario by adding, "At this moment I intend to serve my mandate that I'm seeking from the people of Canada."[40] "Vote for me and I may retire, but then again I might not" was a message unlikely to reassure those voters who were becoming uneasy about voting Liberal. It was certainly not enough to shake the opposition and the press from their hot pursuit on the corruption question.

When it was revealed in the media that Chrétien had called the president of the Business Development Corporation about a loan it was considering for a Saint-Maurice constituent, Stockwell Day alleged that the Prime Minister had engaged in a criminal act. When Day and Clark continued this vein of attack even after the federal ethics counselor had cleared Chrétien of inappropriate behaviour, he brought out the blameless victim defence he had used with diminishing effect in the previous two campaigns. "Mr. Clark and Mr. Day have overstepped the accepted bounds of fairness and decency, which have been our tradition in Canadian elections. Instead, they have sought to destroy my reputation and in so doing have demeaned the political process."[41] In an end-of-campaign interview with CBC TV's Rex Murphy, he took another run, with comically infelicitous syntax, at the same wounded warrior defence: "I have been in public life a very long time and my name is very important and *to attack my integrity after a long career based on nothing* — it was very sad, but for me it was a sign of desperation."[42]

Jean Chrétien is clearly the most important party leader in the period following the breakdown of the third party system, yet his behaviour hardly seems to correspond with what the Carty, Cross, and Young analysis would lead us to expect of the fourth system. On the contrary, his qualities seem to connect more with each of the previous systems. The incessant reporting of probable corruption linked to his sponsorship of federal grants to his constituency may have enraged the opposition parties and the media, but clientelism and patronage echoing Macdonald or Laurier elicited no apologies from him. His tendency to reach into the ranks of provincial premiers past and present as recruits for his cabinet smacked of Mackenzie King's brokering regional differences within the bosom of the federal cabinet. His championing of national values that are polarized against his opponents recalled Trudeau's style in the third system when parties presented "consistent and coherent messages to voters in all corners of the country and ... inevitably reinforced the long-standing importance of the party leader's appeal in electioneering." (21) As for the more democratic, pluralistic, grassroots-centred style of the fourth party system, Chrétien seems in his autocratic practices to be its antithesis. And while he and his colleagues were adept at responding to local demands in proportion to their electoral needs, the entire thrust of his personal campaigning was pan-Canadian. Indeed, the overwhelming focus on the leader by the media is itself a nationalizing rather than a balkanizing force.

IV The Use of Policy by the Liberal Party

Carty, Cross, and Young may have paid little attention to leadership but they make policy central as an indicator of change from the third to the fourth party system. They see a greater diversity among the political parties and a highly regionalized political climate pushing the parties to produce more substantial platforms for the consideration of better educated and more participatory voters, who are demanding a new level of account-ability of their representatives. The Liberals' 1993 campaign platform exemplified the new paradigm. Their "Red Book" allowed "the party leader to offer voters a checklist — a kind of political guarantee — for which, he promised, a Liberal government could be held accountable. In doing so, the party was signalling that it understood growing voter mistrust and that Liberals could offer a real response to meet it." (81) Although Carty et al. acknowledge that "the party's membership played no direct role in decid-ing what would be included" in either the Red Book or its less meaty suc-cessor platform in the 1997 campaign, (118) these documents' transformative role lay in signalling "the increasingly common practice of publishing detailed policy plans during election campaigns." (9)

Opportunity for All: The Liberal Plan for the Future of Canada con-firmed the Liberal Party's non-conformity with the new campaign behaviour identified by the Carty team. At thirty pages in length and small in format, the Liberals' platform statement was so much less weighty than its two predecessors that it was quickly dubbed the "Red Leaflet." Developed following informal consultations with cabinet, cau-cus, and the extra-parliamentary party by a small group led for the third time by Chaviva Hosek in the PMO, the brochure was as slight in sub-stance as it was light in the hand. Apart from recycling as electoral promises the contents of the September Health Accord ("we will invest $500 million for health information technologies") or the 2000 budget ("the Liberal government is doubling maternity and parental benefits from six months to one full year"), the "planks" were notably pulpy.

- "A new Liberal government will champion community action on ill-ness prevention, health promotion, and wellness."
- "A new Liberal government will work with partners from across the country to enable citizens, experts, and officials from all orders of government to engage in a dialogue on the opportunities and chal-lenges facing our urban regions."
- "We will increase access to capital through the Business Development Bank of Canada and the Farm Credit Corporation."

More important than the substance of policy, as far as Carty et al. are concerned, is its function as a yardstick for accountability. Far from

being marketed as a symbol of accountability, the Liberals' 2000 platform document barely made an appearance after its initial launching in
Week 2. Following some desultory media discussion, the Red Leaflet,
and the party's brochure on its corollary, the October mini-budget, virtually disappeared from the news, although the Prime Minister had it in
his hand at every speech.

It is not that feelings of distrust and cynicism about politicians had
disappeared. Instead, from the beginning of the campaign, the Liberals
presented the election as a choice between theirs and the radically different *values* represented by the Alliance. Since the media bought into
this view of the election as an ideological polarization — marginalizing
as a result the "other parties" outside Quebec — the Liberal Party's specific positions on policy questions for which it was to be held accountable became largely irrelevant.

While this decline in accountability as the central focus of the campaign might be thought to weaken the Carty, Cross, and Young argument, the switch of campaign discourse to a debate over values
confronts their analysis with a more substantial counterfactual. So great
has been the balkanization of campaigns following the collapse of the
third party system, in their view, that they have lost any semblance of a
"national discussion of politics" in the fourth system. (224) To the
extent that the campaign in 2000 became a polarized fight over values,
it was indeed a national debate. However much its discourse may have
degenerated into personal attacks on the integrity of Chrétien and slurs
on the religious views of Day, there is no denying that this was a national, rather than a regional conversation.

Carty, Cross, and Young maintain not only that "the parties' policy
positions are increasingly influenced by their membership" but that they
are "tailored to specific segments of the electorate." (9) As with the earlier
editions, Red Book III bucked this putative trend, showing a strong desire
to present the Liberals as a national party with policies designed to serve
all Canadians across the country. As its introduction proudly stated, "Our
vision sees a strong national government as essential to serving the broader public interest" and "Canada needs a vision for the future that recognizes a national perspective and the aspirations of all Canadians." As the
Liberals' effort to control the political discourse, their policy platform was
presented as a national, pan-Canadian document. Naturally, some promises in the Red Leaflet applied specifically to some regions (anti-gang law for

Quebec) or interests (native peoples) rather than to others. But the platform was a single compendium prepared to be read in all parts of the country and by all interests. For their part, the media reinforced the role of party policy in helping foster some national political debate.

V The Media of Communications and the National Political Debate

Carty, Cross, and Young note that, in the third party system, "television initially had a nationalizing effect on campaign communication in that it encouraged and facilitated the simultaneous delivery of the same partisan message to Canadians from coast to coast." (200) Although the mainstream media are not the focus of their research and reflection on the fourth party system, one could expect from their argument that the mass media would now treat federal election campaigns as regional contests rather than as single, overarching competitions and so focus on regional issues as they went about setting the daily agenda for their readers, listeners, and viewers.

In fact, the coverage of the 2000 campaign was far more national than regional. The daily press was more national thanks to Conrad Black's *National Post*, whose unashamedly right-wing bias had helped turn coverage of the Reform Party's slow transformation into the Canadian Alliance and its subsequent leadership race into a months-long media obsession. By the time the writs were issued, the electronic media supported the Liberals' view that the 2000 election campaign consisted of a pair of two-party contests between the Liberals on the one hand and the Bloc Québécois in Quebec and the Canadian Alliance in the rest of Canada on the other. On the CBC's initial election broadcast, news anchor Alison Smith lumped the PCs, the NDP, and Bloc together as "the other three parties."[43] Verbal marginalization heralded quantitative discrimination. Compared to the 1997 campaign, the media gave much more coverage to the Liberals and the Alliance than to the PCs, the Bloc and the NDP. CBC's "National News" gave the Liberals and Alliance roughly three times as much attention as they gave the three other parties. In 1997 the equivalent CBC coverage favoured the Liberals and Reform by just 30 percent.[44]

Canadians spend more time watching TV news coverage of the election than partisan advertising during commercial breaks, so how campaigns are presented on the news has a huge influence on voters' decisions. Thanks to cost cutting in the media, which had reduced the resources they devoted to local and regional news coverage, television news coverage became more centralized, focussing on the national campaign in general and the leaders' tours in particular. For example, in September, 2000 the CBC effectively cut its locally produced television news in half, which meant it could focus less on the local and regional aspects of federal campaigns than before. Similarly, the other television networks aired more and more segments produced by national reporters for their national newscasts during their local suppertime newscasts. Radio and newspapers, which have both been hit by deep cuts in recent years, increasingly turned to wire services for their stories.

Instead of national issues being displaced by regional ones, the 2000 campaign saw local issues becoming national. In their watchdog mode, the press are on the lookout for inconsistencies in the parties' messages, so a faux-pas by a low-profile candidate fighting a losing battle for election may be deemed newsworthy nationwide. For example, when Alliance candidate Betty Granger (Winnipeg South Centre) made some unfortunate comments about people of Asian descent to a political science class at the University of Winnipeg, it became an issue that the Liberals could exploit in their national campaign. Faced with four opponents with regionalized support bases, the Liberals profited from what Carty, Cross, and Young identify as television's role in the third party system to have a "nationalizing effect on political communication," which enabled it "to set a national agenda" and "to present a common front to all voters." As in the third party system, "all Canadians, regardless of their location ... were provided with a base of common political information." (180)

It would be inaccurate to affirm that there were no regional issues in the campaign. It is also true that some of the national issues had a different salience in different regions. Employment Insurance was only a serious concern in Atlantic Canada, organized crime was a major issue only in Quebec, and farm subsidies were only salient in Saskatchewan and Manitoba. Since pan-Canadian policies such as gun control tend to evoke different responses in different regions, the Liberals' success in turning the campaign into a question of "values" helped them avoid taking stances on potentially divisive issues and so present themselves as the most "national" of the parties. In sum, the media helped the LPC make "a mass appeal to the Canadian electorate through network television" (224) — Carty, Cross, and Young's description of media campaigning in the third party system.

VI The New Technologies and the Liberal Party's pan-Canadian message

Admittedly, television broadcasting is the communications medium that differentiated campaigning in the third party system from that of the second, so it is not surprising that it continued to infuse politics in the 1990s with a strong nationalizing character. If there is a technology to set the fourth party system apart from the third, it is the microprocessor-based capacities that have spawned the World Wide Web, consumer profiling, e-mail, and the wireless telephone. Given the fragmentation of the fourth party system into "a series of regional competitions, each with its own issues."[45] Carty, Cross, and Young maintain these new instruments allow political parties to target "relatively small groups of voters" with "specially tailored messages ... in specific areas of the country." (8, 181)

There are solid theoretical and empirical grounds for the Carty group's Orwellian fears about the "national campaign dialogue" (181) of the third party system being undermined by the parties, which can now "deliver different messages to voters in different regions or provinces, and do so without the transparency and accountability inherent in the traditional media." (210) For print, radio, and television, the cost of producing and distributing content is high: a small amount of content is distributed to vast audiences so that the media companies can recoup their investment.[46] Since the production and distribution costs for new media content are much lower, it is feasible to produce content for viewing by very small audiences. New communications technologies give political candidates an opportunity to engage in direct, private communication with voters, without being distorted or monitored by the media.

Carty, Cross, and Young importantly recognize that the "use of more sophisticated polling techniques [is] providing the party with detailed information on subsets of voters." (200-1) and e-technology gives them the capacity to engage in private, customized communications with a much larger number of small groupings of voters than ever before at much lower costs. (210) What is questionable, however, is whether the parties are making use of this technology effectively to court "relatively small groups of voters with specially tailored messages." (8)

World Wide Web

Carty et al. see the Web as one of "three computer-based technological advances that parties are using to communicate with targeted groups of voters." (200) They quote the former national director of the Liberal Party, who "views the technology as essentially an extension of direct mail, in that the message can be tailored to the demographics of the likely user group." (208) Since the cost of producing and distributing content is very low on the Web, it is ideal for sending messages that "may be tailored to both region and a nearly endless number of sociodemographic characteristics." (200) In particular, the parties believe that the "Web offer[s] a unique opportunity for the parties to reach young voters," since young people account for a disproportionate number of Web surfers. (208)

Carty, Cross, and Young point out that parties can enhance their credibility by posting background and supporting materials on their Websites so that people interested in these issues can find details. (206-7) Since every bit of information on the Web is available to anyone, anywhere with an Internet connection and a late model computer, it is an excellent tool for making party politics more accessible and transparent. This is in keeping with the general distrust of élites and the demands for more grassroots participation characterizing the fourth party system. (107-09) With these two functions in mind, we can examine the three kinds of Websites deployed by Liberals in the recent campaign — the national, the regional, and the individual candidate sites.

On October 22, the day of the election call, the LPC replaced their old, rather stodgy Website with a more up-to-date version that greeted Web surfers with a picture of the Prime Minister working a crowd in a Trudeaumanic pose. The site contained information on the leader's tour, copies of the policy platform in a number of formats, biographies and pictures of all the candidates, and a number of self-serving press releases generated by the campaign war room. During the campaign, press releases and a new picture of the prime minister looking his best were added daily. Interestingly, the national site was not used to target the LPC's message to youth or any other particular group. Youth issues did not appear among the nineteen policy fields listed as "Your Issues" on the home page — a list that included seniors, women, aboriginals, and Canadians with disabilities.

Consistent with Carty, Cross, and Young's analysis, the LPC Website did increase the transparency and the accessibility of the campaign. Candidates report that they often referred individuals with detailed policy questions to the national Website, where an abundance of information on policy matters could be found.[47] Neither the Liberals nor any other party made any real use of multimedia in presenting this information, which led one observer to describe the various party Websites as "banal, offering up little more than brochure ware."[48] Missing another opportunity offered by e-technology, the Liberals failed to include a facility on their Website for making secure online donations via credit card until just before election day.

Since candidate Websites are aimed at narrow audiences — the electors in a riding — they are ideal for sending targeted messages. If different issues and messages are dominating the campaign in different parts of the country, they should be reflected here. Although the Liberal Party provided Website templates for candidates, along with tools for helping them construct their own sites, most were as primitive in 2000 as in 1997, featuring a picture and biography of the candidate, the campaign office's street and e-mail addresses, and, sometimes, a schedule of events. Very few of them made any reference to policy beyond the occasional hyperlink to the Red Leaflet's electronic version on the party's national Website. Most incumbents chose to highlight their parliamentary record, while most challengers concentrated on their accomplishments in the community. Only 29 percent of Liberal candidates nationwide had campaign-relevant Websites, from a high of 44 percent in Atlantic Canada to a low of just 6 percent in Quebec. Even though nearly half of Canadians are now online, as compared to just 10 percent in 1997, Liberal candidates did not take the time and effort to create Websites. Many candidates probably realized that few people would visit their Websites, so they decided to create only the most rudimentary sites, if they had one at all. The low number of hits reported on most sites with visible hit counters seems to confirm this theory, but then again, candidate Websites were exceptionally difficult to locate.[49]

If blatantly contradictory messages are put online by candidates in different parts of the country, it is much easier for the media and even the general public to detect than if the message was delivered using local media or conventional door-to-door methods. For example, if a newspaper ad for a Liberal candidate in the *St. John's Telegram* contradicts what the Liberals are saying in Toronto, it is difficult to discover this. If the statement is made on the Web, however, it can be accessed anywhere. Contradicting the ideas of most theorists, Warren Kinsella, a communications adviser to the Liberal Party, reported that it actually used the Web to "ensure consistency of message" across the country, and not to appeal to narrow audiences.[50]

Voter Tracking Software

With recent advances in computer power, it is now possible to use polling data to isolate small pockets of potential supporters within a riding. This is the promise of the new voter tracking software, which Carty et al. see as another of the "computer-based technological advances that parties are using to communicate with targeted groups of voters" in three principal ways. (200)

First of all, the software gives parties and candidates the ability to identify small clusters of potential supporters and even individual supporters by using PSYTE codes generated from census data by Statistics Canada or by merging data from commercial databases with the Elections Canada voters' list. (202) PSYTE codes give a sociodemographic snapshot of every postal code in the country. (204) Once supporters are located, the party can then identify their likely interests and emphasize its relevant policy in all communications with them. Finally, since a large amount of data had to be collected to make the software useful in 1997, its real potential would be demonstrated in the subsequent elections, when the previously collected information on volunteers and donors could be used to give candidates a running start to the campaign. (203-4)

Although the power of the ManagElect software created for the LPC is tremendous, the system was only used to track party supporters in the riding and to mobilize these supporters on election day. The electronic version of the Elections Canada voters list was merged with an electronic version of the local telephone white pages to generate a database containing the name, address, and telephone number of every registered voter in a riding. This information was then printed and distributed to street and phone canvassers, who marked the party affiliation of the voters they contacted on computer-generated lists. Party affiliation information was then re-entered into the computer using a barcode scanner, and a new list of committed and potential Liberal supporters was generated for use on election day. Scrutineers used these lists to keep track of who had voted during the day. Should supporters fail to materialize at the polls, volunteers could mobilize the vote by phoning the electors identified on the list.

In practice, the effectiveness of this operation was hampered by inaccuracies and omissions in the voters' list and in the electronic phone book data. In the Liberals' urban riding of Willowdale, whose electronic behaviour was monitored for this study, the system administrator for the voter tracking software estimated that only two-thirds of the records in the database were accurate enough to be useful to the campaign.[51] The ManagElect software had the capability for creating new fields in the database and thus exploiting PSYTE code or information from commercial databases to identify potential voters and the issues they were interested in, but using these features was both difficult and unnecessary. It was difficult, since it was costly to acquire the data and time-consuming to analyse it; both time and money are in short supply in a campaign. It was unnecessary, because campaign volunteers, who are familiar with the riding, have an intuitive sense of where their supporters reside.

Assuming that candidates did make use of the software's power to identify individuals that are likely to support them, there is little time in the campaign to respond by sending these individuals information on the issues that interest them. Preparing literature on specific issues and mailing it out to interested individuals is not feasible in a thirty-five-day campaign.[52] Nor was the data collected during the previous federal election campaign useful either, both because of difficulties in importing this information and because the data quickly goes out of date since people in an urban area move with great frequency.[53] The unpredictable timing of Canadian elections and the strict limits on campaign spending and financing also reduce the effectiveness of this software — unlike the United States, where election dates are fixed and the flow of campaign funds is mightier than the Mississippi.

Electronic Mail

Carty et al. make three statements on the uses of e-mail in campaign communications with voters. They anticipate that bulk, unsolicited e-mail (known as "Spam") could well replace conventional bulk mail for sending specific messages to specially targeted groups of potential supporters. (209) For example, parties can purchase an e-mail address list from an environmental group and send these individuals information on how they propose to protect the environment. E-mail is also an effective way for citizens to engage in a dialogue with candidates and parties. (208) In the last campaign, thousands of e-mail messages were sent to parties, which welcomed the opportunity to communicate "with real voters about issues that they are concerned about." (208) This is consistent with the grassroots demands for increased accessibility that characterizes the fourth party system. Finally, Carty, Cross, and Young recognize that e-mail, like the other new communications technologies, allows parties to engage in private communications with voters away from the watchful eyes of the press. (210)

There are many logistical barriers which prevent the effective use of e-mail as a campaign tool. The biggest stumbling block is the difficulty in finding accurate e-mail addresses for the targeted population. A party or a candidate could purchase lists of e-mail addresses from Internet service providers or other commercial sources and then send a uniform message to all electors, but this option fails to capitalize on the ability e-mail gives senders to customize their communication with a large number of receivers. In the 2000 federal campaign, unsolicited bulk e-mail was not used as a substitute for bulk mail by the LPC or by any Liberal candidate.

Few voters seem to be sending e-mails to candidates to ask them questions. During the course of the campaign in Willowdale, only about 30 e-mail messages were received from constituents. Ten people sent good wishes, eight volunteered their time, and the rest asked general questions about party policy and the candidate.[54] Since the most common way of finding candidates' e-mail addresses is from their Websites and since the Websites of the candidates were very difficult to find, candidates might very well have received more e-mails if more people knew where to send them.

In one simple test during the campaign, two e-messages were sent to each of the five national parties. The Bloc answered both queries within an hour, the NDP replied to one query after two weeks, while the PCs, the Alliance, and the LPC did not manage to respond at all. As far as democracy-enhancing interactivity was concerned, the Liberal Party seemed to have given a very low priority to dealing with e-messages from the voters. Canadian parties also failed to make use of the e-mail addresses that fell into their laps when they received messages from the public — as is common practice in the United States — to add them to mailing lists for partisan newsletters and press releases.[55] Since the parties hardly used e-mail in this campaign, Carty's third point about it being used to send communications that could go undetected by the press remains valid in theory but moot in practice.

Though Carty et al. do not mention the value of e-mail for campaign management, it appears to have had three main applications for the LPC's organization in 2000: to keep the national headquarters in touch with local campaigns and vice-versa, to mobilize the grassroots for the campaign and on election day, and to communicate with journalists covering the campaign. E-mail was used by the LPC in this campaign as in any other large organization, that is, to send memos and jokes (in this case, about the Florida recount) around the office.[56] E-mail communication between the LPC national office and campaign staff in the ridings was infrequent. Local campaigns are still run autonomously, so only rarely require the assistance of the national office. For example, Willowdale received less than one e-mail per day from the LPC during the campaign, and most of the messages sent by e-mail were low priority items such as polling results and talking points. Almost as many faxes were received in Willowdale from the LPC headquarters as e-mails, and these faxes were also low priority items.[57]

The Liberals did not maintain an electronic mailing list either for its party members or for interested citizens. It could have made more mileage out of its press releases by judiciously sending them to Liberal partisans or to interested citizens, as do most candidates for high office in the United States. Nor did the LPC send press releases or other information to journalists via e-mail. Sacha Petricic of CBC news did not receive a single e-mail from any party during the campaign.[58] For the first time, Liberal and Alliance campaign buses were equipped with data ports at every seat where journalists could access the internet from their laptop computers, and all CBC reporters were issued Blackberry wireless e-mail devices. Yet the parties failed to take advantage of this technology to get their message out to the reporters. For example, the LPC war room could have easily sent some damaging information about the Alliance to a reporter on the Stockwell Day tour via e-mail, but this opportunity was not exploited. Instead, party war rooms bombarded newsrooms with faxes, and journalists on the tour with the leader were handed sanitized versions of these faxes by campaign staff.

Wireless Communications

In their chapter on campaign communications, the Carty team does not consider the role of wireless technology, although it has significant implications for their thesis. Pagers, cellular telephones, and wireless e-mail devices have become an indispensable tool for party operatives and for political reporters by making information available anywhere in an instant. There are pedestrian uses for this technology in all aspects of a campaign, but its greatest significance is for the entourage accompanying the leader's tour, which used to be isolated from the rest of the campaign while it was on the road. Just ten or fifteen years ago, information on the activities of other parties and other breaking news could be learned in detail only at the end of the day, when the tour staff retired to a hotel for the night. Today, the leader, the leader's staff, and the media covering the tour are continuously updated on developments elsewhere in the campaign by various electronic gizmos.

The speed with which electronic messages travel back and forth has fostered the emergence of campaign "war rooms" which respond instantly to every move of the other parties. When information took longer to travel across the country, such a capacity was neither possible nor as valuable as it is today. This instantaneous electronic communication across the country is also creating a "ping-pong effect" in the campaign's daily routine. Whereas in the past a leader could only respond to another leader's charges or missteps the next day, now there are three, four or even five cycles of exchanges in a single day. One result in 2000 was to make the campaign much more acrimonious than before.[59] In the words of Roy MacGregor, "a leader barks in Saskatoon and the sound has not even faded when another leader yelps back in Halifax," and "very often by the time a day comes to an end the reaction has so far outstripped the original news that no one can even remember where the day began."[60]

49

The implication of this for the Carty, Cross, and Young thesis lies in the fact that all these exchanges of invective between leaders are considered to be newsworthy by media nationwide, which only serves to increase the amount of coverage the leader and the leader's tour is receiving, compared to the coverage that might be given regional issues. Furthermore, the emergence of the war room has increased the importance of the LPC's national office in campaign communications, which means there is even less opportunity for the media to focus on local issues and messages.[61]

In sum, the Liberal Party, along with its opponents, failed to make effective use of the new communications technologies, even though they are conducive to "targeting relatively small groups of voters with specially tailored messages." (8) At the same time, these technologies are forcing parties to be consistent in their messaging, since contradictions can be easily spotted when information is available anywhere in an instant. (200) The unpredictable timing of Canadian elections, their short duration, and the strict limits on campaign spending are frustrating the use of these new technologies, but attitude is just as much of a barrier. Despite its successful use in the United States, the Web has not arrived in Canada as a legitimate political tool yet.

The Results

"No one has more at stake in the result than Jean Chrétien," warned Peter Mansbridge somewhat lugubriously on the CBC TV news on October 29th. "It was his decision — and his decision virtually alone — to call the election ... No one has bothered to hide the fact that many in his own party are sceptical and worried that, on election day, the Liberals won't be able to match their current standing in the opinion polls." At the end of a gruelling campaign in which a beleaguered and seemingly failing prime minister had sustained continual political attack and been dubbed "King Lear" in the media, he had vanquished his foes outside his party and confounded his critics within it. He returned to Ottawa virtually impregnable. Beyond the question of their leader's personality, the Liberals were felt to have done a good job in managing the economy by 59 percent of the electorate, especially in creating jobs and reducing the national debt.[62] Overall, they had managed to maintain their control of the political centre, with moderation and balance their watchwords.

The results comfortably met the party's own goals. In the Atlantic provinces they picked up seven seats, going from four seats to five in Newfoundland, from zero to four in Nova Scotia, from three to six in New Brunswick, while again carrying all four seats in Prince Edward Island. In Quebec they picked up eleven ridings, four from the Conservatives — thanks in good part to former Tory members of parliament André Harvey, David Price, and Diane St-Jacques — who all ran successfully as Liberals — and seven from the Bloc, which fell to parity in seats with the Liberals (at thirty-seven each). Despite Duceppe's solid campaign, his moral support from the ever popular Premier Bouchard, and his material support from the Parti Québécois organization, the BQ faltered. In what had become a two-party race, the Liberals took 44 percent of the provincial vote, which meant 90 percent of the ethnic vote, 80 percent of the anglophones, but just 35 percent of the francophone voters — up from one quarter in 1997.[63]

While the Liberals carried off moderate gains in Quebec, they held their ground in Ontario, knocking off the Conservatives' sole MP and the independent Nunziata, while losing only one riding to the NDP in Windsor and two seats to the Alliance in eastern Ontario. That they kept a hundred seats as the core of their parliamentary majority was in large measure thanks to the Canadian Alliance's failure to unite the right: twenty-four Grit seats were won from the vote being split between the Alliance and the PCs.[64]

The Liberals' net loss of one seat in Ontario was duplicated in Manitoba where they retained five seats and so kept ahead of the NDP and Alliance, who took four each. Further west, the pickings were very slim. Like Manitoba, Saskatchewan has fourteen seats in parliament, but the Liberals only won two of them, having kept Goodale's and gained Laliberté's — which meant they could claim to have doubled their representation in Ottawa. In Alberta the Liberals held on to the two they won in 1997. And in BC, the Alliance picked up two more seats, one from the NDP and the other from the Liberals, whose caucus fell to five of the province's thirty-four constituencies. They also picked up Yukon's single seat.

Overall, Jean Chrétien returned to Ottawa with 173 seats, eighteen more than he had won in 1997 thanks to 2 percent more of the vote. This gave him a resounding mandate for the status quo that he had proposed in the Red Leaflet. It suggested as well that, if the party system was

51

in transition from its third to a fourth system, this transition was showing signs of having stuck in neutral.

Conclusion

Already by 1995 there were good reasons to consider that the Canadian
state had moved into a new phase. The exogenous, market-driven forces
known as "globalization" had reconstituted participating states within
new forms of continental and global governance. Most notably for
Canada, the North American Free Trade Agreement and the World Trade
Organization had shifted many state powers to these new continental
and global authorities. At the same time as national sovereignty was
being truncated from the outside, globalization's ideological counterpart
had driven public officials to embark on a two-decades-long campaign
to shrink government from the inside. Neoliberal budget-cutting under
prime ministers Mulroney and Chrétien also worked to wean a welfare-
dependent population from its reliance on the nanny state.

Political parties give voice to class and other social struggles and so
provide the conduits for social change. If globalization and neoliberalism have transformed the post-war nation state, it would only be natural to find that the party system — which is the chief and most
legitimate medium linking the state to civil society — has changed in
response. To the extent that the third party system serviced the legitimacy needs of the Keynesian welfare state and the Fordist industrial
relations on which its prosperity had been based, one would expect a
successor party system to express the politics of the globalized state.

These political economy factors support Carty, Cross, and Young in
positing a sea change to have occurred from a system with two national
parties plus one minor one to a regime with one national and four minor
parties. Nevertheless, the evidence produced by the Liberal Party in 2000
does not confirm a general transformation in either the nature of
Canadian parties or their campaign practice. Far from showing a "failure
to accommodate the forces of political, social and governmental change,"
the Liberal Party proved once more to be the master at responding to the
electorate's broad desire for balance and moderation. Far from failing to
"dominate party competition," it enhanced its dominance of the political stage in the face of the concerted fire of its four opponents. Far from

having to "wrestle with the problem of finding a way to reposition the party as the core of a new national party system," (82) the Liberals have remained, as they proved in 1993 and 1997, the sole credibly national player, albeit dependent on their quasi-monopoly in Ontario.

Not only had the "old" Liberals succeeded in the fourth party system more than their rivals, they achieved this feat by notably old-fashioned means. While denounced in the media for practising first-party-system clientelism, Maritime and Quebec voters rewarded them for a campaign laced with patronage-style promises, whether EI for the seasonal fishery workers in the Atlantic provinces or bridges for the riding of Salaberry-Beauharnois. In BC the riding of Victoria was helped by a direct promise. Running a campaign against Alberta was a tactic that echoed Mackenzie King's second-party-system campaign in 1940 against the Quebec government. Even the Liberals' use of new technology was "old." It was used to enhance communications within the campaign organization, but not to displace fund raisers or communicate tailored messages to select groupings.

As for general campaign practice, the 2000 campaign suggested that the national consensus, which characterized the third party system, was being reconstructed. In Quebec, the BQ shied away from sovereigntist talk. In the rest of Canada, Stockwell Day made every effort — from holding up his awkwardly lettered "NO TWO-TIER HEALTH CARE" sign during the leaders' English debate, to routinely speaking some French at press conferences, to fielding visible-minority candidates, and abandoning his party's flat tax proposal — to move towards the liberal mainstream in his effort to court central Canadian voters. Both these new parties judged their campaigning by an old-politics standard: Duceppe prided himself on his well-run, disciplined campaign, just as Day apologized for a poorly organized, incoherent one. Parties, as the Carty group reminds us, adapt to the successes of their opponents. The 2000 campaign showed the four minor parties adapting to the Liberals' national focus rather than the Liberals adapting to their challengers' regionalizing practices.

The Grits are too successful a party to be dismissed as the exception proving the new rule. So much of the LPC's behaviour was rooted not just in the third party system but in the second and even the first, that it must be considered a multi-system party in Canada's new multi-party system.

NOTES

1 This study was prepared with the capable assistance of my students at the University of Toronto, Jane Abrahim, Cheryl Auger, Josh Koziebrocki, VIvek Krishnamurthy, and Graeme Norton. I am grateful to them, to Gordon Ashworth, National Campaign Director of the Liberal Party of Canada, and to Priya Suagh for their criticisms and comments on its earlier drafts.

2 Kenneth Carty, William Cross, and Lisa Young, *Rebuilding Canadian Party Politics* (Vancouver: University of British Columbia Press, 2000).

3 Jeffrey Simpson, "The Masters and the Slaves," *Globe and Mail* (Aug. 19, 1998), A16.

4 Geoffrey E. Hale, "Managing the Fiscal Dividend: The Politics of Selective Activism" in Leslie A. Pal, ed., *How Ottawa Spends 2000-2001: Past Imperfect, Future Tense* (Toronto: Oxford University Press, 2000), 60.

5 Shawn McCarthy, "Liberals on the knife edge," *Globe and Mail* (Nov. 26, 2000).

6 Amy Smith, "Chrétien almost says sorry for cuts," *Halifax Herald* (Oct. 27, 2000).

7 Jim Brown, "EI cuts a mistake, says PM," *Halifax Herald* (Nov. 5, 2000).

8 Don Macdonald, "Beware of Grits — indeed, all parties — bearing gifts," *Halifax Herald* (Nov. 3, 2000).

9 One hundred of Chrétien's most infamous malapropisms were collected by Pascal Beausoleil and published as a best-selling booklet, *Les Chrétienneries* (Montréal: Les Intouchables, 2000).

10 Philip Authier, "Bloc backs away from referendum," *The Gazette*, (Nov. 1, 2000).

11 Valérie Dufour, "Deux ponts et des kilomètres de route pour battre Daniel," *Le Devoir* (15 nov. 2000), A4.

12 David Gamble, "Help us to block the Alliance: Pettigrew," *The Gazette*, (Nov. 3, 2000).

13 Ipsos Reid poll, www.angusreid.com

14 Hugh Winsor, "Martin one-ups Day in budget battle," *Globe and Mail* (Oct. 19, 2000), A1, A9.

15 Phinjo Gombu, "The fight of her life," *Toronto Star* (Nov. 1, 2000), A7.

16 William Walker, "Romanow looks set to jump to Liberals," *Toronto Star* (Sept. 20, 2000), A6.

17 Larry Johnsrude, "Mar accuses Chrétien of politicking with Bill 11," *Edmonton Journal* (Nov. 2, 2000).

18 John Cotter, "West may be Liberal write-off," *Edmonton Journal* (Oct. 23, 2000).

19 Vaughn Palmer, "Loyalty runs shallow with BC Liberals," *National Post* (Oct. 14, 2000).

20 Peter O'Niel and Scott Simpson, "Liberals offer transit money, but levy will remain," *Vancouver Sun* (Nov. 1, 2000).

21 Yvonne Zacharias, "Tight races heat up campaigns in B.C.," *Vancouver Sun* (Nov. 1, 2000).

22 Ibid.

23 Barbara Yaffe, B.C.'s six Liberals face uphill battle in Ottawa, *Vancouver Sun* (Nov. 3, 2000).

24 Paul Willcocks. "Beware of Liberals bearing gifts for votes," *Vancouver Sun* (Nov. 3, 2000).

25 Liberal Television Advertisement, "Health Care," Campaign 2000.

26 Liberal Television Advertisement, Campaign 2000.

27 Liberal Television Advertisement, "Quality Health Care," Campaign 2000.

28 Robert Matas, "'Scurrilous' ads enrage Alliance: Liberals using Chinese-language media to paint portrait of rival party as 'scary' and 'racist,'" *Globe and Mail* (Nov. 24, 2000), A7.

29 CFRB radio, November 27, 2000.

30 André Siegfried, *The Race Question in Canada* (Toronto: MacMillan Company of Canada Ltd., 1978), 136.

31 Donald J. Savoie, *Governing from the Centre: The Concentration of Power in Canadian Politics* (Toronto: University of Toronto Press, 1999).

32 Anne McIlroy, "Youth wing cheers PM's populist theme," *Globe and Mail* (March 17, 2000), A9.

33 Jeffrey Simpson, "Two scorpions in a bottle," *Globe and Mail* (April 23, 2000), A19.

34 Shawn McCarthy and Paul Adams, "Chrétien defends early vote," *Globe and Mail* (October 23, 2000), A1.

35 John Ibbitson, "Day's plan found in secret paper," *Globe and Mail* (Nov. 7, 2000), A1.

36 *Opportunity for All: The Liberal Plan for the Future of Canada,* (Ottawa: The Liberal Party of Canada, 2000), 2-3.

37 Shawn McCarthy and Brian Laghi, "Chrétien pounded again as Day puts on show," *Globe and Mail* (Nov. 10, 2000), A1.

38 Edward Greenspon, "Straight for the Jugular," *Globe and Mail* (Nov. 11, 2000), A15.

39 Brian Laghi, "Chrétien evokes image of team spirit," *Globe and Mail* (Nov. 14, 2000), A7.

40 Brian Laghi, "Chrétien says he'll consider quitting," *Globe and Mail* (Nov. 17, 2000), A1.

41 Paul Adams and Daniel Leblanc, "PM wins case, lashes out," *Globe and Mail* (Nov. 22, 2000), A1.

42 "The National," Nov. 24, 2000, author's notes and italics.

43 "Sunday Report," (Oct. 22, 2000).

44 Fifty-two percent of the CBC "National News" election coverage was general. Of the coverage devoted to specific parties, 15 percent was on the Liberals and 16 percent on the Alliance, whereas the PCs received 7 percent, the NDP 7 percent and the Bloc 3 percent. (In 1997 the equivalent figures were 59 percent general, 9.5 percent Liberal, 9.4 percent Reform, 7 percent PC, 7 percent NDP and 9 percent Bloc.)

45 Lisa Young, "Comment on Johnston, 'Canadian Elections at the Millennium,'" *Choices: Strengthening Canadian Democracy* (Institute for Research on Public Policy) 6:6 (Sept. 2000), 37.

46 Edward S. Herman and Noam Chomsky, *Manufacturing Consent: The Political Economy of the Mass Media* (New York: Pantheon Books, 1988).

47 Interview with Joanne Pratt, campaign manager for the Jim Peterson campaign in Willowdale, Nov. 28, 2000.

48 Susan Bourette, "Campaigning in the age of the Internet a cyber letdown," *Globe and Mail* (Oct. 30, 2000).

49 Those candidates whose sites had visible hit counters reported 400-600 hits total by the final weekend of the campaign. Only 67 of 141 Liberal candidate Websites achieved a "top 20" ranking on the Google search engine, and 59 sites achieved a similar score on the popular Altavista.ca search engine.

50 Interview with Warren Kinsella, Nov. 9, 2000.

51 Interview with Paul Mang, manager of information technology for the Jim Peterson campaign in Willowdale, Nov. 28, 2000.

52 Interview with Joanne Pratt, Nov. 28, 2000.

53 Interview with Paul Mang, Nov. 28, 2000.

54 Interview with Joanne Pratt, Nov. 28, 2000.

55 Gary W. Senlow, *Electronic Whistle-Stops: The Impact of the Internet on American Politics* (Westport: Praeger, 1998), 98.

56 Interview with Warren Kinsella, Nov. 9, 2000.

57 Interview with Pratt, Nov. 28, 2000.

58 Interview with Sacha Petricic, reporter for CBC news, Dec. 5, 2000.

59 Interview with Petricic, Dec. 5, 2000.

60 Roy MacGregor, "Wired media have changed the message: A leader barks on the West Coast, one yelps back from the East," *National Post* (Nov. 25, 2000), A6.

61 Warren Kinsella reports that more and more journalists are contacting the LPC national office for information to use in their reports. Interview, Nov. 9, 2000.

62 Richard Nadeau, Neil Nevitte, Elizabeth Gidengil et André Blais, "Pourquoi les libéraux ont-ils gagné?" *La Presse* (2 déc. 2000), A21.

63 Pierre Drouilly, "Le vote nationaliste toujours solide," cyberpresse.ca (1 déc. 2000).

64 This compares with 42 seats won by the LPC from vote splitting in Ontario in 1993 and 26 seats won this way in 1997: André Turcotte, Roundtable on the Federal Election, University of Toronto, Nov. 29, 2000.

Chapter 2

The More Things Change ...
The Alliance Campaign

by Faron Ellis

No party went through more internal machinations and public turmoil in the brief period between the 1997 and 2000 elections than did the Reform Party, as it metamorphosed itself into the Canadian Reform Conservative Alliance.[1] During the inter-election period the party held four major conventions, two-party wide referenda, and a leadership contest, many of these in the year immediately preceding the 2000 election. After all that, the party made only modest gains from the Reform results in the 1997 election. The Alliance broadened its vote base to 25.5 percent (compared to Reform's 19.4 percent in 1997), and it managed to elect 6 additional MPs, (66 as compared to Reform's 60 in 1997). But it failed to achieve any of the more lofty goals it had set for itself. The Alliance failed to reduce the Liberals to a minority government. It failed to reduce the Progressive Conservatives to unofficial party status in its ongoing effort to finish off its conservative rival, once and for all. Most importantly, it failed to make a significant breakthrough into Ontario and therefore failed to actualize its reasons for coming into being.

The Reform-Alliance transformation may indeed have stripped the party of its most important contributions to Canada's new fourth-party system.[2] In attempting to shed its image as a western vehicle dedicated to seemingly radical policy positions, the Alliance project represented a shift away from the regional and policy articulation characteristics Reform helped bring into the new system, back to a more national brokerage politics of the pre-1993 period. In the process, and in the way it conducted its campaign, the Alliance also moved away from what many would argue was potentially Reform's most enduring legacy, the further democratization of party politics and the political system more generally.

The United Alternative

The seed of the Alliance project was planted before the 1997 election. In a showdown with Reform leader Preston Manning, members attending the party's 1996 assembly struck an unspoken bargain with their leadership; either Manning and his campaign team deliver the major Ontario breakthrough they were promising in the 1997 election, or the membership would be looking for accountability in the form of a leadership change.[3] When the election returns were counted and Reform lost its only Ontario seat, both the leadership and the membership acknowledged that changes were going to be required if Reform was to ever become more than a regional protest party. What followed was a fascinating series of developments that were truly unprecedented in Canadian party history. Manning embarked upon a plan that would see him attempt to replace the Reform Party rather than allow it to replace him as leader. Unfortunately for Manning, although he succeeded in convincing Reformers that a new political vehicle was necessary to carry them to government, he was not successful at convincing them he was the man to lead them there.

The Alliance party grew out of an internal Reform evaluation process following the party's 1997 election disappointments. Initially conceived as the Ontario United Alternative, it was proposed as a means to stop the "vote splitting" that appeared to be handing the Liberals almost all of that province's 103 seats. In July of 1997 the party's executive council approved the budgets to organize a number of "campaigns" in preparation for the next election, including an Ontario United Alternative campaign. By March of 1998 Manning had expanded the idea to include national aspirations but was careful to steer discussions away from talk about forming a new party. When a new party was mentioned, it was couched as only one of a number of possible options. Manning had successfully used this multi-choice strategy when he created Reform in 1987, and again when he wanted to expand it nationally in 1991.[4] The strategy involves initially presenting members with a number of options, but structuring the debate so as to eventually eliminate all choices except that which was initially preferred. Even when opposition emerged, and it emerged more forcefully with respect to the United Alternative process than it ever had before, by effectively controlling all of the means of communication and strategy, the leadership proved that it could effectively quash even substantial dissent. In fact, even the last vestige of popular control, the party-wide referendum, was used as an effective tool against the dissidents.

The logic of the United Alternative rested on an intentionally superficial interpretation of vote splitting between Reform and Conservative supporters. It is true that anytime multi-party competition exists, there also exists a split in votes against the winning party. But voters cast ballots against certain parties, and for others, for a variety of conflicting reasons. Simply adding up 1997 Reform and PC vote totals to predict a victory over the Liberals did not do justice to the complexities of Canadian voting behaviour, but it made for simple and therefore persuasive rhetoric. The logic rested on the assumption that the vast majority of Ontario Conservative voters would automatically flock to a new party if it was perceived to be less Western and less radical in its policy proposals than was Reform. For this to occur, the Conservative Party would have to cease to exist, and their previous supporters would have to choose the new UA as their partisan home. Any hopes that the federal Progressive Conservative party would willingly participate in its own demise were quickly dashed when Joe Clark won the PC leadership. And even if the Conservatives could be marginalized, any new entity would still have considerable work to do in recruiting voters. Studies indicated that, largely because of its image, Reform was not necessarily the next choice for most Ontario Conservative voters. In fact, the largest plurality of Ontario Conservative voters would be more likely to choose the Liberals (44 percent) than Reform (18 percent).[5] Be that as it may, armed with the logic of vote-splitting, and post election surveys of Reform members indicating that Ontario "vote-splitting" was thought to be a major problem, Manning brought the United Alternative concept to the floor of Reform's first post-election assembly.

The 1998 Reform Assembly Launches the United Alternative

The United Alternative was one of three major issues discussed at Reform's first national gathering after the 1997 election. Other issues included a planned reorganization of the party's executive council and the constituency associations' financial participation in the party's next national election advertising program. While many members interpreted these latter two initiatives as a power grab, they were not seen as much

more than the ordinary actions of a leadership preparing for an anticipated power struggle. After considerable rancour during a lively debate, a
hallmark of Reform conventions, delegates eventually rejected the executive council reorganization, but not before embarrassing the leadership by
insisting it delay a tribute to the party's founders in favour of more debate
time. Tensions continued to build during the United Alternative debate
with some delegates expressing fears that the leadership was planning
something much grander than they were prepared to admit. Dissidents
also argued that the wild-card UA resolution was unconstitutional, having been sprung on an unsuspecting assembly without being properly
debated at the local level. Proponents assured skeptics that the proposed
United Alternative convention was in no way a "merger or an amalgama-
tion with the Tories ... or a proposal to change the Reform Party name or
leader."[6] Rather, they argued, co-operation with the Conservatives would
most likely occur through joint nominations or some other local co-operative efforts. Manning reiterated these themes in his keynote address to
the delegates. Understanding that there currently existed little interest in
grand institutional change, Manning assured delegates that he preferred
the Reform party's principles, its name, and its current leadership to any
other option. By the time the 1998 assembly ended, Manning had
received 91.3 percent support to hold a United Alternative convention
aimed at discussing how best to build a coalition strong enough to defeat
the Liberals. He also received an 80.9 percent vote of confidence in his
leadership, down from 86 percent two years prior but sufficient to fore-
stall any serious leadership challenges for the time being.

Prior to embarking upon a twenty-five-day Asian and European
tour, Manning outlined his vision of what the United Alternative would
become. He and Reform pollster André Turcotte (see Chapter Twelve of
this volume) argued that Canada had moved beyond the old left-right
ideological labels and was therefore in need of a new vision that represented these new realities. In place of the old left-right dichotomy they
posited a new three-dimensional decision-making axis.[7] The content of
their argument represented more than Manning's latest attempt to shed
the "unite-the-right" label that had already been attached to the UA.[8] His
attempt to articulate a new ideological paradigm was the latest manifes-
tation of his desire to produce a fundamental realignment of Canadian
federal politics. Manning had never viewed his role in Canadian politics
as merely representative of Western, right-wing sentiments in a region-

alized new party system. Nor was he content to simply further the cause of instilling greater democratic participation in the system, changes Reform was successfully forcing on the other parties. Manning's goal was to create a permanent realignment of partisanship in Canada, with him leading one of only two major parties. Reform represented the vehicle to begin, but not necessarily finish the project.[9]

While Manning toured Asia and Europe, the Reform caucus became embroiled in a vicious internal fight over whether its MPs should consider opting back into the parliamentary pension plan they had forfeited when they were first elected in 1993. Manning refused to take action from Asia and by the time he arrived back in Canada the controversy had erupted into a full-fledged leadership crisis. One MP had quit the Reform caucus and others were threatening to quit or being threatened with expulsion by other Reform officials. Once Manning broke his silence he took no stern action, thereby signaling that he was no longer concerned with his leadership of Reform. His attention was focused on the UA and his role in delivering Reform's substantial organizational strength to a new party vehicle. With Joe Clark's steadfast refusal to participate in any Reform-initiated UA process, bringing Conservatives on side meant recruiting primarily from within the Conservative ranks of the provincial legislatures. By the late summer of 1998 the UA had attracted influential members of both the Alberta and Ontario Conservative governments. Alberta treasurer Stockwell Day and strategist Rod Love signed on, as did Ontario's Transportation Minister Tony Clement. An important political endorsement came when Alberta Premier Ralph Klein publicly backed the UA project stating that neither the Tories nor Reform were capable of defeating the Liberals.[10]

The UA steering committee attempted to keep the concept abstract enough to both attract potential Conservative recruits and at the same time not offend Reformers who were suspicious of excessive compromise. The lack of details concerning policy, organization, and direction led to considerable acrimony as Reformers frequently engaged in often wild speculation over each new proposal and counter-proposal.[11] Options such as a confederal party or regional parties with some overarching organization were brought forward and often dropped within days. The speculation led the leadership to order Reform MPs to avoid public debate over the issue. This edict only furthered speculation that the leadership had a hidden agenda and had indeed already decided to abandon Reform for a new party.

The 1999 United Alternative Convention

The UA convention was held February 19-21, 1999 in Ottawa. Alberta Premier Ralph Klein opened the conference by admonishing delegates to build a fiscally conservative but socially moderate party. "We cannot, as those who adhere to a conservative philosophy, declare ourselves to be the party of minimum interference in the everyday lives of everyday Canadians, and then propose to interfere in the most personal of all decisions."[12] Stockwell Day addressed the conference the following afternoon and provided delegates with a "blitzkrieg against the federal government that had delegates swarming him for an hour after the 15 minute address."[13] Day had also spoken to Reform delegates at their 1998 London Assembly and was clearly testing the waters for a possible leadership bid. In fact, given that Day was to speak on the option of forming a new party, yet instead launched into a leadership style speech, he appeared to believe that a new party was a foregone conclusion and the leadership race had already begun.

Manning was the last to speak. Despite the fact that most of the delegates were Reformers (officials estimated that only 300 of the 1,500 delegates were active Progressive Conservatives), Manning's speech was addressed to the potential new recruits rather than the Reform members. In typical fashion he invoked historical images of previous bold new initiatives but added a new element to his UA address. He attempted to "speak from the heart" by invoking the image of a softer, gentler, more caring party than was Reform. He called for a "union of the heart" and "one big family meeting" of Canadians to begin the new millennium. In a similar manner as had Day only hours before, Manning launched his unofficial leadership campaign by recognizing that he would have to improve his abilities and work harder "on expressing [his] affection for Canada and Canadians in a way that connects with the heart as well as the head."[14]

The UA convention adopted three motherhood themes prior to declaring their preferences for starting a new party.[15] Using a preferential ballot, delegates voted on four possible political action options: 1) to create a new party; 2) to support local co-operation initiatives; 3) to unite behind an existing party; or 4) to merge two or more parties. They overwhelmingly chose the first option but the structure of the ballot and the ordering of preferences provided the UA leadership with ample room to manoeuvre. They could begin working on the new party in earnest, behind the scenes, but at the same time assuage Reformers' concerns about abandoning their principles by claiming that a new party was not necessarily the outcome. Organizers were always careful to point out that Reformers would be given not one, but two party-wide referenda on the UA concept prior to any formal changes being made to their party.

Table 1
Political Action Preferences - UA Conference — 1999

	First Choice	Second Choice	Third Choice	Fourth Choice
New Party	665	296	106	27
Local Initiatives	273	409	206	42
Existing Party	252	252	222	96
Merge Several Parties	33	122	171	166

Source: United Alternative Convention

The 1999 Reform Party Referendum

The first Reform party membership referendum was scheduled for May of 1999. The campaign leading up to the mail-in ballot sparked considerable debate, much of which centred around the continuing ambiguity of the concept that opponents argued was intentionally structured into the ballot question. Reformers were being asked if they wanted to continue with the United Alternative process, and given an option of voting "Yes" or "No." There was no direct vote on starting a new party or on local co-operation initiatives. Given that the resolution would not yet change the party constitution, it was considered to be a policy measure thereby requiring only a 50 percent margin of victory overall, and a simple majority in a majority of provinces.[16] Opponents argued that the vague question allowed for unlimited interpretation, a wholesale compromising of Reform's principles, and the eventual end of the party. Supporters countered that members were protected by their ability to reject the finished project in a second referendum down the road. Most opponents, however, correctly viewed the first referendum as their most legitimate chance to stop the initiative. If Reformers formally sanctioned the still fluid process, it was likely that the leadership would be able to create enough momentum to get the project past the point of no return.[17] The referendum process demonstrated the limits of Reform's internal democratic participation. Although Reform members enjoyed many participatory avenues at the branch level similar to those of other party members, Reform members' plebiscitarian check on their leadership in the form of Assembly votes or party wide sanctioning of major strategic decisions was often held out as that which distinguished Reform members' participatory avenues from those of the other parties. It has been argued that this was one of Reform's major contributions to the new party system.[18] In practice, however, with the leadership controlling all of the means of internal communication, including the centralized membership lists and its Reformer newsletter, and a near monopoly on public communication, opponents had few formal resources at their disposal and little ability to structure debate outside of the established paradigm of leadership.

The three-month lag between the time of the UA convention and the referendum did, however, provide opponents with a small window of opportunity to marshal what forces they could. Opponents were energized when a symbolic leader emerged in the form of Alberta MP and Reform folk hero Myron Thompson. His ability to simply articulate opponents' grassroots logic became the dissidents' unofficial slogan. "If the proposed new party is going to keep Reform policies and principles, why do we need it? If they are not going to keep our principles, why would we want it?"[19] But formally organizing the opposition proved difficult. UA supporters controlled the party's budgeted resources and its army of paid staff. Furthermore, while Reform's executive council took an officially neutral position, it encouraged the leader and members of caucus to "make their views on the wisdom of the UA widely known,"[20] and most caucus members were UA supporters.[21] Nevertheless, a small but determined group of dissidents managed to piece together a rudimentary network of web pages, e-mail groups, and subscriber lists. The group named itself Grassroots United Against Reform's Demise (GUARD) and quickly became the media's focal point for dissenting opinion.[22]

Opponents made gains by portraying the UA as a sell-out of Reform's principles in a misguided effort at achieving power. This message appealed to a large segment of the membership who had joined Reform out of support for its principles above the pursuit of power.[23] They also argued, with some success, that the Ontario problems lay not with the Reform vehicle, but with its leader. Dissent continued to build as the party conducted ten regional conferences leading up to the May vote. All ballots had to be postmarked by May 21 and the final results were announced by Manning in Calgary on June 10, 1999. The results at first appeared somewhat ambiguous. Less than half of the members cast ballots, satisfying the 25 percent threshold requirement, but demonstrating the limits to plebiscitarian democracy even within Reform. Only 60.5 percent voted to proceed, more than enough to allow Manning to continue with the process, but less than would be required to dismantle Reform.[24]

Opponents took some comfort in knowing that they kept support under the two-thirds threshold. But they also knew that Manning now had party-wide approval to proceed. Manning quickly let it be known that he interpreted no ambiguity in the results. Using his harshest rhetoric yet, Manning wrote an open letter to the membership admonishing them to unite behind the process and implying that further open dissent ran counter to the practice of democracy and would not be tolerated.

> If there are any members of our party, whether in the Caucus or on the Executive Council, or on a Constituency Executive, or at the grassroots level who repeatedly engage in undisciplined behaviour — attacking fellow Reformers, particularly on a personal level; misrepresenting the positions of others, whether deliberately or thoughtlessly; discrediting the Party's commitment to democracy by failing to respect democratically made decisions; diverting public attention away from the Party's main objectives by being repeatedly "off message" — both you and I should mark them well, and leave them behind as we make the great transition from an opposition to a governing party.[25]

The party's Vice Chairman, Ken Kalopsis, went further in an attached memorandum that was sent to all constituency associations.

> Thus, Executive Council strongly requests that members of the Party refrain from formal internal Party debates until following the receipt of presentations of Action Committee reports, and that all members of the Party and Caucus unite behind Executive Council in pursuing and supporting the United Alternative process.[26]

It was clear that the leadership intended to use all resources at its disposal, including the referendum process itself, to stifle debate until after it had spent the summer organizing its committees, which in turn would not release their reports until early November. But towards the end of a relatively quiet summer, opponents again began to make waves. After the Progressive Conservatives voted 95 percent against any co-operation, dissidents believed they might have one last chance to kill the initiative. This time they took dead aim at Manning and his leadership. They believed that if they could force a leadership review at the upcoming Reform Assembly, it may be possible to damage Manning's credibility enough to eventually defeat the UA.

Starting the New Party

As the UA opposition appeared to be intensifying on the eve of the Reform and UA conventions, Manning decided to confront the leadership question head-on. In another open letter to Reformers he indicated that he no longer had any interest in Reform, and if the UA initiative failed he would not remain as Reform leader.[27]

> It is conceivable that Reformers might reject the UA for a number of reasons. For my part, however, if I believe that Reformers had rejected the UA initiative because of a reluctance to make a special effort to reach out and include others across the country and a desire to simply consolidate our current base in the West, I would not be interested in or able to lead such a retreat. Under such circumstances, I would therefore not want to seek a renewed mandate to lead the Reform Party.[28]

With the leadership issue cracked wide open, many Reformers feared the worst as they headed to Ottawa for back-to-back Reform and UA conventions being held January 27-30. When party chairman Gee Tsang resigned amidst allegations that UA supporters were undermining his authority, and caucus member Dick Harris stepped forward as a leadership contender, it appeared as though UA opponents might be able to mount one last effort at derailing the project. The last stand strategy depended on a large number of UA opponents showing up in Ottawa to support a leadership review. Once the assembly began, dissidents discovered that they were severely out-gunned and would be quickly overwhelmed by the new UA organization. By the time the assembly ended, dissent had collapsed, Manning had received 74.6 percent support for his leadership, and opponents conceded that the last battle had been lost. From this point on, opposition dissipated, putting up only token resistance prior to the final Reform referendum.[29]

With their opponents seemingly down for the count, the UA leadership was not willing to risk a repeat of the first referendum process where the three-month delay allowed dissidents an opportunity organize resistance. The final Reform membership referendum ballots were printed immediately following the convention with members required to return them by March 17, 2000. During the brief promotional campaign that followed, Manning and other UA supporters spoke to increasingly large and enthusiastic rallies and on March 24 it was announced that members had overwhelmingly endorsed (91.9 percent) folding their party into the new Canadian Alliance.[30] Manning had accomplished his first task, delivering Reform's members, organization, and finances to the new party. He immediately set his sights on the second task, obtaining the Alliance leadership.

The Alliance Leadership Campaign

Although Manning and the other leadership contenders waited until after the Reform referendum before officially launching their campaigns, the January UA convention served as the showcase for prospective candidates. Manning clearly had a head start and substantial residual support within the old Reform base. He had, however, alienated significant segments of the Reform membership, and many of the new Alliance recruits were also looking for new leadership. Stockwell Day announced his candidacy the week following the referendum by emphasizing his fourteen years in the Alberta government. Experienced as Day was, most observers agreed that his greatest asset could be found in the simple fact that he was not Preston Manning. Day's "next step" leadership campaign indicated both his personal political journey and the "logic of the new party." His supporters argued that the logic of starting a new party was based on discarding the Reform image and could only be completed by electing a new leader. The paradox lay in that although Day was a fresh face, like Manning he was an Albertan and a social conservative. In fact, in comparison to Day, Manning appeared to be a moderate. This left some Alliance members looking for a leader that could help shed both Reform's western and its social conservative baggage.

Several prominent Ontario provincial Conservatives had been participating in the UA process from the start. Prior to the second UA convention, Tony Clement had been the most visible, but he expressed no desire to seek the leadership. Neither did Ontario strategist Tom Long, one of the most warmly received speakers at the convention. Eventually junior Ontario cabinet minister Frank Klees became the unofficial Ontario candidate. Hoping to be backed by a strong provincial organization, the Klees campaign speculated about delivering half of Ontario's Conservative MPPs to the new party. But when Klees withdrew his candidacy at what many believed would be its official launch, it appeared that Ontario would not be capable of fielding a candidate at all. Eventually Long entered the race and although his campaign would not live up to many of its grand expectations, he helped in recruiting a number of Ontario provincial Conservatives and lent the race a certain credibility that it would not have had without an Ontario candidate. Two-term Reform MP Keith Martin and Hydro worker John Strachow rounded out the field.[31]

As with Reform, every party member would be allowed to cast a leadership ballot. Most would vote at polling stations in their ridings on June 24, 2000. Members residing in constituencies where the party was not yet well organized would be allowed to televote up to three days in advance, as would members in some rural constituencies. Membership sales would be allowed up to one week prior to voting day. This presented organizers with a substantial administrative challenge;

verifying and processing the flood of memberships, producing voter registration lists, and ensuring PIN numbers reached televoting members in less than one week.[32]

For the first half of the campaign Manning kept a low profile, preferring small private meetings that allowed him to showcase his most effective skills, one-on-one dialogue with individual members. Day, and to a lesser extent Long, ran much more high-profile, media driven campaigns. Regularly speaking to large rallies where organizers claimed to be signing up to four hundred potential supporters, Day was the most active in making fresh policy pronouncements. He also continued his practice of directly answering questions about his social conservative views. The four main contenders squared off in a series of debates during late May and early June. Beginning as a polite race that did little to distinguish the candidates, by mid-June the campaign appeared ready to turn on two key dimensions. Initially, there was the need to choose a leader who was electable in Ontario. Day, not Long, appeared to be leading on this score. But a second major cleavage existed over social conservatism. Long occupied the most solid libertarian ground amongst the three main contenders and attempted to use this wedge to separate himself from Day, and to a lesser extent Manning. He bluntly warned that if the party allowed social conservatism to pervade its image, it would lose the next election.

With the membership sales cut-off date approaching it became clear that the Alliance had signed up well over 100,000 new members. Before the party could celebrate its remarkable recruitment efforts, problems began to surface with some of the candidates' tactics, especially Long's Quebec organization. The most publicized problems were centred in Quebec's Gaspé region, where membership went from zero to 2,800 in a few short months. Similar problems were cropping up in Alberta where the Calgary North East membership exploded to 7,200 from a mere 452 prior to the leadership campaign. The membership irregularities led to calls for postponement of the vote but Alliance officials assured anxious members that all was well and the first ballot vote proceeded as planned. The results surprised many observers, including a number of the candidates. Not only had Day bested Manning by over 8 percent, almost 60 percent of the more than 200,000 members participated, thereby legitimizing the recruitment process and the new party's organizational capabilities.

Table 2
Alliance Leadership Contest Vote Totals

	First Ballot (120,557 votes cast)[33]			Second Ballot (118,487 votes cast)		
	Televoting	Polls	Total	Televoting	Polls	Total
Stockwell Day	46.5	42.8	44.2	62.5	64.3	63.6
Preston Manning	38.6	34.6	36.1	37.5	35.7	36.4
Tom Long	13.4	21.0	18.2	—	—	—
Keith Martin	1.4	1.3	1.4	—	—	—
John Stachow	0.1	0.3	0.2	—	—	—

Day's first ballot victory was substantial (44 percent) but not large enough to ensure that Manning (36 percent) would not force a second ballot. Manning immediately ended speculation that he may concede and began what amounted to the most acrimonious two weeks of the campaign. Manning and his advisors unleashed a full assault on Day's social conservatism, some predicting disaster if he became leader. To overcome Day's 9,000 vote lead, Manning attempted to recruit Long's supporters and the large number of members who did not participate in the first ballot. Both goals would prove elusive. Most of Long's support was in Ontario and Day's first ballot victory demonstrated he was capable of beating Manning there. By the time Long eventually endorsed Manning much of his organization had already joined Day's camp. Entering the final week, as Manning steadfastly refused to make himself available to the media and was speaking to smaller and smaller crowds, it became evident that his campaign, and his career as leader, had run their course.

Day handily defeated Manning on the second ballot and quickly announced that he would contest a soon-to-be-vacated BC seat.[34] He then embarked on an effort at making himself better known in Ontario and Quebec. Riding higher polling numbers than the Reform party had ever achieved,[35] Day spent most of the summer touring central and eastern Canada, brushing up on his French and recruiting former Progressive Conservative and Bloc Québécois supporters to his cause. After handily winning the Okanagan-Coquihalla by-election, Day prepared for a media campaign designed to introduce him to voters across the country.

Campaign Organization and Platform Promotion

The Alliance campaign organization differed markedly from the Reform campaigns of 1993 and 1997. Many personnel changes occurred and for the first time the "war room" would be established in Ottawa, separated from the party's national office in Calgary. Alliance MP and former Day leadership campaign manager Jason Kenny served as campaign co-chair along with former Mulroney principal secretary Peter White, who also served as chief fund-raiser. White would get considerable support from former Ontario lieutenant-governor Hal Jackman, who helped raise over $1.7 million in one dinner on the eve of the election call. The leader's dinner went a long way towards meeting the party's goal of an $8.3 million campaign budget and was equally important on a symbolic level. The dinner demonstrated that the new organization could compete with the Liberals in attracting substantial corporate donations. The national council also appointed an executive campaign committee with the power to borrow money if needed.[36]

The campaign was financed through a variety of fundraising activities, many originating with Reform. In total, Reform-Alliance raised and spent approximately $20 million during 2000. About $9.5 million was direct election spending. Revenue came from a variety of sources. Having just completed an expensive UA process, including the second party-wide referendum, very little cash was transferred into the Alliance with the Reform assets. Many of Reform's Western constituency associations, however, were very well financed. The branches contributed approximately $1.5 million to the national TV advertising budget. Six leader's dinners raised another $3 million while membership subscriptions and donations accounted for approximately $3 million. Like Reform before it, the Alliance sold memberships on its web page, which was also equipped to accept contributions. Party officials estimate that the Alliance raised over $19 million during 2000, $11-12 million of that during the campaign period.

The campaign was organized around Day's tour, with Gord Haugh acting as campaign tour director and Phil von Finckenstein serving as Day's press secretary. Kenney was responsible for scripting the leader's tour while White oversaw the arrangements. Noticeably absent from the tour during the first half of the campaign was Day's campaign director and chief of staff Rod Love. He preferred to remain in Calgary, meeting daily with other organizers by conference call and only joining the tour at the half-way mark when it paused in Ottawa for the leaders' debates. The "war room" was run by Hal Danchilla, Day's former special advisor in Alberta. The "war room" was supported by Paul Wilson and the existing Reform/Alliance research department. During the campaign, 25 to 30 staffers worked out of the "war room," some but by no means all of them being veterans of previous Reform campaigns. The difficult task of recruiting 301 candidates fell to Morten Paulsen, who directed constituency development out of the Calgary office. The party had nominated only about 20 candidates by early October and would have only 90 nominated by the time the election was called, most of them in the West.[37] After the first week of the campaign it had nominated 170 candidates and by the time nominations closed, it would field nearly a full slate. Given that many candidates were not nominated until well into the first weeks of the campaign, time did not permit the Alliance to hold national candidate training sessions as had Reform in 1997.

The overall strategy of the campaign was based on the twin pillars of attempting to turn the election into a referendum on Jean Chrétien's leadership, while at the same time improving voters' levels of trust in the Alliance. Although the party attempted to present the electorate with a national campaign in its quest to be viewed as more than a regional party, the Alliance did in fact focus on one region more than any other. But that region was not the West; clearly, the Alliance focus was on Ontario. The party commissioned one pre-election poll and conducted three smaller tracking polls during the campaign period, all of these in Ontario. The pre-election polling and focus group testing revealed that Ontarians had an interest in Day, but wanted more information before making a final determination. Aware that a fall election was possible, Alliance strategists spent the summer devising a two-stage strategy that would optimally involve a spring 2001 election, but could be accelerated should the Prime Minister decide on a fall vote.

The first stage would be implemented in the fall of 2000 and include introducing Day to voters through media coverage of his by-election victory, a series of television commercials, and the party's platform launch. Three television ads were produced and began running in Ontario in early October. The ads were dominated by images of Day engaged in various telegenic activities such as jogging or chopping wood, while voice-overs discussed the Liberal economic record and Day's plan. The intent was to build trust in Day and in the party's economic and tax agendas, areas where polling had indicated the Prime Minister's credibility was greater than Day's. During the campaign period, the Alliance would spend approximately $5 million on television ads. About half of that was spent in Ontario. Another quarter went to national ads while the remainder was spent on regional advertising in the Maritimes, BC, Saskatchewan, and Manitoba. Interestingly, the national campaign made no regional buys in Alberta. Voters in that province saw only the national Alliance ads and those purchased by local campaigns. No region-specific ads were produced, although different ads would run in different regions at different times during the campaign. Approximately another half-million dollars was evenly split between the print advertising and the party's internet site.[38]

The initial run of advertising would coincide with the party's platform launch in Waterloo on October 5. Like the ads, the Alliance's twenty-four-page platform book was heavily dominated by pictures of Day and statements about his vision for the country. The platform book was not originally intended to serve as the main campaign literature. Rather, it was designed as a pre-election introduction of the leader. The party planned to develop more policy-specific literature that would be released during a spring campaign, but the fall election call meant that the leader-dominated platform book would have to suffice. Based on the general themes adopted at the final UA convention, the platform highlighted a number of important characteristics of the Alliance campaign. The platform significantly modified the linchpin of the young party's economic agenda. By unilaterally changing the 17 percent single-rate income tax policy adopted by the convention, the leadership demonstrated that it would allow itself broad interpretive latitude with the direction it had been given by the members. The Alliance platform now promised two rates, a 17 percent rate on incomes up to $100,000, and a 25 percent rate on money earned above that.[39] Other fiscal aspects of the platform included legislated annual $6 billion debt repayments and a requirement that 75 percent of unexpected surpluses be allocated to debt repayment. Although the fiscal agenda was intended to be the centrepiece of the Alliance campaign, when Paul Martin's mini-budget made the Liberals competitive on taxes, and given that the government had already made more than $12 billion in debt payments in one year alone, the Alliance's economic policy did not allow it to significantly distinguish itself from the Liberals. The apparent about-face on tax policy and the overall vagueness of the platform were major deviations from Reform's previous campaigns. Had Manning made such alterations to Reform policy it would have likely produced a significant backlash within Reform's ranks. However, it now appeared as though the Alliance membership was going to allow the leadership much greater strategic latitude than Reformers would have ever allowed Manning. The Alliance constitution grants the leader, in consultation with the caucus and the national executive council, the ability to set the overall strategic direction of the party.[40] If the 2000 election campaign is any indication of how this article of the constitution will be actualized in the future, the Alliance appears to be drifting backwards into a form of leadership-membership relations more typical of leader-dominated parties rather than advancing the participatory elements Reform had ushered into the new system.

In some areas the platform contained old Reform policies. It promised to eliminate regional development agencies, while seeking private investors for the CBC, VIA Rail, and other crown corporations. The party also stated that it remained committed to recall, free votes in the House of Commons, fixed election dates, and to citizen-initiated referendums. This latter policy would make the party vulnerable to charges of harbouring a hidden social-conservative agenda when it was revealed that a candidate briefing book set the initiative threshold at 3 percent of voters. In other areas the platform deviated from previous Reform efforts, most notably in its declaration of support for the five principles of the Canada Health Act, the principle of equalization payments, and bilingualism. Overall, in comparison to Reform's harder edged platforms of 1993 and 1997, the Alliance policy looked anemic, and certainly left the party open to charges that it had abandoned its focus on policy in favour of a style-driven, leader-focused campaign.

The Campaign

In the weeks leading up to the election call, the Alliance leadership regularly made policy adjustments that often appeared inconsistent and confused. While conducting a pre-election tour of the Atlantic provinces, the party was all over the map with its Employment Insurance policies. Also, at the same time the party was trying to build trust by downplaying its social conservative elements, Day made an appearance on 100 Huntley Street, one of Canada's most popular Christian television broadcasts. Day also refused to deviate from his long-standing habit of not conducting politics on Sundays and would therefore be unavailable for media events on the day the Prime Minister made the election call, the final day of campaigning, and for one-seventh of the total campaign. To accommodate his routine, Day decided to get the jump on the Prime Minister by launching his campaign on the Saturday preceding the formal announcement. Using Parliament Hill as a backdrop, Day confidently predicted that the Alliance would make its Ontario breakthrough by winning 20 to 40 seats. More realistically, the party was targeting about a dozen ridings, focusing on the Simcoe county region north of Toronto, the Niagara region, and a few eastern Ontario ridings. Day's campaign launch included a sharp attack on Liberal arrogance followed by the claim that the Alliance represented the only party capable of generating sufficient support to replace the Liberals. Jason Kenny was left to deal with the media on Sunday after the Prime Minister made the official call.

The Alliance campaign got off to a rocky start that lasted through much of the first week. On the first full day of campaigning, when pressed by reporters to explain why his tour had chosen to visit Quaker Technologies, a thriving six-month-old Ontario high-tech firm whose president stated that taxes were not as big a deal for him as they were for the Alliance, Day retorted there were even some success stories in Russia and that the Liberals had nothing to do with the successes enjoyed by some new economy firms. On its own this apparent gaffe would have been insignificant. However, it was only the first in a series of incidents that lent the appearance of a disorganized and at times amateur campaign organization easily taken off-message by its own mistakes. Beyond the bad optics, however, the rhetoric indicated the strategy that the Alliance would use in attempting to weaken the Liberals' credibility on the economy: blame them for the problems while giving no credit for the successes.

Interestingly, it was the same strategy the Liberals would successfully use against Day while attacking his record in Alberta.

By mid-week it appeared as though the wheels were about to come off the tour. The party's own mistakes were moving its main message off the front pages at the same time the Liberals launched what would become a relentless attack on Day and the Alliance's unknowns. Organizational problems were often magnified by Day's frequent deviations from his formal speaking notes. In one twenty-four hour period he demonstrated both his unfamiliarity with Ontario and his organization's lack of preparations by misjudging the flow of the Niagara River and referring to Ontario farmers as Albertans. As the tour visited Quebec and Maritime ridings where the Alliance stood little chance of victory, divisions within the organization began to emerge as both organizers and journalists questioned the wisdom of many campaign decisions. Day continued rejecting some of his strategists' advice and refused to launch sharp negative attacks against the Prime Minister.[41] He chose instead to continue with his "agenda of respect" in spite of increasing invective emanating from the Liberal campaign. Even when Day attempted negative attacks, it appeared that the best the Alliance could muster were rustic critiques of Chrétien's twenty-year-old record as finance minister, attacks that were easily counter-spun by the Liberal campaign. Despite the troubled first week, Day continued to attract large crowds and by week's end, as the tour arrived in Alberta, it received a much-needed boost from the first round of public opinion polls.[42]

The Alliance had entered the campaign with significantly higher poll numbers than Reform had ever enjoyed and after one week *The Globe and Mail* reported an Alliance surge to 28 percent nationally, up 8 percent since the campaign began. They enjoyed 59 percent support in Alberta, 47 percent in B.C., and were climbing in Saskatchewan and Manitoba. However, despite the Liberals' drop of 7 percent, they still enjoyed 45 percent national support and were well ahead of the Alliance in the crucial battleground province of Ontario. Similar polls released over the weekend confirmed the Alliance's momentum and it entered week two under increasingly intense attacks from all the parties.

As Day prepared to go on the offensive, the Prime Minister unleashed some of his harshest rhetoric yet and several Alliance members again got the campaign off-message with their musings about the party's health care policies. In a speech to the 50th Congress of Liberal International,

Chrétien accused the Alliance of representing the "dark side of human nature." At the same time, Liberal attack ads were adding to the uncertainty over the Alliance's health care position. When *The Globe and Mail* ran a headline declaring that the Alliance supported "two-tier" health care, it appeared as though Day would again have to compete with members of his own campaign to get his message out front.[43] Although both Kenny and Alliance health critic Val Meredith had only commented on the current state of Canada's health care system and the possibility of the Alliance continuing to allow private clinics, the damage had been done and the Liberals pounced on what they dubbed the Alliance's "hidden agenda." Fortune briefly intervened when the Liberals released their Red Book and commentary over its lack of substance temporarily relieved some of the pressure from the Alliance campaign. Nevertheless, Day would have to spent the better part of the next two weeks defending his party against what he referred to as a "two-tier smear."

Day came under increasing pressure from within his own organization to become more forceful and directly attack the Prime Minister as per the strategy of attempting to turn the election into a referendum on Chrétien's leadership. But Day refused, and continued to break from his prepared texts and omit some of the hardest hitting segments. He also struggled to provide details about his economic agenda, promising only to provide more information later. Amid reports that the "Harris Conservatives" were beginning to grumble about not being properly utilized, the media began to focus on the campaign's organization rather than its message. As Paul Wells of the usually supportive *National Post* commented after Day's speech to the Business Council on National Issues, whose membership includes the CEOs of the country's one hundred largest corporations, "[the Alliance] campaign needs to ask itself some serious questions about what it's doing, where it's deploying its resources, and whether its leader's sketchy, harried, off-the-cuff style makes him seem a serious contender for a job that has traditionally been reserved for those who do their homework."[44] Other commentary was equally critical. Bill Cameron summed up the media's consensus at the end of the second week: "amateurish handling of the two-tier issue, wasted days, snarled schedules, speeches that are too long and too bland."[45] As the inevitable comparison between the Alliance campaign and Manning's tightly run Reform campaigns began to emerge, Day's resistance to making direct attacks on the Prime Minister appeared to be softening. At a Calgary fundraising dinner that attracted over 1,500 people and raised $500,0000, although Day continued to omit key parts of his formal speech, he began to insert more passion into his presentation and flirted with harsher rhetoric. When the week-two polls indicated that the Alliance had stalled at just under 30 percent, that the Liberals were continuing their domination of Ontario, and that the Alliance had thus far failed to significantly drive up the Prime Minister's negatives, Day finally abandoned his soft approach and spent the weekend attacking Chrétien's credibility and raising allegations of corruption associated with the Prime Minister's lobbying efforts on behalf of his constituents. The change in tone signaled a turning point in the Alliance campaign. Heading into the leadership debates, most Alliance strategists were now confident that their leader would present a more forceful, and more focused, direct attack on the Prime Minister.

Mid-campaign and the Debates

As all the campaigns assembled in Ottawa for pre-debate preparations,[46] Day faced a dilemma that many had predicted would arise because of "debts" he may owe to the social conservatives who had earlier helped him secure the Alliance leadership. On the one hand Day could not ignore the promises he had made to allow social conservative issues such as abortion to be decided by way of national referenda. On the other hand, the Liberals and Conservatives were beginning to make some headway in driving up Day's negatives by arguing that he harboured a hidden social conservative agenda. When the media discovered copies of an "official but confidential" policy background document that had been sent to all Alliance candidates, the campaign immediately reeled back on the defensive seemingly unprepared for the resulting barrage of questions about the party's support for the sale of the CBC, the end of native tax exemptions, and votes on marijuana use and abortion. Of critical importance was the document's commitment to initiating a national referendum if requested by 3 percent of the total number of voters who cast ballots in the preceding election. This issue more than any other would fuel attacks about a hidden agenda. With opponents arguing that as few as 400,000 extremists could take away abortion choice, Day attempted damage control by assuring voters he was not attached to the 3 percent threshold and that consultations with Canadians would determine at what level the threshold would be set. The counter spin only fed suspicion that Day was either indeed harbouring some hidden agenda, or at best that he was willing to override party policy thereby undercutting the credibility of the Alliance platform commitments.

With the referendum threshold issue simmering as the leaders took the stage for their debates, Day was under increasing pressure to perform well in both languages. During its pre-election Quebec recruitment drive, the Alliance had boasted about their leader's bilingual abilities. Unfortunately, as they had done with their Ontario seat projections, the Alliance created unachievably high expectations for itself and for its new leader. In the French language debate, Day failed to deliver. His French was laboured and he often appeared uninterested in becoming fully engaged. During the English debate he performed much better. He aggressively jumped into the fray, effectively challenging the Prime Minister over the Liberal attack ads and the government's criminal justice record. At one point Day demonstrated his love of theatrics by stepping away from his podium and towards Chrétien while challenging him over the Liberals' characterization of Alberta health care policy and the Alliance's platform. "I have said no two-tier health care system. Do one of two things, Mr. Chrétien, call me a liar or pull those U.S.-style negative ads." He followed-up with a "hand-crafted" sign declaring NO TWO-TIER HEALTH CARE, a move that clearly violated the debate rules and was not easily defended or spun by his team. As the acknowledged runner-up, Day also had to fend off considerable fire from all the leaders, especially over the referenda threshold controversy which had now been solidly attached to the "hidden agenda" charge. For the most part, however, Day effectively defended himself against counter-attacks, the most challenging coming not from the Prime Minister, but from PC leader Joe Clark. By the time the debate deteriorated into a shouting match, Day had left a generally positive image, but had not clearly done anything to warrant declaring him the outright victor.

With the debates helping to raise Chrétien's negatives, the immediate post-debate period saw the Liberals increase both the frequency and intensity of their attacks on Day and the Alliance. In response, and in order to meet its previous commitments to explain its economic policy, the Alliance decided to release its detailed economic platform on the weekend following the debates. Yet again, the desired positive impact of

81

the much anticipated economic blueprint was overshadowed by campaign management issues. Organizers decided to release the twenty-page document on Sunday when Day would not be available for comment. Furthermore, Jason Kenney, who had been substituting for Day on most Sundays, was traveling with the leader and also unavailable. The party left it to their economists to speak to the platform and for Alliance staff to justify why the leader and no senior officials were available for comment. Despite positive commentary from the economists, much of the media either focused on the bad optics of the release strategy or reverted to reporting the party's backtracking on the single-rate tax.

The Campaign's Final Stages

Although the Liberals continued to slip in the national public opinion polls during week four, their slide was not benefiting the Alliance. More alarming for the Alliance campaign was the sharp rise in Day's negative evaluations. The percentage of voters who did not have confidence in the Alliance leader rose from 22.5 percent at the start of the campaign to 31 percent after the debates, the highest of all the leaders. Day was also rated as the least trusted of the leaders.[47] Nevertheless, Day attempted to introduce what Alliance strategists believed to be their most beneficial wedge issues, crime and punishment. But by mid-week Day was back on the defensive, first as a result of CBC skullduggery examining some of his past positions and his religious beliefs, and then when Liberal cabinet minister Eleanor Caplan went on the attack accusing the Alliance of harbouring racists.[48] Day attempted to dismiss the attacks as mere fear-mongering but with the Alliance stalled in Ontario, in what some described as a move born out of desperation, Day launched into his harshest rhetoric of the campaign. He accused Chrétien of potentially being involved in criminal activity while lobbying on behalf of his constituents. Day would continue his attacks on the Prime Minister's ethics until the Ethics Commissioner eventually cleared him. Although the ethics controversy appeared to help bring down Chrétien's personal ratings during the final weeks of the campaign, the Liberals continued to maintain their comfortable lead in the polls and the Alliance campaign continued to be dogged by controversy. While preparing for his final push across the country Day had to engage in more damage control after several of his candidates made controversial race-related statements.

With little momentum and even less time left in the campaign, Day returned to the vote-splitting theme during the final week. He urged Maritimers to unite behind the Alliance so as to not elect Liberals. The problem with using this argument in the Maritimes resulted from the fact that the Conservatives were much better positioned than was the Alliance with respect to Maritime vote-splitting. In a final blitz of key Ontario ridings Day softened his rhetoric in an effort at capitalizing on what advisors believed was voter fatigue with the bitter tone of the campaign. He also urged Ontarians to vote strategically and deny the Liberals a third consecutive majority. Day wrapped up the campaign by traveling West and, as he had done for fourteen years of public life, took the final Sunday of the campaign off. Although he would not campaign live on the final day, he appeared on television in a pre-taped television broadcast that would air only in Ontario.

Conclusion

Although the Alliance's 2000 campaign produced marginal gains from where Reform left off in 1997, the differences between where Reform found itself after the 1997 election and where the Alliance is in 2001 are dramatic. After the 1997 election, the status quo was an option for Reform. Certainly the party would have had to address its leadership issue one way or the other, but there existed a cohesive party unit, organizational structure, and a certain congealment of the various interests that made up the coalition, albeit primarily Western and still somewhat extreme in its policy positions. But Reform was a cohesive party unit, bound together by its membership base as much or more than by its parliamentary caucus.

The Alliance does not find itself in the same position. While some party members have taken comfort in the fact that the Alliance solidified its lock on western seats, and increased its voter support in all regions of the country, the changes that occurred during the transition from Reform to the Alliance left the party with no status quo as a possible option. The early election call and disappointing results caught the party in transition before it had time to congeal into a cohesive party unit capable of binding the often divergent factions it was trying to unite. While some party stalwarts will argue that the party can now complete its transition and live up to its potential in future elections, the immediate post-election period suggests that will be a more difficult task than it was thought to be prior to the election.

The results, especially the lack of a significant Ontario break-through, left many party members devastated. Some have been left with an uneasy sense that all of the effort was wasted and the potential squandered by an inexperienced campaign team and possibly the wrong leader. But those seeking a leadership change have to contend with the argument that it would have been difficult for any leader to accomplish more than did Day. They also have to face the fact that other leadership candidates, especially from Ontario, were not stampeding to become the Alliance leader six months earlier during the leadership campaign, and the election results are not likely to increase the flow of candidates from either Ontario or Alberta. Other members have begun a complete rethinking of the Reform-Alliance project and are again making over-tures to the federal Conservatives. Still others have simply withdrawn from active support. Some of the more radical Westerners, who only grudgingly went along with the transition to the Alliance, have already taken up with new, more radical movements.[49] Other key Alberta sup-porters appear ready to focus their energies on provincial politics and abandon the federal scene.[50] At present, the Alliance appears to be little more than a collection of factions loosely bound together by a party organization where the parliamentary caucus, not the membership base, is the most cohesive element and the driving force within the party. It is here that we witness the greatest changes that occurred in the Reform-Alliance transition: the metamorphosis of a Western, grass-roots, mass-based, extra-parliamentary party into the shell of a more traditional brokerage party. With many of the various factions running off in different directions, and some withdrawing from federal politics altogether, it remains to be seen if the still embryonic organization can coalesce into a stable national party.

NOTES

1   The author wishes to thank the many Reform and Alliance staff, candidates, and volunteers who consented to interviews and provided documentation.

2   For a discussion of Canada's four party systems and Reform's role in helping to bringing about the transition from the third to the fourth systems, see R. Kenneth Carty, William Cross and Lisa Young, *Rebuilding Canadian Party Politics*, (Vancouver: UBC Press, 2000).

3   See Faron Ellis and Keith Archer, "Reform at the Crossroads," in *The Canadian General Election of 1997*, Alan Frizzell and Jon H. Pammett, eds., (Toronto: Dundurn Press, 1997) 111-133.

4   See Faron Ellis and Keith Archer, "Reform: Electoral Breakthrough," in Alan Frizzell, Jon H. Pammett, and Anthony Westell, eds., *The Canadian General Election of 1993*, (Ottawa: Carleton University Press, 1994) 59-77; Also see Faron Ellis, *Reform Party Activists*, (Lewiston, NY: Mellen Press, forthcoming, 2001).

5   Neil Nevitte, Andre Blais, Elizabeth Gidengil, and Richard Nadeau, *Unsteady State: The 1997 Canadian Federal Election*, (Don Mills: Oxford University Press, 2000), 98.

6   Nancy Branscombe, a former Ontario candidate heading the UA project in Ontario as quoted by Sheldon Alberts, "Manning plans puzzles party faithful," *Calgary Herald*, Friday, May 29, 1998, A3

7   Preston Manning and Andre Turcotte, "New Dimensions Shape Politics of the 21st Century," *Calgary Herald*, Friday, June 19, 1998, A19; Faron Ellis, "Reformers Yet To Be Sold On '3-D' Politics," *Calgary Herald*, Saturday, June 27, 1998, H6; and Diane Ablonczy, "Reform's United Alternative looks beyond the labels," *Calgary Herald*, Saturday, July 11, 1998, H6.

8   Manning had unsuccessfully tried to "moderate" Reform in the past. His problem resided in the core ideology of the members he recruited into Reform, which were for the most part right-of-centre. For an analysis of ideology in the Reform membership base see Faron Ellis and Keith Archer, "Ideology and Opinion Within the Reform Party," in Hugh G. Thorburn and Alan Whitehorn, eds., *Party Politics in Canada*, 8th edition (Toronto: Prentice Hall, 2001) 122-134.

9   Manning had insisted that a sunset clause be put into the original Reform constitution. The party would cease to exist in the year 2000

unless the members decided that it still served a purpose in Canadian federal politics. Ironically, the members had to vote to extend the date long enough to ensure an orderly decommissioning of the party. For an insightful discussion of Manning and his quest for a grand political synthesis see Tom Flanagan, *Waiting for the Wave*, (Toronto: Stoddart, 1995).

10 Sheldon Alberts, "Klein backs unite-the-right movement," *National Post*, October 27, 1998, A1. This story ran on the front page of the inaugural edition of the *National Post*, Canada's new national daily newspaper. For the next two years the *Post* could be counted on to report on and often provide editorial support for the UA initiative.

11 Faron Ellis, "United Alternative evolving into anti-Reform," *Calgary Herald*, Monday, February 1, 1999, A12.

12 Alberta Premier Ralph Klein, "Address to the United Alternative Convention," Ottawa, February 19, 1999.

13 Don Martin, "Stockwell may have his day in the sun with new party," *Calgary Herald*, Sunday, February 21, 1999, A15.

14 Preston Manning, "Uniting for the 21st Century: Address to the United Alternative Convention," Ottawa, Saturday, February 20, 1999.

15 The three unremarkable themes that were to define the United Alternative were Economic and Fiscal, Social, and Democratic and Governance themes. See "Report to Reformers from Preston Manning, Leader - Reform Party of Canada," March 8, 1999.

16 The Reform constitution also required that a minimum of 25 percent of the membership cast valid votes. Reform Party of Canada Constitution, Article 8b. If a new party was the result, a 2/3 majority vote overall, and a majority in a majority of provinces would be required to change the constitution. *Constitution of the Reform Party of Canada*, Article 7g.

17 The resolution adopted by the UA convention charged the UA Steering Committee with establishing seven organizing committees including a constitution committee directed to develop a new constitution for a new political entity. See Manning, "Report to Reformers," 13.

18 See Carty et. al., *Rebuilding Canadian Party Politics*.

19 Sheldon Alberts, "Popular Reform MP rejects Manning plan to unite right: Myron Thompson's opposition reflects grassroots resistance," *National Post*, Friday, April 29, 1999, A1.

20 Manning, "Report to Reformers," 20.

21 Eventually 15 of 58 Reform MPs would oppose the initiative.

22 See "GUARD'S 10 reasons to vote no to the UA question," *Calgary Herald*, Saturday, April 10, 1999, A16. Important members of GUARD included former Saskatchewan executive council member Christine Whitaker, and Albertans Bruce Stubbs, Ron Thorton, Real Gagne and Don Reimer.

23 Harold D. Clarke, Allan Kornberg, Faron Ellis, and Jon Rapkin, "Not for Fame or Fortune: A Note on membership and Activity in the Canadian Reform Party," in *Party Politics*, Vol. 6, No. 1 (London: Sage Publications, 2000), 75-93.

24 Of the approximately 65,000 Reform members, 32,099 cast valid ballots, 19,417 voted "Yes" while 12,682 voted "No" (176 ballots were spoiled). Reform Party News Release, "United Alternative Referendum Results," June 10, 1999. The question also passed in all provinces except Saskatchewan, where a majority of Reform's MPs, led by Cypress-Grasslands MP Lee Morrison, had opposed the UA.

25 Preston Manning, "An Open Letter to Reformers," July 19, 1999.

26 Ken Kalopsis, "Update on United Alternative Activity," July 19, 1999.

27 Lorne Gunter, "Taking hostages: Reform leader Preston Manning has issued what amounts to a suicide bomb threat: Give me what I want, or I'll blow this place up and take all of you with me," *Calgary Herald*, Wednesday, January 19, 2000, A15.

28 Preston Manning, "An Open Letter to Reformers on the Leadership of the UA and Reform," January 7, 2000.

29 See Faron Ellis and Ron Thorton, "Vote NO," and Grassroots 4UA-Yes Committee, "Think Big: Vote Yes!," the two essays that were printed with the Alliance constitution and accompanied the Reform membership referendum ballots.

30 Approximately 75,000 ballots were issued and 48,838 were cast (65 percent of the membership).

31 John Stachow, an Ontario Hydro nuclear worker entered the race late.

32 Over the course of the campaign, the Alliance would see its membership swell from the approximately 75,000 Reformers, who were automatically made members of the new party, to over 200,000.

33 Returns indicated that Albertan's were still the single largest group of participants accounting for 33.5 percent of those who cast ballots, Ontario followed closely at 32.4 percent; BC 20 percent;

Saskatchewan 4.8 percent; Manitoba 3.8 percent; Quebec 2.5 percent; the Atlantic provinces and the North accounted for only 3 percent of the vote.

34   Sitting Alliance MP Jim Hart had already announced that he would not be seeking re-election in the British Columbia riding of Okanagan-Coquihalla. It was later revealed that the party paid Hart $50,000 to hasten his departure. Hart won the riding in 1997 with 53.1 percent of the vote compared to 26.4 percent for the second place Liberals.

35   The Alliance was polling up to 24 percent nationally and enjoying a 27 point shift in leadership approval as a result of the leadership change according to Angus Reid pollster Darrell Bricker. See Shawn McCarthy, "Alliance surges, Tories collapse: Day helping new party make gains while Liberals maintain solid national lead, poll finds," *Globe and Mail*, Saturday, July 29, 2000, A1.

36   The executive committee borrowed $2 million to help finance the campaign. See Brian Laghi, "Alliance national council to probe extra spending," *Globe and Mail*, Saturday, December 9, 2000, A8.

37   The party had placed an October 10 moratorium on Ontario nominations.

38   The party's website, while competent, was bland and suffered from the same problems all party sites suffer, a lack of use of the full potential of the net. The dilemma for political parties is that although the net represents the potential to communicate directly with specific voters, the real potential of internet sites is found in their ability to link to and therefore provide multiple information sources. Given that parties attempt to use the net as a medium for unfiltered information transfer, they are reluctant to link up to outside sources and therefore forego much of the net's potential.

39   Canadian Alliance, "A time for Change: An Agenda of Respect for All Canadians," Canadian Alliance 2000 election platform.

40   See Alliance Constitution, Article 7(a)iii.

41   The divisions between strategists occurred along the fault line of those from Day's Alberta camp, who argued for a softer, more positive approach, and others, primarily veterans of previous Reform efforts and Ontario Conservatives, who advocated a more aggressive, negative campaign.

42   The campaign also made some organizational adjustments. Rick Anderson, Reform's '97 and '93 campaign director, was provided

the challenge of instilling greater discipline and consistency in Day's message at each event. Jim Armour, who was recently the Alliance's communications director, was brought back as communications specialist for the campaign. Manning was also set to take a more active role in the Alliance campaign.

43 Shawn McCarthy, "Alliance supports two-tier health care: Government should give provinces leeway in promoting private clinics, co-chair says," *Globe and Mail*, Tuesday, October 31, 2000, A1.

44 Paul Wells, "Liberal tortoise and the Alliance: Day must stop improvising, stick to campaign script," *National Post*, Friday, November 3, 2000, A16.

45 Bill Cameron, "As gentle as the day is long," *National Post*, Saturday, November 4, 2000, A9.

46 Strategists from the Tom Long's failed Alliance leadership bid had been working exclusively on debate preparations for weeks. The team included Dan Nolan, Rohit Gupta, and Jordan Bernamoff, who all had long-standing attachments to the federal and provincial Ontario Tories. Eric Duhaime, a former Bloc Quebecois adviser, helped prepare Day for the French debates. See Jane Taber, "Camps rehearse for televised election battle: Consultants hired, studios booked for mock debates," *National Post*, Tuesday, November 7, 2000, A15.

47 Ian Jack, "Day least trusted among party leaders," *National Post* Thursday, November 16, 2000, A18.

48 The CBC documentary entitled "The Fundamental Day," ran on the National Magazine, Wednesday, November 15, 2000. The piece dredged up a series of past allegations and innuendo without providing a response from Day.

49 Howard May, "Western Separatist parties emerge from infancy," *Calgary Herald*, Thursday, January 4, 2001, A6.

50 See Stephen Harper, Tom Flanagan, Ted Morton, Rainer Knopff, Andrew Crooks, and Ken Boessenkool, "Open Letter to Ralph Klein," *National Post*, Friday, January 26, 2001, A14.

Chapter 3

Some Battles Won, War Lost:
The Campaign of the Progressive Conservative Party

by Peter Woolstencroft

As it entered the Federal Election of 2000 the Progressive Conservative Party of Canada did not even pretend that it would form a government, majority or minority. Even winning Official Opposition status was not the goal. For the Tories, the compelling object was to survive. With rare good fortune coming to the PCs, perhaps the Liberals might be denied a majority. Before the election call, political commentators routinely speculated that the Tories faced elimination as a viable electoral force. Party insiders could not be sanguine, given that Parliament's rule required twelve seats for a party to have official standing, and only one riding — the Saint John redoubt of Elsie Wayne in New Brunswick — was considered safe. With the Tories mired at single digits in public opinion polls and badly trailing the Liberals in Atlantic Canada — the region that had given the PCs a healthy number of seats in 1997 along with roughly the same share of the popular vote as the Liberals — there was little reason to think that the party would achieve official party standing. Throughout the campaign, media stories about the PCs regularly contained references to the party's imminent demise. For the media and the public alike, seemingly only two parties, the Liberals and the fledgling Canadian Alliance, were major players.

This essay discusses critical events in the Conservative Party between the 1997 and 2000 elections, which both created and revealed weaknesses in the party, and the election campaign itself. Running through the discussion is the fact that the Tories were in a strategically and tactically difficult situation: not only were they looking for votes and seats, they had to protect their right flank from a predator born of their loins while squeezed by a centrist party keen on polarizing the choice between themselves and the Alliance, between core Canadian values and extremism, between good and evil. Generally parties attempt to maximize their votes (and thus their seats): in 2000 the Tories tried to minimize their losses — and survive.[1] There were few assets to work with, other than tradition, the experienced hand of the leader, Joe Clark, and widespread disenchantment with the Prime Minister.

The 1997–2000 Period

The 1997 election had been bittersweet. Although they still were only the fifth largest party in the Commons, the Conservatives had recovered sufficiently from the 1993 disaster (in which they won only two seats) to hold official party standing. Moreover, the Reform Party, looking to eliminate the Tories as a viable contender by making a breakthrough in eastern Canada, had been held at bay. Since the PCs' twenty seats came from six provinces, there was some basis for the party's claim — and aspiration — to constitute a national entity. With Jean Charest, the party's leader since the 1993 debacle, enjoying high approval ratings in the polls, Tory partisans reasoned that the survival issue had been settled and it was the Reform party that was doomed to die, either by withering or imploding.

Charest, by establishing residence in Ottawa in December, 1997 and concentrating on party rebuilding efforts, seemed to have committed himself to the long haul, although some claimed he seemed distant and uninvolved. A major theme of his rhetoric was the impossibility of Reform and the PCs coming together since they had a number of fundamental differences. All plans, however, had to be rejigged in March, 1998 with the unexpected resignation of Daniel Johnson, the leader of the Quebec Liberals. Charest, in turn, bowing to enormous pressure, left federal politics to become leader of the provincial Liberals in Quebec.

The effect was palpable: polls showed a big drop in Tory support following Charest's departure. Questions about potential candidates were raised in the context of political marginality. Moreover, the party's leadership selection rules, adopted after the 1993 election as part of the rebuilding process, created an enormous organizational challenge.[2] For the first time in Canadian politics, the federal Tories would choose their leader on the basis of "one member, one vote" rather than through a delegated convention. Democracy, adopted as a demonstration of the party's openness, presupposed financial resources and vibrant constituency organizations; but the party was deeply in debt and lacked riding infrastructures in many parts of the country.

Joe Clark, who had left electoral politics in 1993 after over twenty years in Parliament (including seven years as leader and a short stint as Prime Minister) won a desultory race against four contenders in the late fall of 1998. Even before the leadership election's second ballot, Preston Manning, leader of the Reform Party, invited Clark to join him in the United Alternative (UA) movement that Manning had initiated earlier in the year. The "unite-the-right" issue was to bedevil Clark and the Tories for the next two years. As the party sought to build for the forthcoming election, a competitor sought to eliminate it, either through absorption or domination.

An early decision by Clark not to seek a Commons seat (on the grounds that his attention had to be focused on party-rebuilding efforts) proved to be contentious, a lightning rod of criticism especially for those associated with the Reform party and the UA movement. Nonetheless, through the first nine months of 1999, the party's standing in the polls slowly improved. Progressive Conservative parties won provincial elections in Nova Scotia, New Brunswick, and Prince Edward Island, and showed well in Newfoundland and Labrador. Mike Harris's PC government was re-elected in Ontario. Only in Manitoba was there a stumble, with the long-standing Gary Filmon government losing to the New Democrats. On the other hand, Ralph Klein's government in Alberta was popular and without a strong opponent. To be sure, Harris, silent about his federal preferences in 1997, and Klein, a Charest supporter, were not sharing platforms with Clark, unlike the leaders of the Atlantic provincial Tory parties.[3]

By early fall of 1999, when the Tories gathered at an annual meeting, a poll had them at the 20 percent mark (and Reform far behind).[4] A New Democrat, Angela Vautour, first elected in the New Brunswick riding of Beausejour-Petitcodiac in 1997, defected to — not the Liberals — but the Tories. Buoyed by improving prospects, almost 1500 Tory delegates, with a vote of over 95 percent, rejected the idea of reaching any accommodation with Reform and committed themselves to running candidates in each of the 301 constituencies.

There was some basis for the belief in happier times. Analysis of survey data from the 1997 election contained two important points. First, the Tories were considerably ahead of Reform in terms of "fair" or "strong" party identification (11 to 6 percent); outside of Quebec, the PCs, after the Liberals, were the most popular second choice of voters, far ahead of Reform.[5] Optimism seemed reasonable, especially if Reform did not change leaders. Tory thinking made two assumptions. First, the United Alternative project (see Chapter Two of this volume) was doomed to failure. It would lead either to a split between Reform's support base and new members (perhaps resulting in two parties, both much weaker than the original), or rejection of the very idea itself. Second, in the event of a successful launch of a new party, Manning would be its new leader, resulting in no improvement in their prospects in Ontario or points east. The Tories, then, would have an opening for a substantial challenge to the Liberals.

On the other hand, as had been evidenced during the 1998 leadership election, the party suffered a number of organizational weaknesses.[6] In 1999, only about a third of the country's 301 ridings had fully active constituency associations; Quebec was particularly weak, with many ridings having little or no local party activity.[7] Across the country the party's membership stood at 18,682 (far behind Reform, which was reported to have over 60,000 members) and much lower than the over 90,000 members it had in 1998. Further, UA operatives worked the convention halls and held meetings, with some calling for both Manning and Clark to step aside, so that Harris, Ontario's Tory Premier, could lead the melding of Reform and the PCs. A number of Tories, most notably Jim Jones, Ontario's only Tory MP, and Brian Pallister, who had been a candidate for the party's leadership in 1998, called for the parties to find common ground.

Tory optimism began to fade in late 1999 and early 2000. Various events and departures from Tory ranks led to predictions that the next election would see the PCs' disappearance from national politics. Reform successfully completed its United Alternative process by voting to establish a new party. Its new name — Canadian Reform Conservative Alliance Party — heralded exactly what faced the PCs.[8] In early summer, Manning lost the leadership to Stockwell Day, who despite his deep Alberta roots and social conservatism, was considered to be attractive to a sufficiently large segment of Ontario's electorate that Tory hopes would be demolished. Although Tom Long, an Ontario-based candidate for the party's leadership, had been unsuccessful, his and Day's efforts brought many Ontarians into the party, notably some Tory cabinet ministers and party operatives.[9]

Within the federal Tories, there was little good news. In late 1999, Clark, with no consultation with his caucus, opposed Ottawa's proposed

"Clarity Bill" and its stipulation of conditions for any future separation referendum in Quebec. Caucus unhappiness was exacerbated by Clark's unilateral support of a controversial Alberta bill that opened the door to private health providers and what its opponents described as "two-tier" health care. Early in 2000, Charlie Powers resigned his seat of St. John's West. Through 2000 Tory poll numbers continued to fall and fundraising was increasingly difficult.[10] Party officials and activists at an election planning meeting in March feared that the party was spiralling into oblivion. As the Alliance leadership race was soaking up money, they called upon Clark to signal commitments on the tax issue in advance of the party's policy convention in Quebec in order to bolster Tory fundraising. Clark responded by announcing that the PCs would fully eliminate the capital gains tax. Difficulties continued, however, with a Quebec MP, André Harvey, the party's whip in the House of Commons, leaving the caucus in April and eventually joining the Liberals. According to media reports, members of the parliamentary caucus were unhappy with Clark's leadership and concerned about the party's prospects.[11]

Setting the Policy Direction of the Party

The Conservative Party, following its practice in the post-1993 period, called upon its members to participate in the development of the election platform. The structure was straightforward: constituencies and groupings of constituencies held meetings throughout the 1999-2000 period, with delegates meeting in Quebec City in May to vote on resolutions from the constituency-based meetings. The general tenor of the policy resolutions was conservative: abolition of the capital gains tax; staged reduction of the national debt over twenty-five years; deficit-free budgets; restoration of federal health care spending to 1993 levels; and tougher positions on young offenders and illegal immigrants. The party's "red tory" tradition was manifested in its commitment to increase guaranteed income supplements for seniors and to enhance support for agriculture. Clark aroused his audience with the declaration that for the Tories, unlike the Canadian Alliance, "there are no second-class Canadians"; in fact, equality of all citizens was a fundamental commitment of the party.

Clark continued to send confusing messages about his plans to seek a Commons seat. In mid-May he spoke about contesting a by-election created by a Tory MP's resignation.[12] In late May he changed track by announcing he would not seek to enter the House before a general election.[13] Just before the second CA leadership vote in July the PCs suffered two more defections. Senator Gerry St. Germain, a former MP and party President, joined the Alliance, followed shortly by Jim Jones, MP for Markham, who had been dismissed from the Tory caucus because of his support for the CA project. Finally, after the Alliance chose its new leader, Stockwell Day, and was moving up in the polls, Clark announced that he would stand in the Nova Scotia riding of Kings-Hants, which was to be vacated by the sitting Tory MP. In August the party was rocked by defections to the CA of Quebec constituency officials and party workers. In the King-Hants by-election, Clark's triumph was marred by the news that two Quebec MPs were defecting to the Liberals.[14] Shortly thereafter the party's president, Peter Van Loan, resigned following media reports that he was part of a group that was raising questions about Clark's leadership. Following the Van Loan resignation, a number of Ontario campaign workers resigned their various offices. Their replacements — most notably the Ontario campaign's co-chairs — were not in place until mid-October.

John Laschinger's Campaign Strategy

Tory election planning had presumed a spring election in 2001, but by August the signals were clear that the Prime Minister likely would seek a new mandate in the autumn. John Laschinger was asked by Clark in early August to become the national campaign manager, but his business commitments precluded acceptance before the second week of September — which meant, as it turned out, that he had about six weeks to prepare for the campaign.[15] Laschinger's track record went back to the 1980s: he was the architect of Bernard Lord's upset victory in New Brunswick in 1999, when a young, relatively unknown leader of a party deep in the political wilderness defeated a well-established Liberal government.

The fundamental planning constraint facing Laschinger was money. Because of indebtedness (standing at about $8 million when the election was called), the party's Management Committee, following the lead of its National Council, had limited the national party's election budget to $5 million. In the event, the party spent $4.5 million (far less than its national competitors would spend and less than spending in 1993 or

1997).[16] Media speculation earlier in 2000 that corporate dollars were flowing to the Alliance rather than the PCs proved to be correct, as the party raised only $2.5 million during the election, which led to the contraction in the election budget and expansion of the party's line of credit. Two million dollars was spent on advertising, mostly television.

Laschinger's approach to elections is to prepare a strategic plan based on three pillars. First, there must be well-grounded research. Second, the election plan must be focused in its tactics and goals. Third, it must be followed with discipline, not altered with every bump, hitch, or doubt. Accordingly, one of Laschinger's first decisions was to commit about $200,000 to electoral research (focus groups and polling). Laschinger learned that there was considerable unhappiness with the Liberal government, particularly with the Prime Minister, who was seen as not keeping his promises. Further, no party had been able to coalesce discontent around its standard. The Alliance had enjoyed a rise in the polls, but apparently had plateaued as voters sharpened their knowledge of Day. On the policy front, disquietude flowed from the cuts associated with Ottawa's preoccupation with deficit-elimination, to the detriment especially of health-care funding, and a sense that the country was drifting economically. Strategically, Alliance voters were unlikely to be lured away, especially by the Tories. Many Liberal voters, however, were "soft" and amenable to change, but were cautious about, perhaps fearful of, the perceived extremism of the Alliance. The potential for Tory votes was blunted by the perception that the PCs had little likelihood of victory.

On the policy front, there were few obvious targets, certainly nothing salient to most voters that other parties were not addressing. Health care was obvious, as all public opinion research, including the PCs' internal work, put the issue far ahead of any other matter. The NDP had signalled that health care would be its rallying message. The Alliance would talk about health care, tax reductions, law and order, and the fiscal mismanagement of the Liberals, each of which also were talking points for the Tories. The Liberals, for their part, not only had a robust economy and budgetary surpluses to brag about, they had signed a health care protocol with the provinces in September and in October had introduced massive tax cuts. Moreover, they were not carrying the burden of unpopular cuts to Employment Insurance as they had in 1997; in fact, by reversing many of the cuts after the 1997 election they had tempered much of the Atlantic electorate's anger, which had cost the Liberals many seats in the region and allowed the Tories and the NDP to do well.

The PC analysis of the country's problems focused on health care cuts; education, particularly the brain drain; rising taxes; safe communities; and the Liberal government's financial mismanagement. Accordingly, the Tories promised to "restore the cash portion of the Canada Health and Social Transfer to at least 1993–94 levels" along with legislated guaranteed future funding. They also proposed to introduce a wide range of measures to support post-secondary students, increase RCMP funding, revise the Young Offenders Act, repeal the current gun registration system, and introduce a Safe Water Act and a Safe Air Act.[17]

Unlike 1997, when the platform was devoid of any specific agriculture policy, the 2000 version gave considerable attention to the farm sector of the economy. Stress was placed on a new stabilization fund that would support non-quota based farm products with up to $1.7 billion over five years. The other parties had far less to say about agriculture, which led Clark to challenge the other leaders to a debate on agricultural topics. Again, unlike the 1997 platform, the PCs in 2000 addressed a wider set of issues, such as increased funding for the fisheries, regional development, and social housing. In sum, unlike the 1997 document, which was very much inspired by the Harris government's emphasis on cutting government spending and taxes, the platform in 2000 had a much more centrist tone, reflecting, no doubt, Clark's version of progressive conservatism.[18]

Strategically, the PCs had three fundamental objectives. First, retain official party status. Second, elect Clark in Calgary Centre. Third, blunt the move of the Alliance into eastern Canada, especially Ontario.[19] Laschinger's election plan was built on three elements. First, the party had to establish its policy credentials by staking out territory between the Liberals and the Alliance; the latter's perceived extremism prompted the Tory slogan, "Change you can trust." Second, disparate strands of negativity had to be focused on the Prime Minister. Third, through Clark's performance in the campaign, especially in the debates, the Tories would establish themselves as a viable option, not an easy task given their poor showing in the polls. Part of the strategy was the "low expectations game," which simply requires doing better than received wisdom imagines you will. Clark, so often underestimated in the past, would have to reach deep in 2000, but had the necessary experience, capacity, and determination to shine. This "low expectations" approach was encouraged by party organizers, who avoided hyperbolic projections and did not contradict reports about money problems and operational uncertainties such as the availability of a plane or bus for the leader's tour.

There were ample reasons for low expectations. Although the rhetoric of the party's leaders routinely referred to it as a national political entity, the territorial focus at the outset of its campaign belied these pretensions. In the West and North only Calgary Centre and Brandon Souris were seriously considered to be winnable (and according to local polls Clark was far behind his Alliance opponent). In Ontario, only a few rural ridings in the Southwest and the east were reasonable prospects; there were no urban or suburban ridings where the PCs thought they were competitive. Quebec was barren ground, with just Richmond Arthabaska — the sole PC-held riding in the province — even a possibility given the absence of a vibrant Tory campaign in the province. Only in Atlantic Canada did the party believe that it had growth prospects, but only a handful of seats were in reach. As well some PC seats were vulnerable because of Liberal strength and NDP decline.

The electoral prospects of the party were matched by its constrained organizational resources, with party insiders estimating that about half of the country's 301 ridings had viable constituency associations. Indeed, in 1999 only about a third of associations satisfied the party's constitutional requirements.[20] On the other hand, a good part of the party's social base had remained loyal in 1997. Further, the party's long history meant that in most constituencies there were activists and friends of the party who could rally round the flag, help raise money locally, and recruit candidates.

The party's meagre prospects meant that candidate recruitment was difficult, especially in Ontario where municipal elections in November meant that many prospective nominees demurred. In fact, a number of potential candidates were considering running for the Alliance. In the run-up to the election there were few "star" candidates who could be seen as bringing substance, attention, and support to the campaign. Instead, the Tories comforted themselves with the view that they were running a goodly number of local notables. Still, the party scrambled to have a full roster, which it thought it had achieved, only to have a number of candidates disqualified for missing the filing deadline or having insufficient signatures.[21] In the end, the party had 291 candidates.

Negative and Not Much Else

Negative advertisements are not new in Canadian politics. Such advertisements are directed toward the personal discrediting of one's opponents, often without any effort to claim virtue for oneself. The Tory party had used negative advertising to great effect in the 1988 campaign, but had suffered enormously in 1993 from its utilization of television commercials that focused on Chrétien's facial features.[22] Despite these mixed results, the Conservatives in 2000 decided to use *only* negative advertising throughout the campaign.

Despite his popularity and the Liberal standing, Chrétien had a weakness: the perception that he had lied, especially about the abolition of the GST and the renegotiation of NAFTA. What had to be done was to remind voters why they disliked the Prime Minister. Laschinger's thinking was that it was imperative to move the electorate into an "it's time for a change" mood and that only negative advertising would do this. In a multi-party system, a change in government would only come about if a large number of voters wanted one.[23] Besides, there was nothing to lose.[24]

Accordingly, Tory advertising was sharply negative, starting with a one-time newspaper advertisement appearing in ten papers across the country the day after the election was called. Focusing on the $200 million cost of the election, it portrayed the Prime Minister white-water rafting with the headline, "Hold Tight, Canada. We're Being Taken For a Ride." Readers were invited to call Liberal offices in Ottawa to complain about the unnecessary election. For Laschinger, a sub-text of the effort was a message to party activists that the party was going to be a player in the election. The big challenge for Laschinger was to find some way of breaking through the clutter of television advertisements, political and non-political alike, and attract attention to the PCs. At the start of the campaign's third week, just days before the leaders' debates, the PCs began running two television advertisements across Canada, concentrated in Ontario and Atlantic Canada (except for the Calgary area). One, modelled on television advertisements of the last twenty-five years that sold low-end goods with a rapid-fire, in-your-face jingle, invited Canadians to buy a record album carrying Chrétien's "101 Greatest Lies." The "K-Tel" ad, as it was dubbed, even elicited calls from people wanting to buy the record. The other advertisement picked up on Chrétien's statement that God would strike him with lightning if he failed to keep his 1993 election promises. The "act of God" ad had rain pounding on the Liberal's 1993 Red Book accompanied by heavy thunder, a bolt of lightning, and a burst of flame. Both ads barely referenced the PCs and did not even tell voters what to do. Their production values were minimal, to say the least, but according to Laschinger generated a lot of attention (including a lot of free plays on newscasts) and little criticism.

Unlike the Liberals and the Alliance, the Tories held back their TV advertisements, partly for financial reasons and partly because Laschinger reasoned that the electorate would not be following the election closely in the early going. For him, the election had three stages: the first was the run up to the debates; the second was the debate period itself; the last stage was the post-debate period. The first stage required the party to establish its policy credibility. Party organizers judged this was accomplished, inasmuch as throughout the campaign the platform not only was not criticized by the other parties but also received accolades from the media, leading to a number of editorial endorsements. They also sought to undermine the Prime Minister's credibility.[25] On the latter point, Clark criticized the Prime Minister for calling the election and for his unethical involvement in various government-funded projects, particularly in his own constituency. This was a theme Clark would return to in the last weeks of the campaign. One of Clark's first events was a major fundraiser in Toronto where Brian Mulroney, whose administration had been at the root of the 1993 and 1997 disasters, was prominently featured. Logistically, Clark's tour was smooth but crowds were small and not overly enthusiastic.

"Congratulations, Joe, You Have Saved the Party"[26]

The debate stage of the campaign was difficult but straightforward. Clark had to rise above the crowd by making his points cogently and establishing credentials as a party leader and potential Prime Minister. Given the party's limited financial resources, the debates would be its only real opportunity to validate its claim as a legitimate contender for office. It was imperative that it be Clark's night. Tory organizers had four concerns about the leadership debates. Charest, by all accounts, had won the leaders' debates in 1997 but there had been little positive spillover on Tory fortunes.[27] How, then, to convert a positive night into votes and seats? Second, Clark, by his own admission, was rusty. It had

101

been over twenty years since he had participated in a televised leaders' debate; indeed, since 1993, he had only a couple of weeks of parliamentary experience and direct partisan battling to call upon. The third concern was how to avoid the raucous free-for-all that a debate involving five party leaders could become. Lastly, they tried not to over-prepare Clark, lest his spontaneity be stifled.

Debates, however, are noisy events that can easily turn voters off. It is often hard for participants to differentiate themselves from others. As it turned out, Clark not only performed well in both the French and English language debates, but commentators and survey respondents declared him the winner.[28] Partly, this was due to the aggressiveness of Clark's planned point that Chrétien called the election out of vanity to keep Paul Martin, the Finance Minister, from succeeding him. Partly, it was due to the singularity of Clark's humour, especially with his description of Day who, against the debate's rules, had displayed a hand-written sign about "No Two-Tier Health Care," as trying out for the position of game-show host. Partly, it was due to Clark's avoiding extended entanglements with the other leaders and concentrating on Chrétien, keeping on message throughout the debate. The question was: would there be any change in the polls? The last survey reported before the debates had the Liberals rising and the PCs still in single digits. While the ads were attracting attention, Clark's crowds were small and party operatives had to be sent ahead to generate crowds. Indeed, modeling of various poll results (which generally still had the PCs in single digits) suggested that they were destined to win one seat, which had been the best internal Tory estimate when the election was called.[29]

As part of their electoral research, the Tories conducted rolling polls in twenty-five to thirty constituencies in which they believed they were competitive; the bulk of the ridings were in Ontario and Atlantic Canada. During the campaign some ridings were dropped and added. The poll results provide information about the impact of the Tory campaign, especially Clark's performance in the debates, in constituencies (most of which were Tory-held) where it was imperative the party improve. A clear sign of the desperation of the party's situation was the fact that at the beginning of the tracking in Atlantic Canada the Liberals were ahead of the Tories by nineteen points (50 percent to 31 percent); the final results had the Tories ahead by a point (38 percent to 37 percent). In late October about 55 percent of respondents said that the country was heading in the right direction, while 31 percent thought otherwise; by campaign's end, respondents were divided (43 percent said "yes" and 46 percent said "no"). Whether it was time to maintain the status quo or time for a change showed a similar pattern. The initial round of polling had a break of 56 percent to 44 percent; the last polling reversed the percentages. Sentiment in favour of change peaked just at the time of the debates.

Evaluations of the parties also indicated that the Tory campaign had been productive. After the writ was dropped, the Liberals in terms of net impressions (positive ratings less negative ratings) were far ahead of the other parties. Indeed, the non-Liberal parties shared one thing in common at the beginning of the campaign; higher negative ratings than positive, giving them a minus score on the index. By the last weekend, the Alliance and NDP scores had worsened, but the Tories had improved to the same level as the Liberals, whose scores dropped steadily through the campaign's five weeks.

Overall, net impression of the party leaders had a similar pattern. Initially, Chrétien had a healthy lead over his competitors, who barely were on the positive side of neutral. By campaign's end, Day's scores had seriously weakened, but not as much as Chrétien's, which had tipped to the negative side of neutral. Alexa McDonough of the NDP improved her scores, but had not maintained the high score obtained shortly after the debates. The values for Clark had gone negative in the first two weeks of the campaign, but tracked into positive territory after the debates and improved steadily thereafter to produce the best results for any leader by election day. In terms of "Who would make the best Prime Minister?", only Clark showed appreciable improvement in his ratings (from around 20 percent to 36 percent). Chrétien's high 40s slipped to the mid-30s by voting day and the other leaders were essentially flat.

The PC party's ratings improved considerably throughout the campaign period. For the question "which party has shown the most momentum in the campaign?", the Liberals moved in the 40s, closing at 46 percent. The Alliance fell from the mid-30s to 20 percent, while the NDP was flat at 2 percent, and the Tories moved from mid-single digits to 19 percent. For the question of which party had the most credible program or plan, the Tories were the only party to show significant improvement. At the outset, 10 percent of respondents identified the PCs as having the most credible policy approach; in the last polling the proportion was 23 percent. By contrast, the Liberals fell from the mid-30s to 26 percent and the CA moved in a narrow range between 15 percent and 20 percent. In sum, through the campaign the PC percentages increased on all questions, a record unmatched by any other party. On the basis of the party's polling data, it seems clear that the PC's campaign worked effectively in improving the party's standing in the minds of voters (at least in the ridings surveyed).[30] The task was still gigantic: nationally the party was only inching up in the polls and the Liberals were far ahead of any of their competitors.

The Campaign's Last Weeks

The task in the last two weeks of the campaign was to convert the positives coming out of the debates into support for Clark and the Tories. Unlike the two previous elections, the leader's tour went smoothly. Press relations were positive, with Clark and reporters often chatting casually and watching television together (especially "The West Wing," a drama about the American President). Generally it was thought that the media fairly reported what was happening on the Tory campaign, except for reports about some poorly attended events when the Tory plan had been to highlight an issue by putting Clark in an appropriate setting without having a crowd (what organizers labelled a "process" event). In the campaign's waning days there was a minor diversion with a report from Quebec that made it appear that Clark would contemplate a coalition arrangement with the Bloc. Candidates and the leader were "on message" with only one reported case of a candidate and Clark disagreeing.[31]

One problem facing the Tories was that political commentators were still of the view that the election was essentially a two party contest, with the other parties more or less stuck at their pre-election levels in the polls. The Tories were interesting only because of the survival issue. Another problem was the serious constraint created by the fund-raising shortfalls, which meant that in the campaign's waning days, the party not only lacked money to buy television time, it could not even pay for the production of advertisements. On the bright side, the slide of Ontario Tories away from the Alliance continued as Day and his candidates increasingly engendered fears about the Alliance's social conservatism.

The final stage of Clark's campaign was seen by Laschinger as "politics," in the sense of making pointed and aggressive attacks on one's opponents. Early in the campaign Clark would talk about the platform, his policy commitments, and his view of the country's future. In the last stages the platform and vision were put aside and his speeches were devoted to attacks on Chrétien and Day. The government's spending record, its fiscal mismanagement, and, especially, Chrétien's unethical behaviour in regards to government grants in his riding were the talking points. The Alliance was attacked for its extremism as exemplified by the comments of a number of its candidates. The message was simple: For voters disillusioned with Chrétien's performance as Prime Minister and fearful of the Alliance's agenda, the only option was to vote PC.

Near the campaign's close, Clark all but conceded victory to the Liberals. On the other hand, his opponents no longer ignored the PCs and began to attack him. His appeal took on a different tack: vote for us (especially where we are competitive) because we will provide a strong opposition to the government (and perhaps produce a minority Parliament). This approach was problematic, however, as many voters wish to elect a government rather than an official opposition or even a strong contingent of opposition MPs. Appeals for strategic voting are particularly dubious for a party sitting in the very low teens in popularity, in a weaker position than in the last election.

The party's minimum objectives — official party status; election of Clark; and undercutting the Alliance move into eastern Canada — were met. The party's twelve seats were concentrated in Atlantic Canada (nine), though Quebec, Manitoba, and Alberta each gave one seat to the PCs. In the West and North, however, outside of Brandon-Souris and Calgary Centre, the Tories had little presence, generally running either third or fourth. Of the region's ninety-one constituencies, the PCs were second in only seven (with six located in the Calgary area). While the Tories took comfort in the fact that the Alliance won only two seats in Ontario, they managed to run ahead of the Alliance in only fourteen ridings; of the province's 103 seats the PCs were second in eight. Given that in 1997 there was not much difference between the two parties in their vote shares, clearly the Alliance had made significant gains, although it had failed to deliver a knockout blow to the Tories.

In Quebec, PCs ran second in three of the province's seventy-five seats and only in two did the party reach the 15 percent level. In 1997, the Tory vote was very much based on Charest's personal appeal; in 2000 it was mostly based on André Bachand's personal appeal in Richmond-Arthabaska. Atlantic Canada, of course, was more hospitable to the

Tories. There were losses due to the NDP decline (and concomitant Liberal improvement) and the impact of the CA in certain ridings (which probably cost the PCs three or four seats).[32] Generally in non-Tory seats the party trailed far behind the Liberals or New Democrats. Overall, of their twelve seats, only Calgary-Centre was a gain from another party.

Conclusion: Opposition Parties Defeat Themselves

When the 2000 election was called the PCs were burdened with debt, troubled fundraising, organizational deficiencies, and leadership contro-versies. Low in the polls, the PCs had to confront the Canadian Alliance, the Reform-based attempt to forge a new anti-Liberal coalition, especial-ly in Ontario. With a new leader strikingly different from Manning, who was widely regarded as being unelectable east of Manitoba, and enormous financial resources, the CA was poised to be a formidable challenger to the Liberals. Even with the public's undoubted dissatisfaction with Chrétien, the Tory mood was dark. The essential task for the Conservative Party was to focus on the re-election of incumbents and take advantage of oppor-tunities scattered here and there across the country. At campaign's end, the most optimistic of party insiders talked about winning around twen-ty seats. For the Tories, the ostensible national election was not just regional, but an exercise in micro-level fine-tuning.

In terms of improvement from the beginning to the end of the cam-paign, the PCs ran the most successful campaign in 2000. This judge-ment, however, says more about the low expectations held about it in the first place than its success in any absolute terms. Governments, it is often said, defeat themselves. The apparent dissatisfaction of the elec-torate with the Liberals suggests that the 2000 election was an instance of the opposition parties defeating themselves. They certainly had an opportunity to put the Liberals into a minority situation. This is partic-ularly so with the Canadian Alliance which was deemed by the media at the outset of the campaign as the "government-in-waiting" party. Moreover, it had, compared to the Tories, enormous financial resources and showed signs in the early weeks of the campaign of seriously chal-lenging the Liberals. Before the campaign was over, however, the media began speculating about why the Alliance campaign had failed to expand beyond the base it had at the beginning of the campaign. The limited success of the Tory campaign reflects as much as the Alliance's failure to consolidate and build on its opportunities as it does the efficacy of their own efforts.

As Tories contemplate matters in the post-election period, they have to look at what has happened in the last three elections. The rapid drop in Tory support after Mulroney's triumphs in 1984 and 1988 means that the party failed to consolidate its social base. In 1993 the Tories got 16 percent of the national vote. In the following election, primarily boosted by the appeal of Charest in Quebec, the Tory vote rose to 19 percent. In 2000 the PCs received the support of 12 percent of the electorate. In each province and in the northern ridings (except for British Columbia where there was essentially no change), the Tory vote shares dropped from 1997. The three non-Atlantic constituencies won by the Tories reflected idiosyncratic circumstances and candidates with great personal appeal rather than an enduring commitment to the party. Undoubtedly, with other candidates they would not be in the Tory fold.

The attenuation of the party's support base in the post-Mulroney period was mirrored by the contraction in the organizational health of the party. On the other hand, from 1993 to 2000 the party held a number of national meetings (at various places across the country) which were well attended by delegates, generally in greater numbers than anticipated. Moreover, the meetings had a spirit and determination that did not parallel the party's standing in the polls. That is, the party's stock of activists remained relatively healthy while the party's organizational health deteriorated and voter support was falling.

How long can activists maintain the faith in light of its temporal and financial costs? This is a particularly pressing issue for a brokerage party operating within a parliamentary system based on the first-past-the-post electoral system. Generally, the dominant party benefits from the electoral system in the sense of winning inflated majorities relative to its fraction of the vote. Smaller but nationally oriented parties tend to be penalized by the electoral system that gives them fewer seats than their votes warrant. The exception is for parties that are based on explicitly regional grievances and appeals, in which case their parliamentary representation will be larger than their overall share of the vote would suggest. For the Tories the last decade of the 1900s was a time of contracting opportunities and weakening incentives that have not improved with the avoidance of extinction.

The Tory difficulty is that, despite the rhetoric of being a national party, after the election of 2000 it is primarily a rump entity based in Atlantic Canada, even more than it was after 1997. The party in Ontario has a number of healthy constituency organizations, including a handful that have healthy bank accounts, but from 1993 to 2000 its organizational preparedness has weakened. However, only in forty-two of Ontario's 103 constituencies (compared to seventy-two in 1997) did Tory candidates get 15 percent of the vote, the level required to be eligible for funding rebates and return of deposits. Inasmuch as Ontario Tories have for a long time been the dominant presence in national meetings, the question of whether activists will continue to show up and energize the party is very much up in the air.

Once the post-election period of celebrating being alive passed, various Tory leaders, including Clark and Mulroney, spoke about the necessity of finding some way of working with the Alliance. From the perspective of voters looking for a centre-right alternative to the Liberals, three elections in which their voting strength has been fractured by the PCs and Reform/CA is clearly unpalatable. Corporate Canada, having contributed mightily to Long's leadership bid and the CA campaign, was not opening the vault for either the CA or the PCs, the latter especially feeling the big chill. Yet there seem to be great differences between the two parties, with the Tories in particular fearful of the social conservatism that is so much a part of the Alliance, especially with Day as leader. So any formal merger seems unlikely.

At every gathering of the party its leaders talk about the strength of the Progressive Conservative "brand" name, the efficacy of which is evidenced by the fact that many voters — whatever their first party commitment — chose the PCs as their second choice.[33] The problem is that the party has to convince voters that it is in a position to form a government, a daunting task given the traditional policy flexibility of the Liberals and the determination of the Alliance to eliminate the Tories once and for all. The Tories hope, as they did after the 1997 election, that its right-flank opponent will disintegrate, the likely cause being the clear tensions between fiscal and social conservatives. Whatever happens to the Alliance, the PC party has to find some way to enhance its standing in Ontario in order to become a major contender for office. The proverbial clock is ticking.

Notes

1   The author expresses his thanks to John Laschinger, Bruck Easton, John Fraser, and various other party officials for their time and insight. The author attended a number of pre-election planning meetings in Ontario and followed the election tour through a good part of the province.

2   See Peter Woolstencroft, "Democracy and the Selection of Party Leaders: The Case of the Progressive Conservative Leadership Election." Paper presented to the Canadian Political Science Association, Sherbrooke, Quebec (June 1999). See also Roy Norton, "The 1998 P.C. Leadership Selection Process: A New Model for National Political Parties?" Paper presented to the June 1999 CPSA meetings.

3   Relations between the federal party and the three Maritime parties are especially close; see D.K. Stewart and I. Stewart, "Fission and Federalism: The Disaggregation of Canadian Party Activists," *Publius: The Journal of Federalism*, Vol. 27 No. 3 (Summer, 1977), 108. The three Maritime premiers appeared with Clark at a campaign event in late November.

4   For example, Michael Marzolini, the Liberal party's pollster, reported at an August meeting that the Tories were now the leading opposition party, showing appreciable growth in Ontario, and that Clark's approval ratings were improving; *National Post*, August 18th, 1999, A7.

5   Neil Nevitte, et al, *Unsteady State: The 1997 Canadian Federal Election* (Don Mills, Oxford University Press, 2000), 79-89.

6   *National Post*, October 2, 1999, A7.

7   Peter Woolstencroft, "Staying Alive: The Progressive Conservative Party Fights for Survival," in Hugh G. Thorburn and Alan Whitehorn, eds., *Party Politics in Canada* (Toronto: Prentice Hall, 2000, eighth edition), 258.

8   Tory anger over what was regarded as an usurpation of its name led to an appeal to the Chief Electoral Officer to reject the new party's name; the argument was rejected.

9   The list included Hal Jackman, former Lieutenant-Governor of Ontario, businessman and Tory fundraiser; Bob Runciman, Ontario Cabinet Minister, who became co-chair of the CA campaign in

Ontario; Tony Clement, Ontario Cabinet Minister, who co-chaired the founding meeting of the CA. Among many converts from outside Ontario, notables included Senator Gerry S. Germain (a former national President of the PC party), Alberta Premier Ralph Klein, and Brian Pallister, former Manitoba cabinet minister and former candidate in the 1998 PC leadership contest. As well, eight former Tory MPs came out in support of Day though some claimed that they retained membership in the federal Tories.

10 *The Globe and Mail*, for example, reported that Bay Street was fleeing both the Liberals and Tories in favour of the CA; May 13, A1.

11 For example, *National Post*, May 11, A1.

12 *The Globe and Mail*, May 15, 2000, A7.

13 *National Post*, May 27, 2000, A1.

14 The PCs had won twenty seats in 1997. Charest's seat was lost in a 1998 by-election; Bill Matthews, a Newfoundland and Labrador MP defected to the Liberals in 1999. After the four defections in 2000 and the entry of Vautour into the Tory caucus, Clark led a contingent of fifteen MPs into the 2000 election.

15 Author's interview with John Laschinger, December 21, 2000.

16 In each of the two previous elections the Tories spent over $10 million; see W.T. Stanbury, "Regulating Federal Party and Candidate Finances in a Dynamic Environment," in Hugh G. Thorburn and Alan Whitehorn, eds., *Party Politics in Canada* (Toronto: Prentice Hall, 2000, eighth edition), 194.

17 *The Progressive Conservative Plan for Canada's Future: A Summary*, Ottawa, 2000.

18 For a discussion of the 1997 platform, see Peter Woolstencroft, "On the Ropes Again"; for an excellent discussion of the 2000 platform, see John Lorinc, "Mr. Middle-of-the-road," *National Post*, Oct. 26, 2000, A15.

19 Party insiders early and openly spoke about the party's situation and objectives. Susan Elliott, the party's national director, was quoted about the constrained objectives of the PCs; *The Globe and Mail*, October 23, A9.

20 See Peter Woolstencroft, "Staying Alive: The Progressive Conservative Party Fights for Survival," in Hugh G. Thorburn and Alan Whitehorn, eds., *Party Politics in Canada*, eighth edition (Toronto: Prentice Hall, 2000), 248-63.

21 Quebec was especially problematic and in a number of ridings the party had to "parachute" candidates, a practice also followed in 1993 and 1997.

22 See Walter Romanow *et al*, "Negative Political Advertising: An Analysis of Research in Light of Canadian Practices," in Janet Hiebert, ed., *Political Ethics: A Canadian Perspective*, Volume 12, Royal Commission on Electoral Reform and Party Financing Research Studies (Toronto: Dundurn Press, 1991).

23 A COMPAS Inc. poll in mid-October indicated that 41 percent of Canadians wanted a change in Prime Minister; *National Post*, Oct. 14, 2000, A6.

24 Laschinger interview.

25 Susan Elliott, the party's national director, was quoted in late October: "This week we have to show that we're still in the game, despite the polls." *The Globe and Mail*, October 30, 2000, A1.

26 Laschinger to Joe Clark, the morning after the English-language debate; Laschinger, speech to the PC National Caucus, London, Ontario, January 26, 2000.

27 See Peter Woolstencroft, "On the Ropes Again: The Campaign of the Progressive Conservative Party in the 1997 Federal Election," in A. Frizzell and J.H. Pammett, eds, *The Canadian General Election of 1997* (Toronto: Dundurn Press, 1997), 71-91.

28 *National Post*, Nov. 11, 2000, A1; *The Globe and Mail*, Nov. 13, 2000, A1.

29 *The Record* (Kitchener), Nov. 4, 2000, A3.

30 Various polls reported in the media conveyed a message about improving Tory fortunes, though the party nationally was still in the low teens; *National Post*, Nov, 23, 2000, A1; *The Globe and Mail*, Nov. 25, 2000, A1.

31 The instance involved André Bachand, MP for Richmond Arthabaska and Ottawa-Quebec relationships; *The Globe and Mail*, Oct. 31, 2000, A7.

32 Laschinger expected the PCs to win fifteen seats in Atlantic Canada. The last Tory tracking, compared to actual results, underestimated CA strength in Atlantic Canada by about four points. Both the Liberals and PCs got about two points less than his polling had shown. Laschinger attributed the underestimate to CA voters not revealing what they were going to do. Laschinger, interview, December 17.

33 Laschinger's polling data showed that among voters who have a second choice, the Tories are in much stronger situation than the CA; for example, first choice Liberal voters migrate to the Tories over the CA by a four to one ratio (59 percent to 15 percent); New Democrats do so by greater than two to one (37 percent to 15 percent). While CA voters chose the Tories over the Liberals by over two to one, Tories move to the Liberals over the CA by a similar margin, with one appreciable difference; they are more likely to vote NDP than CA.

Chapter 4

The 2000 NDP Campaign:
Social Democracy at the Crossroads

by Alan Whitehorn

In its first two and half decades (1962-1988) the NDP acquired an average of 17.2 percent of votes and 25.7 seats,[1] and in 1988 Ed Broadbent guided the NDP to its electoral peak with 20.4 percent and 43 seats. The party placed a dismal fifth place in 1993, with its worst ever vote (6.9 percent) and only 9 MPs.[2] The party thus fell below the threshold number of 12 seats required to be recognized as an official party in Parliament. The catastrophic 1993 result[3] precipitated a number of "renewal conferences" commencing in 1994. To generate publicity and regain some populist appeal, the NDP opted in 1995 for a two-step leadership selection process involving a direct ballot primary of all party members and a convention ballot by delegates. Former Nova Scotia provincial leader Alexa McDonough, became the party's first federal leader from Atlantic Canada and led the party to an Atlantic breakthrough in the 1997 campaign. The party won 6 seats in Nova Scotia, two in New Brunswick and a total of 21 nation-wide. The gains came despite the fact that McDonough was not well-known outside of Atlantic Canada and the party had had to run in effect a number of local by-elections.[4]

Problem Areas for the NDP

To a significant degree, the NDP's prospects in recent federal elections have been greatly affected by the popularity, or lack thereof, of NDP provincial governments. The provincial NDP victories in Ontario, British Columbia, and Saskatchewan in 1990-1991 had meant that half of the country's population was under social democratic provincial governments. But in the 1993, 1997, and 2000 federal contests, these NDP provincial governments would prove to be liabilities for the federal party.

In Ontario, the NDP government of Bob Rae (1990-1995), with its controversial social contract legislation, had created grave fissures between itself and the coalition of party members, trade unionists, and social activists. In British Columbia, the surprise resignation of veteran Premier Mike Harcourt[5] had temporarily allowed his successor, Glen Clark, to regain party credibility and momentum and win the 1996 provincial election. However, public support quickly plummeted over controversies about the accuracy of government financial statements and alleged personal kick-backs to Clark for granting gambling licences. Following a televised night-time RCMP raid on the Premier's home, Clark finally resigned, but far too late to allow the NDP provincial government under new leader Ujjal Dosanj to regain significant public support before the 2000 federal election. The fiscally prudent Saskatchewan NDP government under Roy Romanow (first elected in 1991) had in the past been one of the assets for the federal party, and had been key to helping the federal party survive in the 1990s (five Saskatchewan MPs in both the 1993 and 1997 elections). But recent Saskatchewan elections had seen the provincial party lose electoral popularity (indeed, its 1999 vote was even lower than the Saskatchewan Party), particularly in the rural areas. To survive, it had to form a coalition government with members of a small Liberal caucus. Matters were not helped by Romanow's decision in 2000 to resign as Premier and speculate about a possible merger of the federal NDP and Liberals. The NDP's performance in the 1999 Nova Scotia provincial election campaign where it declined in both votes and seats was perhaps a foreboding. The defeat of Piers McDonald's NDP Yukon territorial government also added to the challenge in re-electing the NDP MP from the Yukon.

A second problem area for the party was the labour/party nexus. The NDP had been formed in 1961 as a partnership of the old CCF and the Canadian Labour Congress. Thus the linkage between the trade union movement and the party has been pivotal. However since Bob Rae's NDP government's re-opening of labour contracts, NDP/labour relations have not fully healed. Canadian Auto Workers president Buzz Hargrove continued his feud with both the Ontario and federal NDP, and even with colleagues in the CLC. Even more troublesome was the fact that the Steelworkers Union, given its significant Quebec membership and normally a loyal labour ally, challenged the caucus's controversial stand on the Clarity Bill C-20 on conditions for a Quebec referendum on separation.

Media coverage of the NDP in the inter-election period had been disappointing, and was caused by a number of external factors. The media had been preoccupied with the return of former prime minister Joe Clark to lead the Tories, the transformation of the Reform party into the Alliance, the related leadership contest that saw Manning replaced by Stockwell Day, and the ongoing leadership feud between Liberal Prime Minister Jean Chrétien and his powerful Finance Minister Paul Martin. All this meant it was difficult for the NDP to appear as a key player in any of these issues. Added to the NDP woes was its lower membership,[6] MP base, and public support in polls.

The NDP's parliamentary style and organization did not help to attract positive attention. The leader's national profile was still relatively low. The caucus also seemed unfocussed for much of the inter-election period, a pattern that was not helped by substantial senior staff turnover. The caucus did do better after the government's mini-budget when the NDP focussed on the Liberals' lack of attention to health care. Still it was puzzling that given the shift in the public mood to greater concerns with health care and the environment the NDP still did not do better in the polls. Part of the explanation may rest in strategic voting considerations, where citizens feel the need to vote for the more electorally competitive party, rather than the one they feel closest to on key issues.

Prior to the 2000 campaign, two prominent defections by NDP MPs occurred. In New Brunswick, high profile social activist Angela Vautour bolted to the Conservatives (causing McDonough to refer to her as "Vote Tory") and Saskatchewan MP Rick Laliliberte succumbed to Liberal inducements to cross the floor to the government side. On a more optimistic note, Dennis Gruending had won a by-election in Saskatchewan created when NDP MP Chris Axworthy went over to provincial politics. The party also ran a strong second in two by-elections in Windsor-St. Clair in Ontario (CAW union activist Joe Comartin) and in St. John's West, Newfoundland (social activist-comedian Greg Malone).

Election Organization and Committee Structure

Normally, between NDP conventions, the Federal Executive and Federal Council are the principal decision-making bodies of the party. For Campaign 2000, the Election Planning Committee (EPC) was composed of the Federal Executive and a number of co-opts (e.g. EPC chair [Terry Grier, former MP and past EPC chair for four campaigns in the Broadbent era], the CLC's NPAC representative Pat Kerwin, parliamentary caucus representatives, campaign director Dennis Young, Election Communications director Julie Mason). Starting late in January 2000, the full EPC met only about three times, given the early election call, but took the overall responsibility for designing the strategic election plan. Given the size of the full EPC, a smaller Working Group (composed of party officers and co-opts, with federal staff from Ottawa assigned to assist) convened about every two weeks prior to the election call (often by telephone conference calls) to plan the campaign. The technical staff in Ottawa also met every two to three weeks in the pre-election period. Once the election began, the Working Group met once a week to oversee the campaign operation.

The Election Platform Committee (a sub-committee of the EPC) drawing upon past resolutions and reports from party conventions, drafted an integrated policy platform intended to maximize the party's electoral appeal. The resulting twenty-page platform document entitled "The NDP Commitment to Canadians" was completed in time for the September federal council meeting, just on the eve of the election call.

During the actual campaign, a series of groups supervised and, where necessary, modified the election strategy. At the pinnacle of the decision-making hierarchy was the inner circle of campaign strategists who met (in person or by teleconference) at the end of each day. They included the federal secretary, EPC chair, campaign manager, assistant federal secretary, various section directors from organization, advertising, research, tour coordinator, communication, administration, finance, and the labour liaison. Early each morning and then throughout the day, the campaign director and John Walsh, the chief political person on the plane would look over all major campaign matters and give their final OK. The EPC Working Group, often involving many individuals from the daily group, met once a week for several hours each Sunday afternoon, to assess the previous week's events and plan the next. The committee discussed modifications to the leader's tour, daily tracking of polling results, focus group findings, ongoing testing of campaign slogans and phrasing, the final changes of the ads, when and how to replace the first round of ads with subsequent ones and preparations for the leaders' debates, and heard reports of the various organizational activities.

Election Finances

On the eve of the campaign,[7] the proposed budget was $7 million, more than in 1997 (by about $1 million), but lower than in 1988 and 1993, particularly if inflation is factored. Increasingly, the largest expense for a political party in modern elections is for mass media advertising. The NDP media budget for 2000 was set at $2 million, of which $1.45 million was for buying of media time, and only $355,000 for creative work and production. In the recent past, the largest amount of NDP advertising has been allocated to the powerful medium of television, and 2000 was no different. The second largest category of expenditures was goods and services at $1.7 million (usually involving payment for union labour release). The leader's tour, the third largest portion of the campaign budget, was projected to cost $1.1 million (with $785,000 for transportation, mostly for the plane). The remainder of the campaign expenditures were $750,000 for organization (down from 1997 and which included $260,000 for telephone call centres, $154,000 for candidate support, $122,000 for candidate deposits and $110,00 for riding placement). In addition, $500,000 was projected for administration (of which $150,000 was earmarked for information technology [e.g. computers]) and, $50,000 for the website. Costs for public opinion research were set at $250,000, followed by $250,000 for communications, $200,000 for direct mail and for contingency purposes $217,000.

Income was optimistically projected to match expenses at $7 million. Funds for the campaign were to be raised in the following manner: non-cash goods and services ($1.7 million, down from 1997),8 riding rebates ($1.68 million), central rebate ($1.58 million), labour ($1 million, also down slightly), direct mail ($600,000), "direct ask" contributions ($600,000) and web and miscellaneous contributions at $145,000. The extremely compressed election time period necessitates urgent loans, a problem for a social democratic party which routinely criticizes excess bank profits. Given past obstacles posed by the Bank of Montreal, the NDP sought a $3 million loan from the Citizens' Bank of Canada, an Internet e-bank set up by the BC-based VanCity Credit Union. As collateral, the NDP signed over its election rebates and received a crucial $2 million in loan guarantees from a number of trade unions and the CLC. Without the swift, focussed, and sizable support of the labour movement, the NDP's ability to mount a national campaign would have been problematic. This would be even more evident during a cash flow crisis mid-way through the campaign.

NDP Polling

In 2000, polling was directed by the Winnipeg-based Viewpoints Research. The company had been instrumental in the NDP provincial electoral victories in Ontario in 1990 and BC in 1991 and most recently involved in Nova Scotia and Manitoba. Viewpoints' past federal involvement had been in the ill-fated 1993 campaign.[9] The company was officially hired quite late and only did an important baseline survey (Newfoundland, Nova Scotia, Ontario [portions only], Manitoba, Saskatchewan, and BC) a mere two months before the election call, although Comquest had also done one at the beginning of the year. During the campaign itself, shorter surveys posed questions regarding party standings, the leaders, most salient/effective messages and phrasing, and testing the viability of party commercials and literature.

Given the very tight budget constraints ($250,000), polling focussed only on nineteen incumbent ridings and a modest number of others selected as most promising. Over time the limited number of ridings and even provinces selected for polling declined still further (e.g. Ontario was dropped). The surveys were based on a rolling daily sample of several hundred persons. Viewpoints also conducted a number of riding polls, and at least one was done by Toronto-based Comquest for the leader in Halifax.

Viewpoints' August baseline survey, from the relatively small number of ridings where the NDP was thought to be competitive, offered some troublesome findings for the NDP: the NDP came second to the Liberals and the leader placed third as the person who would make the best PM (indeed she polled more negatives than positives outside Nova Scotia). While the numbers for both would go up later during the campaign in the party's internal polling of selected ridings (the NDP support ranging from about 18 percent to 35 percent and leader preference ranging from about 10 percent to 20 percent), the number of ridings and regions polled actually declined, so that the survey samples methodologically, and thus the results, are not fully comparable. Overall, health care was seen as a good NDP issue, but the gap between the NDP and Liberals was not as great as desired, a fact that the election would later confirm. Viewpoints was emphatic that the primary target was the Liberals and that strategic voter switching to the Liberals could occur if the Alliance looked as if it might win — a central theme the Liberals certainly played on. Viewpoints found that the class-based theme of contrasting choices of tax breaks for big corporations and banks vs. social services for working families tested well. As in 1997, the power of sitting NDP MPs to attract voters in incumbent ridings was noted and became yet again a key part of the by-election nature of the NDP's campaign strategy.

As early as December 1999, the Toronto-based Donegan Consulting conducted small focus groups (about ten persons each in Halifax, Sydney, Windsor, Toronto, Sault Ste. Marie, Winnipeg, Saskatoon, and Regina) exploring images of the party and its policies, the party's main platform, assessing arguments for and against voting NDP, strategic voting, and testing the concepts for party ads. Among its perceptive findings were that the NDP and its leader were "invisible," that a "disturbingly large number of NDP supporters ... would vote Liberal if Reform/Alliance were to emerge as a strong contender for government," that the party's voice is "no longer inspirational" and that potential NDP voters, while concerned about the "power of corporate Canada" to make excessive profits, did not see the Liberals as being "in the pockets of big business."[10] The last observation suggested that even NDP supporters do not see the class cleavage between the corporate-funded Liberal party vs. the labour-funded NDP, a tell-tale sign of brokerage politics blunting working class consciousness. During the campaign, four telephone call centres (Vancouver, Regina, Toronto and Halifax and costing about $260,000) were employed to persuade voters in key ridings. Only target ridings had access to the call centres.[11]

NDP Strategy and Nominations

In some ways, the 2000 campaign strategy was a continuation of the 1993 and 1997 campaigns. The NDP was still fighting desperately for official party status in Parliament. Therefore, the goal was quite straightforward: to win at least twelve seats. On the eve of the election call, the NDP held nineteen seats. The key targeted groups demographically were women (particularly working women),[12] middle-aged, lower middle income, union members or union family members, persons in NDP incumbent ridings, and some regional pockets related to incumbency, particularly in Manitoba, Saskatchewan, Nova Scotia, Ontario, and BC. Once more, the NDP chose to "overwhelmingly" target Liberal voters, particularly soft Liberals, along with wavering or former New Democrats.[13]

The NDP designated only about thirty-two (10 percent) of the 301 ridings as either priority "A" (incumbent/must win) or "B" (potential) in the entire country. Of these, seven were located in Saskatchewan, four each in both BC and Manitoba, and one in the Yukon for a total of sixteen in the West. Only about five ridings were so identified in Ontario, where the greatest number of seats were available and where the largest section of the affiliated trade union movement was located. By contrast six ridings were targetted in Nova Scotia, including the leader's, one in New Brunswick and four in Newfoundland for a total of sixteen in the East. No priority ridings were listed for Alberta, Quebec, or PEI. As the campaign went on, the number of targetted ridings declined to about twenty-five (nineteen incumbents and about another half dozen). Party strategists, as in 1993 and 1997, knew the grave danger of squandering funds and experienced personnel in ridings where there was little hope of success.

Those planning the campaign were confronted with several image problems. The first was that, despite the passage of five years and despite being better known and liked overall,[14] the NDP leader's profile outside of Atlantic Canada was not particularly strong. Alexa McDonough lagged behind her party in that she was selected by only 6 percent as the best person to be prime minister,[15] just barely ahead of BQ separatist leader Gilles Duceppe. While she was ranked best or tied for best in honesty or respect for others, she was last in perception of strength and common sense.[16] Given low numbers for both the leader and the party, the NDP out of necessity was forced once more to place emphasis on its local candidates. In effect, the NDP planned its campaign on a number of simultaneous "by-elections." It was a strategy used successfully in 1997, but was not without cost for a national campaign in terms of visibility, let alone appearance of being a major player in the long run.

Given the early election call and the compressed election campaign period, it was more difficult to nominate a full slate of candidates, but the NDP did run 298, only three short of a full slate. However, many of the Quebec NDP candidates were only nominal[17] and Ontario nominations were further complicated by the overlapping province-wide municipal elections. An indicator of the weakness of many riding associations was the fact that the party paid the $1,000 deposit for over half (154) of the candidates.[18] In candidate selection, the NDP has been a strong advocate of affirmative action. Led by Alexa McDonough, eighty-nine women (down from 108 in 1977) were nominated, as were twenty-two youth, eighteen visible minorities, fifteen lesbian, gay or bisexual, five aboriginals, and four with disabilities for a total of 45 percent affirmative action candidates.[19] Almost a third (eighty-seven) of the candidates had a union background.

NDP Campaign Platform and Main Message

In the past few years, the issue of health care had skyrocketed in importance and was now ranked by Canadians as the most important issue. (See Chapter Thirteen of this volume). The NDP has had a long and heroic history (e.g. T.C. Douglas) in the pioneering of medicare, particularly during the 1962 Saskatchewan doctors' strike. The question would remain how many voters would recall the CCF-NDP's pivotal role. All parties, reading the same polling numbers, tried to position themselves as the saviour of medicare. The NDP polled well on the issue, but it could not afford to be complacent.

The campaign platform document was a twenty-page booklet entitled "The NDP Commitment to Canadians" which also posed a subtheme of "Think how much better Canada could be." Its drafting was under the general supervision of the party's election platform committee, chaired by Nan Armour, but in practice largely penned under the supervision of Ross McClellan of the OFL and Hugh Mackenzie of the USWA and the campaign director, Dennis Young. Completed just prior to the election, it was officially unveiled during the second week of the campaign. About 50,000 copies were printed (a small number for a national campaign), but the document was also posted on the party's website and could be downloaded. A shorter mini-platform was never done, given too little time and resources. However, about a half million small wallet-sized pledge cards were produced which listed five of the key planks:

1)   increase federal money for health care and add home care and pharmacare;

2)   tough national standards for safe food, water, and air;

3) a national plan for jobs as the first economic priority;
4) double child tax benefit, fund for early childhood education and child care;
5) roll back tuition fees and create interest-free loans for college and university students.

Later a sixth plank was added to the special website listing "Our Commitment to Canadians":

6) fight for fair trade deals that put the needs of Canadians ahead of global corporations.

The main pamphlet was entitled "Tax cuts for big banks or fixing health care?" with the subtitle "What is more important to you and your family?" The attempt to contrast Liberal Party tax cuts for the rich vs. the NDP's stress upon the needs of social programmes for families was an attempt at classic left populist positioning. Overwhelmingly, the main focus of the pamphlet was to attack the Liberals and big corporations while presenting the NDP alternative, with only one brief sentence directed at each of the Alliance and the Conservatives. This lack of political focus on the Alliance would prove disappointing to a number of Saskatchewan and BC activists who had had a long history of battling right populism, all the way back to Social Credit days.[20]

The website was listed on the pamphlet, thereby interconnecting the print and Internet. Notably, there were virtually no other secondary pamphlets issued by the NDP (although the labour movement issued some), but for those with access to the website, a growing list of "Fact Sheets" on a variety of topics were eventually available (e.g. health and home care, prescription drug prices). The only problem with this electronic format was that some NDP candidates and voters indicated they had difficulty downloading some of the items. Clearly, not all of the electorate has computer access or sufficient technical software or proficiency.

Advertising

Following the Liberal Party's format, the NDP opted to create a "virtual ad agency" of several suppliers called "Société Nouvelle," co-ordinated out of

Montreal. The NDP's advertising budget was quite small by current party norms, at only $2 million. The budget was comparable to 1997 ($1.5 million) but significantly less than 1988 ($3 million) and 1993 ($3.28 million), particularly if inflation is taken into account. The campaign was of necessity frugal, more regionally and even riding-focussed.[21] No network time was bought except for CBC radio. Over the last several decades, most NDP federal campaigns spent the largest portion of the advertising budget on TV ads.[22] However, given the party's focus on a small number of ridings, the 2000 campaign saw an increased percentage of the budget for radio ads, particularly on local stations, focussing upon incumbent and targeted ridings [see Table 1]. This suggests the greater benefit/cost ratio of radio for a fourth place party in a costly TV-fragmented era.

TABLE 1
NDP Advertising

Year	Print	Radio	TV
1988	5%	15%	80%
2000	5%	40%	54%

The largest sum of TV advertising in 2000 was for BC ($371,000), Ontario ($200,000), Manitoba ($128,000), Saskatchewan ($54,000) and the four Atlantic provinces ($90,000), reflecting the locations of where most of the incumbent MPs were located or in the case of Ontario where a return breakthrough was hoped for. No TV ads were planned for Alberta or Quebec, nor were any produced in French. Given the budget constraints and the early election call, only three television ads were produced. This is not sufficient to achieve flexibility during the evolving dynamics of an election campaign. The most widely distributed TV ad was "Hospital Bed," which showed a patient surrounded by medical staff and equipment which increasingly disappeared leaving an anxious and lonely patient. A second ad was entitled "Weather Map" and dealt with the environment. "Glass Jars" noted the "once in a life-time" "massive surplus" that should not be squandered on $100 billion tax cuts for big corporations, banks, and the rich, which the Liberals and Alliance favoured. Given the leader's low national profile, she appeared only at the close of the first commercials.

A key part of the campaign involved the radio ads. Three radio ads in English and two in French were produced in the first wave. In the second wave, two national anti-Liberal ads were produced. One criticized the Chrétien Liberal choices on how to use the surplus, suggesting the need to fix health care and clean up the environment rather than give tax cuts to the big corporations, banks, and the rich. Another, focusing on health care, suggested the Chrétien Liberals had opened the door to "private for-profit hospitals" in Alberta. Given that regional variations of radio ads are easier, less costly to make, and can be placed accurately in a specifically targeted locale, a couple of regional variations of the English ads were produced. One for Saskatchewan attacked the Alliance party as favouring a "two-tier American-style health care." Another for Saskatchewan and BC suggested that there was "enough money to fix health care — not tear it down." A specific Nova Scotia ad attacked the Liberals and Bernie Boudreau.

The advertising focus on the choice of spending on social programmes such as health care was a natural issue for Canada's social democratic party, both ideologically and given the exceptionally high concern with health care by the public in recent years. However, all five parties had been endeavouring to position themselves on this key issue for some time, and the NDP would not be able to claim the issue exclusively or by default. Given the limited regional scope of the advertising, many party members interviewed did not recall seeing most or even any of the NDP ads. Of those who did recall them, the overwhelming preference was for the health care TV ad with the disappearing equipment and staff as the most memorable and effective. Another feature of the ad campaign was the left populist theme of favouring public social spending rather than tax breaks for corporations, banks, and the rich. For such a social democratic campaign to be mounted successfully, given the prevailing Canadian pro-business culture and media orientation, it probably needed a longer pre-election build up (e.g. a pamphlet or website showing that the primary source of Liberal party funding is from corporations).

As in recent past campaigns, the NDP's primary national target remained the Liberal Party, but NDP strategists did make anti-Alliance second-wave regional radio ads for Saskatchewan and BC. Some Saskatchewan members felt that the NDP ad strategy (particularly the national TV and pamphlets) seemed too skewed to the Liberal party and the East, despite the fact that the main rival in

Saskatchewan was the surging Alliance party, not the Liberals (who provincially were part of an NDP-Liberal Coalition government). In the highly regionalized Canadian polity, the need for more varied regional ads, sooner, was a common complaint.

Internet and E-mail

Just as the mass medium of television transformed the dynamics of election campaigns in the 1960s, so too the Internet and e-mail have begun to alter how campaigns communicate.[23] The NDP had created a website in the 1997 election, but it was mostly a symbolic gesture to show the party was "in the game." In the inter-election period, the NDP operated a website for both the party and the caucus, but with the start of the 2000 campaign a newly formatted, more election-oriented site was unveiled. It was hosted and maintained by Thindata of Toronto. The new site was a key medium for presenting the leader, the party's list of candidates and links to the candidates' own websites (if available; less than 30 percent of candidates had websites listed midway through the campaign), the party's main platform (both the full text and summary list), the latest spin on the news, a focus on the key policy differences and choices between the NDP and its main targeted rival — the Liberal Party, the leader's tour itinerary, a summary of the leader's speeches, fundraising, recruiting new members, and the web addresses for all of the provincial and territorial sections. In short, the website was multipurposed and touched on almost all aspects of the campaign. The web structure involved the following initial headings: latest news, meet Alexa, your candidates, the issues, NDP "surreality" check, the campaign trail, media centre, make a donation, volunteer, join the NDP, email newsletter, and contact us. Within each of these categories, options in the respective menus were available. The party also maintained a restricted and confidential website ("Campaigns Only") for campaign staff in the ridings and provincial offices.

During the first month of the campaign, the main NDP website averaged about 60,000 hits per week. The site generated about a total of six thousand emails. Prior to the election about three persons a day joined the party, but during the campaign the number increased to sixty new members a day. A donation page was created and put up just after the election call, but had some technical problems. It is estimated that the website brought in about two thousand dollars a day. There were also delays in getting the Fact Sheets on key policy areas ready and mounted on the website (at the half-way point only a handful were on the site, which eventually had over forty items). Too little work was done on these prior to the election, and during the actual campaign, there were too few staff to do all the work swiftly enough.

The CLC and its affiliate unions also set up websites, particularly for comparing the five major parties on key policy issues. The costs to remount and maintain the party website and Information Technology equipment were initially estimated at $50,000 (website) and $150,000 (IT), but by the end of the campaign the actual expenditures were significantly higher for the latter at $242,000.[24] Clearly, it is easy to underestimate the cost of this new technology, and in the future costs are likely to be even higher, given that it has been recommended that the party create a new web liaison staff position.[25] Given various ages of computer equipment, software programmes, and technological skills in the ridings, it is not surprising that some had significant difficulty downloading some of the materials and asked for faxes.

The NDP Campaign and the Leader's Tour

Despite a shorter campaign (thirty-six days) and more media pooling, the leader's tour was perceived as a major vehicle for communicating the party's national election message. Usually in a federal election the party leader endeavours to travel to as many regions as possible in order to give the party the greatest media profile. However, with the low expectations for the NDP, the 2000 tour targeted the small number of priority ridings.

McDonough spent the largest amount of time (just over sixteen days) in Ontario, the region with the bulk of Commons seats, much of the English media, and the scene of the leaders' debates. Since the leader's home riding and six of the NDP seats had been in Nova Scotia, the tour spent the next largest amount of time (just over seven days) in that province. Saskatchewan (just under seven days) was next, followed by Manitoba, and BC. The time allocated to Quebec, with one quarter of Canada's population, was virtually non-existent. The party was once more fighting for its electoral survival and attention had to be focussed where there were realistic chances.

The first week of the campaign (October 22–28) opened on the environment issue in Cape Breton at the Sydney Tar Ponds and continued on to Ottawa and Toronto where McDonough was critical of the Liberal government's mini-budget as providing excessive tax breaks for banks and corporations, while not providing sufficient funds for child care, home care, pharmacare, and public transit. As an opening statement, it was a classic social democratic commitment to the social sector. Despite the dominant economic news of the week about the biggest ever TSE losses, McDonough reminded voters that health care was the number one priority and counseled that with different choices — "Think how much better Canada could be." While on her first campaign trip to the West, McDonough attacked the Alliance as "mean spirited." Clearly, the NDP leader had begun to attack the right-populist party early on, perhaps learning from the failure to do so in the 1993 and 1997 federal campaigns. Still, at the end of the first week the NDP was at 7 percent in the public polls, putting them in fifth place, and at risk of electoral oblivion if those numbers could not be improved.

In week two (October 29–November 4) McDonough unveiled the official campaign platform, a twenty-page booklet entitled "The NDP Commitment to Canadians." She contrasted the Liberal and NDP choices, accompanied by a backdrop display listing items on the Liberal vs. NDP choices. McDonough reiterated that the Liberal mini-budget favoured spending only two cents in health care for every dollar of tax cuts for corporations and the wealthy. Alliance spokesperson Jason Kenney's comments about endorsing two-tier health care put the Alliance on the defensive and catapulted health care to the front pages. At the Alberta NDP provincial convention, McDonough bluntly asserted: "Guys, its about health care, stupid." Once more while in the East, McDonough focused her criticism on the Liberals, but when out West, she attacked the Alliance Party, particularly in a BC debate with Stockwell Day, on the issues of women's rights and reproductive choice. At the end of the second week, public polls had the NDP still mired in single digits, with McDonough placing a distant fourth at 8 percent as the leader who would make the best Prime Minister. She was ahead only of Duceppe, and barely at that — a far cry from the peak of former leader Ed Broadbent's popularity in the late 1980s.

The most important domestic events of week three (November 5–11) were the leaders' debates. However, the cliff-hanging US presidential election on November 7 revealed the risk of a progressive third party candidate undercutting the vote of the centre-left major party and allowing a right-wing one to win. It was a powerful cautionary tale for potential NDP voters in Canada concerned about electoral gains by the Alliance party, particularly given Day's comments about the threshold of any referendum on abortion. "Would strategic voting hurt the NDP?" was now more than ever a germane question.

In the French language debate, despite good positioning in the middle of the stage, McDonough was not fluent enough to be a strong debater in French, and thus was at a significant disadvantage. She intervened infrequently and stayed close to the party's platform script on investing in health care, home care, education, and reducing poverty.

The English language debate was extremely important for the NDP, and strategists hoped that McDonough would be able to criticize the Liberal record and woo "soft Liberal" voters and shore up wavering New Democrats. McDonough opened by noting the $30 billion surplus and talking about differing visions and choices as to where the money should go. She attacked both the Alliance and Liberal party leaders — Day for favouring two-tier health care and Chrétien for policies that threatened medicare. She advocated returning federal spending on health care to the 25 percent level and halting privatization. While describing the "enormity of the surplus"[26] she again reiterated the line that the Liberals had spent only two cents on health care for every one dollar in tax cuts for the corporations and wealthy. She also suggested the need for a genuine social progress indicator to monitor the health and environmental debt. Finally, she posed the piercing question, "when did tax cuts build hospitals, educate youth, and provide safe drinking water?" In her closing statement, she reminded the audience that the NDP alone would rebuild our social programmes.

In a debate where four opposition leaders attacked the Prime Minister, Chrétien slipped and Joe Clark was deemed the overall winner. (See Chapter Thirteen.) By most accounts, McDonough was effective on health care, and did not come across as excessively negative, but neither did she excel in the key English debate. The CBC's "Reality Check" segment questioned the NDP research and noted that since the health accord, the two cents expenditure was now twenty cents. In assessing both debates nationwide, polls suggest she placed last (even among women voters), with only 6 percent selecting McDonough as victor. She did, however, receive a higher fourth place ranking outside of Quebec.[27] Post-debate public opinion polls showed NDP support between 8–9 percent. In the days immediately following the debate, McDonough continued to hammer away at the health care issue, even suggesting that Ralph Klein was the "father of two-tier health care," Chrétien the "mid-wife" and Day the "obstetrician."

In the final weeks, McDonough began to suggest that a minority government might be a good thing and a ballot for the NDP was not a wasted vote. She also poked fun at Chrétien's excessively large Ontario caucus as the "101 Dalmatians." McDonough likened Stockwell Day to a "cockroach" and later refused to retract the comment. She was also dogged by questions about who was "rich" in the NDP's view and the lack of the party's consistency about corporate contributions to the NDP. While McDonough continued to hope for a minority Parliament, with the NDP playing the key role of balancer, Chrétien was warning Canadian voters that such a situation would only empower the separatist BQ. Most public opinion polls showed the NDP between 9–10 percent and fifth place (virtually the same percent as on the eve of the election, but more clearly last in ranking).[28] Would it be enough to win twelve seats and regain official party status?

The "by-election" strategy of targetting only selected ridings meant that the leader's tour had to hopscotch across country and created many partial days in a particular city or province. This meant a lot of time in transit, and combined with the dramatically increased cost of fuel for the plane, the result was a much greater overall cost for the leader's tour, which came in significantly over budget (eg. projected $1.1 million vs. actual $1.5 million).[29] The cash flow problems caused by suppliers requiring full payment in advance, higher fuel costs and sluggish revenue flow necessitated a reassessment and reduction of spending in other areas mid-way through the campaign.

According to official statistics provided in the EPC post-mortem on the election, at least half of the scheduled tour events focussed on health care. By the end of the campaign, one recurring comment offered by some activists, media and even party officials was that the campaign was too much a "one note tune." The preoccupation with the health care issue conveyed a lack of breadth in the party's world view (the platform notwithstanding) and seemed in the end to bore both reporters and the public alike. The fact that the party did not move up in the polls,[30] despite the greater media attention provided during an election campaign, is perhaps partial evidence.

Election Results and Analysis

With just over a million votes (8.5 percent of those cast), the NDP 2000 campaign saw a setback from the partial electoral recovery of 1997 and its 1.4 million votes (11.7 percent). The 2000 outcome was only about 100,000 more votes than the near catastrophic 1993 campaign when the party received its lowest vote and number of seats in the entire NDP era. Overall, the NDP's vote in the 2000 campaign went down in every province compared to that of 1997. Whereas in 1997, two provinces gave the NDP a vote of 30 percent or higher, none did so in 2000. Only three provinces — Saskatchewan, Nova Scotia, Manitoba — along with the territories, gave the NDP a vote over twenty percent. (See Appendix for results.) Seven provinces were below the 15 percent rate — a key threshold in our electoral system for riding financial rebates. In the low teens were Newfoundland, New Brunswick, and British Columbia. Below the 10 percent level were Prince Edward Island, Ontario, and Alberta. Inching still further towards oblivion in Quebec, the NDP received less than 2 percent of the vote in the province that had been a key rationale for the birth of the New Party in 1961. Overall it was another grim outcome with serious electoral decline in too many of the NDP's heartland provinces. How deep the party has sunk can be seen by the party's rankings in the riding votes:

Table 2
NDP Riding Placement: 2000 Campaign[31]

1st	2nd	3rd	4th	5th	6th	7th	no candidate
13	26	54	136	36	28	3	3

The data on first and second place finishes suggest that only about forty ridings could be considered ridings in which the NDP stands a reasonable chance of a future success. All of the seventh, sixth, and almost all of the fifth place finishes were in Quebec and suggests the need for serious reconsideration about the rationale of running federal NDP candidates in that province.

Despite the decline in vote, the party did manage to win thirteen seats, a number down by 38 percent from twenty-one in the last election, with a high percent of the loss coming from Atlantic Canada. It was just barely enough to meet the Canadian Parliamentary requirement of twelve seats for Official Party status.[32] All but one of those elected was an incumbent and even the sole newcomer (Joe Comartin) had almost won a previous by-election. A regional breakdown of those elected reveals two from BC (Svend Robinson, Libby Davies), two from Saskatchewan (Dick Proctor, Lorne Nystrom) four from Manitoba (Bev Desjarlais, Pat Martin, Judy Wasylycia-Leis, Bill Blaikie), a solitary MP (Joe Comartin) from Ontario's 103 seats despite several high profile candidates, one from New Brunswick (Yvon Godin), and three from Nova Scotia (Wendy Lill, Alexa McDonough, Peter Stoffer). Thus eight were from the West and five from the East (including Ontario). Clearly the West continues to provide the party with the larger number of seats – a pattern established long ago in the CCF days.[33] The number of women in caucus (38 percent; five of thirteen) continues to be significant, and with a higher percent (71 percent) of female incumbents re-elected than men (62 percent). Perhaps tellingly for the future, of the ten incumbents who had a website, eight were re-elected; whereas of the nine incumbents who did not, only four were successful. Four incumbent seats were lost to the Liberals in the East and North, while three fell to the Alliance in the West, confirming the reality of different rivals across the vast political landscape.

Acquiring 15 percent of the vote is a crucial plateau necessary to receive riding financial reimbursement. Most ridings in Canada have given the NDP less than 15 percent of the vote (e.g. forty-eight in 1993; eighty-eight in 1997).[34] In 2000 the party dropped to fifty-seven in the number of ridings where the party qualified for financial reimbursement. This will significantly hurt the party financially in the post-election period.

Conclusion

The primary goal of the NDP was to maintain official party status and that important but minimalist goal was achieved, but just barely. With fewer MPs elected and fewer ridings achieving the 15 percent necessary for reimbursement, the party caucus has had to lay off staff. In addition, with a smaller caucus, it will be even harder to divide up all the work, let alone achieve a high profile in the media. The future is anything but assured.[35] The stark reality is that if just two defections of MPs occur, as in the last Parliamentary session, the NDP would lose official party status. The central Canadian heartland province of Ontario, a primary target in creating the NDP, is still largely barren of NDP MPs. The NDP is a virtual non-entity in Quebec and probably should stop pretending otherwise. As numerous scholars have documented[36] the NDP, like its predecessor the CCF, suffers from under-representation and regional distortion in seat distribution under our current First Past the Post electoral system. Prominent NDP figures such as Ed Broadbent and Lorne Nystrom are now advocates of some form of Proportional Representation. Questions still emerge about a third straight disappointing election outcome with a female leader from a less populous region. Another campaign heavily reliant on incumbent NDP MPs has not helped settle the leadership question. While McDonough indicated on election night that she would continue to lead the party, clearly there are caucus members who are prepared to succeed her.

Money is crucial in elections, for advertising and conducting a national campaign. Certainly, the NDP 2000 campaign had far too few funds for a national advertising campaign. How does a federal party maintain its national status in the long run without a nation-wide ad campaign? The leader's tour is a key part of a campaign, but increasingly one is left to ponder the growing cost vs. effectiveness. Organizationally, this was a campaign that was far too late in getting ready, particularly given the new shorter campaign period. The troubling question is "why?" With less than a year to go, a veteran team of strategists from the Broadbent era (e.g. Grier, Young, Mason, Kerwin) were brought in and heroically stitched together a spartan and highly focussed campaign and perhaps saved official party status for the NDP. But in the eyes of some, it was driven too much by polls and focus groups, and was uninspiring. Furthermore, the campaign did not in practice cover a sufficiently wide range of issues, despite the breadth of the platform document. Has the party increasingly become beholden to technocrats and bureaucrats who poll, market test, and calculate advertising strategy, but cannot rekindle the visionary message and activism of left populism?[37]

Who determines the direction of a mass social democratic party? If the NDP sees itself as a left-wing populist party, its mirror image is the right wing populist Reform/Alliance party.[38] Interestingly, the 1993 Reform Party breakthrough was achieved with virtually no polling, very few free time ads, and yet achieved an electoral success greater than any NDP campaign in forty years. Why in recent elections has the NDP not captured the public imagination? Part of the answer can be seen in the very polling data party strategists rely so heavily on. When respondents were asked which party best reflected their values and principles, the NDP received the support of only 8 percent of the electorate, tied for last.[39] It seems that gone are the days of Ed Broadbent's bold assertion in 1988 that most Canadians were social democrats at heart. Relatedly, the NDP had the highest number of voters indicating they would not support the party. In campaign 2000 health care was by far the top issue, but the electorate was skeptical about any party's ability to resolve the health care crisis.

In our current five party system, strategic voting is more likely to be a key factor as voters must decide what to do if their preferred choice does not appear competitive. In a polarized political climate, where many centre-left voters are fearful of the right's policy agenda, strategic voting may hurt the NDP, as a minor party, even more.

Canada is a continental polity with vast geographical scale. Much of our identity is made up of regional or provincial loyalties. When respondents were asked which party best represents their province, the NDP came in last.[40] In a polity where regional and provincial identities are often key to how a citizen votes, the NDP seems to have lost its regional electoral base and identity, a serious development given our electoral system. Attitudes to NDP provincial governments certainly dramatically colour perceptions of the federal NDP. To add to the NDP's woes, strategically it cannot run a national campaign targetting a single political opponent. In much of the West, the race is largely against the Alliance; while in the East, it is against the Liberals.

The NDP was founded as a co-partnership of the old CCF and the CLC, and thus, the labour movement is a very special interest group for the party. But Bob Rae's Ontario NDP government drove a catastrophic wedge between the party and some of its affiliated unions that still reverberates, particularly in the comments of CAW president Buzz Hargrove. Nevertheless, the labour movement, including the CAW, provides substantial numbers of candidates, financial contributions, and volunteer labour for the party. But how much longer is labour willing to put in such efforts for diminishing returns?

Over past decades the NDP has developed links with key interest groups such as the women's movement, environmentalists and nationalist anti-free traders. At election time, these groups have not been as supportive as the party would want. In the 2000 campaign, the NDP lost public support of several high-profile figures (e.g. pioneering abortion doctor Henry Morgentaler, internationally renowned environmentalist David Suzuki), and continued to receive extensive criticism from high profile feminist and TV personality Judy Rebick.

In exploring the future of socialism and the NDP,[41] the role of the left intellectuals must be considered. From the CCF's founding in 1932, intellectuals, particularly the League for Social Reconstruction, played a key role. They co-drafted the Regina Manifesto and did pioneering long-range research which the party relied upon (e.g. *Social Planning for Canada*). With the birth of the NDP, again intellectuals played a key role including the publications of *Social Purpose for Canada*. However, since the departure of the New Left Waffle in the early 1970s, the gulf between the left academics and the party seems vast. If the NDP is adrift, does it need the intellectual guidance of the left-wing academics?

One thing is clear. After three sub-par electoral performances, a major reassessment must come and is likely to include NDP elder statesperson Ed Broadbent, media guru Gerald Caplan, new leftist academics such as Mel Watkins, Jim Laxer, and John Richards.[42] But where is the younger generation? Among party and union leaders, CAW president Buzz Hargrove has been unequivocal in his call for a more left-wing stance, while former Saskatchewan NDP premier Roy Romanow has been more inclined to seek a Liberal-NDP alliance, and McDonough steers a more middle course.[43] Whatever ideological direction the party decides, it remains to be seen whether the trade unions and social movements will be co-participants. Even more fundamentally, will the election of 2000, like that of 1958,[44] be the catalyst for a phoenix-like transformation of a social democratic party? In any case, social democracy and the NDP are at a cross-roads.

NOTES

1   I am grateful to the many who kindly consented to post-election interviews and members of the full EPC who allowed me to observe some of their deliberations. I particularly wish to thank Terry Grier and Pat Kerwin, without whose generous assistance, this chapter would not have been possible. Unlike in past elections, I did not have access to the crucial weekly EPC working group meetings or its minutes during the campaign. Figures on the NDP vote and seat percentages are calculated from "Appendix" pp. 263-264, A. Whitehorn, *Canadian Socialism* (Toronto, Oxford, 1992).

2   For details, see A. Whitehorn, "The NDP Election Campaign: Dashed Hopes" in A. Frizzell et al., eds., *The Canadian General Election of 1988* (Ottawa, Carleton University Press, 1989).

3   I. McLeod, *Under Siege: The Federal NDP in the Nineties* (Toronto, Lorimer, 1994).

4   See A. Whitehorn, "Alexa McDonough and Atlantic Breakthrough for the New Democratic Party" in A. Frizzell and J. Pammett, eds., *The Canadian General Election of 1997* (Toronto, Dundurn, 1997).

5   See D. Gawthrop, *Highwire Act: Power, Pragmatism, and The Harcourt Legacy* (Vancouver, New Star, 1996), M. Harcourt, *Mike Harcourt: A Measure of Defiance* (Vancouver, Douglas and McIntyre, 1996).

6   Membership had declined by about 50 percent (from 146,121 to 78,815) from the late 1980s to the mid 1990s. A. Whitehorn, "Alexa McDonough and NDP Gains in Atlantic Canada," in Thorburn and Whitehorn, eds., *Party Politics in Canada*, 8th edition, p. 269.

7   See W. Stanbury, "Regulating Federal Party and Candidate Finances in a Dynamic Environment" in H.G. Thorburn & A. Whitehorn, eds., *Party Politics in Canada* (Toronto, Prentice-Hall/Pearson Education, 2001, 8th edition) pp. 194-195. At the time of the writing of this chapter, final accounting for the 2000 NDP campaign was not complete and so numbers are only preliminary estimates.

8   These were mostly union labour releases. Note that the same sum is on the expenses side of the ledger.

9   A. Whitehorn, "Dashed Hopes" p. 45; "Quest For Survival", p. 45-46.

10   Donegan Focus Group Reports, April 17 and June 20, 2000.

11   H. Fraser, "Report on the 2000 Federal Election Campaign, January 2001.

12 As noted in Gidengil and the 1997 Election Studies team, there is an important gender divide in both public opinion and party support. Women tend to favour spending on health and education (i.e. social issues), while men are more inclined to be concerned with debt and taxation levels (economic issues). Nevitte, N. et al., *Unsteady State: The 1997 Canadian Federal Election* (Toronto, Oxford, 2000) pp. 110-115 and E. Gidengil, "Economic Man and Social Woman? The Case of the Gender Gap in the Support of the Canada–US Free Trade Agreement", *Comparative Political Studies*, #28, pp. 384-408.

13 N.A., "Campaign Positioning" January, 2001. Yet again no mention was made of endeavouring to win over Alliance supporters, a particularly sore point in Saskatchewan. The fear of some strategists was that to attack the Alliance would contribute to the polarization of the electorate and push potential NDP voters to cast their ballots strategically for the Liberals in order to stop the Alliance. The 1999 Ontario provincial election was perhaps a warning in this regard.

14 See Angus Reid, September 29, 2000. In contrast, Ekos reported that a significant number of Canadians indicated a low level of trust in the NDP leader (41 percent vs. 30 percent moderate, 18 percent high) (Ekos, October 26, 2000).

15 She was either in third or fourth place even in her home region of Atlantic Canada. Ipsos-Reid, November 24, 2000 and Environics, November 25, 2000.

16 Compas, October 13, 2000.

17 For example, looking at the party's list of candidates with phone number, FAX number or email number reveals that in Quebec 73 of 75 had none of the above in the listing.

18 H. Fraser, "Report on the 2000 Federal Election Campaign," January 2001.

19 Such candidates were eligible for a grant of $800 from the party.

20 See D. Laycock, *Populism and Democratic Thought in the Canadian Prairies 1910 to 1945* (Toronto, University of Toronto, 1990).

21 The number of ridings designated for radio ads by province were BC-7, Sask.-8, Man.-7, Ontario-8, New Brunswick-1, N.S.-7, PEI-1, Nfld.-4 (along with the Yukon riding targetted by newspaper ads) for a total of 44. This is indicative of the number of ridings given priority and resources.

22 Whitehorn, *Canadian Socialism*, p. 216; Whitehorn, "Dashed Hopes" p. 45; "Quest For Survival" pp. 45-46; "Atlantic Breakthrough" p. 98.

23 See C. Alexander "Digital Leviathan: The Emergence of E-politics in Canada" in H.G. Thorburn and A. Whitehorn, *Party Politics in Canada,* 8th edition.

24 "Financing Campaign 2000," January 20, 2001.

25 "Report on Operations of the Media Relations Group" n.a., n.d. c. January 2001.

26 Still later she suggested the surplus was $100 billion, not the $30 billion she had earlier mentioned. It is not clear that, after years of the public being told repeatedly about the size of the debt and deficit, the voters fully understood the magnitude of the surplus or that NDP comments about spending such vast sums would not play into the public's stereotypes about the NDP as big spenders.

27 Ipsos-Reid, November 12, 2000.

28 "The Polls," CBC Website [cbc.ca], November 28, 2000.

29 "Financing Campaign 2000," January, 2001. The cost was calculated after income was also factored and thus in reality was actually higher.

30 The NDP basically flatlined in the polls ranging between 7 and 10 percent in twenty public domain polls from October 25 to November 25 [CBC website, November 28, 2000]. When Canadians were asked to assess the five major parties performance in the campaign, the NDP's assessment was overwhelming "same" or unchanged (Ipsos-Reid, November 24, 2000).

31 Correspondence with J. Marzetti, NDP federal secretary, December 18, 2001. For comparable data analysis techniques over a number of federal elections, see J. Williams, *The Conservative Party of Canada* (Duke, Durham, 1956) p. 186.

32 It makes more sense to have official party status based on a combined percent of votes (e.g. 5 percent) and at least one seat. This is both a more accurate reflection of the public will and more stable than seats.

33 See Whitehorn, *Canadian Socialism*, chapter #1 and "Appendix" and "Alexa McDonough And NDP Gains in Atlantic Canada" in H.G. Thorburn and A. Whitehorn, *Party Politics in Canada,* 8th edition.

34 See "Atlantic Breakthrough."

35 Gerald Caplan, "Does the NDP have a future?", *The Globe and Mail*, November 29, 2000.

36 For a review of the literature see H. Milner, "The Case for Proportional Representation in Canada" in Thorburn and Whitehorn, eds., *Party Politics in Canada*, 8th ed.

37 Some have suggested placing all of the election post-mortem reports on the party's website for the entire membership to read and discuss and be a catalyst to debate.

38 See F. Ellis and K. Archer, "Ideology and Opinion in the Reform Party", in Thorburn and Whitehorn, eds., *Party Politics in Canada*, 8th edition.

39 Ekos, October 26, 2000. See also Compass, October 13, 2000.

40 Ekos, October 26, 2000; Ipsos-Reid, November 3, 2000.

41 See A. Whitehorn, "Some Reflections on Social Democracy and the New Democratic Party" (paper presented to the NDP Renewal Conference, Ottawa, August, 1994).

42 See E. Broadbent "Social Democracy or Liberalism in the New Millennium" in P. Russell, *The Future of Social Democracy* (Toronto, University of Toronto, 1999), J. Laxer, *In Search of a New Left: Canadian Politics After the Neoconservative Assault* (Toronto, Viking, 1996), and J. Richards, *Retooling the Welfare State: What's Right, What's Wrong, What's to Be Done* (CD Howe Institute, Toronto, 1997).

43 See for example, M. Kennedy, "Hargrove's harangue hampers McDonough", *Kingston Whig Standard*, November 25, 2000; P. Adams, "Romanow calls on NDP to revamp", *The Globe and Mail*, February 1, 2001; V. Lawton, "NDP to side with summit trade protesters", *The Toronto Star*, January 26, 2001; Gerald Caplan, "Does the NDP have a future?", *The Globe and Mail*, November 29, 2000.

44 See W. Young, *Anatomy of a Party: The National CCF 1932-1961* (Toronto, University of Toronto, 1969).

Chapter 5

The Bloc Québécois

by André Bernard

In the 2000 electoral contest, the Bloc Québécois (BQ) elected thirty-eight members of Parliament, six fewer than in 1997. However, the party reaped a slightly larger share of the Quebec votes than in 1997 — 40 percent instead of 39. From the viewpoint of people frightened by the prospect of Quebec separation from Canada, the loss of seats suffered by the BQ is good news, as is the fact that the Liberal Party received a larger share of the votes and almost as many seats in Quebec (thirty-seven). From the viewpoint of those who wish to divide Canada into two countries, the BQ share of the votes, on November 27, 2000, shows continuing strong support for Quebec sovereignty, the BQ's basic objective.[1]

Its basic objective sets the BQ apart. Contrary to the aim of each of the other four political parties in the Canadian House of Commons, the objective of the Bloc Québécois is not to form the government in Ottawa. Rather, the goal is to make Quebec sovereign and, then, to join the Parti québécois in order to govern Quebec as a sovereign country. Precisely, the BQ basic objective is to make Quebec a member of the United Nations, and to keep it, at the same time, a full participant in what is already known as the Canadian economic union and what is becoming the North-American economic union. Because of its basic objective, the Bloc Québécois is not only a strange political party, it is also the object of a lot of concern.

Explanations for the Loss of Seats

The loss of six seats suffered by the Bloc Québécois was explained, in the hours following the voting, by commentators as well as by the leading members of the Quebec sovereigntist movement. Three losses (Quebec-East, Louis-Hébert, and Portneuf) clearly resulted from the dissatisfaction raised by the Quebec Provincial Government's proposal to merge into one single city the various municipalities which make up the Quebec Urban Community.[2] It was easy to link the BQ to the Parti Québécois, which holds the majority of seats in the Quebec National Assembly. To cast a vote against the Bloc candidate was a way to express one's opposition to the proposed forced merger, a merger that was parallel to similar mergers on the Island of Montreal and on the South Shore of the St. Lawrence River. In the region of Montreal, the opposition to the mergers was concentrated in areas where the BQ has never been popular; however, in the suburbs of Quebec City, it was great enough to cause the loss of three seats.

The other seats were lost because the Liberal Party, on November 27, 2000, received the support of many voters who, in 1997, had sided with the Progressive Conservative Party (PC).[3] The best example available of the realignment of former PC supporters is to be found in Bonaventure-Gaspé-Madgalen Islands-Pabok. In 1997, the BQ candidate was elected there with a margin of 179 votes over his Liberal opponent, while the PC candidate had 6,267 votes; on November 27, 2000, there was no PC candidate in that district, and Liberal Georges Farrah was elected with approximately four thousand votes more than the number obtained by the Bloc Québécois challenger.[4]

The realignment of former PC supporters and the reaction to the urban merger project of the Quebec Provincial Government certainly explain a lot, but, the day after the vote, the leader of the Bloc Québécois also put the blame on the old-time tactics of the Liberal Party.[5] The Federal Government ministers had promised $100 million to the Gaspé region if the Liberal candidate there was elected, and they had announced two new bridges in the electoral district of Beauharnois-Salaberry, where they were challenging Daniel Turp, who had become well-known as one of the prominent members of the Bloc Québécois in the House of Commons. Many BQ supporters have been heard saying that the Liberals won the seat of Beauharnois-Salaberry thanks to the two bridges!

According to members of the Bloc Québécois interviewed for this chapter, the failure of their party to gain many new votes is the real explanation of its fate on November 27, 2000. In their view, this failure is partly the result of the coverage given by the media to a few blunders and partly the consequence of the close alliance between the BQ and the Parti Québécois. Among the blunders made by the BQ, one, clearly, had a direct impact on the number of seats gained. It was the decision made by BQ leader Gilles Duceppe to appoint a candidate of his own choice, Noël Tremblay, in Chicoutimi-Le Fjord, instead of endorsing Sylvain Gaudreault, who was the choice of the local organization. That decision led to a confrontation between two groups of sovereigntists, each supporting a candidate of its own, Noël Tremblay, the official BQ nominee, and Mauril Desbiens, an independent reacting to the dismissal of Sylvain Gaudreault. The final consequence was the victory of André Harvey, the candidate of the Liberal Party, who was previously a member of the House of Commons representing the Progressive Conservative Party.[6] Even though the votes obtained by the two sovereigntists do not add up to the total obtained by André Harvey, one can take into account the disenchantment that led many to abstain from voting and, then, conclude that the Bloc Québécois followers could have gained that seat if they had been able to turn out in full muster behind one single candidate. In any case, their defeat in Chicoutimi-Le Fjord was worth thinking over.[7]

As for the impact of the close alliance between the Bloc Québécois and the Parti Québécois, it explains more than the loss of three seats in the vicinity of Quebec City; it apparently shows why many former BQ supporters have chosen not to vote. Among many others, political scientist Louis Massicotte has been quoted saying that some sovereigntists were probably tempted to turn away from the polling-booths because of their disapproval of the policies advocated by PQ leader Lucien Bouchard and by his government.[8] The fact is that, on November 27, 2000, the turnout was much lower than in 1997; the Bloc Québécois received approximately 18,000 fewer votes than in 1997. In addition, the Liberal Party was able to obtain the bulk of the support from voters who had sided with the Progressive-Conservative Party in 1997.[9] In any case, during the Fall of the year 2000, the mood, in the ranks of the sovereigntists, was at low ebb.[10]

Permanent Disadvantages for the BQ

While trying to explain the fate of the Bloc Québécois, one should also look at some of the permanent disadvantages which discourage many voters from giving their votes to its candidates. The main disadvantage for the party is its basic objective: the project to transform Quebec into a sovereign country. This basic objective raises tremen-

141

dous forces against the Bloc Québécois, as well as against its Quebec provincial counterpart, the Parti Québécois. Because of this objective, almost every Canadian organization associated with politics, outside Quebec, is stubbornly opposed to the Bloc Québécois, as it is to the Parti Québécois. In Quebec, the Bloc Québécois and the Parti québécois also have a lot of enemies, as shown by the results of numerous public opinion surveys published over the years. All in all, listening to what is being said of the Bloc Québécois by those who oppose its basic objective, or listening to their own feelings, many voters in Quebec, prefer not to vote for a BQ candidate, whatever their dislike of other political parties or candidates.

The Bloc Québécois is also fundamentally hampered by its position as a political party which, by its very reason for being, cannot hope to have the majority of seats in the legislative body in which it is to be represented. Because of this, among the voters who approve of the BQ basic objective, a few, certainly, prefer to give their vote to one of the other political parties, and many, no doubt, abstain from voting. Because of its stance, the Bloc Québécois looks like the spearhead of a protest movement. Moreover, by their criticism of the federal government policies, the members of the BQ in the House of Commons have contributed to their reputation of permanent protesters. This reputation clearly repels many voters, impressed by the pun which is printed often in some of the Quebec dailies: "le Bloc bloque; c'est tout ce qu'il fait!" (The Bloc blocks, that's all!).

Letters coming from readers and, sometimes, quotations from interviews, printed in English-language dailies and weeklies, occasionally depict the Bloc Québécois as a political party of French-speaking Quebeckers, not as a party open to all Quebeckers. Although the BQ leaders regularly say that their basic objective is meant to ease the relationships between communities, although they say their party is open to all and working for all, and although the number of BQ candidates with English-language credentials is increasing, the mental picture of the BQ, in the minds of many English-speaking Quebeckers, is not yet one with which it is easy to identify. As a consequence, taking into account the fact that many English-speaking Quebeckers do not see how they could benefit from the division of Canada, the BQ is not a choice from the viewpoint of almost all English-speaking Quebeckers. As English-speaking Quebeckers account for one-fifth of the Quebec voters, the BQ is permanently deprived of a relatively large voting base.

The Bloc Québécois is also at a disadvantage, compared to the Liberal Party, because it is not the political party that is preferred by the wealthy. Knowing this, and in line with their desire to restrict the rules pertaining to electoral finance, the leaders of the BQ have shunned donations from corporations and they limited the amount of individual donations they were willing to accept from 1990 to 1999. But then when they decided to act as the others in the 2000 electoral contest, they could not attract large donations, because their party was still not a viable choice from the viewpoint of the wealthy.

The hostility the BQ inspires in business people has many negative consequences for the party. For instance, the BQ cannot count much on the help given, during working hours, by persons who are on the payrolls of corporations. However, it does get help from several persons who are on the payrolls of Quebec Provincial ministerial offices or a few non-profit organizations, as one former assistant to Michel Gauthier (the BQ leader in 1996) has explained in a book published in 1998.[11] And, of course, it is hard to believe that the members of Bloc Québécois are always treated as they would like by radio stations and newspapers owned by some of the known opponents to the project to make Quebec a sovereign country.[12]

Being shunned by the wealthy, the Bloc Québécois does not recruit persons who are already in the limelight. Among the BQ candidates, one does not find any high-profile business leader. The BQ candidates, however, are highly educated and, as a whole, clearly community-oriented. A reading of the 2000 edition of their resumés shows that, among the seventy-five BQ candidates, sixty-seven have obtained a university degree and that, among these sixty-seven, nineteen have reached the master's level or higher. Most of the highly educated, and all of the other eight candidates, have been involved in community work of one kind or another. Unfortunately for the Bloc Québécois, the credentials of its candidates do not overcome its disadvantages.

However, the leading members of the Bloc Québécois have put a tremendous amount of energy and imagination into trying to overcome the handicap of the limited financial resources available to the party. One of their most successful moves has been the maintenance and expansion of the network of allied organizations that provide them with resources and support. Many workers' unions of Quebec, for instance, have sided regularly with the Bloc Québécois, as have most of the organizations involved in the defence of the French language in Quebec.

The Bloc Québécois produced a 177-page electoral platform for the 2000 electoral contest.[13] This heavy book summarized the numerous speeches of the BQ members of the House of Commons between 1990 and the year 2000, and also included a compendium of proposals for the future. The proposals resulted from a series of advisory opinions provided by a number of organizations (the chairperson of the committee that produced this platform, Yvan Loubier, wrote that forty organizations had been consulted). The platform dealt with the basic objective of the Bloc Québécois — the sovereignty of Quebec within the Canada-Quebec economic union, a project that implies a new partnership (*partenariat*) between Quebec and its neighbours.

However, the platform also dealt with numerous topics of contemporary significance: the present-day federal public finances, the federal policies relating to economic development and employment, the problems posed by the present-day lack of social solidarity in Canada, the federal government policies towards Quebec regions, the federal policies relating to the environment, the federal policies in the area of justice, in the area of culture, in the field of agriculture, and so on. Reading the 177 pages of this platform, one cannot be but very impressed by the documentary research that it required, and by the tone of the proposals.

In a way, the Bloc Québécois platform shows that this party has one basic objective — Quebec sovereignty and a new partnership between Quebec and its neighbours — and several secondary objectives — new methods of public finance, better laws against gangsters, and so on. Unfortunately for the Bloc Québécois, this platform did not reached the voters. It was probably used by the BQ election workers as a source of inspiration during the campaign, but it was not distributed at large. Although it was also available to internet surfers (address: www.bloc-quebecois.org), it was certainly not downloaded often, as it was so large.

The Quebec newspapers made few references to this platform, though it was briefly described the day after it was published.[14] A summary of this platform appeared in the Montreal French-language daily, *La Presse*, along with summaries of the platforms of the other main political parties, and that was about all that was really noted concerning this very interesting piece of party literature.

In spite of its limited impact, this platform was a feat and it is a testimony of the energy put out by the BQ leading members in their endeavour to overcome the disadvantages that hamper their party.

The Bloc Québécois also produced a standard, letter-sized, sixteen-page booklet that got wide distribution. This booklet, entitled *le Quebec gagne a voter Bloc*, was based on the main proposals of the platform. In full colour (with blue dominant), and with pictures of various types of faces (showing the diversity of the Quebec population), this booklet was very attractive, compared to the booklets distributed by the Liberal Party and others. It probably had a positive impact, and in any case, its high quality is further evidence of the dedication of the leading members of the BQ. During the campaign, the Bloc Québécois made ample references to this booklet in its television spots. It did, however, have to correct one of these, as it seemed to take advantage of the October World March of Women.[15] But, all in all, the party advertizing was of high quality.

The campaign plan of the Bloc Québécois was to attract the voters who had sided with the Progressive Conservative Party in 1997. In order to gain the support of these voters, the Bloc Québécois leader and his lieutenants took Jean Chrétien as their target, exposing his type of ethics and his attitude towards the majority of French-speaking Quebeckers. Even though it was made repeatedly, the attack on Jean Chrétien does not seem to have influenced many Quebec voters outside the ranks of the Bloc Québécois.[16] In order to lure former Progressive Conservative voters, the Bloc Québécois also put much emphasis on two other themes: the quality of public health services in Canada, and, more often, the war against gangsters. One of the BQ leaders, Yvan Loubier, was able to get the attention of the media on this topic, because he had been threatened by gangsters soon after his actions against them.[17] Again, it is unlikely that the BQ strategy had the desired impact. Indeed, the polls have shown that most voters who shifted away from the Progressive Conservative Party shunned the Bloc Québécois in favour of the Liberals.

While it was trying to lure former Progressive Conservative voters, the Bloc Québécois was anxious to keep the support of the Quebec sovereigntists. In order to get that support, it obtained the co-operation of Parti Québécois leaders to get involved in the campaign.[18] Finally, the leader of the Bloc Québécois, Gilles Duceppe, was indefatigable and, in spite of the stress of the campaign, he was able to avoid the most obvious pitfalls. He performed relatively well in the televised debates and was a winner in French, thanks, partly, to Joe Clark, the Progressive

145

Conservative leader who saw the Liberal Party as the real explanation of the existence of the Bloc Québécois.[19] In the end, commentators awarded very good marks to Gilles Duceppe, but, presumably, these good marks are little comfort for the verdict of the polls.

Conclusion

In her book on the Bloc Québécois published in 1995, Manon Cornellier had come to the conclusion that the Bloc looked more like a movement bound by its veneration for the leader (Lucien Bouchard at the time) and the pursuit of a single mission than a true party.[20] Since 1995, the Bloc Québécois has changed, although it still is a party that looks different from the others. It is no longer a movement bound by its veneration for a leader. And it has become a party with a basic objective and several secondary objectives, a party that seeks power not in Ottawa but in a sovereign Quebec.

Voters in Quebec understand this. Those who would like to see Quebec become a sovereign country tend to give their vote to the Bloc Québécois; the others do not. The results of the 2000 electoral contest show that 40 percent of the votes cast in the province come from persons who are willing to live in (or with) a sovereign Quebec.

NOTES

1   Pierre Drouilly. "Le vote nationaliste toujours solide." *La Presse*, Friday December 1, 2000, page A13.

2   Vincent Marissal. "Turp s'ennuie de Bouchard, les bloquistes blâment les fusions." *La Presse*, Tuesday December 12, 2000, page A8. In the middle of the electoral campaign, the Quebec Provincial Government decided to merge the municipalities of three of the several conurbations of the province: those of the Quebec City area, those of the Island of Montreal, and those of the South Shore of the Saint Lawrence River, near Montreal. That decision was critcized by the mayors of the suburban municipalities doomed to be merged.

3   Katia Gagnon. "Les fusions n'expliquent pas tous les malheurs du Bloc." *La Presse*, Wednesday November 29, 2000, page A6.

4   Jean Guenette. "Georges Farrah est élu." *La Presse*, Tuesday November 28, 2000, page A4.

5   Martin Pelchat. "Duceppe blâme les 'vieilles tactiques' libérales." *La Presse*, Wednesday November 29, 2000, page A8.

6   Paul Roy. "Histoires de chicanes de famille." *La Presse*, Tuesday November 28, 2000, page A4.

7   Sylvain Gaudreault. "Lettre ouverte à Gilles Duceppe." *Le Devoir*, Thursday November 30, 2000, page A7.

8   Louis Massicotte, quoted in Katia Gagnon. "Les fusions n'expliquent pas tous les malheurs du Bloc." *La Presse*, Wednesday November 29, 2000, page A6.

9   Michel Venne. "La bouderie des électeurs." *Le Devoir*, Wednesday November 29, 2000, pages A1.

10 Kathleen Lévesque. "Le PQ est rongé par la démobilisation." *Le Devoir*, Saturday December 23, 2000, page A4.

11 André Néron. *Le temps des hypocrites*. Montreal: VLB, 1998 page 216.

12 It is to be noted that Gilles Duceppe has said that the tone of the media coverage, in his own case, has improved recently. Gilles Duceppe, "Question d'identité," Outrement (Montreal), *Lanctôt Éditeur*, 2000, page 131.

13 Bloc Québécois, Plate-forme électorale du Bloc Québécois. Automne 2000. Un parti pris pour le monde, Montréal, Publication autorisée par l'agente principale du Bloc québécois, 2000, 177 pages.

14 Robert Dutrisac. "Dévoilement de la plateforme électorale." *Le*

Devoir, Saturday October 21, 2000, page A11.

15 Robert Dutrisac. "Le Bloc corrige sa publicité destinée aux femmes." *Le Devoir*, Thursday November 2, 2000, page A5. Françoise David presides the Quebec Federation of Women known in French as the Fédération des femmes du Québec, the organization behind the October World March of Women.

16 A survey has shown that, in Quebec, the Bloc québécois was the choice of 65 percent of those who disapproved of the way the Liberal Party Government favours its friends (a way labelled as *patronage*, in French).

Richard Nadeau and others. "Pourquoi les libéraux ont-ils gagné?" *La Presse*, Saturday December 2, 2000, pages A21.

17 Louise Leduc. "Construire un pays... débarassé de ses criminels." *Le Devoir*, Friday November 10, 2000, page A5.

18 Huguette Young. "Appui à Gilles Duceppe." *Le Devoir*, Thursday November 16, 2000, page A5. Also: François Cardinal. "Les trois ténors à l'unisson." *Le Devoir*, Monday November 20, 2000, page A1.

19 Manon Cornellier. "Coup de pouce à Duceppe." *Le Devoir*, Thursday November 9, 2000, page A1.

20 Manon Cornellier. *The Bloc*, (Toronto: Lorimer, 1995, page 157).

Chapter 6

The Politics of Exclusion:
The Campaign of the Green Party

by Joan Russow

In the 2000 federal election, there were eleven registered parties. Those who follow politics in the media will observe there is a clear distinction between what I will refer to as the "Pentad"—the group of five parties (the Bloc Québécois, the Canadian Alliance, the Conservatives, the Liberals, and the NDP) represented in the House of Commons, and the "Non-Pentad" parties (the Canadian Action Party, the Communist Party, the Green Party, the Marijuana Party, the Marxist-Leninists, and the Natural Law Party), who have no parliamentary members. In Election 2000, the Christian Heritage Party lost its status as a registered party, the Communist Party regained its status, and the Marijuana Party acquired registered party status because they ran candidates in fifty ridings. The criterion that the media seem to use to determine coverage is not what a party stands for, but the standing the party attained in the last election. Often terms like "all parties," "the parties," or "major parties" refer only to the Pentad, while the non-Pentad parties (when they are referred to at all) are called the "other parties," "fringe parties," or the "small parties."

From my perspective, a better distinction is that the Pentad, the Communist, the Green Party, and the Marxist-Leninist parties have a comprehensive program, offering a range of complex, though quite different, solutions, albeit. The Bloc and the Canadian Action parties have comprehensive programs but focus primarily on a specific solution with extensive ramifications: in the case of the Bloc, separation from Canada, and in the case of the Canadian Action Party, fundamental reform of the banking system. Neither of the remaining two parties, the Marijuana Party and the Natural Law Party, has a comprehensive program. Instead, they both offer specific solutions which themselves have complex ramifications; the Marijuana Party through the legalization of marijuana and the Natural Law Party through Yogic flying and transcendental meditation. Citizens at public forums usually expect parties to be able to discuss more than a single issue and deride the candidate who expresses the same solution to every problem, no matter how complex.

At the time of Election 2000, five "national" parties also had provincial counterparts: the Conservatives, the Bloc, the Green Party, the Liberals, and the NDP, though we observe that the Alberta and Ontario "Progressive Conservative" parties are actually more Canadian Alliance than Conservative. Of the eleven registered parties all but the Bloc attempted to run candidates across Canada, but only the Canadian Alliance, Conservatives, Liberals, and the NDP attempted to run in every riding.

Parties or Single Issue Groups?

The emergence of what has been described as "single issue parties" raises the question of how does a political party differ from what is described, at least in the *Elections Act,* as a "third party." One difference between interest groups and political parties is the differential access to status, either charitable or political, and the implication for tax receipts for their donors. Interest groups can receive charitable status, which enables them to issue charitable tax receipts. However, interest groups that are deemed to be "political" cannot receive charitable status. It is interesting to note that an interest group like the Fraser Institute has charitable status, but most activist groups involved with human rights and peace issues are deemed "political" and cannot receive charitable status. Political parties, once registered, can also issue political tax receipts for donations; political tax receipts result in deductions off the tax payable.

A trend is emerging where groups that have usually been described as "interest groups" are beginning to form parties, and unless coalitions are formed among the various parties wishing to change the status quo, these single-issue parties may contribute to the perpetuation of the status quo, or may undermine the status quo, depending on the nature of the issue of the single-issue party. It is often presumed that if a single-issue party is progressive on one aspect of public policy, that the party is also progressive on other issues. However, this cannot be presumed. For example, in my riding of Victoria the representative from the Marijuana Party, shattering the peace-loving, pot-smoking image, spoke out vociferously in favour of the NATO bombing of Yugoslavia. The Green Party, since its inception in 1983, has been a strong advocate of civil and political rights including the decriminalization of marijuana, but the Green Party also promotes other aspects of what I term "the public trust" (social justice, equity, environment, peace, human rights). It is understandable, however, that a political party advocating the complexity and inclusiveness of issues cannot give a high profile to a single issue as the single-issue party can.

The Green Party is not itself a single-issue party, since it stresses the complexity and interdependence of issues. It promotes guarantees for human rights, including civil and political rights, labour rights, women's rights, indigenous rights, as well as the human right to food, housing, corporate-free education, and universally accessible publicly funded health care, while looking for ways to prevent environmentally induced diseases and poverty related illnesses. It works to ensure social justice, and fair and just transition programs to socially equitable and environmentally sound employment. It supports the prevention of war and conflict, reducing the military budget, and rejecting the guise of "humanitarian intervention," and of course it has the fundamental purpose of protecting the environment, addressing environmental racism, reducing the ecological footprint, invoking the precautionary principle and moving away from the current model of over-consumption.

At the federal level, the Green Party is organized with a leader, and a council of administrative chair, financial agent, organizing chair, publications chair, international representative, and representatives from each of the provincial parties. The council and the leader are elected every two years at the national convention by single transferable vote (which includes a "none of the above" option) with all members having a vote, including a mail-in ballot. Essentially no money has been spent on internal elections to this point. A biography and statement by each candidate for leader and for council are circulated with a mail-in ballot to all the members through our publication "Green Canada" — the Green Party publication.

Internationally, the first Green Party was formed in 1972 in New Zealand; it was called the Values Party. In Canada, however, without being registered as a party, candidates did run for the "Garden Party" in the federal election of 1971 and in PEI provincial elections, though the party name was not on the ballot. The Green Party of Canada was founded in 1983. Since then, the Green Party has fielded an increasing number of candidates in each subsequent federal election; it ran candidates in 111 ridings in the 2000 election, and also participates in provincial and municipal elections.

The Green Party of Canada is part of a global Green Party movement of associated political parties usually named "Green" but also named "Ecology," "Integrity," "Del Sol," etc., adhering to a basic set of principles. The Green Party of Canada participates as a member of the Federation of the Green Parties of the Americas, and works with Green Parties on other continents. In September 1999, in Oaxaca, Mexico, an international meeting of Green parties from around the world met and published the Oaxaca Declaration. A Declaration of Actions was agreed, to, which is one of the documents prepared in advance for the Global Green Conference held in Canberra in April 2001, where a Global Green Charter was discussed. Although it is part of government in some countries, and has elected representatives to the European parliament, the Green Party in Canada is still considered a "small" party. One reason for its greater success elsewhere, as in Germany, is the existence of some form of mixed proportional representation where the number of seats a political party attains corresponds more closely to the percentage of the popular vote it attains. Our system, called "first past the post," makes the percentage of the popular vote irrelevant as long as a party attains more votes that any other within an electoral district.

The Green Party Campaign

Although the high profile candidacy of Ralph Nader as the US Green Party presidential candidate resulted in increased interest in the Green Party of Canada in the 2000 election, the ancillary so-called "Nader factor" had a detrimental effect on our campaign. Having spoken out against the status quo, calling for fundamental electoral reform and for fundamental structural socio-political change, Nader was then unfairly blamed for electing George W. Bush by siphoning off Democratic votes. During the Canadian federal election, Jean Chrétien and Liberal candidate David Anderson in my riding of Victoria tried to take advantage of this situation, describing a vote for the Green Party as "a wasted vote." Mr. Chrétien is reported to have said, "Here, especially here in B.C. I ask you not to waste your vote on a third party. This is very, very important, a party that has no chance to win. Look at Florida at this moment and think of the people who voted for

Ralph Nader there."[1] As Green Party leader, I was constantly asked about the "Nader factor," and how I would feel about being responsible for the election of the Canadian Alliance. Near the end of the election, when asked about the "Nader factor," I referred instead to the "Bush/Day factor" — blaming the problem not the solution.

The Green Party fielded seventy-eight candidates in the 1997 Federal Election, and there was some discussion within the party about what levels we should then strive for in 2000. We had ambitious plans, but unfortunately with little time to prepare for the election we wereable to run only 111 candidates. We ran candidates in every province except Newfoundland, and for the first time we ran a candidate in Nunavut. For the next election expected in 2004, we hope to run a full slate, with candidates selected far in advance. Until now, candidates generally have been chosen only when the election was called, on what I believe to have been the misguided notion that the proximity of the election would generate interest in our candidates. As it was the intention of the Green Party of Canada to have candidates nominated in advance of the federal election, I had planned on traveling across Canada in the summer of 2000 to work on setting up riding associations, and to encourage the nomination of candidates for the federal election which I anticipated would occur in June 2001. Unfortunately, I became caught up in running in the Okanagan by-election against Stockwell Day.

The usual procedure for selecting candidates in the Green Party depends on whether or not there are Green Party members in the ridings. When there are Green Party members in a riding they are contacted and the candidate is selected, usually from members living in the riding, at a meeting of members. Where there are no Green Party members the organizing chair in conjunction with provincial parties searches out potential candidates and the candidates are recommended to the organizing chair and leader. The recommendations are rarely opposed. We are moving towards increasing the number of constituencies at the provincial level and ridings at the federal level so that a more consistent practice of selecting candidates can be established. Although the Green Party has advocated that the provision for a $1000 deposit be removed from the Elections Act, the revised provision in the Elections Act of complete reimbursement of the $1000 deposit on the completion of the auditing requirement regardless of what percentage of the vote the candidate received certainly helped the Green Party this time in attracting candidates.

For this election, the Green Party of Canada office printed 100,000 copies in "tabloid" format of a summary of policy (our "platform") and distributed them to various candidates. The bulk of the campaign material was up on the website. This included: a Green Book (a compilation made by Don Ferguson of all the resolutions made over the years through Green Party of Canada conventions); the *Green Guide* (selected items of policy for the Platform 2000); the *Green Public Trust Budget* (a Department by Department set of proposals for redirecting and relocating government funds); and the 1997 platform set up department by department. Individual candidates and riding associations also printed up a wide variety of campaign literature based on Green Party principles, platform, and policies. Policies of the Green Party have been developed over the years through resolutions presented either at policy conferences or at Annual General Meetings. Since the last federal election, I had been compiling policy that had been passed by the Green Party federally and provincially since 1983. The policy document just with the "statements of action" ended up being at least 400 pages and was subsequently reduced to 180 pages. I placed the various policies within a framework of federal departments.

Because of the name "Green," there has often been the presumption that the Green Party is only concerned with environmental issues. Although the party emerged out of the peace and environment movements, it has become more involved with seeking solutions within the complexity and interdependence of issues through furthering the public trust. On the other hand, "ecological integrity" is one of the fundamental principles of all Green parties. The Green Party of Canada emphasizes the environment as a core issue linked with other issues and recognizes the inherent worth of nature beyond human purpose. We linked human rights and legal and ethical obligations and commitment through calling for the implementation of fundamental principles such as the "precautionary principle," the "reverse onus principle," and the "reduction of the ecological footprint principle." We linked human rights and the environment through addressing the human right to a safe environment, including safe drinking water and clean air, with the right of future generations to their ecological heritage, including the preservation of old growth forests, conserving biodiversity, enacting strong endangered-species legislation, and establishing a more extensive publicly managed park system with conservation corridors. We linked energy to transportation and then to health, by calling for the conversion to environmentally safe and sound renewable energy, and moving away from car dependency.

Health care was a major issue in the 2000 election. We linked health and environment issues by calling for increased funding for a universally accessible, publicly funded, non-two-tier, not for profit, health care system with due consideration given to environmentally induced diseases. We linked environment and poverty through addressing poverty-related health problems, and affirming the fundamental human right to unadulterated food and safe and accessible housing. We linked environment, health, and equity by calling for the banning of genetically engineered foods. We called for the banning of uranium mining, and phasing out civil nuclear plants. We linked labour and environment by supporting fundamental labour principles and calling for the banning and phasing out of socially inequitable and environmentally unsound practices, coupled with a fair and just transition program for affected workers and communities. We linked trade with the environment, calling for the dismantling of the WTO, the implementation of other international agreements (including international environmental law), and the revoking of charters and licences of transnational corporation for violating the public trust (including for destroying the environment and denying social justice). We linked human rights, economic justice, and the environment by addressing the issues of environmental racism.

Financial Limitations on the Smaller Parties

There are numerous limitations that are experienced by the non-Pentad parties, including questionable regulations on political funding, inadequate media coverage especially because of the media pools, unfair polling, a seriously flawed electoral system, inappropriate third party intervention, the inequitable reimbursements from the public purse, and institutional bias against the non-Pentad parties.

Political parties that accept donations from corporations, unions, and individuals in unlimited amounts are at a considerable advantage. In submissions to the Senate Committee on the Elections Act, the Green Party along with the Communist and Marxist-Leninist parties raised the issue of corporate funding of political parties and proposed that there be a clause in the Act prohibiting donations from corporations. To support this recommendation I pointed out that it is considered illegal for Canadian companies to give money to elected officials outside of Canada because it is construed as bribery, and individuals or regimes accepting money from corporations are perceived to be engaging in corruption. In Canada, there is a difficult-to-appreciate distinction between corporations giving money to a candidate and leader before the candidate and leader are elected and corporations giving money to elected officials once elected. Under Canadian law, the former is described as a political donation; the latter is condemned as corruption. In some other countries, this fine distinction is not recognized and all contributions coming from entities that do not vote are banned. The legislation regarding donations has to be completely reformed so as to prevent this form of corruption. Although there is no required disclosure of donations when given to the leader and candidates outside of the election period or to the constituencies or riding associations, there is the requirement to disclose donations made to the political party itself and to candidates and leaders during the election period. While, at this time, we are not able to ascertain the nature and extent of these forms of corporate donations during Election 2000, we can extrapolate from the reported Election 1997 donations. During the 1997 federal election, the Reform, Liberal, and Conservative parties received donations from the following institutions and corporations: banks and financial institutions, the tobacco, coal, oil, gas, automobile, forest, chemical, mining and nuclear industries, arms producers, agribusiness, pharmaceutical, military arms producers, and in the case of the Reform, the gun lobby. The NDP also accepts corporate donations provincially, and it has been reported that the federal party currently accepts corporate donations as well. It would appear that some of the non-Pentad parties also accept what would be categorized as "corporate donations." The Canadian Action Party reported accepting a donation from Magna.

The Green Party of Canada at its convention in Ottawa, in August 2000, supported the call for prohibiting corporate donations, and defeated a resolution calling for the acceptance of corporate donations in the interim until the Act is changed. I ran in the election stating that we do not take corporate donations but it would appear that some Green Party candidates did accept donations from small businesses that engage in practices that are supported by the Green Party. The influence of corporate donations is evident in the nature and extent of grants and contributions from government to industry, in spending priorities, in policy development and implementation, in determining what constitutes "economic well being" (GDP), and in the relaxing of regulations (deregulation and voluntary compliance). I firmly believe that only individuals vote, only individuals should be able to contribute to campaigns, and that individual contributions should be limited.

Smaller parties are also disadvantaged by the public subsidies, which are skewed to the Pentad parties. In the Elections Act there is a formula that places limits on election spending. Under section 441, a party can spend $2.07 for each of the first 15,000 electors, $1.04 for each of the next 10,000 electors and 0.52 for each of the remaining electors. These "limits" fail to create a level playing field, as the Pentad spending is far in excess of that of the non-Pentad parties. We are often somewhat amused when we receive the Elections Canada statement saying we are only allowed to spend about $70,000, when we might only have a few thousand to spend.

There are also other inequities that perpetuate a vicious circle where the Pentad parties receive subsidies from the public purse, while the non-Pentad parties get nothing. Under Section 435 of the Elections Act, if a party obtains a certain percentage of the vote in a previous election, the party is reimbursed from the public purse for 22.5 percent of their election expenses (if candidates endorsed by the registered party received at least 2 percent of the number of valid votes cast in the election or 5 percent of the number of valid votes cast in the electoral districts in which the registered party endorsed a candidate). Further, in sections 464-6, if a candidate obtains 15 percent of the vote in an individual riding, he or she then receives 50 percent of election expenses from the public purse. Thus, when an election is called, the Pentad parties have considerable funds already at their disposal, since they can borrow money from banks against the likelihood of getting these subsidies. Rather than encourage political parties to spend to their limit, it would make more sense to reduce the allowable expenses by at least half, discontinue all reimbursements, and set up a public fund for political parties that could be allotted through individual assignment of public funds each year.

Almost all registered parties except the governing party lament the lack of fixed election dates. The parties that accept major corporate and union donations and substantial reimbursements from previous elections have substantial funds to launch a campaign. The Green Party, along with most of the non-Pentad parties, starts out an election with a national budget of several thousand dollars in contrast to the several million that the Pentad parties have. The challenges of an election campaign without funds creates a whole different world from the privileged Pentad parties. For example, it is difficult to attend multiple events if one doesn't have a charter aircraft. After the Democracy Channel debate, in Toronto, I was supposed to be in Vancouver at a 7 a.m. forum, in Halifax at 2 p.m. for one on health and women's issues, and back in Toronto at 7 p.m. to seek yet again to be part of the women's debate.

Other Sources of Discrimination

The Leaders' Debates are often seen as the cornerstone or turning point in election campaigns. The practice of only including registered political parties that have elected members in the House of Commons contributes to the continuation of inequities in the current electoral system and to the perpetuation of the status quo. Whether a party has elected members to the House of Commons, however, often depends on the nature of the Election Act and the media coverage of the registered parties during the previous election. During the last federal election in 1997, I was invited to participate as the sixth party leader in a debate on First Nations issues. I read through the five thousand page Royal Commission report on Aboriginal Issues and flew to Ottawa to debate with the leaders of the Bloc, Conservatives, Liberals, NDP, and Reform. When I arrived in Ottawa, I found out that I was the only leader present for the three hour debate; the others must have all agreed among themselves that they were not prepared to discuss First Nations issue and the Royal Commission report for three hours, so they sent a page with their picture and a comment along with a substitute. The Pentad leaders refused to participate in issue debates if non-Pentad leaders were invited to participate. In the 2000 election, to address the failure to include all registered political parties in the debate, Greg Vezina organized an all-registered political party debate on the "Democracy Channel." As was expected, the Pentad did not participate in the debate. When the non-Pentad leaders arrived at the debate, we shared the stage with five empty chairs. Although the debate was broadcast on CPAC, and partially broadcast on CBC Newsworld, the other national print media, such as *The Globe and Mail* and the *National Post*, trivialized the event.

158

In 1997 there were only two female leaders of registered political parties in Canada. The National Action Committee on the Status of Women (NAC) organized a debate but did not include me. Subsequently, the former director, Joan Grant Cummings sent me a letter of explanation and apology. In 2000, again I was excluded from the debate. Thinking incorrectly that I was still the only woman leader other than Alexa McDonough, I lobbied for my inclusion in the debate. (I later found out that the leader of the Marxist-Leninists was also a woman.) I contacted NAC and was told by the new president that they could not include me because they were only including the parties that were "framing politics in Canada." I was also told that only two leaders were going to participate: Alexa McDonough and Joe Clark. I went to the Debate at Hart House, at the University of Toronto, still hoping that I might be included, but was not. I was the only leader present anywhere at Hart House that night — Alexa McDonough and Joe Clark in the end did not appear. Before the debate I talked with Judy Rebick who told me that NAC had wanted to include me, but that one or more of the "major" political parties had said that they would not participate if I were included. Ironically, the last time I was at Hart House was in 1958 while attending the University of Toronto. I was told that I had to leave because no women were allowed in Hart House.

In this election, as leader, I was included much more by the media and by organizers of public meetings than in 1997. For example, I was on CBC, Terry Milewski's Newsworld report, CPAC, CTV's morning show, the David Ingram Show, Counterspin, CTV's Chat Room, CHEK TV interviews, Shaw cable, Much Music, TV Ontario, Radio-Canada, numerous radio stations in French as well as English, Co-op Radio in Vancouver, and the University Radio in Victoria. *The Globe and Mail* printed a position piece by me on the debate, and there were features by the University news service, the *Ottawa Citizen, Montreal Gazette,* the *Victoria Newsgroup, Monday Magazine, Le Soleil,* and the *Hamilton Spectator.* I was invited to attend the McGill forum on the Environment,

This coverage, however, pales compared to that received by the leaders of the Pentad parties through the media pools. From the media coverage in Election 2000, it would appear that the journalists assigned to the different Pentad leaders' campaigns were reluctant to raise issues that were not already predetermined by the Pentad itself. The polling results and the election results complement, reinforce each other, and determine essentially the nature and extent of the media coverage.

It can be said that the Election Act is fundamentally flawed but scrupulously fair in its application whereas the Canadian Radio Television Corporation (CRTC) regulations are fundamentally sound but unfairly applied. Under the CRTC regulations, the media are not to determine which parties are of worth. The CRTC regulations state, "The broadcaster does not enjoy the position of a benevolent censor who is able to give the public only what it 'should' know. Nor is it the broadcaster's role to decide in advance which candidates are worthy of broadcast time." Presumably, the intention of the CRTC provision was to give fair coverage to all the registered parties. In this election as in many others, the media determined that what really constitutes worth was which parties had elected seats in the last election, and which parties were substantially likely to win future seats. Under the CRTC regulations the purpose of the requirements is clearly stated: "The purpose of the requirements is to ensure the public's right to be informed of the issues.... This right is a quintessential one for the effective functioning of a democracy, particularly at election time. The broadcaster's obligations as a trustee of the public air waves is seldom greater than it is in respect of the exercise of the most fundamental democratic freedom." The lack of compliance with CRTC regulations must be more fully examined. I raised the lack of compliance with CRTC regulations at the February 2001 meeting of the Advisory Committee for registered parties.

Often in the media, "media pundits," including academics, would make comments such as "'no party' is addressing this issue," or "'all parties' have proposed this," when 'no party' or 'all parties' were designations that excluded all parties other than the Pentad. For example, at one CBC "Town Hall Meeting" with four Pentad parties present, a CBC commentator proclaimed that the NDP had the best environmental policy of ALL the political parties. Mirroring the media in their determination of worth were numerous third party groups that purported to be concerned with fairness, equality, equity and non-partisanship. The performance of some of these groups during this election brings into question what constitutes non-partisanship. In election 1997, the Council of Canadians sent a questionnaire out to only the Pentad. In Election 2000 the Council of Canadians did not send out a questionnaire but instead issued two reports: *This Election Take Back the Agenda*, and a report on genetically engineered foods and crops. In both reports the Council reported on only the Pentad. By only evaluating the Pentad, the Council gave the impression that the only choices in the election were parties of the Pentad and that only the Pentad had policy on the issues that the council believed to be important. In the categories chosen, the NDP was shown to have the strongest policy because the Canadian Action, the Communist, the Green, and the Marxist-Leninist parties were excluded. The strategy of reducing the domain in order to give credibility to the one included in the domain is a public relations tactic that should be beneath the Council.

Exclusion Through the Electoral System

The current electoral system perpetuates the status quo by failing to reflect the percentage of the popular vote and the multiplicity of concerns by citizens and groups. The Election Act was actually revised during the last parliament, yet all attempts to change the entrenched system based on what has been described as the "first-past-the-post system" failed. This system results in governments being elected with less than 50 percent of the popular vote. Moreover, there are cases where a party is elected with an even lower percentage of the popular vote than another political party, as in the most recent elections in B.C. and Quebec. The current system condones, encourages or justifies the odious practice by politicians of calling for strategic voting, prevents the election of members of small parties, and disenfranchises segments of the population. In Election 2000, this practice was carried to a new high in the politics of fear fostered by the Liberals. Even the Bloc, Conservatives, and NDP were impacted by the clarion call for not wasting the vote.

Currently the Green Party is working with two law professors from the University of Toronto, David Beatie and Ed Morgan, on a Charter challenge to the current first-past-the-post system (article 313 in the Elections Act). This case will be arguing that the current system discriminates against women, First Nations, visible minorities and small parties and thus could be deemed to be in violation of the equality clauses in the Charter of Rights and Freedoms. We propose a system where a proportion of the seats are selected on the basis of an altered first-past-the-post system (using a run-off or single transferable vote), and a proportion of the seats are selected according to the percentage of the vote. A mixed proportional representation such as this would reflect the popular vote, while continuing to provide for regional representation. For example, there could be two hundred ridings where regional representation could be maintained through a modified first-past-the-post system. The remaining one hundred seats could be proportionally distributed according to the percentage of the party vote. Citizens would have an opportunity to vote twice within each riding, first for the candidate selected through single transferable vote, and second, for the party itself.

Conclusion

Parties other than the Pentad won 1.8 percent of the vote in the 2000 election. (See Appendix.) The Green Party won a record-high .8 percent. Outside of Quebec where the Green Party ran candidates, the party generally came in 5th place after the Liberals, Conservative, Canadian Alliance, and NDP. In one case in B.C. the Marijuana Party was ahead; in another riding the Green Party was ahead of the Conservatives, and in another riding in Vancouver, the Canadian Action Party was ahead. In Quebec, the Green Party was ahead of the NDP in four ridings, and behind the Marijuana Party in several ridings, and in some cases the Marijuana Party was ahead of the NDP and the Green Party. These results indicate that hundreds of thousands of people are willing to vote for parties which present an alternative to the Pentad. The fact that they are willing to do so despite the discouragement offered by the current electoral system and other factors as described in this chapter is testimony to the need for new parties entering the political arena.

According to *The Globe and Mail*, from 1945–1988, 75 percent of eligible voters in Canada took the time to vote and cast a ballot for the federal party of their choice. On November 27, 2000, 62 percent of those eligible voted. If you include all those eligible to vote but who were not on the voters list the turnout dropped to 53 percent. One reason for voter alienation may be Canada's first-past-the-post system, and the realization by many potential voters that the Pentad parties do not represent the change that is necessary to move towards a society that supports the public trust. Voter dissatisfaction might be alleviated by changes to allow greater participation by non-Pentad parties who present issues otherwise ignored or watered down by the major parties.

Many opponents of the status quo as represented by the Pentad withdraw from participation in the political system altogether for numerous reasons, some principled, some whimsical, and some questionable. Anti-status-quo activists and anarchists have forsaken political parties because they see over and over again the discrepancy between rhetoric and action. Many ordinary citizens distrust politicians because they have seen a consistent discrepancy between pre-election rhetoric contained in platforms and post-election action. Citizens also distrust politicians because they delude the public into thinking they are what they are not. For example, the Canadian Alliance deludes the public into thinking that it is a "grassroots" party. Yet an analysis of its 1997 party donations reveals that it accepts donations, as do the Liberals and Conservatives.

Election 2000 was an election not of solutions, but of missed opportunities to advance fundamental change. Canadians could have addressed the need to shift from risk management to the precautionary principle — to build on the full range of implications arising from Walkerton. Election 2000 could have given Canadians the chance to make the environment, economic justice, equitable distribution of resources, peace, health, and human rights higher priorities than they are presently. It was an election of "could have been," a lost opportunity to endorse an alternative economic system of prevention, precaution, and limits to growth.

NOTES

1   *Vancouver Sun*, November 18, 2000, p A7.

Chapter 7

Covering Campaign 2000

by Edward Greenspon

Live by the photo-op. Die by the photo-op.[1]

On the second day of the 2000 general election, in what would become one of the campaign's defining moments, Stockwell Day's bus caravan made its way to Niagara Falls for no other reason than to illustrate his contention that Canadian tax policies were driving our best brains to the United States. The election was in its infancy and the public impression of Day remained unformed. Polls showed Day with a generally positive rating, although many Canadians said they were still taking his measure. Certainly, though, his "negatives," as pollsters say, were not as great as those of his main opponent, Jean Chrétien, whose disapproval rating had fallen to its lowest point in his prime ministership.

Day already had quite a reputation for theatrics, most notably for his pre-election gambit of jet-skiing to a press conference on the shore of Lake Okanagan and fielding questions dressed in a wet suit. The episode garnered him tons of publicity and the experts debated end-lessly whether it harmed or helped him.

Even before the Niagara Falls fiasco, it was apparent that Day intended to live by the photo-op. He had decided he would not cam-paign on his Sabbath, and therefore would not be available when Chrétien dropped the writ on Sunday, October 22. In order to get into the news cycle, he invited the press to a scrum on Saturday outside the Museum of Civilization in Hull. The site had been chosen by Day's son, Logan, who was doing advance work in the campaign — scouting out locations for the leader's encounters with the media. The museum sits just across the river from the Parliament Buildings, providing a strong visual backdrop for Day's message about government waste. Unfortunately, Logan Day had checked out the site at a different time of day. The late afternoon press conference, he would later confide, proved a bit of a disappointment because of the bad angle of the sun, which put the Parliament Buildings into silhouette.

Oh well. Beginner's bad luck.

The Alliance leader's real campaign tour kicked off Monday morning. Jean Chrétien, with no compunction against campaigning on Sunday, had flown off to his home riding of Shawinigan and then down to the expected key electoral battleground of southern Ontario. For both men, it would prove a day of gaffes, at least according to the media portrayals. Chrétien would be accused of insulting the majority of Canadians who had not completed high school with his comment that his childhood friends in Shawinigan could have been great citizens "if they had had the occasion to go to university." Everyone seemed to know what the Prime Minister was really saying — that an education is an increasingly important asset — but election campaigns are unforgiving, and he was roasted for having treated non-university educated Canadians as lesser lights.

Meanwhile, Day, intent on driving home his point about the brain drain, took reporters to Quake Technologies Inc., a high tech company just west of Ottawa. The accompanying media duly grilled the company's president, Daniel Trepanier, about the brain drain only to discover that he was part of a reverse flow back into Canada. He had returned to Canada eight years earlier from the United States and, moreover, had recently lured four others from jobs down south. "Ottawa seems to be a land of opportunity," remarked the high tech entrepreneur, who seemed at that moment to be a Liberal Party *agent provocateur*.

Oh well. Sophomore jinx.

The Day campaign bus snaked its way through Southern Ontario and across the Niagara escarpment, the reporters feeling pretty good about turning the tables on the Alliance leader. (Nothing personal — it's just that political leaders employ a legion of communications strategists and media spinners to get out the lines they want. The media grunts always feel a measure of independence when the spin whirls out of control.) Day hadn't given up on the brain drain or the need for tax cuts, however. Many commentators figured the Liberals had taken the sting out of the issue with their quickie mini-budget on election eve. It was carefully crafted with the Alliance tax-cutting platform in mind. The minions in the Department of Finance designed measures specifically aimed at the "new economy" and went so far as to cut the low-income tax rate to 16 percent from 17 percent so they could wag their finger at their opponents and accuse them of tax favouritism toward the rich.

Stockwell Day was up for a good day. His advance team prepared an irresistible photo-op to bring home the point that high taxes were driving Canadians to the United States. They were headed to Niagara Falls for the same reason everyone heads to Niagara Falls — for the view. Alliance intended to use the scenic Rainbow Bridge as the backdrop on a postcard-perfect pitch. The tag line for the day was to be "Bridge to the USA" — and Alliance strategists had stashed a sign in a hotel room with precisely those words emblazoned on it.

But this is Canada, a land defined by weather as much as politics. Fog rolled in before the great event. Day's handlers frantically reached for their cell phones. They checked with the weather office. They talked to headquarters, informing them the Rainbow Bridge was not visible. Someone had a brain wave — that they could use the flow of the water itself as their metaphor. The Bridge to the USA sign was put away. A call went back to a researcher in Ottawa to prepare some lines for Day — pronto. Meanwhile, the team on the ground tore through the hotel looking for a room with a good visual. They found a suite with floor-length windows looking out onto the falls. The media horde was summoned. The cameramen assembled their equipment and pasted up filtered papers so their shots would be sharp. The candidate arrived and delivered the lines faxed down from Ottawa: "Just as Lake Erie drains from north to south, there is an ongoing drain in terms of our young people," he intoned with Shakespearian gravity. "We would like to see that stop when it is a case of people feeling forced to move because of high levels of taxation."

Unfortunately for Day and the Alliance strategists, his traveling entourage included on this day the quick-witted CBC reporter, Eric Sorensen. Sorensen grew up in nearby Port Colborne and while he's no expert on the brain drain, he knows a thing or two about local geography. He listened to the sound bite crafted for his use on that night's newscast and immediately thought, "That's not right, is it?"

"Excuse me," he challenged Day, "the lake actually drains into the Niagara River, which travels North, not South." The Alliance leader's demenour underwent an immediate metamorphosis. His tone turned to ice. "We will check the record," he said. "If someone has wrongly informed me about the flow of this particular water, then I will be having a pretty interesting discussion."

Hmm. Third whiff. Could be something wrong with this team's batting mechanics?

All these unforced errors were messing up the Liberal game plan. Team Chrétien's chalkboard called for the stigmatization of Stockwell Day as scary, not incompetent. Ever since the summer, long before anyone's mind had turned to a Fall election, the Liberals had been talking up a campaign based on competing values — their Canadian ones versus Day's supposedly alien set of beliefs.

The Liberals went into the election having digested some lessons from the 1997 campaign. Although they'd won a second majority, the governing party had dropped nearly two dozen seats in 1997 and had hung on to a bare majority with just 38 percent of the popular vote. Liberal strategists talked now of the need to run on more than just their record. The 1997 campaign had been largely planned as some sort of ticker-tape parade to celebrate the beating back of the deficit. The lack of Liberal message and vision had created an opening for the Reform Party, which defined the agenda for most of the campaign.

From election night 1997, Liberals debated the return message sent by voters. Two results in particular disappointed the party: the loss of twenty of their thiry-one seats in Atlantic Canada and the failure to make inroads in Western Canada (in fact, the party's 1993 gains were rolled back) despite the government's fiscally conservative orientation. "If you look at the results in Atlantic Canada, I think the message to us was we have to reinforce our Liberal roots," Sheila Copps told me the day after the 1997 campaign. Another minister, on the centre-right of the party, surprised me in a private conversation some time later with his vehement declaration that Western Canada had been given its chance to embrace the Liberals and had refused, "So forget the West. We're going to appeal to the East now," he said.

And so as the second term moved along and deficits turned to surpluses, Liberal rhetoric tilted leftward. Prime Minister Chrétien had particular eyes for Atlantic Canada, injecting $700-million into the region in the form of an Atlantic economic development strategy. Then, with days to go before his election call, he reversed one of the most contentious aspects of his government's 1996 unemployment insurance reforms — the so-called intensity clause that clawed back benefits from repeat users. The calculation was clear — even though Western Canada contains two-and-a-half times as many seats as the Atlantic region, the east provided greater a prospect of making gains. The seasonal workers, traditional Liberal supporters who had turned their backs on the party in 1997, were the prize pupils. Western Liberals would have to make do.

A second lesson from 1997 cited by Liberal strategists was the difficulty of fighting a multi-front war. They found the regional nature of post-1993 electoral politics in Canada extracted a particularly heavy toll on themselves. As the only party competitive in every region, the need to fight different enemies in different places made it difficult to communicate clear national messages either through their leader's tour or advertising.

I was at first surprised when a top aide to the Prime Minister told me in the run-up to the election that the party's main target in Atlantic Canada would be Stockwell Day. On the surface, that seemed irrational given the fact the Alliance barely registered in the region. But the idea was to portray Day and his party as bogeymen who imperilled the livelihood of the region — an approach fortuitously assisted just before the election when an Alliance pollster described Atlantic Canadians as lazy. The word went out that the Alliance must be stopped at all costs, even if it meant foresaking Tory and New Democratic allegiances for the safe harbour of Jean Chrétien's Liberals. To this end, Chrétien recruited Newfoundland premier Brian Tobin, one of the country's best communicators. The election was to be about a stark choice: the Canadian way or the Americanized-Alliance way. The Liberals intended to demonize Day and polarize the electorate; Tobin was their polarizer of choice.

The Liberals knew that Canadians yearned for some kind of change. Satisfying this desire would obviously be difficult for a two-term government led by a profoundly conservative politician. Pre-election polls demonstrated a fatigue factor with Chrétien. Canadians were not discontented with his party or policies, but they wanted something different. They consistently told pollsters they felt the time had come for the sixty-six-year-old Prime Minister to retire — a choice he didn't intend to give them, especially after seeing off a half-hearted challenge to his leadership the previous March by supporters of Finance Minister Paul Martin. So, the Liberals needed to establish that they represented change, moderate change to be sure, but change that resonated with the real-world experiences of ordinary Canadians. They planned their leader's tour around "new economy" themes, with visits to many of the companies, such as Vancouver's Ballard Power, that were prospering with the help of government assistance, the kind of programs the Alliance would eliminate. Chrétien was to overcome his image as tired and staid by turning himself into a hip, "new economy" kind of guy. At the same time, the Liberals hoped their demonization of Day would neutralize his ability to benefit from the change card. The message, the Liberal strategist told me, was simple: Day doesn't represent change but rather rupture.

Meanwhile, the newly minted Alliance was salivating at the prospect of getting at Jean Chrétien. The right in Canada would prove itself immature in this election in a breath-taking number of ways, prominent among them their inability to detach their personal animus toward Chrétien from their political analysis. Discussions with an array of Alliance strategists always came back to the single belief that Canadians wanted to be rid of their tired, old-style prime minister and would embrace the fresh face of the new kid on the block. Call it a form of political fundamentalism.

Stockwell Day, a rookie with more than a little vanity, would get carried away with his penchant for putting the spotlight on himself. Victory, especially pundit-defying victory, has a way of playing cruel tricks on the victors. They get spoiled. They come to over-estimate their intelligence and under-estimate the advice of the losers. Weren't those others the very ones who got it wrong last time out? So it was with Day. His leadership victory had been a surprise even to many of his own backers. Knocking off Preston Manning, the Reform Party founder and the architect of its replacement party, was no mean feat. But Day misinterpreted his win as a personal endorsement from the Canadian people. In fact, it marked the triumph of clever organization. His leadership campaign had tapped into the energies of the Christian right and built bridges to other conservative religious groups. That and the desire for the new party to start life with a new leader propelled him to victory. Canadians, by and large, still had no idea who he was.

At that point, hubris kicked in. Day failed to reach out to his vanquished rivals, the coterie of now hardened political professionals who had served Manning faithfully and the equally hardened Ontario team loyal to Tom Long. He clashed particularly with Rick Anderson, Manning's Mr. Everything. Anderson, a hardball campaigner, had gotten down and dirty against Day in the late stages of the leadership contest. Now the new leader wanted not just a transfer of loyalty but an apology. None was forthcoming. Day wanted as little as possible to do with Anderson. As for Long, he felt increasingly marginalized by Day.

Ostensibly, he served as National Strategy Chairman, but he remained outside the loop on important strategic decisions. His loyal followers were never fully engaged.

To make matters worse, as the election call approached — a call Day's team expected would come in the spring — his own campaign chief, Rod Love, informed both leader and led that he would be returning to Calgary for the main event. Pressures on the home front made it impossible to contemplate five weeks living out of a suitcase in Ottawa. Love would participate in the daily strategy sessions and be available at the end of a phone line. But in the fast-paced environment of a national election campaign, he may as well have been in west Africa. His inexperienced campaign team lacked the hands-on leadership it required.

Several less than compelling aspects of his make-up emerged in short order, starting with his beachfront press conference in Kelowna. Three further incidents stood out for me. The first was a letter Day wrote to the provincial premiers in the run-up to their September conference with Prime Minister Chrétien on health. Day essentially offered them the shop, more than even most Premiers would have dared demand. I described it as a love letter to Lucien Bouchard. His stance would have entirely removed the Federal Government from the health care field, music to the ears of the most radical Premiers but a discordant note to the vast majority of Canadians. The lesson: he hadn't yet learned to think like a national politician.

The second episode occured at his party's end-of-summer caucus retreat in Saskatoon. On the eve of the meeting, a journalist asked Rod Love about the GST; the chief of staff took a whack at the lobbed ball and floated out the possibility of scrapping the dreaded tax. Day joined him on the base paths, never really saying he would get rid of the tax, but toying with the possibility. The problem was that the GST didn't figure into the party's tax-cutting positions at all. The Alliance was trying at that point to build up its brain drain argument: that Canada's punishing tax rates were impeding our competitiveness in the global economy by discouraging our best and brightest and by driving away corporate investment. The problem was that the GST didn't fit the story line. It was simple opportunism and had nothing to do with Alliance strategy. Lesson 2: Day was undisciplined and non-strategic. He made it up as he went along.

The third incident flowed directly from the death in late September of Pierre Elliott Trudeau. Members of Parliament gathered in the House of Commons the following day to pay their tributes. Corsages of red roses, in tribute to Trudeau, had been left in the lobbies for the MPs. Most members chose to wear them, but some non-Liberals, including Joe Clark and Alexa McDonough, obviously felt uncomfortable and foresook the gesture. Day, too, appeared without the corsage, but he couldn't let the omission pass unnoticed. When it came his turn to speak, he produced one of the roses and placed it on a small silver serving tray. He then summoned one of the House of Commons pages and asked her to walk the tray down the corridor and place it under the famous portrait of Trudeau with his coat draped over his shoulders like a cape. "I honour those who wear the rose today as a sign of respect and trademark," he said. "I did not ever know him. I do not feel that closeness." Within half-an-hour the tray was gone, retrieved by an Alliance aide and returned to Deborah Grey's office, from where it had been borrowed. Lesson 3: Day, despite his cocky exterior, was uncomfortable in his new setting. And when in doubt, he would always resort to a stunt.

The Pre-Campaign

Chrétien, his wife, Aline, and a phalanx of aides and security officers crossed the street from his residence to Rideau Hall on Sunday morning, going through the motions of asking the Governor-General to dissolve Parliament so he could seek a new mandate. The decision to go to the polls in the fall had been his and his alone. His party had been gearing up ever-so-gradually for a spring 2001 vote, when Chrétien suddenly concluded the stars were in alignment for a lightning strike. Day was still getting established and remained unknown. Liberal polling suggested his freshness and likeability could work to his advantage even though his flat tax and provincialism were welcome putty in the Prime Minister's hand. Best to move fast and use a campaign to define him before he could define himself, Chrétien reasoned. (Inexplicably, Day would lend a helping hand by veering off script in the House of Commons and daring the Prime Minister to call an election for which the Alliance was completely unprepared.) Chrétien was a bird-in-the-hand kind of guy. He could see that the country abounded with economic optimism after two consecutive years of nearly 5 percent growth. The upbeat mood could only get worse over a long winter, especially with rising gasoline and home heating prices scaring the living daylights out of everyone with a car or home. The Opposition parties were actually making headway on that issue in the Commons.

Chrétien's advisers and ministers initially thought the old guy had lost it. They were fixed on the last war, and the difficulty he had experienced in justifying an early election call in 1997. How would they again justify going to the electorate early and unnecessarily? Wouldn't it just exacerbate a growing Liberal reputation for arrogance? But "the boss" shrugged them off and issued private instructions to Finance Minister Paul Martin to get a snap budget ready.

The budget — the Liberals preferred to call it an economic statement or mini-budget for legalistic reasons — came down on October 18, four days before the election call. It was a work of beauty. Martin had been roundly criticized by business groups and the right-wing press in his February budget for the timidity of his tax reductions. Now he heaped on an extra helping, bringing his tax-cutting package in its entirety up to a nice round figure of $100-billion over five years. He also addressed just about every concern the high tech community had voiced about the brain drain and he stole the Alliance's thunder with a large, one-time pay down of the national debt. The budget pleased fiscally conservative Liberal MPs from the several dozen small-town Ontario ridings where Alliance was thought to have a decent shot. Once again, a lid was placed on overall spending despite the rhetoric of new programs. The lion's share of spending in the budget went to finance the health accord the Prime Minister had signed with the provinces in September.

Martin used his budget speech to launch a blistering attack on the Alliance proposal for a flat tax, charging it "would deliver to upper-income earners tax relief that rightly belongs to the middle class, and that's wrong." The flat tax — a name Day and his handlers detested — was destined to become a non-issue in the official election campaign, but at this phony-war stage it remained a major point of debate. The original Alliance proposal had called for a straightforward 17 percent income tax on all working Canadians, with increased up-front deductions that would take hundreds of thousands of low-income Canadians off the tax rolls altogether. But the move at the bottom end did not disguise the obvious fact that the biggest winners of the flat tax would be high-income earners. The Liberals prepared their attack lines, employing much the same language that Democrat Al Gore was using against George W. Bush in the U.S. election then underway.

When Day unveiled his party's platform in Kitchener on October 5 — a couple of weeks before the Martin mini-budget — he fudged on the flat tax. The newscasts that night were saturated with coverage of a protestor throwing chocolate milk on Day (a situation he handled with class and aplomb, leaving the stage to change his shirt and then joking that he could have used his wet suit). But the more substantial development of the evening concerned the climb down from one of the central planks adopted at the party's founding convention six months earlier. Day now committed only to introducing the 17 percent rate for low and middle income earners. High income earners would still be subject to a 25 percent rate, at least during a first Alliance term. Party spinners put out the word that these changes would remove the flat tax as an issue in the upcoming campaign.

To most of my colleagues, this made perfect sense. They viewed the flat tax as an albatross — one the Liberals would twist around Alliance's neck until the party fell to the ground gasping. But some Alliance strategists, particularly the Ontario crowd, wondered if Day, in his quest to appear moderate, was losing his moorings. After all, Mike Harris hadn't won Ontario in 1995 by compromising on his convictions but rather by looking as though he were setting out strong policy positions and contrasting his principled stands with the rootlessness of his main opponent.

My colleagues Brian Laghi and Hugh Winsor and I were scheduled to interview Day the next morning in his hotel suite at the Harbourcastle Westin on Toronto's waterfront. "Day backs off flat tax," read the headline in the morning's *Globe and Mail*. Day did not hide his displeasure with Brian's story. First off, it wasn't a "flat tax," he interjected, which was an American term of no relevance to Canadians. What he'd been proposing was a "single tax," and even that was out for now. Moreover, he hadn't backed off; he simply couldn't afford to proceed immediately because of the demand to provide relief against rising gasoline costs. Sure, we thought.

Brian and I headed out to Mississauga for a noon speech Day was to deliver to a business group. On our way into the banquet hall, more Alliance staffers blasted us over *The Globe*'s use of the term flat tax. I was by now in full agreement with an unnamed Paul Martin aide, who'd been quoted in Brian's story the previous night saying "they blinked."

The luncheon speech dispelled any remaining doubts. Day's performance was extraordinarily, er, flat. "Suddenly, this politician of convictions is fudging his convictions," I wrote in the next day's paper.

The incident foretold Day's surprising tendency to back away from controversial policy stances. When I got back to Ottawa, I arranged for coffee with an Alliance source, who showed me the party's polling on the flat tax. It was more popular than one might have supposed. Moreover, the Liberals knew this, too, since this Alliance stalwart also showed me favourable Finance Department polling he had obtained under the Access to Information Act.

Chrétien also was having a bad run of things as the election date neared. He had been taken aback by the negative reaction against his unilateral decision to change the name of Mount Logan to Mount Pierre Elliott Trudeau. Then he grabbed the wrist of a bothersome reporter in a scene repeated on television almost as often as his famous chokehold on a protester in 1996. The so-called Human Resouces Development Department boondoggle, and the related question of grants to friends and supporters in his own riding, refused to die down.

Chrétien took a calculated risk that week in keeping the House of Commons in session long enough for the Auditor-General to release a hotly anticipated report into HRD's spending habits. Chrétien could have called the election a week earlier, ensuring there would be no Parliament in which the Auditor-General could table his report. But that would have invited charges the Liberals had something to hide and were manipulating the system. He chose instead to keep Parliament sitting and allow the release of the report, confident it would not be as damning as expected. The Auditor-General was to appear late in the week before the Commons' Public Accounts committee, a last pre-election chance for the Opposition to make hay out of the issue. But somehow none of the Liberal MPs made it to the hearing room, denying the committee the necessary quorum to proceed. Liberal House leader Don Boudria was full of lame excuses for what went wrong. He refused to countenance suggestions that the Liberal absence may have been part of a carefully orchestrated strategy. All of this would ensure the prominent display of the words "Liberal arrogance" in newspapers across the country on the eve of the general election.

Early Days

Chrétien's stay inside Rideau Hall was brief. Soon he was standing before the microphone and informing Canadians they would be going to the polls on Monday, November 27. The press had been waiting for this moment for several weeks now — the chance to trip up Chrétien, à la 1997, with the question of why the early election call. Of course, since every journalist in Ottawa could speak about nothing else, the Liberal leader wasn't exactly going to be taken by surprise. The first question came: why an election now? Unsurprisingly, the Prime Minister appeared prepared.

Perhaps he was over-prepared. He offered more than a half-dozen reasons for the earliest election call by a majority government since 1911.

- A phantom election campaign had already been going on for some time.
- A mandate was needed to validate the important choices arising out of the age of budgetary surpluses (different choices, one supposed, from those rendered a few days earlier in the mini-budget).
- Opposition politicians were expecting a fall vote so why not deliver.
- Canadians want to avoid extended American-style election campaigns.
- Nothing is more democratic than an election.
- Clear alternatives are being offered.
- And, finally, the weather was exquisite and, who could tell, it might be awful on February 27.

I found this all unconvincing and defensive. But it worked — the predictability of the entire ritual rendering the matter anti-climactic and therefore lacking in newsworthiness. The networks delivered their judgement: the Prime Minister had sailed through. Over at Alliance headquarters, campaign co-chairmen Jason Kenney and Peter White stood in for the seventh-day resting Day. Kenney lit into the Prime Minister for his arrogance, the word on everyone's lips that day. Then White, the money man behind the new party, launched into a rant in French about the early election call, working himself into a populist frenzy. This puzzled the reporters, who quickly reminded him that his leader had actually asked for the election himself.

Which brings us back to Niagara Falls, where the Stockwell Day phenomenon first began showing signs of flowing backwards. We have since learned that Day was actually playing pretty well with the regular folks in regular places in those early days. As even the Liberal polls recorded (see Chapter Eleven of this volume) the public liked what it saw in the fresh-faced newcomer to the tired old federal scene. Still, Day and his handlers understood he remained an unknown quantity and that the Liberal would try to paint him as intolerant and scary. They decided to get out of the starting blocks first in "defining" Day to the public. In the weeks leading up to the campaign, his party spent heavily on television ads, one of which featured Day holding his granddaughter, Janessa, who happens to be of mixed Caucasian and Filipino blood. The script had Day talking about the heavy debt burden being imposed on the next generation, but the real message was clear: a guy with a mixed-race granddaughter obviously can't be deemed intolerant.

The public polling, while nowhere as intensive as Michael Marzolini's efforts for the Liberals, told a similar tale of openness to Day. The first opinion sampling of the campaign, a *Globe and Mail-CTV-Ipsos Reid* poll, was released on the evening of October 26. It showed the Liberals with a big lead, but the momentum resting clearly with Day. Respondents were asked if their opinions of the party leaders had improved, stayed the same, or worsened over the previous several weeks. Chrétien had negative momentum; Day was moving in the right direction. His ratio of approvals and disapprovals were also superior to the Prime Minister, thanks to significantly lower negative appraisals. He seemed to have shaken off much of the negative baggage associated in the 1997 campaign with Reform leader Preston Manning. Incidentally, the poll also showed that Joe Clark, as the accompanying *Globe and Mail* article put it, "appears to be coming back from the dead." But it would require Day to falter for Clark to be able to take advantage of his improved public ratings.

The first days of the campaign were relatively inconsequential. The public had not yet focused on the election, and at times it seemed neither had the leaders or parties. Before the writ was dropped, the general expectation had been that the instantaneous nature of all-news television and increasingly the web would produce an almost minute-by-minute campaign dialogue in which claims and counter-claims, charges and counter-charges, played themselves out on a single stage. The truth in those early days was that the five distinct campaigns barely engaged one another.

All that changed on the morning of October 31, when a front-page headline in *The Globe and Mail* infused the campaign with its missing focus. The headline, big and black, read: "Alliance supports two-tier health care." Shockwaves immediately rippled across the political landscape. The genesis of the article by Ottawa bureau chief Shawn McCarthy (and an accompanying column by me) lay in the appearance on the previous Friday night of campaign co-chair Jason Kenney on the *CBC-TV* program, *counterSpin*. I was casually watching the program at home when I thought I heard Kenney endorsing a European-style parallel health care system in response to a question from host Avi Lewis. I phoned Lewis the following morning and asked if he could get me a transcript as quickly as possible. It arrived Monday morning and, to my thinking, all but said two-tier health care. Shawn had watched the same program and had also been surprised Kenney had gone so far.

The interpretation is important because the Alliance would complain long and loud about our coverage, particularly the front page headline. One senior strategist would complain bitterly that running against the Liberals was tough enough — how was he supposed to run against a newspaper? A couple of weeks later, Kenney and I appeared together on a political panel on *ROB-TV*. The host, Michael Vaughan, asked me about media coverage of the campaign. I replied that I thought the *Globe* had been aggressive, which I intended as a positive comment. Kenney angrily demanded to know whether by aggressive I meant misleading headlines on two-tier health care etc. etc. I continue to believe our coverage was fair, impartial — and aggressive. The real authors of the two-tier health care controversy were Kenney and Love.

In my column, I quoted Kenney's remarks in their entirety so that readers could judge for themselves. Shawn's story also quoted other senior Alliance figures on the subject. Here was the *counterSpin* exchange:

Avi Lewis: "Hold on Jason, please. I want to insist that you answer the question. You told the *Calgary Herald* in regard to Bill 11 that you support private health care. I just want to know if the Alliance party does. Simple."

Jason Kenney: "...I'm sure what I said because what I believe is that people should have choices available to them, but I believe in public health care. The two are not a dichotomy, believe it nor not, Avi. You can have a quality universal public health-care system available to all, everyone, and allow some people some choices, like, for instance, every Western European country does. But that would be up to the provinces as long as the federal government would guarantee that not a single person goes without quality care because they can't afford it."

To me the key phrases were "and allows some people some choices" and "guarantee that not a single person goes without quality care." This clearly implied different levels of care.

Either way, the issue landed on the campaign like an atomic blast. The Alliance's biggest vulnerability lay in the suspicion of many voters that it harboured some kind of hidden agenda. The same complaint had dogged Reform, too, as its former pollster André Turcotte reported. He would always try to tease out in focus groups what people meant by a hidden agenda. Invariably, they would look at him as if he were from Mars and reply "We don't know. It's hidden."

Was this it — the hidden agenda exposed? Chrétien and Clark, two experienced opportunists, pounced. "Now the cat is out of the bag," Chrétien responded. "I think the cover has been ripped off the face of the Reform-Alliance Party now," Clark concurred. Day gingerly distanced himself from Kenney's comments, saying Canadians should not be able "to buy their way up the line." But Love threw fuel on the fire by declaring he would welcome a debate over the fact we already have a parellel system. The political benefits of inviting a debate on weak policy terrain for his party were not immediately apparent to outside observers.

The senior advisers around Chrétien, experienced campaigners with an iron will to win, harboured no disinclination to look a gift horse in the mouth. They couldn't care less what Kenney really said or really meant or why Love was seeking a debate or that the health care system had gone downhill under their stewardship or that two-tier health care was breaking out in key areas like diagnostic imaging out of neglect. They just wanted to keep the heat on Day. They ordered up television commercials to drive the point home. Meanwhile, Chrétien, who communicates values much better than policy, was let loose to defend the principles of the Canada Health Act against those with alien values.

The Liberals were scheduled to release their platform, *Red Book III*, the following day. They were so enamoured of the turn of events over health that they debated postponing their big press conference. But with criticism already mounting that Chrétien was bereft of ideas, they decided to proceed with the show, but also use the gathering to drive some more two-tier stakes into their opponents.

The two-tier mess inflicted tremendous damage on the Alliance. But it did not immediately bolster the Liberals, at least according to the public polling. An *Ipsos-Reid* poll published in *The Globe and Mail* on November 3 indicated a slow leakage of Liberal support, although not enough yet to cost them their majority. But the really bad news was reserved for the Alliance. In the previous poll, the party had reached 28 percent support in the critical Ontario battleground, just on the threshhold of the level needed to start bagging significant numbers of seats. But this second sampling showed the Alliance actually falling back four points in Ontario. All these movements were within the margin of error of the poll, but the trendlines seemed clear. The Liberals owned the heartland; the Alliance remained a Western party.

On the Doorsteps

The day before the poll came out, I went to Burlington, Ontario for some door-knocking with Liberal MP Paddy Torsney. Each election I like to pick a couple of ridings and canvass with the candidates. When they leave the doorstep, I stay behind and try to find out what's really on the minds of voters. I always start off with very general questions, such as "How are you finding the election so far?"

It's quite amazing the insights you can gain. One of my favourite conversations in the 2000 election took place with a middle-aged working woman home for lunch. She started out by telling me she wasn't following the election too closely yet, but she sure was angry about immigration. The government was soft, she said, letting in too many people and the wrong kinds at that. Then she went on to pillory the softness of the prison system and its molly-coddling of criminals. Both these issues were Alliance hot buttons. I figured I knew where she was leaning. "So what do you think of Stockwell Day," I asked. "Oh I don't know much about him," she replied. "All I know is he wants to cut taxes for the rich. The middle class, we always get it in the neck." She knew one thing about Mr. Day and that was the Liberal propaganda about his tax cut. I changed my mind about her probable vote.

180

Torsney and I were in north Burlington, an area I had also visited in the 1997 campaign. Up and down the several blocks we visited, I heard the same story over and over again. People were unhappy with Chrétien. They felt the time had come for him to retire. They desired change. But they didn't know Day well enough. Did he represent change, or as the Liberal strategists hoped people would believe, rupture? Because times weren't too bad. And the last time these Burlington voters had taken a flyer, they'd ended up with Bob Rae and the NDP, an unhappy memory for most of them.

The person who really impressed me was a man named John Gill, one of many voters who said he was just beginning to pay attention but hadn't yet made up his mind. He was clearly troubled by the choices before him. We talked for a while and then I asked him what he thought he would do (reporters should never ask how someone intends to vote; that's far too intrusive). "I believe it's time for change," he replied after an eternity. Then he thought some more. "But Day's not offering very much so therefore you don't know if it's the right time for change." He paused again, playing with the conundrum in his mind. "Yes," he finally concluded, "it's time for change, but is it the right time for change. We don't know. Who is Day? Is he someone good enough?"

I mentally catalogued him as a hold-your-nose Liberal voter. And I became a disciple of the theory of the electoral disconnect — that Liberal poll numbers did not relect the true level of dissatisfaction with the government and desire for change. All the polls suggested some kind of disconnect between voter satisfaction and voting intention. And the anecdotal evidence also suggested an undercurrent of discontent. Everywhere voters were talking of how they felt trapped. The question of this alleged disconnect would become a recurring theme in election analysis. Journalists, including myself, could see by the poll numbers that the Liberals were safely in the lead. We could see the Alliance self-destructing. But how to account for the dissatisfaction, particularly with Chrétien? How would this play out?

The Abortion Referendum

By all rights, the next major campaign event should have been the French-language and English-language leaders' debates, which the

Liberals had succeeded in scheduling earlier rather than later as an insurance policy against a poor Chrétien performance. If the debate went badly, as it had for Brian Mulroney in 1988, they wanted enough time to mount a counter-attack and regain lost ground, as Mulroney had.

But before we reached the debates, Stockwell Day was to be severely tested again — and found wanting. The issue was abortion, a very un-Canadian topic of discussion. Unlike Americans, for whom a politician's views on abortion are always an important litmus test, moral issues rarely enter into Canadian electoral discourse. But the door had been thrown open by Day in the Alliance leadership campaign. He had courted anti-abortion groups, and they had delivered for him. They expected a pay-off. In the run-up to the election, Day had attempted to divert attention by saying his strong personal opposition to abortion would not influence him as prime minister. Instead, he would be guided by citizen-initiated referenda on such issues. And he was always vague about how these referenda would be organized.

The Liberals knew abortion was a soft spot for the Alliance. By and large, Canadians had put the matter well behind them a generation earlier. It was the kind of issue that made Day seem like a throwback to the early days of Social Credit in Alberta. It illuminated the values-divide the Liberals were intent on exploiting. The issue was especially resonant among women, a key segment of the Liberal coalition and a weakness for Day.

In his analysis (see Chapter Eleven) Michael Marzolini writes of the importance of the abortion issue and gives credit to the Liberal team for deftly putting it on the agenda in a speech the Prime Minister delivered to about a thousand women in Laval, Quebec on Sunday November 5. "We have social peace on the question of abortion," Chrétien said, adding that he didn't think Canadian women would be happy if Day revived the issue through a referendum. For me, it was odd to hear Chrétien talking of abortion. I had nearly fallen off my chair the previous March, when he went after the new Alliance party before delegates to the Liberal biennial convention by saying: "Canadians do not want a party that threatens a woman's right to choose." Not only was this not part of normal Canadian political debate, but I had never heard the conservative Chrétien utter anything on the subject other than to joke that as the second-to-last in a long line of children he was glad his mother hadn't believed in abortion.

In any case, Chrétien sensed his advantage and took it. But it wasn't the Laval speech that blew the abortion issue into the open so much as the exclusive in the November 7 *Globe and Mail* by Queen's Park bureau chief John Ibbitson. He had obtained a policy background document that had been sent to Alliance candidates. The briefing book was chock full of the sort of details Day preferred to duck. Prominent among these was an elaboration of the policy that a citizen-initiated referendum would be triggered by "three percent of the total number of voters who cast ballots in the last election." John calculated that to mean, based on 1997 election returns, fewer than 400,000 votes. In other words, with just 400,000 signatures on a petition, the country would be subjected to gut-wrenching debates on everything from abortion to capital punishment to, well who knew, maybe a Quebec sovereignty referendum.

Day took a bad situation and exacerbated it at his daily press conference that morning. He sought to repudiate his own party's policy document, blaming it on junior researchers who hadn't checked with the top before sending out the position paper. He refused to stand behind the 3 percent figure, saying only there would have to be widespread support for a referendum and that he would have to consult with Canadians on the proper threshhold. (That raised the intriguing possibility of a referendum on the right number for a referendum.) He insisted he didn't want to reopen the abortion debate. "Abortion is not even on the platform," he said. "It's been discussed, but it's not on the platform." What was one to believe? The party's document said one thing. The leader claimed another. Could anyone be blamed for wondering if the dreaded hidden agenda was at play here?

I asked Day's senior staffers why, once the policy book was in the open, he hadn't stood behind the stated policy. I got back two answers: first, that he'd made it up as he was going along and they'd been as surprised as anyone; and second, the simple explanation that the 3 percent figure didn't accurately reflect their thinking. But which causes more damage — standing behind a flawed policy or looking like you're hiding something? Day could have defended the policy. Some advisers thought he should have just said that unlike this arrogant Liberal government that gathers all power in the Prime Minister's Office, the Alliance intends to listen to the people. It will share power. It would rather be democratic to a fault than anti-democratic. Instead, he made himself look either like a man with something to hide or someone simply unprepared to govern. Even Chrétien, in his first press conference after the election, would marvel over his opponent's unwillingness to defend his referendum policy. The Prime Minister noted that while he didn't agree with the policy, similar approaches existed in many jurisdictions, such as California, and that they were perfectly defensible.

Day now headed into the debates battered and bruised over abortion and two-tier health care. A credible performance would no longer suffice. He needed to strike a knockout blow.

The Debates and their Aftermath

The French-language debate took place first. Bloc Québécois leader Gilles Duceppe looked confident and in control this time out. The Bloc seemed to be on a roll in Quebec. Jean Charest had polled very well in his home province in the previous election despite a largely successful and cynical effort by the Liberals to polarize the electorate. But without Charest this time, the Conservative vote was in freefall in the province. The best evidence lay in the pre-election decision of three Conservative MPs to defect to the Liberals. The big question in Quebec was where would those centrist Conservative votes go — to the hard-line federalist Liberals or the hard-line separatist Bloc?

The sovereigntists were credited with running a good campaign in talking about issues other than sovereignty. Duceppe spent a good deal of time attacking the Liberals for being too lax on biker gangs and too hard on youth offenders. As always, the separatists cockily felt that Jean Chrétien represented their strongest asset, especially given his tough-love approach in the Clarity Act. The Liberals seemed to accept the reality that Chrétien still played badly in his native province. In Quebec, their ads gave equal prominence to Paul Martin and Chrétien. And Martin was kept especially busy working his adopted province.

The English language debate would prove the real revelation. Joe Clark, who had been gamely waging the best campaign of the five leaders, used his one shot at a big audience to maximum advantage. He was passionate, funny, tough, in command. He cut Day to the quick by comparing him to a game show host for his stunt of holding up a hand-written sign saying "No Two-Tier Healthcare." But the night was mostly a gang-up on Chrétien, and Clark led the way. He accused the Prime Minister of only having called the election to stymie the ambitions of Paul Martin. He sadly said that Chrétien had been changed by power. He challenged the Prime Minister to name the true lasting achievements of his seven years in power, a simple question Chrétien seemed unprepared to answer.

Clark's closing statement was masterful. After pounding Chrétien throughout the evening, he essentially conceded the election to the Liberals but told the audience that Day simply wasn't up to the task of holding the government to account. They needed him. The post-debate consensus gave the evening to Clark, just as Charest had been deemed the winner in 1997. But the Tories then, weak on the ground and a fifth wheel, hadn't been able to translate the earlier victory into lasting momentum. Now that same challenge would fall to Clark. Meanwhile, the Liberals, concerned over Chrétien's weak performance and continued softness in his personal numbers, moved to low-bridge the leader and emphasize the team.

Liberal numbers nudged downward again in the aftermath of the debate, led by the Prime Minister, according to the *Ipsos Reid* poll. The proportion of Canadians saying their opinion of Chrétien had worsened rather than improved kept growing. The percentage thinking he would make the best prime minister tumbled. Day was also on the downswing. Only Clark showed upward momentum. Clark's post-election roll was best captured by the woman who approached him in Trenton, Ontario to say she had always been a Liberal, but that he had converted her in the debate. "You're not Joe Who anymore," she said. "You're Joe Somebody."

Of course, he wasn't really Joe Somebody, which explained part of his success. In a campaign of unprecedented negativity and nastiness, Clark looked decent and reasoned. But the fact of the matter was that he had been as negative as anyone else, or more so. His campaign ads featured outlandish attacks on the Liberals. Campaign manager John Laschinger, challenged about the ability of these ads to sell a product, corrected a reporter that his task was actually to destroy a product, one called Jean Chrétien. Clark benefited from being a nobody in the campaign; he was not held to the same level of media scrutiny and accountability as either Day or Chrétien.

The Tory veteran was making up ground. But mostly it was the ground he had lost with his poor showing in the year leading up to the election. Nonetheless, as the campaign headed into its final stretches,

Clark was eating sufficiently into Liberal and Alliance votes that both Chrétien and Day took to attacking him. A weird dynamic was at work. With Day losing credibility by the hour, the Liberal strategy of polarizing the electorate was under threat. Atlantic Canadians, in particular, felt relaxed enough now to turn back to the Conservatives and, to a lesser extent, the New Democrats. That seemed to spell further problems for a Liberal majority.

Meanwhile, the Alliance finally began to play its wedge issues. All election long, it was apparent that one of the few areas of competitive advantage for the party lay in the apprehension of Canadians on justice issues. As the wheels fell off the party's campaign, commentators wondered when Day would roll out law and order. The time now had arrived. At the start of the second to last week of campaigning, he systematically trotted out wedge issues — those that separated him from most competitors — such as immigration and natives and justice. By now, the challenge was to galvanize his core, not to win over disgruntled Liberals.

Day caught a rare break early that week. At the same time he was putting out his party's position that three-time sex offenders would be put away for life under an Alliance government, a notorious child molester who had been released into a halfway house was re-arrested in Toronto in the company of an under-aged boy. Under the Alliance plan, the offender would never have been released from jail in the first place. Now that he was into red-meat politics, Day seemed to be finding his voice. On Tuesday night in Regina, the reporters traveling with him were taken aback by the strength of his performance. The crowded hall (Alliance always had crowded halls) brimmed over with energy. As he spoke, passionately and fluently, about child molestors and pornographers and governmental waste and arrogance, the reporters kept making eye contact with each other. They'd never seen Day this good. They wondered afterwards if he'd finally turned a corner.

But the moment was over almost as soon as it began. That evening, CBC ran a documentary on Day's early political life in Alberta. Mostly it covered familiar ground until a professor from the local community college recounted an event at which Day, then an Alberta government minister, had publicly spoken about how he believed the world was 6,000 years old and that humans had co-existed with dinosaurs. And it got worse yet. That evening, in Toronto, Liberal immigration minister Elinor Caplan leveled the worst kind of accusation at Day, accusing him of consorting with neo-Nazis. The charge was widely condemned, but it damaged Day by reviving the old concerns about intolerance and knocking him, once again, off his agenda.

By early the next morning, the tide had turned against him again. The reporters at his morning press conference weren't interested in child pornographers. They wanted to know about Nazis and dinosaurs. Day accused the CBC of cheap-shot journalism and refused to answer questions about his personal beliefs, although later in the day, he would issue a statement on the subject. In short order, the CBC comedy show, "This Hour has 22 Minutes," satirized his referendum policy by initiating a petition on its website to get the Alliance leader to change his name to Doris Day. Suddenly, this once daunting political challenger had become the subject of widespread ridicule.

There wasn't much public polling available that week, but it looked as though Day was done. Indeed, the knives already seemed to be coming out with a week still to go in the campaign. It was not at all difficult to tease out critiques of Day's campaign performance from Alliance stalwarts. And the Liberals weren't done with their paint job yet. They got hold of a tape of an Alliance candidate in Winnipeg named Betty Granger referring to an "Asian invasion" on the West Coast in an appearance before a political science class at the University of Winnipeg. The Liberals arranged for the tape to fall into the hands of the media.

The Betty Granger episode underlined the weakness of the Alliance team and the skill of the Liberals. Once again, the Alliance managed to take a bad situation and make it worse. The tape began circulating on Friday, leaked by the Liberal war room. The Alliance strategists read the entire transcript and thought Granger was getting a bum rap. On Saturday, they put the inexperienced and nervous candidate before the microphones to explain herself. Her performance convinced the Alliance brass she should resign after all. At first she said yes. Then she complained publicly that she'd been pressured. Then, with the issue finally dying down, Day waded in to say that as a father-in-law of a Filipino-Canadian, he'd been personally hurt by the Asian invasion remark. That kept the story alive through yet another news cycle. The Liberal war room couldn't believe its luck.

Having failed to dispatch Granger quickly and cleanly, he and his handlers paid the price. Intolerance was back on the agenda. Meanwhile, the Liberals ordered up Chinese language ads to run in Vancouver and

187

Filipino ones in Winnipeg so they could wring maximum advantage out of Granger's comments.

The election had taken on an extraordinarily negative cant. But its descent was not over yet. Once again, with the Liberals seemingly coasting home free, the media turned the play. The former head of the federal government's Business Development Bank declared in a wrongful dismissal suit that Chrétien had lobbied him to approve a loan to a hotel in Shawinigan in which he had once held an interest. Earlier in the campaign, Day, after withstanding criticism that he was being too soft on Chrétien, had raised the temperature by calling him corrupt. But he quickly became mired in his own controversies and rarely got back on the message of Chrétien's alleged abuses of power.

Now the issue was back on the front burner, particularly because Chrétien's office had previously denied that any such lobbying had taken place. The Prime Minister stood typically unbowed. He maintained he had only been helping out a local businessman. "We work for our constituents," he said. "It's the normal operation." He had called the BDC president twice and buttonholed him on a third occasion during a visit with a group of young executives to 24 Sussex Drive. "You call who you know," Chrétien said.

His opponents went after Chrétien hard. They knew this would be their last chance to mark him up before Canadians voted. They attacked him all week long, demanding investigations by the RCMP and the federal ethics counsellor (who happened to report to Chrétien). In a stunning development, Day went so far as to suggest Chrétien had violated a Criminal Code section on corruption. The ethics counsellor agreed to a speedy investigation that would be completed before the election. With six days left until Candians cast their ballots, he pronounced that Chrétien had not done anything wrong because there were no rules against phoning a Crown corporation president. Chrétien's opponents dismissed the finding as a whitewash, but the Liberals jumped on it as exoneration. An emotional Chrétien spoke about how his father had told his kids that, at the end of the day, all they had was their good name. He demanded apologies from Clark and Day. They spoke instead of the need for a public inquiry.

The final election polls were a muddle. They all pointed to a Liberal win, but the margin of error either translated into a safe majority or a narrow one. And nobody knew what effect the mud flung at Chrétien might have as Canadians prepared to go to the polls. *The Globe and Mail* said "PM's majority on knife's edge." Many of us in the media were still entranced by the disconnect theory. Chrétien returned home to Shawinigan to cast his ballot and await the results. At an off-the-record dinner on the Sunday night, he advised several of the journalists traveling with him that their predictions for their office election pools were too low. They were under-estimating his strength in Quebec. He told them he was going to win 172 seats, as bullish a prediction as anyone was willing to make.

Chrétien, of course, was right. He had felt in his bones, and had seen it validated in his private polling numbers, that something was up in Quebec. He and his top advisers never accepted the conventional wisdom that they would be punished for the Clarity Act. Their polling showed that Quebeckers thought greater clarity a commonsense proposition. Many theories would be proferred over the coming weeks for the fact that the federalist alternative outpolled the sovereignist choice. The Bloc's apparent strong campaign proved to be a mirage. Some people said it was due to a low turnout, which hit the separatist side particularly hard. Some said it was due to the Bouchard government's introduction late in the campaign of a municipal restructuring plan that particularly outraged Bloc Québécois voters around Quebec City. For his part, Chrétien believed the turnaround was due to an increasingly grudging respect for him and his policies. Whatever, the Quebec story was the one the media missed. It would prove to be the big election surprise.

Election night couldn't have been sweeter for the most under-estimated prime minister in Canadian history, who now could claim the feat, unmatched by Pierre Trudeau, of having won back-to-back-to-back majorities. In so doing, he'd increased his majority handsomely, a fitting testament to his political instincts in calling a fall election. In every region of the country, the Liberal result was either better than expected or as good as could be expected. As economic confidence sagged over the winter, the move looked all the more astute.

Despite the deflation of their polarization strategy in the final ten days of the campaign, the Liberals managed to restore their fortunes in Atlantic Canada sufficiently to gain a majority of seats in the region. Chrétien took his greatest satisfaction from the result in Quebec, where, in besting the Bloc, he had defied the pundits who had predicted his Clarity Act would come back to haunt him. In Ontario, the Liberal heartland, the economically contented once again gave his party nearly every seat — 100 out of 103. The Alliance assault had netted just two seats, with the NDP picking up one. The story wasn't as rosy in Western Canada, but the returns surpassed most expectations. His political ministers in each of Saskatchewan, Alberta, and British Columbia had looked vulnerable. They all survived.

On the other side of the aisle, the election results left the NDP questioning not just its leader but its very essence, and the Tories and Alliance still locked in a political stalemate. And then the greatest satisfaction of all. Within six weeks of the election, the separatist hero, Lucien Bouchard, would announce his resignation as Quebec Premier, citing the federal election result as a confounding and dispiriting experience. Chrétien had seen off his greatest political nemesis, the man who had nearly taken the country apart in 1995.

For Stockwell Day, the sniping hardly waited twenty-four hours. His erstwhile friends in the Ontario right made it plain they had little faith in the Albertan leader or even necessarily the new party that had been expressly created to take down Jean Chrétien. As the winter wore on, Day's position would grow weaker and weaker. He'd been leader of his party for little more than six months, and already the expectations were that he wouldn't last past his party's convention in March 2002.

As for Chrétien, he had felt the pressure of the disconnect throughout the campaign. He had heard all the media voices and ordinary voters saying how much they wished they could vote for Paul Martin. At one point, he had even felt it necessary to float the notion that he might well resign two or three years after an election victory. Now safely returned to power, his tone changed. "The people have passed their judgment. It was a very clear mandate I have received in my judgement," he crowed the day after the vote. What about his remark about leaving? "I'm elected," he said, "and I intend to serve my term." His audacious autumn 2000 election gamble had paid off, putting him into the history books alongside Mackenzie King and his great hero, Wilfrid Laurier.

NOTES

1   Thanks to Hugh Winsor for reading a draft of this chapter.

Chapter 8

Facts and Arguments:
Newspaper Coverage of the Campaign

by Christopher Dornan and Heather Pyman

The 2000 federal election was marked not simply by the presence of a new and prominent political party, the Canadian Alliance, but by the presence of a new and prominent national newspaper, the *National Post*. Launched in October 1998 by Conrad Black's Hollinger Corporation, which at the time controlled the Southam chain of broadsheets, and very much the child of Mr. Black himself, the *Post* was designed from the outset as a national paper that would compete in anglophone Canada with *The Globe and Mail*. As well, the *Post* gave the Southam corporation a daily title in Toronto, the country's largest newspaper market, which the company had heretofore lacked.

The arrival of the *Post* ignited a newspaper war in the Toronto market — and indeed nationally, between the *Globe* and the *Post* — as the new title attempted to establish itself with readers and advertisers, while the three older Toronto dailies (the *Star*, the *Sun* and *The Globe and Mail*) moved to defend their respective market advantages in the face of additional competition. From the start, the *National Post* was in many ways a formidable entrant. With the acquisition of the *Financial Post*, the new daily boasted a comprehensive and professional business section capable of competing with *The Globe and Mail*'s *Report on Business*. The paper was staffed by hand-picked reporters, columnists, and editors, many of whom were lured from positions with other papers by offers of substantially higher salaries, and whose morale was galvanized by the collaborative effort of launching the first new Canadian English-language daily in a generation. Even a seeming disadvantage – the comparative lack of advertising in the early days – meant that the paper had far greater space to devote to editorial content than *The Globe and Mail*, and could therefore offer readers richer and more varied content.

The *Post*'s natural competitor, both in Toronto and nationally, was *The Globe and Mail*. Both offered themselves to an up-market readership as business-oriented dailies with a clear emphasis on federal politics and national affairs. *The Toronto Sun* and *Toronto Star* remained much more parochial in their emphases on the local affairs of greater Toronto: the former with its distinctive brand of tabloid populism and the latter as the dominant omnibus broadsheet of the middle class household. Nonetheless, the turbulence created in the newspaper market by the arrival of the *Post* buffeted both the *Sun* and the *Star*, as each took steps to guard against declining readership and advertising revenue.

By October 2000, two years after the launch of the *National Post*, the convulsions in the newspaper industry in Canada were such that *The Globe and Mail* had a new publisher and editor-in-chief; *The Toronto Sun* had been purchased by Quebecor, with attendant changes in the management hierarchy; *The Toronto Star* had acquired broadsheets in urban markets adjacent to Toronto; CanWest Global, the broadcasting company, had agreed to purchase the remaining Southam dailies along with 50 percent of the *National Post*; and *The Globe and Mail* would come into the fold of the new corporate alliance of Bell Canada Enterprises and the CTV network.

The advent of the *Post* was in no small part the catalyst for these realignments in Canadian media ownership. From its beginnings, however, the paper was also of consequence for political discourse in the country. The proprietor, Conrad Black, is a man who makes no secret of his own political convictions, and it was widely assumed that the paper was created at his behest in part to give voice to a certain stripe of conservatism that Black found lamentably lacking in the mainstream of public discourse. Admirers applauded what they saw as a lively and welcome new organ that championed an emergent brand of political change. Detractors decried what they viewed as an overtly ideological mouthpiece for a constellation of hard-right prejudices. In some quarters, the *Post* was seen as an affront to the traditions of non-partisanship in Canadian journalism. Black, it was said, had imported a style of advocacy journalism from England, where he owned the *Daily Telegraph*, the largest circulation quality broadsheet and a conservative bastion, both small-c and large-C.

It is true that from the editor, Kenneth Whyte, to many of its high-profile contributors such as Ezra Levant, David and Linda Frum, and Donna Laframboise, the *National Post* featured a roster of writers and staff identified as right-wing in their political beliefs. However, the paper also featured equally prominently reporters and columnists of no particular political bent, such as Christie Blatchford and Allen Abel, or whose sensibilities if anything shaded toward a left-leaning humanism, such as Robert Fulford and Roy MacGregor. As well, it is unfair and misleading to accuse the *Post* of having somehow polluted the Canadian journalistic Eden by introducing a journalism of perspective. All newspapers develop and maintain a character of their own, a point of view and mode of address they bring to the passing scene, and this personality emerges as a consequence of the people who write and edit the papers, in concert with their respective market positioning. The *Star*, for example, long distinguished itself from its two earlier Toronto competitors, not merely because it sought to cover the city with all the resources of a full-service broadsheet and circulation giant, but because it carried itself as a paper with a social conscience, as opposed to the conservative *Globe* and *Sun*. In practice, this meant the *Star* was identified as a small-l liberal paper with close affinity for the policies of the large-L federal Liberal party. The *Sun*, meanwhile, as a fiesty tabloid aimed at blue-collar readers, was coloured by a populist conservatism that was manifest, for example, in staunch support for the police forces, a profound distrust of the nanny state, and an unapologetic recognition that the lads on the factory shopfloor rather enjoy seeing pictures of scandily clad, buxom young women. *The Globe and Mail*, for its part, has long been a conservative journal of a different hue. Though it can advocate social reforms that might be seen as leftist causes (decriminalization of soft drugs, rights for gays and lesbians), these are equally consistent with a conservatism that places priority on the rights of individuals to do as they please as long as they harm no one else. As well, throughout the 1980s under its previous editor, William Thorsell, the paper consistently supported the policies and administration of the Mulroney Conservative government.

Therefore, to accuse the *National Post* of having imported a new and odious form of journalism, in which news coverage and commentary — the choice of stories to pursue, the emphasis of play accorded different issues, the packaging of headlines, and so on — are conducted according to a perspective the paper wishes to advance, is to misunderstand the more nuanced realities of newspaper journalism in Canada. It may have been true that the regional Southam dailies — *The Hamilton Spectator*, *The Edmonton Journal* and the rest — traditionally eschewed any single or overt political point-of-view in their contents, but this was likely a result of the fact that these papers enjoyed near-monopoly status in their markets. In their bid for universal circulation in their home towns, such papers could not risk alienating potential readers, and so strove to be all things to all people. The result was an anodyne product with an ill-defined personality. In a market such as Toronto, by contrast, with more than one paper competing for different types of readers, it is no accident that each paper comes to acquire a vivid and distinctive character.

Whether by design or by happenstance — though one is forced to conclude the former, no matter how insistently some of its employees may deny it — the *National Post* quickly emerged as an advocate for a new brand of social conservatism in Canada. Adamantly opposed to the Liberal regime, the paper recognized that if the Liberals were to be unseated, conservative opposition could not continue to divide itself between the Tories and the Reform party. From the outset, then, the paper championed a movement to "unite the right" under a single political banner. Again, this was done not simply via editorial harangues and the opinionated commentary of columnists, but through the choice of news stories the paper pursued and the play accorded to the issue. Some, no doubt, saw this as a rich man using his wealth to exercise influence in national political affairs. One can equally see the *Post*'s actions as perfectly consistent with the historical role of the newspaper in a free society: it used its resources and whatever influence it might claim in order to advance a cause it believed to be in the public interest. All newspapers — and indeed all political parties — claim to defend the public interest. Democracy, at its root, is nothing more than a contest over who gets to define what *is* in the best interests of the public.

Though the unite-the-right movement failed, the *Post* can no doubt claim some responsibility for the creation of the Canadian Alliance party. Certainly, going into the 2000 federal election, the paper was widely perceived as pro-Alliance. Indeed, Peter White, Conrad Black's longstanding partner in Hollinger, served as co-chair of the Alliance campaign. On the night of the vote, CTV assembled a panel of pundits, each of whom was associated with one of the major parties, to analyze the returns as they came in. Bob White, for example, the former union leader, represented the NDP. The Alliance was represented by Ezra Levant, then a writer for the *National Post* and the only journalist on the panel. The message was clear: as the unions are to the NDP, so the *Post* is to the Canadian Alliance.

Advocacy and affiliation, however, are not the same as deliberate efforts to skew news coverage in order to favour a sectarian interest. What one reader may see as evident "bias," another may greet as refreshing candour. Consider the headlines that appeared in the *National Post* and *The Globe and Mail* on October 19, just before the election writ was dropped. The previous day, the Minister of Finance, Paul Martin, had introduced in the House a mini-budget clearly intended to pave the way for the election call. Its centrepiece was a series of tax cuts — something the Alliance had been loudly promoting — that the Liberals boasted was the deepest in modern Canadian political history, but that the Alliance derided as insufficient. The *Post*'s headline read: "Liberals deliver Alliance budget." The equivalent headline in the *Globe* (on a front-page article by Hugh Winsor, labelled "analysis") read: "Martin one-ups Day in budget battle."

How is one to interpret these two readings of the same event? Both are perfectly accurate, though it seems obvious that the *Post* headline implicitly favours the Alliance via the suggestion that the Liberals had resorted to stealing the ideas of their major opponents and, indeed, were about to launch an election campaign by running on Alliance policies. By the same token, the *Globe* headline would appear to implicitly favour the Liberals, via the suggestion that the Minister of Finance had outmanoeuvred the Leader of the Opposition; it was not that the Liberals had stolen Alliance's ideas, but that they had stolen the Opposition's thunder. It is not a matter of which headline is right and which is wrong, but which of the two one would find more satisfying, and that in turn depends on one's own political inclinations.

In that vein, a reading of all four of the Toronto papers' major election headlines during the campaign reveals the different characters and emphases of the respective papers. The *Sun*, for example, as a Toronto-centric tabloid, paid the least attention to the election. Indeed, the election made the front page only infrequently and only in the aftermath of major campaign events such as the leaders' English-language debate; or when accusations of criminal wrongdoing were levelled ("Clark, Day: PM broke the law" — Nov. 18), crime being a preoccupation of the *Sun*; or when a local angle could be found to the national story of the election, as in "Mayor: I fear Stock Day; but Lastman says he's never even met Alliance Leader" (Nov. 8) and "T.O. Grits: PM's our big problem" (Nov. 15).

For the most part, the *Sun*'s news coverage was relegated to a page or two per day tucked inside the paper, typically on page 10, and the headlines merely documented the major developments of the previous day's campaigning, as in "PM sets sight on Day; targets Alliance stand on gun-control issue" (Nov. 7), and "Mounting accusations; PM hindering RCMP probe: Day" (Nov. 14). The *Sun*'s distinctive campaign coverage innovation — again, perfectly in keeping with its demographic — was the daily feature "Catherine Watch," in which the paper would run a photograph of Catherine Clark, the Conservative leader's attractive daughter, with accompanying text detailing what she had been wearing the previous day on the campaign trail.

The other three papers mapped a spectrum of interpretation, at least in their headlines on the election, with the *Star* leaning in favour of the governing Liberals, the *Post* decidedly disapproving of the Liberals, and the *Globe* somewhere in between depending on the day. For example, on October 23, the day after the writ had been dropped, the *Star*'s headline ran: "'Two visions of Canada' choice on Nov. 27: PM" — presumably precisely the sort of headline the Liberals were looking for, since this is exactly how the election call had been framed by the party strategists: as presenting voters with a choice between the known quantity of the Liberal government and an ostensibly ominous social conservative agenda at odds with core, mainstream Canadian values. The headlines in the *Post* on the same day, by comparison, in the multi-deck style the paper favoured, ran:

"PM Attacked for Fall Election 'Vanity'";
"Chrétien accepts Liberal nomination in hotel cited in critical
    Auditor-General's report";
"Cuts off questions";
"Chrétien concedes he is taking advantage of lead".

A further headline, on an accompanying piece by correspondent Paul Wells, read simply: "Tests patience, tempts fate". *The Globe and Mail*'s headlines on the day were notably more neutral: "Chrétien defends early vote; PM says choice is between two distinct visions of Canada, argues Alliance had already begun advertising." An accompanying piece by Jeffrey Simpson, labelled as analysis, carried the headline "History is not in the Liberals' corner."

It is not difficult to find *Star* headlines throughout the contest that would seem to cast the best light on the Liberals' campaign or accentuate the misfortunes of their major opponent, e.g.: "Chrétien 'most trusted' leader; poll puts him at top of trust ratings, ahead of Day" (Oct. 29); "PM accuses Day of threat to rights; Alliance will eventually destroy Charter, Chrétien says" (Oct. 31); "Liberals pledge 'smart' billions; Platform calls for $6.6 billion in research, housing" (Nov. 2); "Chaos theory, Alliance-style; Campaign team takes a while to find footing" (Nov. 4); "Day says he believes biblical story of creation; Claims there is scientific backing" (Nov. 16). Even something as patently obvious as the sheer slenderness of *Red Book III* became, in the hands of the *Star*'s front page headline writers, a backhandedly good-news story for the Liberals: "Red Book Lite: The Liberal platform gives voters no concrete reasons to abandon Chrétien government" (Nov. 2).

Again, none of these headlines is inaccurate. Nor did the *Star* ignore the difficulties that beset the Liberal campaign. The paper duly noted the accusations of pork-barreling in the Prime Minister's home riding, for example, and that the "controversy continues to dog PM's campaign" (Nov. 18). However, as a whole, and particularly in comparison with the *Post*, the front page of *The Toronto Star* was a good deal kinder to the Liberals and the Prime Minister than its competitors.

If the *Star* offered examples of headlines one might deem favourable to the Liberals, the *Post* offered plenty that conceded no comfort to the government. For example:

"PM briefly encounters his public;
Shushes reporters" (Oct. 26)

"Scandal eating into Grits' lead, poll finds;
Minority 'plausible'" (Oct. 28)

"Millions in aid up for grabs in Gaspé, Liberal says;
Party lost riding to Bloc by a mere 174 votes in 1997" (Oct. 30)

"Big crowds give Day hope in Ontario;
Outdrawing Chrétien;
Alliance leader tapping into changing mood" (Nov. 1)

"Farmers' problems are their own fault, Liberal candidate charges" (Nov. 1)

"Dollar is headed for 60 cents: CIBC
Banks says global downturn could sideswipe the loonie;
PM says it's not his department" (Nov. 3)

The paper also hammered away at the allegations of impropriety and wrongdoing on the part of the Prime Minister, as one might expect from the newspaper that had done more than any other to reveal such allegations in the first place. As well, this was presumably the Opposition's strongest suit, particularly given Stockwell Day's repeated stumblings. If the Prime Minister could be shown to be arrogantly corrupt, voters would have cause to abandon the Liberals and turn to alternatives. Hence:

"Boardwalk of shame;
The leader of the Bloc Quebecois takes a bus tour of sites of Liberal largesse in PM's riding" (Oct. 25)

"Leaders' debate: Rivals gang up on Chrétien over grant abuse;
Grant suspended to business in PM's riding" (Nov. 9)

"PM lobbied for disputed loan;
PMO's defence is that he was just doing what 'MPs from every party do'" (Nov. 16)

"'It's the usual operation': PM;
Defends intervention in federal loan to inn;
Clark would fire a minister for such conduct" (Nov. 17)

"Clark, Day seek criminal probe;
Tory leader says RCMP should examine 'all relevant circumstances' of disputed loan" (Nov. 18)

"Leaders press case for PM probe;
Clark raises five points;
'Was it ethical?' Day's letter asks of Chrétien's lobbying" (Nov. 21)

"Grits slump amid ethics row;
Lead over Alliance shrinks to eight points, majority government
could be in doubt" (Nov. 23)

Interestingly, after Nov. 16, when the *Post* reported "Day's 'negatives'
up sharply, poll finds," the paper began to feature Joe Clark more often
in its headlines, occasionally ahead of the leader of the Official
Opposition, as it became apparent even to those who wished to unseat
the Liberals that Stockwell Day was not performing to his party's expectations. This may have been simply a reflection of the fact that, against
all initial expectations, Clark waged a superior campaign. However, for
a newspaper by that time firmly identified with the Alliance and its fortunes, it was difficult not to wonder whether the *Post* was attempting to
distance itself from Day, on the grounds that a national newspaper too
closely associated with a rump party runs the risk of being dismissed as
a rump newspaper. Or was the paper merely covering its conservative
bets? Just before the *Post*'s newfound attention to Mr. Clark, however, on
Nov. 15, in what seemed an over-reaching attempt to damage the
Liberals with a fusillade of negative publicity, the *Post*'s front page featured the following headlines:

"Liberals 'Sliding Big-Time'"

"Party loses eight to nine points in tracking polls"

"Prime Minister accepts responsibility for two-tier health"

"Grit MPs in Toronto say Chrétien a liability"

"Liberal polls show party support in decline"

"Federal banker claims political interference"

"Grand-Mère Inn at heart of dismissal lawsuit
Prime Minister denies involvement"

"MRI threat alienates Liberal donor
Owns private clinics"

And, on an accompanying opinion piece by Andrew Coyne on the Auberge des Gouverneurs in Shawinigan: "Political Ponzi-scheme unravels".

The difficulty, however, was the banner headline in block capitals: "Liberals 'Sliding Big-Time.'" The accompanying story, though it twice repeated the same quotation from an anonymous source, offered next to no evidence of the Liberals' supposed collapse in public opinion. Indeed, apart from a passing reference to internal party polls in the second and then autepenultimate paragraphs, the story did not mention this catastrophic Liberal decline. It appeared as though the paper were merely projecting via the headline its fondest wishes onto the governing party. All journalism — or at least all responsible journalism — is founded on a contract between the news outlet and its public, in which the former promises it has done all that it can to ensure the reliability of its news content. That is how mainstream journalism distinguishes itself from a supermarket tabloid such as the *Weekly World News*, which merely promises its readers it has done all that it can to *pretend* that its contents are true. It is one thing to interpret the facts; it is quite another to build "facts" out of thin air. In this instance, the "sliding big-time" headline seemed crafted simply for bombastic effect. If the *National Post* said so vigorously enough, perhaps it would prove to be true. The following day, even the *Post*'s own Paul Wells made fun of the hyperventilated headline.

Perhaps, though, the *Post* merely thought it was doing to its opposition what the Alliance believed *The Globe and Mail* had done to it. As Edward Greenspon relates in Chapter Seven of this volume, on Oct. 27 Alliance campaign co-chair Jason Kenney had appeared on CBC Newsworld's *counterSpin* with Avi Lewis. Pressed by Lewis, Kenney appeared to concede that an Alliance government would permit some private medical care to exist in parallel with the public health system. Both Greenspon and his colleague Shawn McCarthy took notice. After poring over a transcript of the broadcast, alerting the national desk in Toronto, following up with their own calls to Alliance officials, and filing, respectively, a column and a news story, this became the *Globe*'s Oct. 31 banner headline: "Alliance supports two-tier health care; Government should give provinces leeway in promoting private clinics, co-chair says."

The headline played directly to fears that the Alliance harboured plans to "privatize" health care — an accusation that had already been levelled by the Prime Minister, and that indeed had prompted Avi

Lewis's line of questioning in the first place. As well, the headline resonated with those who suspected that what the Alliance said publicly
was a script calculated to make the party appealing or palatable to the
largest number of voters, but that if elected to power it would enact
much more drastic change. That is, there was the suspicion that the
Alliance could not be forthright about its genuine legislative intentions
because, stated plainly, these would dash the party's chances of electoral
inroads. Hence the leitmotif throughout the campaign of the Alliance's
supposed "secret agenda." The *Globe*'s headline added powerful credence to such scepticism. It appeared that senior party officials had
admitted in their own words that the Alliance favoured crucially significant changes to the Canadian health care system that were nowhere
mentioned in the party's platform.

Clearly damaging to the Alliance, the headline immediately made
health care the campaign's front-burner issue for the next week at least.
No matter that it was not clear what was meant by "two-tier"; no matter that the issue was complex and convoluted; no matter that neither
the Liberals, the Tories nor the Alliance had much interest in clarifying
it, since it was far too volatile a political issue. In the end, the Alliance
leader was reduced to holding up a hand-written card during the
English leaders' debate, ardently trying to reassure Canadians that he
did not advocate "two-tier" health care, whatever it might mean. As
Liberal strategist Warren Kinsella remarked in a speech at the National
Press Club three months after the election: "At that point, there was only
one way we devil Grits could have managed the dialogue better — and
that would have been to make up the little sign ourselves, and demand
that Mr. Day hold it up on TV."

Newspapers, like political parties, compete to command attention.
The "two-tier health care" headline significantly contributed to the
course of the campaign dynamic. It was a headline of clear political consequence. And in its rivalry with the *National Post*, the effect was to signal that *The Globe and Mail* was a player in the election; that it was the
paper of record, the one that set the metronome of what mattered.
Whether the headline was justified — and Alliance members most
strenuously insisted it was not — it was at least based on evidence to
which the paper could point, unlike the mere innuendo of the *Post*'s
"sliding big-time" banner, and it provided the Alliance's political opponents with the cudgel they needed. As the other parties fell on Stockwell

Day and his strategists, the *Globe*'s competitors in the news media craned forward to document the fray.

The Toronto Newspaper Coverage

Headlines may communicate impressions and reveal the emphases and different characters of newspapers, but they do not capture the nature, range or content of newspapers' coverage of the election. With that in mind, we conducted a content analysis of the four Toronto papers' attention to the 2000 campaign. This study is a continuation of the analyses begun in 1974 in the first of the Carleton University series of publications on the elections, and replicated in the 1988 and 1993 volumes.[1] The previous examinations of newspaper coverage had shown that very little real difference in election coverage existed regionally between newspapers, and that it would be useful to introduce some new dimensions to the analysis. While the analytical variables would remain the same — measures of extent of coverage, coverage of leaders, definition of the issues, etc. — the selection of papers would change in order to shed light on differences that may exist between papers with different readership, styles and ownership.

For the current analysis, four Toronto newspapers were selected: *The Globe and Mail, The Toronto Star*, the *National Post* and *The Toronto Sun*. These four newspapers were selected to allow for an examination and comparison of coverage by Canada's two anglophone national newspapers, as well as Canada's largest city newspaper, and the founding tabloid of the *Sun* chain. It is regrettable that by focusing exclusively on the Toronto market the study neglects to take into account how coverage may have differed in francophone Canada, for example, or how a Western-based party such as Alliance may or may not have received different coverage in different regions of the country. However, given limited resources, the Toronto media battle seemed to present the most interesting new development of press coverage of Election 2000. With the arrival of the *National Post* and accusations that the paper's coverage is ideologically driven, we wished to explore to what extent analysis and interpretation featured in the news coverage of the various papers, as opposed to straightforward stenographic reporting of campaign events, and whether this element of opinion consistently favoured one party over the others or consistently played to the disfavour of one party over the others, and how this varied from paper to paper. Hence, as in previous analyses, every journalistic item dealing with the election (excluding Sunday coverage, which was not consistent between papers)[2] was analysed and coded, for a total of 2,458 items. These included news reports, news with analysis, background news, editorials, columns, special submissions or op-ed articles, photographs, cartoons, and letters to the editor. The "news with analysis" category was added to the previous years' categories of items in order to distinguish straight news reporting from pieces that also contained an interpretive element.

TABLE 1
EXTENT OF COVERAGE: Number of stories by newspaper

	Toronto Star	Globe and Mail	National Post	Toronto Sun
1984	1035	812	Na	Na
1988	1378	922	Na	Na
1993	822	484	Na	Na
2000	522	764	710	462

In the 1993 study it was noted that the quantity of coverage had dropped in each successive election from 1984 to 1988 to 1993. While the 2000 election was even shorter than the 1993 election — 36 days as compared to 47 days in 1993 and 57 days in 1984 — the proportional amount of coverage again dropped in *The Toronto Star* but increased markedly in *The Globe and Mail*. *The Globe and Mail* and *National Post*, the two national papers, had significantly more coverage overall than *The Toronto Star* and *Toronto Sun*. This may reflect the fact that, as national newspapers locked in competition, the national story of a federal election became an occasion for both the *Post* and the *Globe* to showcase their attention to national affairs. They were competing, in part, through the comprehensiveness of their coverage.

TABLE 2
TYPE OF COVERAGE

	Toronto Star	Globe and Mail	National Post	Toronto Sun
News	42%	38%	50%	39%
News background	6	5	5	1
News with analysis	12	18	7	5
Editorial	7	4	6	5
Column	10	14	10	13
Op-ed	1	6	7	3
Letter	18	13	12	21
Cartoon	2	1	3	8
Photo with caption	1	1	2	4

Note on Column percentages: Figures may not add to 100 due to rounding

Also noted in the 1993 analysis was a swing from straight news coverage to opinion-based coverage — including news with analysis, editorials, columns, op-ed articles and letters. In the 1984 analysis 73 percent of the election coverage was straight "news". In 1993 this figure dropped to 60 percent of the coverage. When adding "news" and "news with analysis" together (as had been done in the previous studies) in this election, straight news coverage dropped to an average of 53 percent. The *Toronto Sun* generated the least news coverage, 44 percent, while all three other papers were closely grouped to around 55 percent of their coverage. (Table 2)

By separating "news with analysis" from the "news" category a new emphasis in coverage becomes apparent. *The Globe and Mail* led the way with the most "news with analysis" reporting, although unlike the other papers, in most cases it clearly identified the items as such via the explicit label "analysis." The *Toronto Sun* had the least proportion of "news with analysis". When looking at what topics dominated the news analysis category, social issues — predominantly health care — were most common in all four newspapers, followed by all economic issues. "Letters to the editor" also increased significantly from previous elections, up from an average of 10 percent in 1993 to 15 percent. *The Toronto Star* and *Toronto Sun* had the highest proportion of letters with 18 percent and 21 percent, respectively.

In terms of the length of all items in the analysis, the *Toronto Sun* and *Toronto Star* had the highest percentage of stories under five hundred words. Conversely, the *National Post* and *Globe and Mail* had much higher proportions of lengthier articles over five hundred words. When looking at the "locale of the report", an average of 17 percent of the stories originated from Ottawa. The *Toronto Sun* had the lowest proportion of stories originating in Ottawa, at 14 percent. Understandably, both the Toronto *Star* and *Sun* had a higher proportion of Ontario stories as each of these papers covered the campaigns in the Toronto area. Both *The Globe and Mail* and the *National Post* used their own staff for more than three-quarters of the election coverage in all reporting categories, while only two-thirds of the coverage of the Toronto *Star* and *Sun* was generated by staff writers. Both the *Star* and *Sun* relied more heavily on Canadian Press and letters to the editor to round out their coverage.

TABLE 3
COVERAGE OF LEADERS

More than 60 percent of the coverage in all four newspapers had the leaders of the parties as the "principal actor" in the item, 40 percent had "other" or "no" individual as the "principal actor". The *Sun* had the highest percentage of stories overall that had the leaders as the "principal actor", while the three other papers had an equal proportion of stories which focused on other "principal actors".

	Globe and Mail	Toronto Star	National Post	Toronto Sun
Jean Chrétien	34%	39%	42%	45%
Stockwell Day	38	41	29	33
Joe Clark	15	7	11	15
Gilles Duceppe	5	5	7	1
Alexa McDonough	9	8	11	5

Note on Column percentages: Figures may not add to 100 due to rounding

When looking at just those items that had the party leaders as the "principal actor" (table above), more than 70 percent of the coverage in all four papers focused on Jean Chrétien and Stockwell Day, although there were some differences in the emphasis each paper placed on each leader. (Table 3.) *The Globe and Mail* and *Toronto Star* evenly split their coverage between Chrétien and Day while the *Post* and *Sun* ran a higher percentage of stories about Chrétien. Joe Clark was of slightly more interest to *The Globe and Mail* and *Toronto Sun* than the *Post* and *Star*, but very little attention was paid to Gilles Duceppe and Alexa McDonough by all four papers.

From Table 4 we can see that in all four papers the largest proportion of items that had a principal actor were unfavourable stories as opposed to favourable or neutral stories. The *Toronto Sun* and *Star* had the highest proportion of unfavourable to favourable stories while *The Globe and Mail* and the *National Post* had the most balance between the three categories. The coverage across all four papers was generally negative in tone.

By looking at all stories that had the leaders as the principal actor by the readers' impression of the stories, across all four papers, this negativism can be examined more closely. Overall, Chrétien had the highest proportion of unfavourable stories written about him in all four papers: 65 percent unfavourable to 14 percent favourable and 22 percent neutral. Fifty-one percent of the articles about Day were unfavourable and only 18 percent of the stories about Clark, McDonough and Duceppe were unfavourable. So, while the coverage in general was focused on Chrétien and Day, the tone of the majority of these articles was unfavourable. But, was this negative focus consistently applied to Chrétien and Day in all four papers or did different papers have different emphases?

TABLE 4
READERS' IMPRESSION TOWARD PRINCIPAL ACTOR BY PAPER

		Jean Chretien	Stockwell Day	Joe Clark	Gilles Duceppe	Alexa McDonough
Globe and Mail	Favourable	21%	15%	42%	305%	54%
	Unfavourable	52	50	15	25	14
	Neural	27	36	42	45	31
Toronto Star	Favourable	19%	14%	44%	25%	56%
	Unfavouralbe	53	65	30	13	20
	Neutral	28	22	26	63	24
National Post	Favourable	7%	25%	44%	23%	35%
	Unfavourable	62	40	8	15	22
	Neutral	30	35	49	62	43
Toronto Sun	Favourable	8%	27%	40%	25%	35%
	Unfavourable	80	51	18	–	17
	Neutral	13	23	42	75	39

Note on Column percentages: Figures may not add to 100 due to rounding

Although the pattern of coverage of the two major story-makers was consistently negative, there were variations of the proportion of unfavourable coverage from paper to paper. The *National Post* and the *Toronto Sun* carried a much higher proportion of unfavourable stories about Chrétien than *The Toronto Star* and *Globe and Mail*. However, even the latter two papers gave heavily unfavourable coverage to Jean Chrétien, the leader of the party they supposedly supported. In the *Sun*,

80 percent of the articles about Chrétien were unfavourable. Both the *Sun* and *Post* carried a higher percentage of favourable stories about Day. Clark, McDonough, and Duceppe had higher proportions of favourable versus unfavourable stories written about them in all four papers; notwithstanding that all three leaders only generated 30 percent of the total coverage.

When looking at another analytical variable, "the object of attack" — of those stories which were coded as having a direct attack on a leader — Chrétien had the highest proportion of stories at 53 percent, followed by Day at 32 percent and the rest of the leaders below 5 percent. *The Globe and Mail* and *Toronto Star* had the lowest proportion of stories attacking Chrétien while the *Post* and *Sun* had significantly lower proportions of stories that attacked Day. Fifty percent of the stories had no major object of attack at all.

TABLE 5
TYPE OF COVERAGE

	1984	1988	1993	2000
Issues	26%	37%	31%	51%
Process	74	63	69	49

Note on Column percentages: Figures may not add to 100 due to rounding

There were more items about issues in election 2000 than there were in past elections. The "process" category takes into account all stories written about the campaign, including: polls, debates, voting behaviours, timing of the election call, and party strategies and platforms. All remaining stories were about issues. The coverage by all four papers was relatively similar.

TABLE 6
ISSUES COVERED

	2000
Economy	20%
Social Issues	18
Patronage	12
Leadership	9
Moral Issues	7
Law and Order	5
Constitutional Issues	4
Immigration/racism	3
Environment	1
Native issues	1
Other	21

Note on Column percentages: Figures may not add to 100 due to rounding

In articles that did not focus on the workings of the campaign, a number of old issues were carried over from previous elections but new issues also emerged. Falling under the "economy" heading were articles that dealt with the deficit, government spending, the economy in general, taxes, and employment. In previous elections the economy had always been of varying interest, generating a high of 40 percent of the issue-related stories in 1993 and a low of 8 percent of the stories in 1988. During the 2000 election, even in a time of comparative prosperity and economic stability,

articles about unemployment, debt and tax reduction were still newsworthy, although they did not have the same focus as in the 1988 campaign,
which was dominated by free trade. It is interesting to note, however, that
the dominance of "health care" in the public issue agenda (see Chapter
Thirteen of this volume) is not reflected in the media coverage. Health
care predominated in the "social" issues category, which also included
articles on housing, education, and poverty; however, these social stories
in total were fewer than those dealing with economics. Firing the health
care debate were articles about Chrétien and the Liberal record of "systematically destroying the health care system" and Day's defence against
the phantom "two-tier" health care accusations. Patronage and associated
scandals created additional problems for Chrétien as opposition leaders
tried repeatedly to get something to "stick" to him. This, however, also
created a new set of problems for Day as his criminal accusations were
deemed to have taken an inappropriate form.

A new issue that emerged in this campaign questioned the leadership
abilities of all the leaders of major parties: Was Chrétien too old to lead the
Liberals into another election? Was Clark washed up and then reborn as
leader of the Conservatives after his performance in the debates? Did Day
have enough experience to "unite the right"? And was McDonough sufficiently dynamic to lead the NDP back from political obscurity? The
Canadian Alliance platform of social conservatism generated debates on a
number of moral issues including abortion and capital punishment. The
Alliance platform also generated debate on constitutional issues including
stories about referenda and constitutional reform. Absent from the campaign were articles on women's issues, national unity, and agriculture —
which were represented in previous elections — and all but absent was
attention to the environment and native issues.

The Globe and Mail had the largest proportion of stories on social
issues, the *Star* and the *Sun* on economic issues, and the *National Post* on
the patronage issue. When looking at the timing of the coverage of the
three main issues — economic, social and patronage — all three were
present from day one of the coverage but had different peaks in proportion of coverage. Almost one-quarter of stories on economic issues were
written between days eight through twelve. Social issue stories experienced two peaks, between days ten through twelve and days twenty-two
and twenty-three, while the majority of patronage stories were written in
the waning days of the campaign, day twenty-seven through thirty-three.

Conclusion

The most immediately notable aspect of the newspaper coverage of the 2000 election, in comparison with the previous studies, was that the competition between the two national papers clearly resulted in greater attention to the election. Previously, the volume of coverage as measured by number of stories and other items had been dropping, and for this election continued to drop in *The Toronto Star*. If one believes that vigorous attention to the electoral process is advantageous to a democratic society, then the redoubled coverage that resulted from the competition between the *Post* and the *Globe* is a welcome development.

The 2000 campaign coverage saw greater attention to election issues than to the manoeuvrings of the "horse race," again reversing a previous trend. Complaints that the media concentrate on which party is ahead and why, to the detriment of substantive coverage of the issues, have been common in the past, but in this election our content analysis would seem to suggest that the newspapers attempted to provide both a running account of how the parties were jockeying for advantage along with dutiful attention to their various positions on a range of issues. It may have been that this attention shed more heat than light, but that may also have been because the front-running parties themselves either shied away from clear and explicit statements on issues they believed to be too volatile or deliberately raised the temperature of the campaign by trading inflammatory rhetoric.

Interestingly, though the issue of health care emerged at the end of the first week as a defining aspect of the campaign, in terms of volume of coverage it was not the most persistent. Economics was the single issue that garnered the most overall attention.

It is also plain from our analysis that the newspapers concentrated on the Liberals and the Alliance, and paid comparatively scant attention to the NDP, the Bloc, and the Tories. This was no doubt a consequence of the fact that for the media the central concern in an election campaign is the outcome, which is to say, who will win. In that regard, the "story" for the newspapers was whether the Liberals would be returned with a majority. That, in turn, would depend in largest measure on how the Alliance would fare, and in particular whether it would make significant electoral gains in Ontario. The Bloc and the NDP were secondary elements in such a story: they featured only insofar as they might influence the Liberals' election fortunes. Would the NDP deny the Liberals a resurgence in the Maritimes? How many seats would the Bloc take in Quebec? The Progressive Conservatives attracted coverage as the campaign wore on, in part as a result of the strength of leader Joe Clark's performance in the debates and in part because of the faltering campaign of the other party of the right.

Finally, although the trend toward greater analysis or interpretation in news coverage continued in this election, it is interesting to note how this was actually manifest. Since the *National Post* enjoys a reputation as a newspaper that promotes a certain agenda in its coverage, one might have thought that it would feature the highest proportion of stories in which news reporting was laced with "analysis." Certainly, its detractors commonly complain that the *Post* "torques" or skews its coverage to favour a particular perspective. However, the paper that carried the largest number of "news with analysis" items was *The Globe and Mail*. Indeed, the *Globe* played up this aspect of its campaign coverage. Straight news reports were often accompanied by analytical pieces by the paper's political writers on the campaign trail — neither columns nor deadpan reportage — and these were explicitly labelled "analysis."

It is true that the *National Post*'s coverage was far less favourable to the Prime Minister than that of the *Globe* or the *Star*, but by the same token, 40 percent of its coverage of Stockwell Day was also coded as "unfavourable" (although, admittedly, this was the smallest percentage of unfavourable coverage of Day of all four papers). As well, the paper with the highest percentage of favourable coverage of Day (27 percent) and the highest percentage of unfavourable coverage of Jean Chrétien (a quite remarkable 80 percent) was the *Toronto Sun*. Be that as it may, for all the bluster of its occasionally overheated headlines — and what newspaper does not from time to time run overexerted headlines? — and for all its supposed reputation in some circles as a paper that cannot be trusted in its political news coverage because its own political agenda infects the news content, the fact remains that 50 percent of the *Post*'s election coverage was coded as straight news, the highest of all four papers. Most certainly, the paper brought a perspective to bear on the campaign, but it also offered the largest volume — in both percentage terms and in the sheer extent of its coverage — of unadorned and unadulterated reporting. One could despise the *National Post*'s editorial posture and still read it as a valuable source of election news.

In the end, then, these four papers between them offered what voters and readers most require in a free society: choice between meaningful alternatives. True, the papers did not map the political spectrum in its entirety. There was no newspaper to defend and promote the agenda of the left, the way the *Star* allied itself with the Liberals and the *Post* with the parties of the right. But the four papers were far from lockstep in the packages of coverage they offered readers, and the competition between the *Post* and the *Globe* enlivened both election coverage and the election itself. And all that should be counted in their favour.

NOTES

1   See Alan Frizzell and Anthony Westell, *The Canadian General Election of 1984* (Ottawa: Carleton University Press, 1985), Chapter 3; Alan Frizzell, Jon H. Pammett and Anthony Westell, *The Canadian General Election of 1988* (Ottawa: Carleton University Press, 1989), Chapter 4; and Alan Frizzell, Jon H. Pammett and Anthony Westell, *The Canadian General Election of 1993* (Ottawa, Carleton University Press, 1994), Chapter 7.

2   The *Sun* and *Star* published on Sundays, while the *Globe* and *Post* do not.

Chapter 9

Television, the Internet, and the Canadian Federal Election of 2000

by Paul Attallah and Angela Burton

The federal election of 2000 may well be remembered as a key transitional period in the coverage and circulation of political information. Indeed, its most outstanding media event may well have been the emergence of the Internet as a new and legitimate source of information capable of challenging television as the dominant information medium. But it remains a challenge rather than a fully realized victory, for the Internet stands today where television stood in the 1950s and radio in the 1920s: a new medium, still overshadowed by its predecessors, and still seeking its own voice and form.

Nonetheless, television clearly remains the dominant medium for covering federal election campaigns. The reasons for its dominance are easily understood. In a country so vast as Canada, it is extremely unlikely that any candidate could ever meet more than a fraction of voters or that any but the smallest number of voters could ever meet more than a few candidates. Indeed, if the same political programs are to be conveyed to everyone, if the same leaders are to campaign effectively everywhere, if dominant electoral themes capable of focusing attention are to emerge, then some form of instantaneous mass contact becomes a logical solution to a logistical problem. Television is merely the preferred form of instantaneous mass contact, as radio was from the 1920s to the 1950s, and as the Internet may become in the future.

The use of television has not only allowed political parties to project consistent images to the entire electorate, it has also allowed campaigns to be considerably abbreviated. As a result, the campaign of 2000 lasted only thirty-six days. But this fact merely underscores the centrality of television: as campaigns are shortened and compressed, it becomes increasingly important to stage or to plan events with television in mind, precisely in order to obtain the maximum coverage.

Consequently, the political parties' TV advertising campaigns become a focus of attention. Likewise, the debates of the party leaders are staged for television. Furthermore, on election night virtually the entire population turns to television to obtain what is widely regarded as the best coverage, the best commentators, the best information, etc. On election night, therefore, television is hugely preferred to all other media, and election night coverage is traditionally a time when television can foreground its technological and research capabilities in order to establish itself further as an important medium to which viewers should return again and again. Indeed, election night coverage constitutes an example of what Dayan and Katz call "festive" or "ceremonial" television:

> those historic occasions — mostly occasions of state — that are televised as they take place and transfix a nation or the world ... [they employ] the unique potential of the electronic media to command attention universally and simultaneously in order to tell a primordial story about current affairs. These are events that hang a halo over the television set and transform the viewing experience. (Dayan and Katz, 1994, 332.)

Finally, the centrality of television also means that any intervention for or against the parties or the political process must also occur as a television event. This was manifestly the case of the spoof referendum campaign conducted by Rick Mercer of the "This Hour Has 22 Minutes" aimed at forcing Stockwell Day to change his name to Doris Day. But it is also the common currency of protests — usually staged for television — marches, demonstrations, pie throwings, etc.[2]

The plainly dominant role of television has naturally generated a discourse of alarm and concern. The question is always asked — and the campaign of 2000 was no exception — whether television is accurate and fair: does it give equal coverage to all parties and all views?[3] Does its mere presence in some way drive the political agenda or alter the nature of politics?[4] Do the media trivialize politics?[5]

All of these concerns grow out of what Daniel Boorstin, as early as 1961, called "the graphic revolution" and the concomitant rise of "image politics." They appear to form the permanent background of discussion about the media generally and television specifically and it would not be surprising to see them carried over into future discussions of the

216

Internet. Whether that is the most fruitful avenue to follow will be disputed by this chapter.

Organization of the coverage

As in the 1997 federal campaign, the major television networks agreed to pool their resources but also to divide campaign coverage amongst themselves. Consequently, the various networks would concentrate on specific parties but would make their coverage available to everyone. On the English-language side, therefore, the CBC focused on the Canadian Alliance (CA) and the Liberals, CTV on the Progressive Conservatives (PC) and Global on the NDP. On the French-language side, Radio-Canada focused on the Liberals and TVA on the Bloc Québécois (BQ).

The reason for the sharing was primarily economic. Political parties charge news organizations for seats on their planes and buses. Additionally, the media must cover the daily cost of hotels and meals for their camera crews, which can consist of up to four people (reporter, producer, camera, sound). The daily cost can, therefore, reach $1,000 per day per media representative (see Lawton and Thompson, 2000).

Additionally, though, the sharing of coverage can help neutralize charges of bias. If all the networks use the same feed, it becomes considerably more difficult to claim that one network in particular is favouring a given party or candidate. On the contrary, it creates an onus on the originating network to provide a feed that is as neutral as possible, precisely because it must be used by several organizations whose priorities and judgements might conflict.

The sharing, though, also indicates a structural change in the nature of the television industry. For example, in the United States, the major networks no longer provide gavel-to-gavel coverage of political conventions, leaving that to specialty channels such as CNN or C-SPAN. The same shift is occurring in Canada. Not only are there two English-language all-news channels — CBC's Newsworld and CTV's Newsnet — but there are also two French-language all-news channels — Radio-Canada's RDI (Réseau de l'information) and TVA's LCN (Le canal Nouvelles). These are not only alternate windows for exhibiting news content, they are also outlets that demand an enormous amount of content in their own right. It becomes strategically efficient, therefore, to leave some news and some types of news to the all-news channels which, in turn, free the main networks for different types of political coverage. As a result, while the main networks pool their coverage, there is in fact more overall election news and more types of election news.

The availability of more types of news is well illustrated in the case of the CBC which, during the campaign, devoted the documentary and investigative part of its 10 p.m. main news broadcast entirely to election news. The coverage was no longer of breaking news but concerned more in-depth investigations and commentary. The most outstanding example of in-depth analysis was probably provided by Allan Gregg's nightly appearances on the CBC. And the most memorable of the investigations was broadcast on Tuesday, November 14, 2000, at the midway mark of the campaign. It reported that Stockwell Day, leader of the CA, believed in creationism. This caused a subsequent firestorm of debate over the role of religion in public life, over whether or not the CA would seek to have creationism taught in schools, over a possible hidden agenda, and so on.

The second main organizational aspect of the election coverage — also an innovation of the 1997 campaign — was the daily provision of a morning news conference to all the political parties. These news conferences were carried live and in full every day on Newsworld. The parties were free to put forward whomever they wanted. The daily news conference served several functions. The first was to counter the oft-repeated criticism that television deals only in insignificant sound bites and never lets politicians speak in their own voices. Here was an example of precisely the opposite. The second function was to provide the all-news channels with content to feed their voracious appetites. It may be added that, from television's point of view, news conferences are both an easy and inexpensive event to cover, especially as many of those attending the conferences and posing the questions would be reporters from other media (radio, newspapers, websites, magazines).

The advertising campaigns

Television advertising has assumed critical importance in any federal election campaign. These ads constitute virtually the only moment of the election campaign when the parties and their leaders exercise total control over their image and message. Indeed, at all other times — press conferences, scrums, debates — the ever-present danger is of some unexpected event casting a bad light on the party or leader. In their ads, however, the parties control absolutely every parameter.

Additionally, the ads reach a national audience. This makes them a highly prized form of communication and underscores the importance of controlling them. Consequently, the ads are a highly anticipated part of any federal election campaign and they usually form the object of their own press coverage and commentary. Indeed, not only do the television networks air the ads, for their usual fees, but they also comment upon them in their news programs.

Finally, the ads are important to the political parties in another way. They show that the parties are serious contenders precisely because they can command a national audience and because they possess the financial clout to produce and air them. A party that can not provide national advertising is not a serious contender in the Canadian political system.

Each major party adopted a different advertising strategy that played to its strengths and attempted to capitalize on the weaknesses of its opponents. Their various strategies also indicated who they took as their main opponents at various points in the campaign.

The Liberals ran a big budget campaign with richly produced advertising. They also had the largest number of campaign ads. Their ads, however, focused on "pan-Canadian" themes, stressing visually the diverse ethnic make-up of Canada, its various regions, and insisting on positive, upbeat messages. For example, one ad used as its tag line "I believe in a Canada where everybody wins." Another ad showed the Prime Minister and the Minister of Finance, who were reputedly no longer on speaking terms, strolling through a park and pausing to wave at smiling children. The theme of the Liberal ads was "togetherness" and a positive sense of collective winning. They focused not on the Prime Minister, widely regarded as the party's greatest liability, but on an idealized notion of "us." The Liberals also ran a different series of ads in French that specifically targeted young or first-time voters. One ad, in particular, showed three young university-aged people in a café. The young man muses about whether or not he should even care about federal politics. Immediately, though, a young woman reminds him that the federal Liberals have made lots of good contributions to the quality of their life.

The CA ran a more hard-hitting campaign with the twin aims of foregrounding the party's main issue — tax reform — and introducing the leader, Stockwell Day, to a wider audience, especially in Ontario where the party hoped for a major breakthrough. The CA ads, therefore, adopted a two-part structure. In one part, the party's theme would be foregrounded; in the second, Stockwell Day would address the camera directly. The goal was to present him as a trustworthy manager and he invariably appeared in a shirt and tie (no jacket), looking like a young, modern, efficient executive. Overall, though, the CA ads lacked the lush visuals of the Liberal ads and, unlike the Liberals, focused on the individual leader rather than an idealized collective "we." The CA ads also directly targeted the Prime Minister, attempting to make him an issue even as the Liberal ads avoided any unnecessary mention of the Prime Minister.

The NDP ads were, like the Liberal ads, visually appealing, and foregrounded the party's main issue, health care. The problem for the NDP, however, was how to combine a threatening message of declining health care conditions with an upbeat, positive image of the party itself. This it largely achieved through effective production values that managed to show the degradation of health care services in a serious but non-threatening manner.

The Bloc Québécois ran a campaign seen only in French. It stressed the qualities of its leader, Gilles Duceppe, and the value of solidarity amongst French-speakers. One typical ad showed a young man in long shot sitting by a misty lake wondering at the "distance" he felt from federal politics — which, indeed, was the theme of BQ ads.

The PCs ran the most memorable, and likely oddest, ad campaign. There were only two PC ads and they only began to air quite a bit later than those of the other parties. Plainly, the PC party, given its parlous financial state, could ill afford the cost of an advertising campaign and could ill afford to forgo one. A failure to advertise would have been a tacit admission that it had fallen to third party status. Nonetheless, its two ads can be characterized as humorous attack ads. The first was conducted in the style of a K-Tel record commercial of the 1970s. Over what appeared to be a credit roll of hit songs, but was actually a list of broken Liberal promises, a "wild and crazy" announcer called out the promises as though they were song hits. The second ad showed a book open on a table. It could have been a Bible but turned out to be the Liberal Party's campaign book. Across the bottom of the screen scrolled a statement from the Prime Minister claiming that only "an act of God" would prevent him from fulfilling his promises. At that moment, a thunderbolt erupts from the heavens, strikes the book, and sets it on fire. While star-tlingly memorable, the ads appeared to be inconsistent with the image of the sober statesman projected by party leader Joe Clark and while they gave reasons to distrust the Prime Minster, they failed to provide any to vote for the Tories. Their main function, it seems, was to draw attention by any and all means possible to the continued presence of the Progressive Conservative Party.

Finally, it should be noted that the ads all drew upon a common ver-nacular of television advertising well-known to the television audience. While the Liberals drew upon the imagery of the large corporation — per-haps an insurance firm or a oil company — with a reassuring, feel-good message to deliver, the CA drew on the imagery of car ads with their promise of performance, reliability, and simplicity. The Tories, as stated, drew upon the hawking commercials of the 1970s, whereas the NDP and BQ seemed to draw upon music video and romantic cologne ads respec-tively.

The debates

The leaders' debates have become a ritualized part of any federal elec-tion campaign. Although the Canadian debates were originally mod-elled on the US Kennedy/Nixon debate of 1960, several factors distinguish them. Unlike that most famous of US debates, which was actually organized by the League of Women Voters and simply covered as an event by the networks, the Canadian debates are organized by the CBC and are carried by virtually all the networks. This then puts the Canadian networks in the business of simultaneously staging and cov-ering an event. It also generates a requirement that the networks, as a demonstration of fairness, invite all the main party leaders when, in fact, many viewers might prefer to see only two or three of the leaders. Over the years, the parties have exercised ever greater control of the debates, determining everything from the background colour of the set to the order of questions. The leaders prepare extensively for the debates and they are widely watched.[6]

As in other recent federal elections, there were two debates in 2000, the first on November 8, in French, the second on November 9, in English. Both debates were characterized by the usual degree of incomprehensible squabbling and neither produced a truly defining moment. In neither debate did the Prime Minister stumble badly, thereby losing the election. In the French-language debate, Jean Chrétien and Gilles Duceppe, speaking their mother tongue, performed well as would be expected, and Alexa McDonough and Stockwell Day, both of whom speak French with barely describable clumsiness, were virtual non-entities, also as would be expected. There was a general consensus, however, that Joe Clark performed surprisingly well.

In the English-language debate, everyone performed roughly as expected, except for Joe Clark who, again, exceeded expectations. Indeed, his success in the debates seemed to mark his rehabilitation and lent a boost to the Conservative Party.

The debates were received differently by the two main language groups. A headline in *La Presse* captured response to the French-language debate: "Le débat n'a guère passionné les téléspectateurs" (Thursday, November 9, 2000, *La Presse*, p. A13). Indeed, French-language columnists virtually ignored the debate on the next day, preferring such topics as the music industry, tainted meat, and Quebec television. On November 14th, 2000, when Vincent Desautels of *Le Devoir* did comment on the debate, it was to dismiss it: "Exercice démocratique, le débat télévisé? Laissez-moi rire. Il ne s'agit que d'un test public pour vérifier le charisme médiatique des politiciens." (Desautels, *Le Devoir*, November 14, 2000, p. B7). Significantly, this response to the debate also characterized the attitude of most French-speakers to the election: an unnecessary and uninteresting exercise.

The English-language debate sparked more comment but by now the main news topic was not the Canadian election but the inconclusive result of the US presidential election, which just happened to coincide with the debates. Much sober second thought, therefore, was devoted to the satisfying observation that the American electoral debacle could not possibly happen in Canada. Nonetheless, approximately 2.75 million viewers watched at least some of the English-language debate (*Toronto Star*, November 11, 2000, p. A11). The most consistently highly rated program on Canadian television, "Hockey Night in Canada," usually scores about 3.2 to 3.5 million viewers. A rating of one million viewers is considered successful. The level of exposure to the English-language debate indicates its continuing relevance to English-speakers, their ongoing interest in the political process, and the distance that separates them from French-speaking viewers.

A third "debate", featuring the Natural Law Party, the Marijuana Party, the Green Party, the Canadian Action Party, the Communist Party, and the Marxist-Leninist Party, occurred on November 19 and was broadcast in part on Newsworld (MacKinnon, 2000). However, rather than engage one another in political disagreements, the various small party leaders used the event as an opportunity to present their party platforms.

The Audience

Whether there is any correlation between the amount of air time received by a party, its advertising, its expenditures, and its electoral success remains a moot point. In 1993, the Conservatives, with a huge war chest, massive advertising, and more free air time than any other party, achieved the worst electoral results in Canadian history. In 1997 and 2000, with roughly the same campaign style, the Liberals moved from a bare majority to a respectable majority. With minuscule resources compared to 1993, the Conservatives in 2000 greatly improved their visibility. Despite increased coverage and resources, the CA remained stagnant. Many of our concerns about the role of the media generally, and television specifically, grow out of that moot equation. Can't television bias the outcome of an election? Shouldn't we institute safeguards, rules or guidelines to ensure a "good" outcome? Unfortunately, from the point of view of television research, the discourse of alarm and concern that characterizes so much of our inquiry into television and politics appears both dated and underpinned by unspoken presuppositions.

The unspoken presuppositions are (1) that at some point in the past, politics was a more thoughtful, more genuine, more democratic exercise than now, (2) that the modern media by their pervasiveness and nature set the parameters of knowledge and therefore virtually exhaust everything that voters can and do think, (3) that voters are therefore easily misled and in need of protection or guidance, (4) that electoral results are naturally suspect and contestable, and (5) if only the media behaved as their critics demanded, the world would be better.

Significantly, embedded within the unspoken presuppositions that motivate much criticism of television, there appears to lie a mistrust of the electoral process that keeps producing bad results. Much of the crit-

223

icism, while aimed at the media, therefore actually appears to be concerned with guaranteeing the type of electoral results that the critics deem appropriate.

However, the unstated presuppositions, while quite understandable, tend to be out of keeping with contemporary television research.[7] Indeed, studies of audiences caution greatly against the assumption that viewer behaviour is mapped, determined or controlled by television content. They indicate rather the enormous cultural inventiveness of television viewers who are apt to interpret television content in unintended ways, to insert it into unexpected patterns, to judge it according to unanticipated parameters, and so on.

Indeed, a greatly and fatally overlooked fact of television is that its audience is enormously sophisticated in both the forms and history of the medium. No one nowadays watches television naively or innocently. All viewers come to it from the depth of their own highly textured cultural knowledge and background. It is a commonplace to state that the audience has become highly fragmented and that this fragmentation is reflected in the explosion of specialized media outlets. But that very fragmentation is also the index of increasing audience sophistication as viewers seek their pleasures and meanings in increasingly self-defined genres and patterns, away from and beyond traditional patterns. This is characteristic not only of the modern television audience but is also the very hallmark of the Internet. The failure to interrogate political coverage from the point of view of audiences causes us to ask questions about "the impact" of television when, in fact, audiences increasingly view television coverage of election campaigns as another type of "genre," an artefact about which to display one's cultural knowledge and sophistication, a media event open to multiple interpretations and transformations. This was indeed the whole point of the Rick Mercer spoof of Stockwell Day and it merits attention for that very fact.

Rick Mercer is a performer on one of the CBC's most popular television shows, "This Hour Has 22 Minutes." The program consists of a series of comedy sketches, almost exclusively on political themes. As such, it presumes a high degree of political awareness on the part of its viewers. Indeed, without such awareness, the program would be virtually unintelligible. Yet, it is one of the CBC's most consistent ratings generators. Furthermore, the political awareness that it requires is not merely "reportorial" or "documentary"; it is not exhausted by a factual recounting of events. On the contrary, the program also presumes that viewers will know *how* political events are reported in the media and about the *range* of responses that the events can generate. The program, therefore, is not only about politics but also presumes considerable intertextual knowledge concerning *the way in which* political information and images are manufactured and circulated. Naturally, it can do that successfully only if the audience also possesses the same degree of intertextual sophistication. It makes little sense, when confronted with this degree of sophistication, to ask only or primarily what the impact of television might be, for clearly, television content becomes an occasion for the exercise of pre-existing knowledge and attitudes.

During the course of the campaign, Rick Mercer seized upon an item in the platform of the Canadian Alliance Party, that a referendum could be launched if three percent of voters signed on. Many suspected that the Alliance Party would use the provision to introduce legislation criminalizing abortion, legalizing gun ownership, directing public money to religious education, and so on. In the context of one broadcast, Mercer launched a spoof referendum. He invited viewers to sign on to his website where, with 3 percent of voters, he would launch a referendum forcing Stockwell Day, leader of the Alliance Party, to change his name to Doris Day. The response was immediate and overwhelming. The website very rapidly collected approximately one million signatures.[8] Mercer's point was political: he wished to demonstrate his opposition to the referendum measure by showing how it could lead to mischief. It is fair to say that he achieved his goal in a highly effective manner.

From a media perspective, however, the Mercer spoof also demonstrated several other aspects of the campaign. The first is that many television viewers are also Internet users. A television audience, therefore, can also be one of the many audiences of the Internet. The audience can bring its skills, attitudes, background knowledges, and so on, from one medium to another. The event also demonstrates the ease with which an audience can give a political item — one particular plank of a political party's platform — an utterly unintended inflection. Not only was Mercer's use of the platform unintended by the Alliance Party, and unexpected by voters, but there was virtually no support for it in other media: no orchestrated advertising campaign urged voters to sign on to the website, no political personality spoke in its favour, no other media covered the event as more than a curiosity, etc. And yet, it was probably the defining moment of the 2000 campaign because it showed not only the merging of television and the Internet but also because it emphatically demonstrated the sophistication of the television audience, its *unavailability* to traditional modes of persuasion and its *distance* from the presumption that what it consumes determines what it thinks. This was an entirely oppositional political act that also undermines the thesis that oppositional voices are always shut out from the media.

Consequently, while it would be foolish to deny absolutely the possibility of television impact, it would be equally imprudent to dwell upon it as a sole or determining factor. Audiences are more sophisticated than the discourse of alarm and concern allows. Indeed, by now, television coverage of elections has reached a level of maturity in which television producers and audiences are fully aware of the criticisms and respond to them in their very production and viewing practices.

But the sophistication of the audience, characterized by its fragmentation, its ironic relationship to content, its awareness of the history of the medium and its forms, its conversance with the style and grammar of television merely raises new questions about a new medium, the Internet.

The Internet

The general election of 2000 was Canada's inaugural Internet election simply by virtue of the fact that all actors in the political process were present and active online throughout the campaign. From the five dominant political parties to fringe parties, and from the traditional news media to entertainment media, upstart independent website operators, and even many individual voters, the volume of Canadian online political content continued to grow throughout the campaign. The general election of 2000 was particularly noteworthy for the introduction of an unofficial new "beat" to traditional election campaign coverage — the politics in cyberspace reporter. Emerging from this new beat was a groundswell of coverage on how the election campaign was played out online.[9] While the wealth of coverage of politics in cyberspace was clearly in response to a novel development in Canadian election campaigns, and therefore deserving of journalistic attention, media interest in the Internet during the campaign also served to meet growing demand for content from the increasingly fragmented spectrum of Canadian news and specialty television channels.

While politics in cyberspace was a "hot topic," the limitations of current technologies, as well as limited understanding — and maybe even imagination — as to how they might be used to cover Canadian election campaigns mitigated some of the great expectations placed on their possibilities prior to the campaign. Technological failure at critical junctures in the campaigns served as timely reminders that long-established patterns of conducting and reporting on politics will not be quickly or easily replaced. However, the traditional media players and some independent political websites achieved a critical success in election 2000 by first recognizing, and then creating, products and services to meet the growing demand of the political Internet audience. This success suggests that the Internet will likely play an even more prominent role in future campaigns. In many ways election 2000 demonstrated that the fragmented niche market of Canadian political news consumers is large enough to justify the development and provision of specialized news products.

While it is not clear that the Internet will displace television as the dominant medium for delivering political news coverage, it is now obvious that the reach of traditional media can be complemented, and even extended, by directing audiences online for a more interactive, expanded, and converged multimedia news experience.

Jumping on the Online Bandwagon

Canadian household Internet use statistics for the month of November 2000 revealed significantly increased traffic at many political web destinations, including the Elections Canada website (Elections.ca) and the official Canadian Alliance party website (CanadianAlliance.ca), both of which had never before registered on the Media Metrix web measurement tracking system.[10] This occurred in the context of a year in which PricewaterhouseCoopers reported that per capita Internet use by Canadians has surpassed per capita use by Americans for the first time ever.[11] All five political parties with official party status had a web presence during the election campaign; indeed some form of web presence is clearly not a strategic decision anymore, but rather a bare necessity. On the whole, though, the parties' online offerings were lacklustre, suggesting that they accept the reality of the new medium and the need to meet a bare minimum but that they have not fully thought through its true political utility or value.

Capitalizing on their advantage in determining the timing of the election call, the Liberals demonstrated the importance they placed on their website by relaunching Liberal.ca the day of the election call. However, the Liberal web strategy for election 2000 did not capitalize on any of the unique features of the Internet. Consequently, the Liberal website contained no interactive elements, such as discussion forums, and no multimedia such as real audio or video files. Liberal.ca also provided no contact information beyond an e-mail form that allowed visitors to express an interest in volunteering or donating to the party. But the form allowed only the *expression* of interest, not an actual donation of time or money. The omission of an online credit card donation function was particularly surprising given the online fundraising success of United States Senator John McCain a few months earlier.[12] It also illustrates the distant embrace which characterized political party use of the Internet in election 2000.

The Canadian Alliance, which in its previous incarnation as the Reform Party had been positioning itself at the forefront of Internet use as a strategic political tool, ran a surprisingly status quo online campaign, perhaps being caught off-guard by the timing of the election. CanadianAlliance.ca was plagued by over-ambitious web design that in many cases served only to alienate Internet surfers using less sophisticated computers and web browsers. While the Canadian Alliance homepage was undeniably attractive, featuring cool blue and green tones, it often took several minutes to open, far longer than the average household Internet user is prepared to wait. And while the Canadian Alliance did surpass the Liberals in employing some of the unique features of the Internet, such as signing up volunteers and accepting online credit card donations, it also failed to embrace the hallmark feature of the Internet, namely interactive discussion forums and chat.

On the content side, demonstrating their considerable financial and human resources, both the Liberals and the Canadian Alliance offered copious fresh written content, updating their respective sites almost daily throughout the campaign. New content generally consisted of an occasional photograph from the campaign trail, but more often consisted of written political spin documents such as talking points, press releases, backgrounders, and quote documents, all aimed at countering their opponents' campaign trail claims. To its credit, the NDP countered this activity with a section on NDP.ca called a "Surreality Check." Most of the material in these sections may have been targeted directly at journalists rather than the general public, as the minutiae of these partisan campaign tactics likely escaped the interest or attention of all but the most politically active Internet users.

The Progressive Conservative party attempted, if not always successfully, to offer some multimedia and interactive features on its party website. PCParty.ca offered video links to its American-style attack television ads and to a speech by party leader Joe Clark. The site also featured the ability to accept online credit card donations, and an extensive photo gallery. However, it provided no space for discussion forums or chat. It is perhaps not surprising that the party with the most to gain and the most to lose in the campaign tried to explore the potential of this cost-effective yet controlled-image medium. The key failure of PCParty.ca was that it was not maintained as the campaign progressed. With little fresh content added over the course of the thirty-five-day campaign, the site seemed to fall by the wayside in the face of limited resources and more pressing campaign matters.

The Bloc Québécois ran an interesting online campaign. Tightly focused on its core constituency, BlocQuebecois.org was for all practical purposes unilingual French. The site design and content demonstrated a somewhat more sophisticated knowledge of Internet user demographics, specifically targeting those who may be more likely to go online for political information, namely younger voters. Of course, the Bloc did have the advantage of only having to target one quarter of the Canadian population and a much more limited Internet user base. Of the 12.3 million Canadian Internet users, only 2.3 million are francophone.[13] The Canadian Alliance ran a significantly more sophisticated online *advertising* campaign than any of the other parties, including a high volume of targeted banner advertising on election pages of traditional media websites. Later in the campaign, the Liberals also twigged to the concept of online advertising, running some click-through banners on both traditional media and independent political websites.

One significant online development in this campaign was the rather sophisticated organization demonstrated by some of the fringe parties, most notably the Marijuana party (Marijuana.org) and the Green party

(Green.ca). Both parties were keenly attuned to how the election was playing in cyberspace and devoted considerable resources to promoting their respective agendas online and via e-mail. While their efforts clearly did not translate into electoral success, they did succeed in employing a Web strategy to raise awareness by generating coverage in the traditional media.

Consistent with findings from studies of how the Internet was used by American politicians in the 1996 presidential campaign, the five major Canadian political parties approached their website strategies much like an advertising tool, featuring carefully chosen photographs of leaders, party platform documents, and critiques of their opponents. There was nothing to offend or alienate party loyalists, and as such party websites would tend to reaffirm decided voters, not sway the undecided. Also similar to observations of how American news organizations used the Internet in the 1996 presidential race, in the federal election of 2000 Canadian news organizations tended to make rather civic-minded and innovative use of the web to enhance their role as key providers of political news and enhancing that role by providing other information useful in the democratic process as well as forums for information and opinion.

For example, *The Globe and Mail* website featured an "Election 2000 Hub," a specialized election homepage from which it offered online access to the election news stories from the print version of the newspaper, as well as some original online election coverage, and a variety of other resources including leader profiles, a "riding finder" searchable database keyed by postal code, a "candidate finder" searchable database, voter registration information, discussion forums on campaign issues, an election photo gallery, and numerous other features. Following the election, the hub remained active and featured a week by week headline review from the election campaign. The CBC.ca portal website also featured an election hub which, in addition to news content from the various CBC services, featured analysis by CBC reporters, leader profiles, Canadian election history, a campaign calendar, discussion areas, riding profiles, and many other voter resources. CBC also used its website to recruit people to attend town-hall meetings held in Halifax and Vancouver.

Nearly all major Canadian media organizations, including most large market daily newspapers, the major broadcasters, and many radio stations offered some form of special online election feature. Not surprisingly, the traditional media broadcasters led the way in providing streaming audio and video via their websites. CTV, CBC, and Global TV all featured written news items derived from their television (and radio in the case of CBC) content as well as audio or video on demand links. Many traditional media websites also featured some unique content that was not broadcast or did not appear in print. CTV profiled technology correspondent Mark Schneider's commentary on the election in cyberspace and the CBC website featured guest election columnists Larry Zolf and Rex Murphy. The continuous updating of election news on GlobeandMail.com, with reporters filing in real time and appearing to work around the clock, complemented the news material from the print edition and elevated the quality of the online coverage above that of its competitors. Cnews, which is operated by Canoe.ca and includes the Sun newspaper chain and a few other daily newspapers, also featured a dedicated election page under the banner Decision 2000. One of the more simple, yet effective features offered by virtually every large media organization was a headline summary service, sent daily via e-mail to subscribers, generally before 8:00 a.m. or at the end of the business day. The summaries, which featured brief story teasers and direct links to the election coverage featured on a given media organization's website, served the dual purpose of providing additional and targeted specialty news products for hosting banner advertising and creating a returning user-base to the media websites.

In sum, online campaign coverage by the traditional media of the general election of 2000 provided a glimpse of the potential of the Internet for reducing the time, effort and cost required by individuals to gather political information, if not analyze it and put it to good use.

A New Political News Beat: Politics in Cyberspace

The Canadian general election of 2000 may best be remembered for introducing a new beat to Canadian news consumers: politics in cyberspace. In most cases it was an unofficial beat, but there were a few reporters uniquely assigned to cover the role of the Internet in the election campaign. Whether assigned full or part time to covering this beat, whether posted online only or also included in traditional news delivery, journalists across the spectrum of traditional media produced volumes of content on the subject.[14] Media coverage initially focused on how political parties were using the Internet as a strategic political tool, but quickly shifted to coverage of fabricated Internet "events" and independent Internet entrepreneurs and enthusiasts when it became apparent that the political parties were not doing much. Considerable media coverage simply focused on small independent websites that featured innovative political twists on a standard Internet application such as databases, polling technology or the aggregation of existing online information and into more organized or user-friendly formats.[15]

Some of the more notable online events of the campaign, however, involved the major parties, especially the Liberals and the Canadian Alliance, running up against upstart Internet entrepreneurs, spoof site operators, and cybersquatters. In a move rather contrary to both their typical freedom of speech posturing and their previously avant-garde approach to online politicking, the Canadian Alliance came out swinging at one spoof site operator who, under the domain name CanadianAllianceParty.net, created a site with the same look and feel as the official Canadian Alliance site, but featuring content strongly critical of the Canadian Alliance.[16] The Liberals also ran into an Internet entrepreneur cum cybersquatting company who had purchased the domain names of fifty-two Liberal candidates and wanted to sell them back to the Liberal party for $35,000.[17]

The Canadian federal election of 2000 saw its share of negative online content in the context of what was widely reported to be one of the most negative campaigns in Canadian history. Spoof and attack websites drifted in and out of national media coverage throughout the election campaign. Narrowly focused, often on a single issue or politician, many of these sites were more notable for their colourful domain names than the content they featured. Prime Minister Jean Chrétien was targeted, as were Justice Minister Anne McLellan, Human Resources Minister Jane Stewart, and Health Minister Allan Rock. But the greatest online venom was directed at Canadian Alliance leader Stockwell Day. One of the most extreme examples was one that likened Canadian Alliance leader Stockwell Day to World War II Italian fascist leader Benito Mussolini, including a photograph of Stockwell Day's head superimposed on a photograph of the body of a marching and uniformed Mussolini.[18]

As the Internet matures, some predict it may increasingly become an outlet for more extreme political discourse than is found in the traditional mass media. As one politics in cyberspace commentator noted, "when the political Internet was in its nascent stage, do-gooders and political Dudley Do-Rights of the world touted the medium as a savior that would solve all sorts of problems. With the [year 2000 U.S. presidential] election season on us, it's clear that the medium has grown up. Not only are there hundreds of parody sites, there are some not-so-nice things going on online."[19] Online activity during Canada's election 2000 suggests this trend is not unique to the United States.

Hitting the Wall: The Unrealized Potential of
Canadian Politics in Cyberspace

While enthusiasm for the novel and innovative offerings online in the Canadian federal election of 2000 was inspiring, it did not go unchecked. At two critical junctures in the campaign — English debate night on Nov. 9 and election night on Nov. 27 — the limitations of the Internet in Canadian politics became glaringly obvious. A widely promoted CTV News — Ipsos-Reid joint Internet experiment to superimpose the results of instantaneous Internet polling of a 500 viewer-strong web audience onto television screens following each of the major ten to fifteen minute segments of the English language leaders' debate failed. Slow servers were identified as the "technical problem" that resulted in the plan being abandoned after the first segment of the debate on social justice issues.

Server problems were also the culprit on election night, as most major media websites were completely overwhelmed when voting results began pouring in from across the country between 10:00 and 10:30 p.m. CBC.ca took several minutes to load and CTVNews.com crashed at around 10:15 p.m. Canoe.ca was slow throughout the evening and NationalPost.com crashed numerous times beginning around 10:30 p.m. and went off-line altogether around 10:50 p.m. Interestingly, the only major media website not to crash, GlobeandMail.com, used this fact to market itself in the days following election night.[20] Any discussion of the Internet supplanting the dominance of established media in election coverage is premature until such time as the Internet is more technically reliable. At the same time, however, the current technology does offer the opportunity to enhance traditional coverage and expand specialized news products for growing and increasingly fragmented niche news markets.

The Internet Audience:
Growing Demand in the Political Niche Market

News organizations used the traditional media, television, radio and newspapers, to great effect to promote their websites. The lead election story on the nightly newscasts invariably concluded with a cross-media promotional phrase suggesting viewers "visit our website at www-dot ... for more election campaign coverage," giving their own websites valuable free advertising.

Nowhere was the power of cross-media promotion more evident than the now infamous "This Hour Has 22 Minutes" petition to trigger a referendum on having Stockwell Day change his first name to Doris. By tapping into the popularity of their own brand of political satire, both the novelty and the unique features of the Internet and the broader spectrum of Canadian popular culture, "22 Minutes" turned a joke — albeit one with political impact — into one of the more significant political Internet stories of the election campaign, if for no other reason than because 900,000 people logged on to sign the petition within the first week. This remarkable movement would not have been possible without the loyal television audience the show enjoys.[21] A more promising and perhaps meaningful way in which the entertainment media used cross-media promotion to capitalize on the broad appeal of popular culture and higher notions of promoting democracy could be found on the Canadian popular music channel MuchMusic and its website MuchMusic.com. During its regularly scheduled after-school "RapidFax" segment, MuchMusic aired a daily "news" feature on the election campaign, tied in with its special online election package, MuchVote 2000. In addition to basic voter information for younger voters, such as how to get on the voter registration list, the MuchMusic.com election package featured the results of a survey of the five official party leaders on issues geared to a younger constituency.

Given that the time required for new sites to become registered in most search engines is far longer than the duration of the election campaign, traffic to these sites was generally a function of the attention they received from the traditional media. In the online versions of traditional media coverage, direct links to sites being reported on were often imbedded within the text of the story making it easy for the news consumer to check out the site in question for themselves. This in turn led to marked increases in traffic to those sites lucky or strategic enough to be featured in the traditional media. As traffic to independent sites increased, what would otherwise have been just one among billions of sites on the World Wide Web became all the more newsworthy, not necessarily because of their content or catchy domain names but because they were now overnight success stories.

Clearly, the new voices that emerged online during this election campaign, many sponsored by neither major political parties nor traditional media, provide some evidence of the potential of the Internet to enhance and expand upon the community-building role of traditional media. However, the proliferation of single-issue, narrowly focused spoof and attack sites and the fringe views and lack of substantive debate that overwhelmed many discussion forums during this campaign suggest that in its nascent stage the Internet may in some cases be little more than a semi-anonymous, quasi-public space for airing extreme views within like-minded groups.[22]

Conclusion

The Internet is indeed changing the established political media ecology in so far as it is having an impact on the way news organizations organize, collect, report, and present political news. Further, the Internet demonstrated just how effectively it can cater to the ongoing fragmentation of the news market and the growing niche of political news consumers.

Although the legitimacy of the Internet as a means of political communication increased considerably during the course of Election 2000, the impact of this new medium was mitigated by some key factors. From a technological perspective, the Internet proved to be only semi-reliable at critical, high demand moments. Until such time as the approach and applications are refined, expectations for the Internet to pose a significant challenge to the dominance of television, or other traditional media for that matter, will go unrealized. While it is not clear that the Internet will displace television as the dominant medium for delivering political news coverage, it is now obvious that the reach of traditional media can be complemented and even extended by converging news audiences online for a more interactive, expanded and multimedia news experience.

Backed by big budgets and the competitive spirit, the traditional media demonstrated in this election that they are at the forefront in Internet use, offering innovative online political coverage and voter resources; tools and resources that would not have otherwise been available to Canadians over the election campaign. Further, Election 2000 did demonstrate that the Internet may facilitate an increased presence of third party voices in the electoral process. Third parties proved that the Internet, if approached strategically, can garner significant media attention and coverage for their issues. The overall impact at this point in the evolution of the Internet, however, remains unclear. This uncertainty over the utility and reach of political communication on the Internet is the common thread in how all actors in the political process approached this new medium in Election 2000. From the conservative, minimalist approach of the major political parties to the experimental, aggressive approach of large traditional news organizations, to the innovative, novel approach of Internet entrepreneurs, politics in cyberspace post-Election 2000 will give rise to higher and more specialized expectations among Canada's online political news audience.

Works Consulted

Bonisteel, Steven. "Canadian Election Colors Web-Traffic Stats: Report." *Newsbytes.com* (December 20, 2000).

Calamai, Peter. "Internet attacks with a serious thrust: Political protests on Web a far cry from heckling." *TheStar.com* (November 15, 2000).

Calamai, Peter. "Panel of Web experts name their favourite political sites: PoliticsWatch.com and Policy.ca top the list." *TheStar.com* (November 18, 2000).

CBC.ca. "Websites put the 'e' in federal e-lection." *CBC.ca* (October 24, 2000).

Dayan, Daniel and Elihu Katz. "Defining Media Events: High Holidays of Mass Communicaiton" in Horace Newcomb (ed.), *Television The Critical View*. New York, Oxford University Press, 1994 pp. 332-351.

Desautels, Vincent. "Les règles du jeu." *Le Devoir*, November 14, 2000, p. B7.

Kapica, Jack. "Alliance spoof sites threatened." *GlobeandMail.com* (November 2, 2000).

Kapica, Jack. "Websites defy broadcast ban, others crash." *GlobeandMail.com* (November 29, 2000).

Kershner, Vlae. "Finding serious political discourse among all the online illiteracy." *SanFranciscoChronicle.com* (August 2, 2000).

Kinsella, Warren. "The spin doctor strikes back." *The Ottawa Citizen*, November 28, 2000, p. A15.

Lawton, Valerie, and Allan Thompson. "Media watch a two-horse race." *The Toronto Star*, November 3, 2000, p. A7.

McGregor, Glen. "'Cyber squatter' buys up Liberal domain names: Firm asks candidates for $35,000 for rights to their names." *OttawaCitizen.com* (Oct. 20, 2000).

MacKinnon, Mark. "Fringe debate features less yelling, more yogic flying." *The Globe and Mail*, November 20, 2000, p. A1.

Newcomb, Horace (ed.). *Television: The Critical View* (1994). New York: Oxford University Press.

NUA Internet Surveys. "Language divides Canadian Web users." *NUA.ie/surveys* (Dec. 11, 2000).

PoliticsOnline.com. "Most Valuable Internet Player of the Year 2000." *Net Pulse: The e-journal of politicking on the Internet* 5(1) Jan. 2, 2001.

PoliticsOnline.com. "Dirty dancing: Online campaigning grows up." *Net*

Pulse: The e-journal of politicking on the Internet 4(13) July 5, 2000.

PoliticsOnline.com. "Neat idea: Satire petition." *Net Pulse: The e-journal of politicking on the Internet* 4(23) Dec. 4, 2000.

Power, Bill. "Protesters target CBC debate." *The Chronicle-Herald*, Sunday, November 12, 2000.

Sikstrom, Mark. "Coolest campaign clicks on the Web." *CTVNews.com* (Nov. 12, 2000).

Wall Street Journal. "Business Bulletin: The Internet is hottest in the Great White North." *WSJ.com* (Dec. 21, 2000).

NOTES

2   For example, on the night of the English-language leaders debate held in Ottawa, "placard-waving members of a mix of advocacy organizations" marched on the CBC studios in Halifax in order to make themselves heard (Power, 2000). The television studio, rather than some other venue, appeared to be the most logical place to stage a demonstration.

3   *The Toronto Star* raised the issue explicitly on November 3, 2000 (p. A7) under the headline: "Media watch a two-horse race, Reporters scarce on campaign buses of NDP, Tories." To this may be added the complaints that the media ignored or gave insufficient coverage to arts funding, health care, the environment, and smaller or "third" political parties.

4   This was specifically the concern of Hugh Winsor's column of November 27, 2000 (*The Globe and Mail*, p. A7) titled "Media laid minefields in race" in which he stated: "There is only one undisputed winner in this election campaign — the media ... every other major development in the campaign has been initiated in some way by the media rather than the political actors themselves."

5   Liberal campaign advisor Warren Kinsella said as much in *The Ottawa Citizen*, November 28, 2000, p. A15: "I can count on one hand the number of times a reporter called up to discuss actual bona fide policy issues. It did not matter, it seems, that 60 percent of Canadians were saying that they considered health care to be their biggest concern. It did not matter that a sizeable number also wanted to discuss taxation. No, what interested reporters were trivialities."

6   The election 2000 debates in both French and English were watched by roughly 55 percent of voters, a remarkable number for a single-occurrence television event in Canada. (The 55 percent number is also reported by Marzolini while Pammett mentions 53% (page 308).)

7   Examples of this type of television research can be found in David Morley's *The "Nationwide" Audience* and *Family Television: Cultural Power and Domestic Leisure*, Lynn Spigel's *Make Room for TV*, Ellen Seiter's *Remote Control: Television, Audiences and Cultural Power*, William Boddy's *Fifties Television*, Ien Ang's *Desperately Seeking the Audience*, amongst others.

8   This figure should be treated with some caution, however. Web users could go directly to the "22 Minutes" website to register their vote or reach it through various links on other sites. However, it was also possible for a single person to vote several times. The figures, therefore, contains an unknowable number of repeat votes.

9   For example, as Editor of PoliticsWatch.com, Angela Burton was asked to comment on federal political party websites in a piece that ran on CBC's "Sunday Report" the night of the election call. The piece was subsequently posted online at on October 24 under the headline "Websites put the 'e' in federal e-lection." She was repeatedly called on to participate in panel discussions and to comment on a variety of different issues related to politics in cyberspace throughout the campaign, up to and including an interview on election night, November 27, on CBC Newsworld "Today."

10   Bonisteel, *Newsbytes.com* , Dec. 20, 2000.

11   Business Bulletin, *The Wall Street Journal* , Dec. 21, 2000.

12   Upon naming Senator John McCain their Most Valuable Internet Player of 2000, PoliticsOnline in *Net Pulse: The e-journal of politicking on the Internet* 5(1) Jan. 2, 2001 commented: "Sen. John McCain's New Hampshire primary win served as the spark that made politicos realize the importance of online fundraising. McCain, who raised $1 million online in just two days after the [New Hampshire primary], raked in the bucks and became every campaign's bellwether to measure online fundraising success."

13   NUA Internet Surveys, *NUA.ie/surveys*, Dec. 11, 2000.

14   According to the PoliticsOnline.com *2nd Annual Media Index of Politics and the Internet in the News*, the total number of politics in cyberspace news stories jumped 170 percent from 1999 to 2000 in

the United States. Internationally, coverage of online politics also increased, up 130 percent from 1999.

15 For example, CTVNews.com politics in cyberspace reporter Mark Sikstrom and *Toronto Star* reporter Peter Calamai both featured the same two sites www.CanadianDebate.com and www.Politics Watch.com in these types of articles. CanadianDebate.com organized the party platforms of all political parties (large and fringe) into a database that permitted users to compare where the parties stood on the issues. PoliticsWatch.com offered up a daily cross-media headline review and the PM Picker Vote Selector Quiz where users could fill out a survey to assess their stance on 15 key election issues and then see how their views compared with those of the five major party leaders.

16 Jack Kapica reported online at on Nov. 2, 2000 that the owner of CanadianAllianceParty.net received a letter from Canadian Alliance lawyers by e-mail ordering him to shut the site down because it "constitutes a serious infringement of the rights of the Canadian Alliance." At the time site owner / operator Mike Gifford said he would keep the site up and running. True to his word, more than a month after election day the site is still up.

17 Glen McGregor, a reporter for *The Ottawa Citizen*, wrote on Oct. 20 that the company, Toronto-based Computer Edutainment Canada, had initially bought the domain names hoping to get a contract to develop Websites for the 52 candidates in question for $2,500 each. However, Liberal party national director Terry Mercer refused the offer, saying the party intended to develop candidate Websites in-house. When the company then threatened to sell the domain names to opposition candidates instead, Mercer called the offer "blackmail."

18 As *Toronto Star* political reporter Peter Calamai wrote in an article headlined "Internet attacks with a serious thrust" on Nov. 15, the site goes much further, drawing comparisons between Day and Mussolini, noting that both were pro-life and both called for a united alternative to left leaning politicians. The site also features mock Canadian Alliance propaganda resembling that produced by Italian fascists during World War II, and a graphic photo of Mussolini's dead body hanging after he was executed.

19 *Net Pulse: The e-journal of politicking on the Internet* 4(13) July 5, 2000.

20 Kapica. Nov. 29, 2000.

21 Incidentally, the "22 Minutes" petition was also featured as a 'Neat

Idea' by PoliticsOnline in *Net Pulse: The e-journal of politicking on the Internet* 4(23) Dec. 4, 2000 which noted: "Que sera sera. A Canadian cyber-petition that started as a political satire took on a life of its own. A TV show (www.22minutes.com) launched a petition that demanded Canadian Alliance leader Stockwell Day change his name to "Doris" after the party said it would pass legislation to put any petition signed by more than 3 percent of voters on a national referendum. Within a week, the petition had 900,000 signatures — 9 percent of the electorate."

22 Commenting on online political discussion stemming from the Republican National Convention, *San Francisco Chronicle* journalist Vlae Kershner wrote on August 2, 2000 that "one of the Internet's biggest disappointments is that while it is supposed to empower individuals to discuss issues seriously, much of the discussion that really occurs is illiterate ranting."

Chapter 10

After the Polls Closed:
The Race to Publish Results

by Mary McGuire and Janice Neil

Election night 2000 promised to be very different from other election nights for people who want results quickly and for the journalists who provide them. By the year 2000 all major national news organizations were providing breaking news online, competing to be first on their websites with major stories such as the death of Pierre Trudeau or the election call. Until the 2000 election, real-time election results, as the ballots were counted, had always been the exclusive domain of traditional broadcasters. Television anchors, reporters, analysts, pundits, and even comedians provided play-by-play reporting of the results as they came in. Networks raced to scoop each other to declare the winner first. Newspapers weighed in the morning after with context, analysis, commentary, and details of riding-by-riding results. All that changed with the 2000 election. Now that the Internet had allowed newspapers to join the game once dominated by broadcasters, Canadians had more choices on election night than ever. In addition to, or even instead of, watching their favourite network, they could log on to the Internet to follow the results provided online, by national broadcasters such as the CBC, CTV, and Global, by national newspapers such as *The Globe and Mail* and the *National Post*, by Internet-based companies such as Sympatico, by Elections Canada itself, and even by a rebel with his own website. And they did, in numbers that surprised even people in the online news business.

Getting individual riding results promised to be a lot easier online than on television. Because of the linear nature of a television broadcast, riding results could only be pumped out one riding at a time in a graphic on the screen. The non-linear nature of the Internet, on the other hand, meant online users should be able to call up the results of any riding, any time.

The reality on election night was somewhat different. Going online for results proved disappointing for many who found pages that wouldn't load, sites that were not available, and results that seemed slower than what was available on television. Many of those who went online found most, though not all, news organizations failed to live up to expectations for reasons both within and beyond their control. Still, some Internet-savvy Canadians hungry for early results managed to find them, thanks to a software developer in British Columbia out to challenge the Canada Elections Act. And, although the Internet did not provide the competition it might have for election night viewers this time, it did have a clear and distinct influence on the nature of the television coverage.

One of the biggest challenges faced by the news media on election night is the Canadian law prohibiting the publication of election results in any region where the polls had not yet closed. While Americans living on the West coast have always been able to tune in to live coverage of election night results as soon as the polls closed in the East, hours before their own polls closed, Canadians have not. Election law prohibits anyone from publishing results from the east in places where the polls are still open. Section 329 of the Canada Elections Act states:

> No person shall transmit the result or purported result of the vote in an electoral district to the public in another electoral district before the close of all of the polling stations in that other electoral district.[1]

To break the law is to risk a fine of up to $25,000.

Broadcasters have traditionally complied with the law by blocking their election night feeds to regions where the polls are still open. So, when the polls close in Atlantic Canada, people living there can tune in to live election night specials while Canadians elsewhere can only see regular programming. When the polls close in Central Canada, the election night feeds are extended to include Central Canada. It is a practice that has worked for years and was followed again on November 27, 2000.

For online news producers, however, complying with the law was more challenging. Access to websites cannot be blocked by region, though news organizations tried to find a way to do it. They concluded there was no way to publish election results from the east and prevent people living elsewhere from reading them.

Some online news organizations such as the CBC had been providing breaking news online for a few years. Others, like CTV News and

The Globe and Mail had only set up separate online news operations to produce breaking news online in the year 2000. The *National Post* was also expanding its online news operation. For all of them, election night was an enormous opportunity. It would give them a chance to try to satisfy and even cultivate the growing appetite of Canadians for news online; to establish themselves as leaders in the business of providing news online; and to provide new kinds of coverage not available on television or in the newspaper.

They were stymied, in part, by Elections Canada blackout rules. They knew that the nature of the Internet meant anyone with a computer and Internet access could spread news about the election results as soon as they were made public in Eastern Canada and probably escape detection. But if newspapers did it, they would be caught. Neil A. Campbell, the man in charge of *The Globe and Mail*'s online publication, said "If I lived in Newfoundland and wanted to set up a small results reporting website with friends across the country, chances are nobody would ever notice. But if I were a maverick in B.C. who had a site and put out a press release bragging about it then I would expect to get caught. And, if I were *The Globe and Mail*, I would be sure I was going to get caught."[2]

In the end, none of the major news organizations took the risk. Instead they waited until all the polls had closed in British Columbia before publishing any results on their websites. That meant, for example, that Eastern Canadians had the results on television and radio shortly after the polls closed at 7:30 EST but would find nothing at media websites until 10 p.m. EST. Similarly people living in Quebec, Ontario, Manitoba, Saskatchewan, and Alberta were getting results on television shortly after the polls closed at 9:30 EST but could not get the results at media websites until after 10 p.m. So, the possibilities offered by the Internet on election night were not realized in full, thanks to Elections Canada.

The Early Blackout Period

Not surprisingly, Elections Canada was not entirely successful in preventing the spread of early results online. The biggest challenge came from an unlikely source — a thirty-year-old software developer in Burnaby, B. C., Paul Bryan. He saw section 329 of the Elections Act as an unreasonable restriction on freedom of speech. He said "The gag law is a serious threat that could infringe on our rights on the Internet. I take freedom of speech very seriously."[3]

He took up the cause following the federal by-elections in September 2000. In two separate by-elections on the same day, Joe Clark, the Progressive Conservative party leader, was elected in the Nova Scotia riding of King's Hant and Stockwell Day, the Canadian Alliance leader, was elected in the B.C. riding of Okanagan Coquihalla. At the time, results from the Nova Scotia by-election were published online before the polls closed in B.C. A few days later, police confiscated the computer of Ivan Smith, a Nova Scotia man they believed was responsible. It was enough to motivate Bryan to launch his challenge. He said, "If we don't stand up for our rights, they go away. I wasn't willing to sit idly by and watch that happen."[4]

He set up a website at electionresultscanada.com and promised to post early results on November 27th. He kept his promise. The page displayed results shortly after the polls closed in Newfoundland at 6:30 p.m. EST and updated them every few minutes for the next three hours. Bryan is coy about exactly where he was on election night but says he got the results by watching the CBC television's feed to Atlantic Canada from a satellite dish. He typed the results in, by hand, on his web page, which was hosted on a server in San Antonio, Texas.

He managed to keep up until the results came pouring in from Central Canada, and he could no longer type fast enough. At that point, he had hoped to connect to the Elections Canada website, which had promised to post results at 10 p.m. EST. But he found the same problem anyone else visiting the Elections Canada site that night did — the site was unstable and very slow to post results. When he found better results at media websites, shortly after 10 p.m. EST, he created a page that read "Mission Accomplished" and directed his visitors to visit media sites for further results.

During the time Paul Bryan was posting results, his page was accessible, popular and simple. He provided no stories, no analysis, no photos, no fancy graphics, and no declarations of likely winners — just raw results from individual ridings showing who was leading and how many polls had reported. He says he had 500,000 "page views" that night. A page view is a record of a web page being requested by an Internet user. On newsgroups such as can.politics there were also a number of postings from people asking for the address of his or any website where early results were being posted.

Days later, he, too, was visited by the police who seized two of his hard drives and his VISA card statements because they included charges for the server he used in Texas to publish the results. While he has yet to be charged, as of February 2001, he said some people are raising money for him so that he can fight any charges as unconstitutional. He also said authorities may have a difficult time proving where he was on election night and, if they can't verify that he was in Canada, he may argue he was not subject to Canadian law.

Paul Bryan succeeded where the media organizations did not. He was first with results and his site survived the stampede of Internet users in search of early news.

He wasn't entirely alone. Other brief stories about early results appeared on Yahoo Canada a full hour and a half before the polls closed in Central Canada; in a story by the international news service, Reuters, published on various websites; in a story dated 9:10 p.m. EST from Associated Press, which was picked up by several American papers and published on their websites; and, in a story published by ABC News on its website before the polls had all closed in Canada. News about early results was also published in messages at sites such as cnn.com from Eastern Canadians who wanted to spread the word.

There was also a Cape Breton radio station broadcasting live results on the Internet for a time, but when a *Globe and Mail* reporter called to ask about the decision to break the law, the station was quickly silenced. The station manager later said the broadcast was accidental.

Complying with the law posed a different challenge for television and radio networks on election night.

Until the election in 1997, polls closed at 8 p.m. local time across the country, which meant there were four-and-a-half hours between the time they closed from one end of the country to the other. The election night shows started in Newfoundland and extended west as the polls closed in Eastern, Central, and Prairie Canada and eventually in British Columbia. The three-hour period between the time the polls closed in Ontario and B.C. was always the most critical one. As the results from Ontario and Quebec poured in, staff at CBC, CTV, and Global examined the voting patterns and declared which party would form the next government and whether the government would be a majority or not.

So, in the past, by the time polls closed in B.C., election coverage would almost always begin there with the declaration of a winner — before a single ballot in the province had been counted.

In 1997, in part to reduce the risk of early results leaking out over the Internet, the law was changed to provide staggered hours for voting across the country. So, in 1997 and, again in 2000, polls closed in Newfoundland at 6:30 p.m. EST; in the Maritime provinces at 7:30 p.m. EST; in Ontario, Quebec, Manitoba, Saskatchewan, and Alberta at 9:30 p.m. EST and in British Columbia at 10 p.m. EST.

For broadcasters that meant they had hours to fill with nothing more than background reports and results from Atlantic Canada, then only half an hour to deal with a deluge of results from Central Canada and the prairie provinces before all the polls in the country closed. It meant each broadcaster had plenty of time to introduce many of the elements of their productions during the first few hours and, in some cases, that would be the only time those elements got to air, so viewers in the rest of the country would never see them. For instance, CBC's Atlantic desk with anchor Norma Lee McLeod in Halifax, had assembled a panel of analysts to talk about the region. She went on the air at 7:42 p.m. EST for almost ten minutes but no one west of the Atlantic saw the panels, nor did they return that night. An hour later, CBC TV assembled political operatives (for instance, the Progressive Conservative's Susan Elliot, the New Democrat's Tessa Hebb) to offer their partisan perspectives. Hebb returned to air at 00:21 after the polls closed in all the other regions and the Liberal majority was solid, and Elliot, ten minutes later. CTV had the same problem: "We used about one-fifth of the resources (we had set up)," Kirk Lapointe, Senior Vice-President of CTV News, reflected. "We had three dozen remotes [reporters in various around the country], we had extra people [pundits and other guests] ready to come into the studio but they never got on the air. We never got everything on the air that we wanted to."[5]

At 9:00 p.m. EST, when viewers in Quebec, Ontario, Manitoba, Saskatchewan, and Alberta signed on, there was still sixty minutes before the polls would close in B.C. (Viewers in Atlantic Canada continued to get a different live show with results.) Instead of results from the thirty-two eastern polls, viewers were treated to a "pre-game" show: CBC, which broadcast from Parliament Hill, showed off its majestic "set" (the Hall of Honour inside Centre Block), introduced its reporters, and aired taped pieces on how it would collect and report poll results and a segment on government trivia including the fact that 27 MPs with the surname MacDonald have been elected and almost as many (twenty-six) Smiths. Global News aired a piece in which random interviews with people on the street are asked "What would you do if you were Prime Minister?" and had its pollster of the evening, Conrad Winn, examine the results of public opinion polls taken during the fall. CTV News introduced some of its segments, pundits, and comedian Mike Bullard. They all reminded viewers that they were prohibited from reporting on the preliminary results of the polls in Eastern Canada. It was all an effort to fill airtime and to build suspense (CBC, CTV ran countdowns) to 9:30.

Dusk: After the Polls closed in Ontario

At 9:30 p.m. EST, when the polls closed in Central Canada, but remained open for another half an hour in B.C., online news producers could still do little but wait. Broadcasters, however, shifted into high gear. That slow, analytical pace on television evaporated as soon as the 234 polls in Ontario and Quebec polls closed. CTV's Lloyd Robertson was ebullient: "4, 3, 2, 1! Here are the results from Atlantic Canada." And so was the CBC: "The Liberals rebound in Atlantic Canada. They get an Atlantic cushion. But is it enough to lock in another Liberal majority? Good evening, I'm Peter Mansbridge...." Suddenly the anchors energetically bounced on air as they could finally reveal the preliminary results from Eastern Canada. The graphics from the Atlantic (with vote counts up to two hours old) were ready and displayed within seconds. Later, it took only six minutes after the polls closed in Manitoba before CBC TV displayed its first result from Winnipeg Transcona. CTV was slower, although its total MPs elected/leading began reflecting the new poll counts within four minutes and the first riding result was reported at 9:35 p.m. EST. Global TV was much slower; it didn't display any specific riding results west of the Atlantic until 9:58 p.m. EST.

Television networks, for most Canadians, beat the media news sites by a wide margin simply because they could produce results within Elections Canada rules by targeting the region where their signal was broadcast. So, Eastern Canadians could watch results for almost three hours as they were broadcast on the regional feeds of the national broadcasters — long before they could find them online at media websites.

249

The Blackout's Over: All the Polls close

As the moment arrived when the doors were being closed on all the polling stations in British Columbia, the online news sites were finally able to display what they had been hiding for hours.

The Globe and Mail site snuck in a few moments early with three stories indicating how well the Liberals had done in Atlantic Canada. Then, it provided a breakdown of the number of ridings where each of the parties was leading. It seemed to mirror what was available on television at the time. At 10:06 p.m. EST the *Globe and Mail* site led with a story that CTV News had projected a Liberal majority — just two minutes after the network became the first to declare the winner. It would be another sixteen minutes before CBC Television would project a Liberal majority, at which point the *Globe* refreshed its story with that news, too.

Throughout the night, *The Globe and Mail* site provided a series of stories about the latest developments. It also offered a number of interactive features such as charts, maps, and links for details about the popular vote, riding results, candidate information etc. For users interested in following the results of specific ridings, the *Globe* site made that easy to do. Internet users visited the site in record numbers. *The Globe and Mail*'s Neil Campbell said it got 1.26 million page views that night and 1.68 million the next day. He says on an average day the site gets 300,000 to 400,000 page views.[6]

What set the site apart from all the rest, though, was that it was accessible all night long. Before the election, Campbell said "We've put a massive effort into having a site that doesn't break down. We're expecting a surge in traffic that night and have added extra server capacity. We're also cutting back a little on some of the extras normally on the site so we can make the page easier to load. I don't know how much thought other sites are putting into this but we've been obsessed by it, because if nobody can get in the door, then it doesn't much matter how great your content is."[7]

It was an effort that made globeandmail.com the winner among online news sites that night. At almost all of the other online sites, pages would not load, connections timed out, and it became enormously frustrating for any user interested in following the election online or getting specific riding results.

When *The Globe and Mail* went online with breaking news in June of 2000, its biggest competition was cbc.ca, the CBC's online news operation. The CBC had been providing breaking news online for a number of years and was the veteran in the field. Despite all its experience, though, the CBC site did not work well on election night 2000. Our attempts to reach it at 10 p.m. EST resulted in network error messages. After several tries over a few minutes, we finally managed to load a page with four short stories about the results from Atlantic Canada. The link to the results page, however, yielded a message that the "server was busy." The link to a chat (a page where visitors join others in a discussion conducted through typed messages in real time) with Ralph Benmurgi did not work; nor did it ever seem to work that night. Another link to a general chat with other users failed and, although we tried it every fifteen minutes, we did not get through until 11:49 p.m. EST, though when we did get in, it was clear others had been there chatting for some time.

At 10:23 pm. EST a new headline appeared that read "Liberals will form a majority government." But the link to the full story took users to an old story about Ontario and Quebec being the keys to the election — a story that had been posted on the site before the polls closed and results were available. The link to what was the key story of the election call did not actually take us to a story about the declaration of a winner until 11 p.m. — almost an hour after the election had been called by CTV and posted on the *Globe* website, and almost forty minutes after it had been called by CBC television.

By 10:25 p.m. EST we were finally able to connect to the CBC results page where we were told the page would be updated every thirty seconds. The problem, however, was that every thirty seconds a message would appear saying the server was too busy to update the results. When we tried to link to individual ridings to track results, we often got messages saying the server was too busy to provide them. We also found more strange links to outdated stories. Under the main results table we found a headline at 11:09 EST which read "It's a Liberal government but too soon yet to say whether it's a majority or a minority." That was a full half hour after the site had posted a headline declaring a Liberal majority. For anyone who wanted to follow the election results, it was a most frustrating experience.

It was equally frustrating for the people responsible at the CBC. Ken Wolff, a producer at cbc.ca, said "technically we were not nearly as good as we should have been. The technical people screwed up."[8] He insists that the content they produced was excellent but admits too few people got to see it. Wolff said the CBC servers never actually crashed, though they were incredibly slow. Despite the problems, he said they still recorded the highest number of page views ever that day at 1.6 million, more than *The Globe and Mail*. He said he can only imagine how high the numbers would have been if error messages hadn't sent visitors clicking away to other sites.

While the *National Post* does not offer a lot of breaking news at its website yet, it set out to provide up-to-the-minute election coverage and real-time results on election night. But it, too, encountered technical problems that made it difficult for users to access information or follow results. Shortly after the polls closed, it posted stories about the Liberals making big gains, and the NDP and the Tories almost falling off the radar. By 10:30 p.m. EST, the pages were slow to load and we could not access the text of the stories. Ten minutes later a Canadian Press story appeared whose lead read: "Ontario's Liberals pulled out to an early lead in today's federal election, but remained far from another sweep of Canada's most populous province." By now both major networks had declared the Liberals the winner of a majority government. A few minutes later error messages appeared when we tried to reach the story. By 10:57 p.m. EST the Post was finally running a story headline that read "Chrétien to win majority government." But the Post did provide useful interactive features such as ways to find the results from individual ridings.

The producer of the *National Post Online*, Nancy DeHart, said the site never crashed, though it was slow at times. Still, the site had seven times more traffic than normal that night with 700,000 page views recorded on election day. She also reported that 10 percent of the traffic came from points outside Canada. According to DeHart, the *Post* simply didn't have the server capacity to handle the surge in traffic on election night. She said new servers had been ordered but such purchases had been frozen for a time when CanWest Global bought 50 percent the *National Post*.[9]

Canoe.ca, a website that showcases papers in the Sun Media chain owned by Quebecor, was also providing results on election night. As soon as the polls closed, Canoe's main page offered links to stories about the Liberals poised for a majority and the NDP's fortunes slipping in Eastern Canada. By 10:09 p.m. EST, there were numbers posted indicating how many seats each party had won. Results were also broken down by province and riding. The results were updated regularly through the next few hours. The stories, too, were updated regularly but it was not until 11:16 p.m. EST that we found a story declaring the Liberal victory. Art Chamberlain, the executive producer of Canoe's Cnews site, said the site was as quick to declare a winner as the networks, but he admitted the site was painfully slow to load for many visitors. He, too, said Canoe was not set up to handle the incredible surge in traffic it received that night. He said the site had 3.4 million page views on election day and 1.2 million on election night itself.

Sympatico provided some coverage, too. Its election page was not easy to find from its main page. It had links to several stories and to the CTV News website. After the polls closed, its pages were slow to load and the general results did not show up on the table until 10:53 p.m.

On election night, CTV News had ambitions to produce editorial synergy with its website, CTVnews.com. Launched in September 2000, the site is currently the most sophisticated broadband broadcast site in Canada providing real-time news stories, newscasts, background text, and video clips. The plan for election night was to turn the resources of the broadcast network loose on the website to provide "a complete package of materials for viewers: streamed video; background reports on polls; profiles of candidates; humour columns; analysis, reporter notebooks, chat rooms and searchable results.[10] But the service is demanding, technologically, because it operates best on high-speed service (cable or ADSL). While CTV said it received 42,000 unique visitors on election night,[11] our monitors and others outside of our site reported major problems loading the site. (Lapointe said visitors using a slower, 56k modem had fewer problems accessing at least some of the information.) What is impressive about the site is the enhancement of the information text with video clips. So, before 10:00 p.m. EST our monitor could read stories and watch video news clips about election day with excellent screen resolution (made possible through the broadband, 300k facility) and finely co-ordinated sound. After the polls closed in Newfoundland, the site posted a story on polls closing in Newfoundland with a video link but the link was misdirected to an older version about voters heading to the polls. By 10:04 p.m. EST, after all the polls in the country were closed, CTVnews.com was very slow to load or loaded only half a screen or text only, with a lead story quoting the CTV call for a majority government. A box on the right hand side of the screen offered "Election results." It lead to globeandmail.com (a link that *The Globe and Mail* purchased as an "advertisement"). By 10:35 p.m. EST the CTVnews.com site was frustrating to our monitors; the video screen did not work and only some of the text articles appeared when loading. It then became inaccessible for the rest of the broadcast period.

While the Internet did not live up to its promise, it did have a major impact on election night television coverage — on the way some information was gathered, and on the graphic style in which broadcasters presented their information.

Sensitive to charges that television news was produced by and for the elite, producers in the last two decades have attempted to become more populist by including views of "the voters" (in the newsroom vernacular, the "real people") in their programs. One common approach (non-scientific, somewhat random) was to send a reporter into a "family living room" or bar and capture the reactions of the viewers as they watched the election unfold. The reporter would probe as to how they voted and ask them to speculate as to why other Canadians voted the way they did. The Internet, then, provided another vehicle to "reach out" to the public, to gauge reaction and to try to understand the voting decisions. The three national broadcasters monitored for this study embraced the concept of interactivity, available to them via the Internet, in a diverse array of ways.

The most popular method of reaching out to viewers was simply asking them to telephone or e-mail their opinions. But without the visual backdrops of noisy bars or cluttered living rooms, they needed to make the two-dimensional responses leap onto the screen. So, two of the networks hired prominent network hosts to read out their mail (CBC TV assigned Rex Murphy while CTV assigned Wei Chen). "It's an outlet for viewers to say something, it gets more voices onto the show," said CBC TV's Chris Waddell, who said CBC TV received about 3,000 e-mail reactions on election night. He pointed out it has distinct advantages over the instant feedback from viewers at a house party. "Both ways are being highly-selective but this [e-mail comments] has the potential to have a broader range of material." CTV agreed, insisting that Wei Chen's selection of e-mail messages were from viewers who lived in centres away from Toronto and other large cities, which normally get covered, because TV stations are only located in cities. But it was a dispensable item when airtime was limited during election night 2000. For instance, while viewers in Atlantic Canada saw Rex Murphy read viewer e-mail five times before polls closed at 9:30 p.m. EST, he was squeezed out by results and analysis until 10:39 p.m. EST (for the entire country) when the Liberal majority was confirmed.

Aside from the unscientifically gathered opinions of rural Canada, there was one significant foray into using the Internet to more meaningfully understand why people voted as they did earlier in the day. CTV conducted the first-ever election night online poll and then broadcast the results. CTV reporter Lisa LaFlemme and Ipsos-Reid president and CEO, Darrell Bricker, appeared throughout the night to report on the results of the same-day, public opinion poll completed by 2,350 respondents (the sample group was pre-selected before election night to balance the sample according to demographics and region).[12] Each of the respondents was sent a twelve-question survey, by e-mail, to be completed after they had voted. They were asked how they voted this time and last, as well as their opinions on issues such as abortion and party leadership (e.g. "Do you believe Canadian Alliance leader Stockwell Day had a hidden agenda?").

The base of information allowed CTV to provide context and depth to the otherwise simple reporting of voting results. "It was more or less a typical family's living room on a mass scale using the technology," said Lapointe in an interview. "We wanted to talk psychologically about the vote. What were their issues, what was driving people? We wanted the opportunity, in discussing the results, to say that Canadians were driven by this feature or that feature or that image or that personality. To that extent it was useful." He argued that it gave CTV the confidence that the information garnered by its team of reporters and producers was accurate and up to the minute. "It gave us a final reality check. [The election campaign] could come down to the last three days and it could be an attack ad or a last minute messaging from one of the leaders or a regional issue that knocks the legs out of a party. So it gives you that kind of data [and it gives you] empirical material so you're not winging it with anecdotes heard on the campaign trail." It allowed CTV to flesh out its analysis. For instance, it allowed LaFlemme and Bricker to discuss why the Liberals had amassed a surprisingly high level of support in Quebec or explain that although Ontarians' support for the Alliance was weak, it had more to do with the leadership of Stockwell Day. "It wasn't a massive revelation from the political science point of view but when it comes to daily journalism, it was a better bedrock of information and better than doing 50 interviews on election day," said Lapointe. He is adamant that it was not an exit poll, the kind of instant poll that broadcasters in the U.S. have suddenly soured on, given their experience in the November 2000 presidential election. CTV first used the sample group for online polling during the campaign when the party leaders debated each other in English. Respondents sat by their TVs, then dashed to their computers to answer questions such as "who won" and "who lost" at periods throughout the debate. While the answers flooded in after the first question, Lapointe said one server could not produce results for any of the succeeding questions until after the debate. The story was ready in time for the 11:00 p.m. newscast. It failed as a real-time poll about whether the debate was influencing viewers, but Lapointe said CTV found better servers on election night.

The impact of the Internet on television went beyond information gathering and disseminating; it also influenced the way broadcasters presented their information in graphic images.[13] Many specialty channels, particularly those broadcasting all-news and business news, run at least one graphic component on their screens all the time (e.g. quotes from the stock exchange) so it is fair to assume that many viewers are used to seeing layers of dynamic visuals on TV. The graphic on CBC TV was packed with information: with Peter Mansbridge or reporters talking in the middle the screen, bars and columns were placed on the sides and bottom to relay a vast array of information; at times there were four different elements: an anchor, and four graphs, charts or maps. It was informative: at a glance viewers could read overall party standings, the province standings and results from ridings as well as the popular vote or the CBC website and e-mail address and toll-free phone number. It most resembled a web page: a busy, information-dense page. One television critic congratulated the CBC on "being armed with the most eye-catching graphics."[14] However, it was also occasionally confusing, as candidates in fourth or seventh place could appear to be "leading" or "elected".

CTV had simple graphics: party standings on the right side of the screen (CBC's were on the left) and riding results on the bottom — but only the first and second place winners had displays. "There was no doubt that CTV carried the day in terms of the visual battle," declared a next-day review in *The Toronto Star*.[15] Global TV had the simplest graphic display of all: riding results alternated with regional and national totals on a white background along the bottom of the screen, leaving plenty of room for anchors. That meant some candidates (and some fringe parties) never got their moment on Global's broadcast. "We decided to only show the top three candidates in that riding, unless Jean Chrétien was in fourth place," said Cal Johnstone, the results producer for the Global TV election night program,[16] adding that the network assumed those were the only races people were interested in. "If you wanted to know how the Green Party was doing, then you could turn to the Internet," he added.

There was some reluctance at the CBC to venture further into interactivity, said Chris Waddell, of CBC TV.[17] "The Internet was not factored in [to our planning of the show]," he conceded. "We still look at the Internet as a way for people to get more detailed information than we can give them on the screen. What we can do is give people a sense of the big picture, what it means, how it got there. You can't get that from the Internet. I'm skeptical how active you want to be when you're watching TV. It's so passive."

Lessons learned

1) THE BLACKOUT: The advantages of providing local riding results on the Internet cannot be fully realized, and the Internet cannot compete against coverage on television, as long as staggered voting hours and the legislated blackout continue. One would think, then, that the Internet news services would be lobbying Elections Canada to change the law. None admitted to such a campaign, hoping that private citizens would take up the charge instead. And, none in our survey admitted they were even tempted to break the law. "No one wants to go to jail for telling a British Columbian who was elected in Crowfoot (Alberta)," said Lapointe. "We were all pretty well warned and took advice from legal counsel, so we didn't even think about it." However, CTV did, in a roundabout way, enable Canadians to get results before 10:00 p.m. CTV has a co-operative arrangement with ABC News in the U.S., allowing ABC News to take CTV video feeds (even from the Atlantic) and turn them into text and video clips for its website. That meant anyone in the world with Internet access could view CTV material before 10:00 p.m. EST at abcnews.com Policing the blackout proved difficult this time and promises to become even more difficult in the future. As Lapointe

noted, "It's the wild west out there. The Internet gives everyone a broadcast licence."

2) LOCAL RESULTS: One disadvantage of the linear, sequential fashion in which TV broadcasts news and other information is that viewers have to wait for the programmers to serve up results on specific ridings or candidates. Since national broadcasters focus on the national race, the big names and the big picture, it can be difficult to follow a riding—especially if there was no big name or no particular news angle in the race. Still, some viewers want to know what happened in their local ridings or region. National broadcasters have accommodated that in the past by providing "local cutaways": cutting away from the national broadcast every half hour for a five-minute segment produced out of each local newsroom.

CTV, with twenty-five local newsrooms, provided the best local information with reporters at local campaign headquarters and the anchors updating results in the region. "People need to see people locally, hear from the winners and losers in their region. It's not a national election for a lot of people. You're not voting for Jean Chrétien, you're voting Stan Keyes and you want to see if Stan Keyes won," argued Lapointe. Global TV, for the first time, included local cutaways from its twelve stations (this was the first "national" broadcast for Global TV). But its ability to cover the "local" depended on the region. In Ontario, for example (with 103 ridings), the entire province was covered out of the Toronto-area, which meant the only campaign headquarters visited by reporters were two newsworthy races: John McCallum (former chief economist at the Royal Bank) and John Nunziata, (renegade independent candidate). No specific information was provided for viewers in Ottawa or Sudbury, for instance. After years of providing local cutaways, CBC abandoned them for its 1997 election coverage. Waddell argued that the staggered hours have squeezed air time between 9:30 p.m. EST and 11:00 p.m. EST, at which point party leaders start making their concession and victory speeches, so there is no longer any time to cut to local races and away from the national one.

Clearly, if viewers want detailed riding results, the Internet can provide a superior service. Broadcasters focus on the big picture, the trend (so that each is in a race to "call" the election)[18] and keep updating and summarizing for viewers who may tune in and out. However, it is likely the look of the TV election specials will change in the future. With staggered voting hours there was less time to listen in on the pundits: CBC TV featured no one except the anchor, the lead correspondent (Jason Moscovitz), and other reporters in the studio and scattered across the country from 9:30 p.m. until 10:43 p.m. EST (when former pollster Allan Gregg was interviewed to provide analysis).

3) POPULISM: As American political scientists Richard Davis and Diana Owen have written, the great promise of the Internet was that it would involve more people in how their nations are run. "The most optimistic, and perhaps most unrealistic, perspective sees new media as a force in a democratic revolution, with new media stimulating a political interest and activism among citizens. Media populism abounds, as ordinary citizens work their way into a political arena that once was primarily the domain of elites." [19] Election 2000 embraced that hope as news sites and broadcasters had the potential to involve Canadians. CTV's Lapointe: "The degree to which you can involve voters on the night, the better you are. I don't mean that as a sop to 'vox populi'; it legitimately has a purpose in understanding the country if you can put the emotion of the people onto television." In this election that meant reading aloud e-mail messages from viewers; the next election could see viewers' reactions on video clips, captured by their web cameras attached to their home computers then transmitted to the broadcasters and websites. "When you do too few of them you sound like an open-line radio show but if you can involve people in your broadcast (and in your campaign coverage) much more than that you're serving a better purpose."

4) CONVERGENCE: This election year also saw a flurry of media mergers in the country. While the news operations were still running distinct operations, there were signs of media convergence: globeandmail.com bought an ad on the CTV News program as well as a link on the ctvnews.com Internet site. (Shortly after the election, BCE finalized the deal to own both media companies.) Over at Global TV, when the website, globaltv.com, faltered around 10:37 p.m. EST, visitors clicking on stories were linked to the *National Post* page. (CanWest Global had recently purchased Hollinger Inc. and 50 percent of the *National Post*). "We're looking at doing more co-operative ventures, and that means sharing more resources during an election broadcast and campaign," said Global's Cal Johnstone.

5) TECHNOLOGY MATTERS: Broadcasters have long known that the best research and plans mean nothing if your program goes to black or dead air. Most Internet news sites learned a similar lesson on election night — that if they do not have the server capacity, it hardly matters if they have the fastest results and the best journalism. CBC's Ken Wolff said the CBC has now hired an outside company to conduct a huge technical audit to determine why its set-up failed so many visitors on election night.

The 2000 election could be seen as a test run, so that providers could determine the appetite for Internet coverage and results online. It also means gearing up with more servers or gearing down, as is the case with CTV, to accommodate visitors with modest Internet access (dial-up modems). "The lesson learned out of this is that you have an enormous instrument in broadcasting and hundreds of thousands of people are in front of it. When you encourage them to turn from one screen to another you have an opportunity to pull a lot of people in so you have to be ready for them," said Lapointe.

NOTES

1 Elections Canada On-line. The New Canada Elections Act, section 329. 17 Jan. 2001 http://www.elections.ca/

2 E-mail interview, Neil Campbell, globeandmail.com, Toronto, November 25, 2000.

3 Telephone interview, Paul Bryan, Burnaby, December 15, 2000.

4 Telephone interview, Paul Bryan, Burnaby, December 15, 2000.

5 Telephone interview, Kirk Lapointe, CTVNews.com, Toronto, January, 2001.

6 Telephone interview, Neil A. Campbell, globeandmail.com, Toronto, December 11, 2000.

7 E-mail interview, Neil A. Campbell, Toronto, November 25, 2000.

8 Telephone interview, Ken Wolff, executive producer, cbc.ca., Toronto, December 12, 2001.

9 Telephone interview, Nancy DeHart, producer of the National Post Online, Toronto, December 20, 2000.

10 E-mail interview, Mark Sikstrom, CTVnews.com, Toronto, Wednesday, November 29, 2000.

11 E-mail interview, Jennifer Humphries, Managing Editor, CTV Corporate Communications, Toronto, January 18, 2001.

12 IPSOS-REID was confident that it was representative of Canadian voters, although it was unusual in two respects: there was a high correlation of previous voting (about 85 percent of the sample had voted in 1997 compared to 67 percent of the general population) and that every respondent in an Internet poll was an Internet user. (between 60 and 65 percent of Canadians are "Internet enabled") (BRICKER, HILL TIMES, Jan 15, 2001).

13 RATINGS: TV (English) 1.7 mil (CBC Research, January 16, 2001), CTV News & Newsnet 1.2 million (CTV Corporate Communications, January 18, 2001), Global (Ontario only) (CBC Research, January 16, 2001).

14 Brad Oswald, *Winnipeg Free Press*, November 28, 2000 B10.

15 *Toronto Star*, November 28, 2000.

16 Telephone interview, Cal Johnstone, Assistant News Director and Results Producer, Global TV Toronto, January 19, 2001.

17 Telephone interview, Chris Waddell, Ottawa, December 20, 2000.

18 CTV "won" the election calling by declaring a Liberal majority first

— at 10:04p.m. EST. Global was second at 10:13 p.m. EST and CBC TV called it at 10:22 p.m.EST.

19 Davis, Richard and Diana Owen, *New Media and American Politics.* New York: Oxford University Press, 1998, p. 256.

Chapter 11

The Politics of Values:
Designing the 2000 Liberal Campaign

by Michael Marzolini

Courageous decisions are usually avoided in politics. Politicians are by nature risk-averse. They don't tempt fate, and they rarely play fast and loose with public opinion, that all-important commodity which keeps them in office. To refer to a political decision as "courageous" is a polite way to condemn it as fool-hardy and risky. When Prime Minister Jean Chrétien directed POLLARA, his private polling firm, to assess the potential for calling an early election in the fall of 2000, many of his advisors, ministers, and members of parliament shrugged.[1] It would not happen. It would be too courageous. After all, the public was clearly in a mood for change. Media polls were showing that large majorities of the public felt the Prime Minister should retire. The new Canadian Alliance Leader, Stockwell Day, was enjoying a honeymoon with the voters and becoming increasingly popular. The Liberal government was in damage-control mode over the accounting and spending practices of its HRDC department, while at the same time a majority of Canadians thought it was dragging its feet on tax cuts, especially for middle-income earners. The public health care system was in dire need of repair. Most Canadians felt that their standard of living had fallen during the Liberals' seven years in office, and that the government lacked the ideas, creativity, and vision to turn things around. Calling an election too early in the mandate, many Liberals felt, would be tempting fate and giving the public an opportunity to embrace the new Canadian Alliance. Better to complete the full term, wait for Stockwell Day's electoral honeymoon to pass, give him time to make some political errors, allow the HRDC "scandal" to fade in public opinion, give the government an opportunity to include further middle-income tax cuts in its spring budget, and start fixing the health care system.

The fall atmosphere, though, was not necessarily grim for the Prime Minister. Liberal support had been stable at the 43 percent level since 1997, high enough to return a good-sized majority. But horse-race numbers are not as important as the foundations of this support, the underlying public attitudes toward the parties, leaders, issues and policies. And while those foundations had been weakening steadily since 1993, as they will with any government over time, there was some encouraging news for the Liberal Party. Prime Minister Chrétien was still seen as the best leader to govern the country, and there was no bleeding of Liberal support to the Alliance. The Alliance may have been surging, but they were only winning votes away from the beleaguered PC Party, seen to be lacking strong leadership under Joe Clark. No other party posed a significant threat to the Liberals. The New Democratic Party under Alexa McDonough was perceived by most Canadians to be a non-entity, with left-wing policies and values that were out of touch with the post-1995 trend of fiscal conservatism. And the Bloc Québécois under Gilles Duceppe, still holding half the vote in Quebec, suffered because Quebeckers were far more concerned with their province's health care system and economic situation than they were with Quebec's status in Canada.

The two-edged sword for the Liberals was the emergence of the Canadian Alliance as the one serious threat to their hegemony. Under the leadership of Stockwell Day, the Alliance had quickly surpassed the 19 percent support level of their previous Reform Party incarnation, and was now up to 24 percent in the polls. This Alliance momentum, however, actually served to benefit the Liberals in many different ways. First, "political honeymoons" after a leadership change always provide a short-term boost to public opinion, but raise expectations to a point where they are higher than the leader and party can ever deliver. Kim Campbell discovered this in 1993 when her honeymoon gave the PCs confidence in the early stage of the election but her vote collapsed when she couldn't keep up the momentum. There was therefore an expectation that when Stockwell Day's honeymoon ended, many of his voters would return very suddenly to the PC fold.

More importantly, during previous elections the Liberals had always been satisfied with four weak opponents rather than one strong opponent. However, as the POLLARA pollsters explained to the Liberal National Caucus in August 2000, the Liberals would benefit electorally from having one main target to campaign against and contrast themselves with. This would be especially true with a target like the Alliance, seen as having rigid views, values and thinking. A campaign based on Liberal versus Alliance "values," the pollsters said, would have traction.

264

In 1997, the Liberals had won only a narrow majority while playing "whack-a-mole." They targeted the Reform Party whenever it gained support, whacked the PCs when they emerged briefly after the debate, and attacked the NDP and BQ when they each had their individual moments in the sun. In 1997 the Liberals could not hope to direct their efforts against one major opponent. Such an opponent, especially with such a different agenda and set of values as the Alliance, could be expected to act as a foil for Liberal messages to the voters, and allow the party to concentrate its resources.

With the Alliance as the key opponent, the Liberals would have the opportunity to run one strong national campaign, rather than dilute the effect by running five or more regional campaigns as in the previous election. This would allow for consistency of communications, and more effective and better understood messaging. The differences between the Alliance agenda and values and those of the Liberals would be more visible and defined, and this is usually to the benefit of the party closest to the centre of the political spectrum. The values and agenda of Stockwell Day and the Alliance were not unpopular with many of the electorate. Indeed, the fact that the CA policy of a flat tax was endorsed by fully a third of all Canadians showed they had room to grow. And their bottom-line approach to improving Canadians' standard of living rivaled in popularity the Liberals' approach to improving quality of life. Stockwell Day was seen to be likeable, dynamic, fresh, and exciting. The more Canadians saw of him, the more they liked him and what he stood for.

But if the Liberal electoral foundations had weakened during their term in office, they were still stronger than the shaky foundations of Alliliance support. There was a lurking suspicion, voiced in many POL-LARA focus groups, that Stockwell Day was too good to be true. The same voters who compared him to a "young Pierre Trudeau" also ruminated that "maybe he wasn't telling us everything." They worried about "a secret agenda" and the more that people were told about his alleged social policies, such as his anti-abortion and anti-gay rights views and positions, the more this bothered them. This worry was reinforced, certainly in Atlantic Canada, when an Alliance National Council Member alleged in public that Atlantic Canadians, being lazy and only supportive of governments who would guarantee their subsidies and welfare cheques, wouldn't warm to the Alliance. Atlantic Canadians, who had previously been only lukewarm to the Liberals as well, now viewed the

Alliance as a major threat to their way of life. The suspicion that the Alliance harboured unsavoury values and agendas grew, as did Liberal support in Atlantic Canada.

The Alliance's public opinion "Achilles' heel" was in their values, both stated and unstated. The strength of the Liberal Party was in its own values, built and witnessed historically through many generations. The state funeral of former Liberal prime minister Pierre Trudeau shortly before the election was called concentrated more focus on these values, but contrary to the views of most pundits, had no direct impact on electoral support. The decision of the Prime Minister to call an early fall 2000 general election, while at first controversial even among his own candidates, many of whom at first thought the decision was "courageous" in the worst possible way, was based on this perspective on public opinion. Values would form the basis of the campaign, and the ballot question would be the most important a voter can ask, "Does he think like me?" For those Liberal candidates who were nervous of the early election call, the Liberal Party shared some of the confidential pre-election POLLARA poll, projecting a Liberal victory of between 170 and 180 seats. Some however, dismissed this as propaganda and would not lose their nervousness until the last weeks of the campaign.

The "Values Campaign" started, as do all Canadian election campaigns, with a two-week "phony war" period. Only one-third of Canadians pay much attention to the opening salvos, and most tend not to "tune in" until the leaders' debates mid-way in the campaign. Those who do follow the election closely are usually the opinion leaders, people whose way of thinking usually predicts the movement of the rest of the general public. But for the Liberals, the attitudes and behaviour of these opinion leaders in the first week of the campaign was not at all favourable. Liberal support was slowly sinking and Alliance support was surging. For many opinion leaders, Stockwell Day was a very new product, one that they were immediately attracted to. They liked what he was saying. It was new, fresh, and dynamically delivered. They liked him, and they liked his values: honesty, integrity, compassion, humility, and sensitivity. His attitude toward taxation was well liked, though it had largely been neutralized by the Liberal's pre-election mini-budget that promised tax relief, especially for the middle-class, who were most sensitive to this issue. Liberal criticism of the Alliance proposal of a flat tax rate was in turn countered and somewhat neutralized when Day changed the policy to make it more "progressive" —

that is, sensitive to low income Canadians. The public did not perceive this as indecisive, but rather welcomed the change. For some, it showed that the Alliance had flexibility and would listen to public opinion. For others it meant that an obstacle to voting Alliance had been removed.

One week into the campaign, support for the Alliance was higher than at any point in its or the Reform Party's history. After reaching 30 percent four days before the debate, it gained a point a day for the next four days. More worrying for the Liberals was the fact that among the third of all Canadians following the election closely, the Alliance had the support of 37 percent of those classified as "opinion leaders," versus only 42 percent for the Liberals. And Stockwell Day was making significant gains on the Prime Minister in terms of image, and was perceived as the most likeable of the leaders, the most honest, the most sensitive to the needs of each region, the most compassionate, and the most likely to bring about positive change. He was also the least likely of all the leaders to threaten the Medicare system. This state of affairs was not publicly known, so the Alliance received little boost in momentum. It was counter-intuitive. The Alliance leader and campaign had made many gaffes and errors in their first week, but these did not impact on the public.

Canadians were paying little attention to Jean Chrétien in the opening days of the campaign. They had heard him before and he was a known quantity. The new Liberal Red Book platform promised good government, but included nothing radically new, and so received little attention. All the innovations could be found in the Alliance campaign. The Liberal campaign was coming dangerously close to being a referendum on whether to reward the Prime Minister with another majority. This is never a good ballot question, and not the one the Liberals intended. The ballot question had to be "Which of the leaders and parties thinks like me?" And for the Liberals, the vote choice had to be framed as "light under the Liberals" and "darkness under the Alliance."

The Alliance's "secret agenda," their right-wing positioning on both social and economic issues, had to be put on the table for public discussion. However, this could not be bluntly stated without the Liberal campaign being perceived as "going negative" or acting in desperation. Liberal attempts to use the single tax rate as an element of a hidden agenda to benefit the rich over the poor had only mixed results. The hidden agenda charges would not be believable until more had been done to "flush out" Stockwell Day on additional issues. At the outset of

267

the campaign, he was to Canadians what he wanted to be, and what they wanted him to be. The adversaries were still circling each other, and most Canadians were not focused on the campaign. However, with increased support comes increased public and media scrutiny, and the Liberal party judged that by debate night, the secret agenda issue would have more resonance. In the meantime, the Liberals made use of their popular Finance Minister, Paul Martin, who crossed the country to show the strength of the "Liberal team," while at the same time shoring up support in Quebec, which appeared in the early days of the campaign to be unusually volatile for all parties. Former Newfoundland Premier Brian Tobin did the same nationally, with concentration on Nova Scotia and New Brunswick where the Liberals had to make gains to hold a majority. Record high Alliance support in Western Canada meant that the Liberals could expect to lose seats in British Columbia, and they would have to be made up east of Ontario, especially if the Alliance was able to make an impact in Ontario itself.

With the Alliance support on an upward trend, and the debate approaching, it was unfortunate for Stockwell Day that his Campaign Chairman, MP Jason Kenney, appeared to voice support for a two-tier health care system early in the second week of the campaign. This gave the Liberals, as well as the other parties, an issue to focus on and an opportunity to raise once more the "hidden-agenda" and "values" side of the campaign, which had to have credence if they were to win. Though Kenney claimed to have been misquoted, actually saying he would support private-sector health care providers only if they were not permitted to bill the patient directly, the excuse made no impact on the public. For them, it was the thin edge of the wedge, and the number of Canadians believing Stockwell Day to be the most likely to threaten Medicare surged by 10 percent overnight.

The Liberals embraced this issue with an immediate advertising campaign, using it to reveal Day's "real agenda" and values. Most public polls showed that Canadians' top concern was their health care system. They wanted it fixed but did not know how to fix it. Most Canadians are indeed open to private sector involvement in the health care system, and most would even endorse some form of user fee to curb system abuse, but they demand a chance to discuss these issues in depth if they are to be raised. An election campaign is too short a time for the scope of far-ranging public discussion required. And with the media "exposing" this Alliance policy, complete with values contrary to those of the old policy, the public reacted towards Day and his party with suspicion and reservation. When this issue was raised, opinion leaders grew slightly more hesitant about the Alliance. At the same time however, Alliance support from the general public continued to grow, illustrating the time-lag between opinion leader and general public beliefs. It would take most Canadians a few more days to catch up; unfortunately for the Canadian Alliance, they would start to catch up around the time of the leaders' debate.

The ground for the leaders' debate was prepared, not only by the Medicare dispute, but by one of the key events of the election campaign, a carefully placed reference to the abortion issue in a speech delivered by the Prime Minister to one thousand women the weekend before the debate. He outlined his pro-choice position on abortion, and quietly dropped the issue on the table. He neither concentrated on the issue, nor attacked Stockwell Day directly with it, but merely ensured that the issue, which the Liberals judged to be a ticking time-bomb for Stockwell Day, was placed on the agenda and therefore fair game for discussion at the leaders' debate. Liberal polling by POLLARA before the election was called indicated that the abortion issue was a "magic bullet" to use against the Alliance. In surveys and focus groups, the public had reacted very strongly and negatively towards the Alliance when they were exposed to Stockwell Day's own words on abortion, gay rights, and single-parent families. The "value issues" had the ability, once they were discussed in the public domain, to terminate Alliance electoral momentum and shut them down as the key threat to Liberal re-election.

There was a problem for the Liberals in using this "magic bullet"; if Alliance momentum was indeed shut down too early in the campaign, the Liberals were in great danger of losing their chance of winning a majority government. A non-threatening Alliance would create the same situation that faced the Liberals in the previous election of 1997, which resulted in a swift drop in their electoral fortunes outside of Ontario. That is, most Canadians were of the view that the Liberals would win a large majority government, and approved of this outcome, as a majority of voters in every province perceived the Liberals as the best to serve the national interest. However, in every province save Ontario, the Liberals were not seen as best to serve the regional or provincial interests. From British Columbia to Manitoba, the voice of the west was the Alliance, and to some extent the NDP in urban centres. In Quebec, the Bloc Quebecois

269

spoke for Quebeckers, both federalists and nationalists. And in Atlantic Canada, the PCs and NDP shared the regional voice. Only in Ontario were the Liberals seen as best to represent both the national and provincial interests. Without a serious threat to the Liberals, Canadians would anticipate the result of the election as a foregone conclusion, as they did in the previous election, when there was no national alternative party that could be considered a credible replacement for the Liberals. At that time, the Liberals had a strong lead in the media opinion polls, and very few Canadians believed that they would not win a majority. Voting based on regional interests, therefore, could be indulged in totally risk-free, as the national interest would still be served. The problem that could arise, and almost did, was the possibility of all Canadians voting on regional rather than national interests. This came close to triggering a Liberal minority in 1997, and could potentially have resulted in a Liberal defeat, a paradoxical outcome that would have been perceived by the public as being against its own self-interest.

If the "values campaign" was too effective, and shut down Canadian Alliance momentum before the mid-point of the campaign, the Liberals would have been haunted by an ever-declining support trend. They would again have to play electoral "whack-a-mole" and run at least five diluted regional campaigns rather than one strong national campaign. They would have had to play defensively rather than offensively, and few goals are scored playing defence. Internal polling indicated that if the Alliance disappeared as the national alternative government, PC and NDP support would rise in Atlantic Canada at the expense of the Liberals, Bloc support would rise in Quebec, and even Alliance support would strengthen, though only in the West. The Liberals could not afford to vanquish the Alliance too soon, assuming that their plan to make abortion a "wedge issue" actually worked.

The French and English Leaders' Debates were viewed by a total of 55 percent of eligible Canadian voters. The winner, according to all the public and private polling, was PC leader Joe Clark (see Chapter Thirteen of this volume). The loser, at least in the public polls, was the Prime Minister, who was in the position of being the target of all four other leaders. This interpretation was highly misleading. The common survey question "Who in your opinion won the debate?" yields data applicable to performance only. The Canadian people judged Joe Clark as the big winner, and improved their perceptions of the performances of BQ leader Gilles

Duceppe, Alliance leader Stockwell Day, and NDP leader Alexa McDonough. Each performed well, but in electoral politics this means very little. The media polling data did not measure or reveal the changes to the attitudinal "mind-map" of the electorate. The public may well have designated Joe Clark and Stockwell Day as debate winners, and felt that the Prime Minister at best held his ground, but they also took away something completely different and far more relevant. They now suspected or believed, and many strongly feared, that Stockwell Day's Alliance Party had a secret agenda, an agenda that included not just introducing a two-tier health system, but even worse, restricting abortion rights. The day before the election, *The Globe and Mail* had published excerpts from the "confidential policy briefing book" provided to Alliance candidates, in which it was alleged that a national abortion referendum would be triggered by a petition of no more than 3 percent of eligible voters. Day's alliance with Campaign Life and other anti-abortion groups was well known to the media and to his political opponents, and this fact and the policy book revelations gave their debate attacks on Day the necessary credibility. Each of the other leaders attacked Stockwell Day throughout the debate on his policy for an anti-abortion referendum, and it was clear to the public that all except for Day were on the side of majority opinion in Canada, being pro-choice to varying degrees. A majority of Canadians saw and heard the four leaders make this issue stick, and saw Stockwell Day unable to decisively refute it. The "take-home" value of these exchanges would far exceed the impact of which of the leaders had the smoothest debate delivery.

By the end of the debate, while the media and pollsters uselessly discussed the question "who won the debate?" in shallow terms only reflecting "who was the most forceful speaker?", the ballot question had been firmly planted in the minds of the electorate. "Does Stockwell Day think as I do?" In most cases across the country, the answer was "no, he doesn't." Almost immediately following the debate, Alliance support plummeted. From their historic high of 34 percent, they dropped to 26 percent in less than a week. Stockwell Day had lost the chance of forming a government. The beneficiaries were Joe Clark's PCs, who edged from 7 percent up to 10 percent, Jean Chrétien's Liberals, who went from 44 percent to 47 percent, and the NDP and BQ, who each rose 1 percent each to sit at 8 percent. In addition, the number of Canadians who believed that Stockwell Day would make the best prime minister also fell in the same proportions, from 27 percent to 18 percent in less than a week.

The question remaining for the Liberal campaign was whether the Alliance fortunes had died too soon. Was that party now beyond recovery? Was the electorate, once the media published its opinion polls, going to take a Liberal majority victory for granted and once again drift off, region after region, to the other parties? Liberal polling indicated that Stockwell Day had the ability to resurrect his campaign, at least partially. The government was vulnerable on many issues he could have raised, including the Young Offenders' Act. Before the election, Day had improved his standing every time he raised such law and order issues. For Day, reforming the YOA was a perfect "wedge issue" to act as a foil for his leadership and values. Like capital punishment there was majority support, but unlike capital punishment, reforming the YOA did not require the voters' strong emotional commitment to the policy. Most Canadians will not vote for a political party advocating the death penalty, as they do not want the responsibility attached to the issue. But they would endorse making the Young Offenders' Act more strict, which was undisputed Alliance policy. It was anticipated that by the second week of the campaign Stockwell Day would be utilizing the YOA issue. However, by that time he was already embroiled in a controversy over whether he endorsed a two-tier health care system, and once the debates were concluded he was forced to try to explain his conflicting referenda policies.

For the Liberals, the abortion issue was a perfect wedge-issue. Certainly it was not as important an overall issue concern as health care, but it was more effective politically. Indeed, less than 2 percent of Canadians polled named it the most important issue facing Canada, while fully half named health care. Abortion was a surrogate issue for the values campaign. It was more effective than health care, which Canadians were concerned about but found too complex a problem for widespread understanding of potential solutions. For abortion, depending on one's position on the issue, there was both a problem and a solution. The differences between the parties on health care, even with the two-tier debate, were shades of grey. The difference on abortion was black and white. By asking themselves the question "do you want to return to the '60s and '70s and fight for your right to choose all over again, or do you want to move on into the new millennium?", women voters abandoned the Alliance en masse. Indeed, women made up some two-thirds of all those who deserted the Alliance during the campaign.

If the Liberals were worried about the electorate taking a Liberal victory for granted in the last two weeks of the campaign, and then melting off to support other parties they viewed as more regionally sensitive and representative, they had a right to be concerned. The electorate in fact began to do exactly that, but not until the very last week of the campaign, by which time it could not swing the balance away from a Liberal majority. Liberal victory was not generally realized nor taken for granted in the week after the debate, for the simple reason that both the media and the electorate were confused. There was little public or media understanding of what was actually happening in the second-last week of the campaign. The media polls were few and far between in this period, and quite erratic depending on the pollster being used. A front page headline in the *National Post* trumpeted "Liberals 'Sliding Big-Time'," ten points in one night, based on a fraudulent leak from somebody who had claimed to have seen the POLLARA overnight tracking. (In actuality, fewer than five people in any party's campaign are ever privy to the overnight polling data.) The media were at sea, and were under varying impressions of the campaign, most of them inaccurate, and based largely on perceptions of debate performances. The most widespread view was that Liberal fortunes were damaged after the debate, that Joe Clark and Stockwell Day were on the rise, and that Gilles Duceppe was gaining much new ground in Quebec. This misperception masked the reality of the Alliance slide and the new gains that the Liberals were making in Quebec and Atlantic Canada. What the public and the media didn't realize, they could not react negatively toward; as a result, Liberal support was solid in the second-last week of the election.

During the final week of the campaign, it was the turn of the Liberals to brave an ordeal by fire. The Prime Minister was under attack for lobbying the Business Development Bank on behalf of a constituent. All other party leaders concentrated on this issue, Stockwell Day going as far as accusing Jean Chrétien of criminal conduct. This was the final phase of the campaign, and though the federal ethics counsellor would absolve the Prime Minister of any impropriety, damage was done. The voters reacted with the same "no smoke without a fire" attitude that had hurt Stockwell Day on two-tier health. The Liberals dropped by 4 percent almost immediately after the allegations were raised, and while they recovered slightly after the ethics counsellor ruling, it is progressively more difficult to change voter choices the closer they get to election day.

One very positive effect of the BDB lobbying allegations was that it kept the status of the campaign up in the air. By the last week of the campaign, the public and media were seeing polls that were finally showing the Liberals with a strong lead, the Alliance going nowhere, the Bloc in their usual tie in Quebec, and the other parties also-rans. Nobody knew, however, how the BDB controversy would impact on the election.

The Liberals were continuing to pursue a policy of targeting Stockwell Day and the Alliance Party. They realized that Day could no longer pose a threat to forming a government, but knew that if they removed the pressure, admitting the lack of national opposition would "nickel and dime" their support in every region outside of Ontario. Voters rarely vote "for" a party; they tend to vote "against" a party. The Alliance had to continue to be treated seriously as a national alternative, one that Canadians could vote against, by voting for the only party that could effectively block them. However, by this last week and the publication of the new media polls, it was clear to everybody that the Alliance would not form a government. Liberal support started to soften right across the country, but the impact was greatest in Atlantic Canada where the Alliance threat had been a buttress against the PCs and NDP. Joe Clark's PCs surged up two points nationally, to 12 percent. The NDP went from 8 percent to 9 percent. The Bloc went from 9 percent to 11 percent. The Liberals gave up 3 percent in the final week, declining from 44 percent to 41 percent.

The final hurdle for the Liberal strategy was to survive the last wave of media polls the weekend before voting day. If these polls all agreed that the Liberals would win an easy majority, 170 seats as the private Liberal POLLARA polls were predicting, then there would likely be some last minute attrition as the regional voting behaviour pattern gained momentum, which would jeopardize the majority. If the polls were mixed, and a Liberal majority government was in dispute, the electorate would sacrifice their regional interests to the national interest, thereby ensuring a Liberal majority. The election-eve media polls were very indecisive. Most purported to show a Liberal majority but there were key exceptions. Forty-eight hours before the vote, *The Globe and Mail* headline shouted "PM's Majority on Razor's Edge" based on an Ipsos-Reid poll showing the Liberals with only 39 percent of national support, and tied with the Bloc in the province of Quebec. Though this was the same media poll that had over-estimated PC support by 6 percent (outside the stated accuracy of 2 percent) in the previous 1997 general election, it was given much weight, and put the election outcome in doubt. The more reliable CBC-Ekos poll, though overestimating Liberal support by the same amount as the Globe-Ipsos-Reid poll had underestimated it, similarly had the Liberals only tied with the Bloc in Quebec. Indeed, of the eight media polls released in the last four days of the campaign, five had the Bloc ahead of the Liberals in Quebec, two had them tied, and only one had the Liberals marginally ahead. The Prime Minister, however, was certain that he would win Quebec by a significant margin; his own polling was based not on general public interviews, but on interviews with Quebeckers who were absolutely certain to vote. Many of these were senior citizens, strongly federalist, who cast 28 percent of the ballots, despite constituting only 13 percent of the population. Their impact, combined with the low turnout from nationalists in Quebec, delivered Liberal seats that few in the media expected. And it was this seat gain, combined with similar gains in Atlantic Canada, that boosted the governing party's seat total to 172 from the 156 they had won the previous election.

Taken collectively, the election-eve media polls, as they had in 1997, provided an element of confusion to the media and to the public that kept the election outcome in doubt until the very end. The effect was to dampen the impact of the "by-election style" of regional voting that nearly cost the Liberals their majority in 1997. The electorate desired a majority government and if that was in doubt, which it was, they would put regional voting on the back-burner. They may not have loved the Liberals, but they could endorse and be comfortable with Liberal values. The Alliance values were not as attractive. The Alliance had been enticing, and Stockwell Day had excited them as a dynamic potential Prime Minister. They liked his opinions, and they also thought, early on, that they liked his values. Only when they discovered, under the intense scrutiny of a campaign, the Alliance leader's public and personal positions on abortion, Medicare, gay rights, and progressive taxation, did they return to the party whose values had been forged by Pierre Trudeau and preserved by Jean Chrétien.

NOTES

1   This public opinion and strategy overview, recounted from the per-
    spective of the pollster to the Liberal Party, may be read as a sequel
    to "The Regionalization of Canadian Electoral Politics", Chapter
    Ten of *The Canadian General Election of 1997*. As with that earlier
    chapter, I gratefully acknowledge the contribution of Donald Guy
    of POLLARA, the co-pollster of the Liberal campaign, whose inter-
    pretation and strategic analysis of election polling data is second to
    none. I would also like to thank the 60,000 Canadians who freely
    gave us their opinions during the course of the election campaign.
    Public attitudes, opinions, beliefs, and values are the most impor-
    tant component of both an election campaign and good represen-
    tative government. Survey respondents do a great service to all of us
    whose views they represent.

Chapter 12

Fallen Heroes:
Leaders and Voters in the
2000 Canadian Federal Election

by André Turcotte

Every election is about leadership.[1] It is during the few weeks of an election campaign that the citizenry's search for compelling leadership crystallizes around the individuals who may lead the country. In this sense, the 2000 Canadian federal election was no different from its predecessors. Jean Chrétien, Stockwell Day, Alexa McDonough, Joe Clark and Gilles Duceppe spent five weeks attempting to persuade the Canadian electorate of their respective leadership credentials. In the end, one was more successful than the others, and Jean Chrétien was re-elected as Prime Minister of Canada.

However, there was also something special about the 2000 federal election. In many ways, Pierre Elliott Trudeau's death on September 28, 2000 cast a long shadow over the current state of leadership in Canada. While people from around the world praised Canada's "Renaissance Man,"[2] there was a sense that today's leaders were failing to measure up to the leadership standards set by Trudeau. In fairness, time had been kind to the former Prime Minister who was better regarded at the time of his death than when he retired from politics in 1984. Nevertheless, it was generally observed that Canada was experiencing a decline of leadership, and the passing of Pierre Trudeau exacerbated this sentiment.

It will be the aim of this chapter to explore the leadership issue in the 2000 Canadian federal election. The primary objective of this analysis is to examine the electorate's evaluation of the party leaders, with a special focus on the impact of the campaign. To achieve this objective, I will first assess how the Canadian electorate perceived the party leaders prior to the start of the election campaign. Since Canadian electoral politics is increasingly regionalized,[3] I will look at leaders' evaluations from both a national and regional perspective. Secondly, I will concentrate on how these perceptions evolved as a consequence of the campaign. The election results suggest that the Liberals made significant gains at the expense of the other four main parties, and we will determine if the aggregate results mirror the evolution of leaders' perceptions. Moreover, for the third consecutive election, the Reform Party – now the Canadian Alliance – has failed to make significant inroads east of the Manitoba border. I will examine the extent to which this failure can be attributed to the perception of the performance of the Alliance Leader. But I will first place the present analysis in its broader theoretical context.

The Study of Leadership

The importance of leaders in the political process is not new. One only has to think of Lenin, Churchill, de Gaulle, Mao, and Eisenhower to appreciate the historical centrality of the role of leadership in bringing or accelerating fundamental societal change. To some extent, leadership is increasingly important, with television encouraging voters to make their voting decisions on the basis of media-driven individual performance — it has been argued that our evolving understanding of free, empowered individuals being the fundamental units of society helps explain the heavy emphasis we put on leadership in modern politics.[4] While there is little questioning of the importance of leaders in the political process, systematic theoretical and empirical analysis of the electoral importance of leadership has generally lagged behind that devoted to parties and issues.[5]

Recently, however, new approaches to leader assessment have begun to appear. First, political leadership is increasingly analyzed as a product of the interaction between leaders and the leadership environment with which they are faced. On the one hand, political leaders are motivated by particular ambitions and their actions are guided by certain modes of behaviour. On the other hand, the leadership environment is comprised of many interlinking elements, which may be either mutually reinforcing or countervailing and which can be classified under two headings: institutional structures; and the needs of the society. Leaders are able to shape their environment, but the environment will also shape their ambitions and behaviour.[6] An implication is that leader evaluations are not necessarily superficial, irrational, or purely short-term. Voters may focus on the personal qualities of a leader to gain important information about characteristics relevant to assessing how the individual will perform in office.[7] A similar perspective rooted in social psychological theory contends that criteria used in judging candidates reflect relatively general and enduring tendencies.[8] This was important in the 2000 federal election since voters had to assess how political newcomer Stockwell Day would perform if elected as Prime Minister of Canada. Without previous federal experience to rely upon, voters had to focus on Day's personal characteristics as a judgmental shortcut to assess his potential prime ministerial capabilities. For this reason, Day was put under closer personal scrutiny than the others who had already demonstrated their leadership potential.

The study of leadership in Canada has generally considered leader images to be short term in nature. For instance, in "Leaders and Voters: The Public Image of Canadian Political Leaders," Lawrence LeDuc probed the substance of the images of the two most successful party leaders of recent times in Canada, Pierre Trudeau and Brian Mulroney.[9] He pointed out that personality characteristics tend to predominate among frequently mentioned attributes of Canadian party leaders.[10] In another approach, Steven D. Brown, Ronald D. Lambert, Barry J. Kay, and James E. Curtis also looked at leader images in Canada.[11] They expected that the common prototypical structure exhibited by the citizen would remain quite stable over time despite the emergence of new circumstances and new leaders. Indeed, they suggested that this structure might be more useful to citizens when they are confronted with new leaders on the political landscape[12], as was the case in the 2000 election. They found that Canadians show evidence of possessing a prototypical leader role schema that informs their perceptions of the major party leaders in any one election period, and that remains stable from one election to another, despite turnovers in leadership personnel. Accordingly, Stockwell Day was faced with an electorate focusing on his personal character as a way to predict his behaviour in federal office, while the other four leaders were able to stress their ability to handle the task-relevant features of leadership. The leaders also had to contend with a reality of Canadian politics which suggests that leaders' evaluations inevitably deteriorate as the electorate becomes more familiar with them.

In *Absent Mandate* (1991), Clarke and his colleagues pointed out that public evaluation of party leaders does influence voting choice. However, the actual effects of leaders on voting choice and on the outcome of elections vary from election to election, and leader and issue effects on voting are intertwined.[13] Furthermore, they described party leaders as "fallen heroes," emphasizing the point that there has been a steady erosion of public support for party leaders, both as individuals and collectively.[14] They showed that every party leader between 1968 and 1988 has declined in public esteem from the benchmark established in his first election as leader, no matter how popular or unpopular the leader was at that juncture.[15] Thus,

> From the heady spring of "Trudeaumania" in 1968 to the bleak February of 1980, positive feelings toward Trudeau declined sharply and steadily...[Similarly] Robert Stanfield was less well-liked by the public in 1974 than in 1968, Joe Clark was more poorly regarded in 1980 than in 1979; John Turner was rated even lower by the public in 1988 than in 1984. Taken as a group, the party leaders were all less popular than they had been four years earlier.[16]

Building on the previous findings, Pammett has demonstrated a sharp decline in the influence of party leaders on voter's choices in Canada. (See also Chapter Thirteen of this volume.) Specifically, Pammett suggested that the "heyday of the party leader" in guiding the vote came with the final elections involving Pierre Trudeau, those of 1979 and 1980. He went on to propose that it was the appeal of Trudeau himself which limited the extent of the Liberal defeat in 1979 and propelled the party back to power in 1980. From that point on, leaders have declined in importance in actually motivating voters' choices, even while they have dominated the media coverage of the electoral debate ever since.[17] It is within this theoretical context that the present analysis will be conducted.

Leaders at the Starting Gate

If leaders have been a declining influence in motivating Canadians' voting behaviour, the media did not seem to notice. The media coverage of the 2000 federal election focused predominantly on the party leaders, seemingly crowding out other important elements of the campaign. This media emphasis on leadership began with the selection of Stockwell Day as leader of the Canadian Alliance on July 8, 2000. Day defeated Preston Manning in large part because he was able to effectively make the case that the newly-formed Canadian Alliance also needed a new leader. (See Chapter Three of this volume.) After the leadership convention, the party strategy was to capitalize on the apparent appeal of their young and telegenic new leader to improve the party's standings at the beginning of the campaign: to position the Canadian Alliance within "striking distance" of the Liberals. Day and the Alliance would then be able to build upon this improved positioning during the election campaign. It was believed that the appeal of the new leader would translate into an increase in party support and more seats for the Alliance. Above all, the party was expecting an electoral breakthrough in the East. However, while the media appeared initially besotted with Day, the electorate did not share the same enthusiasm.

When we examine the leaders' evaluations a few weeks before the start of the 2000 election campaign, it appears that Day had indeed successfully put himself "within striking distance" of Chrétien. Using a 1 to 10 scale of overall impression where 1 signifies "not at all impressed" and 10 is "very impressed," impressions of Day stood at 4.8, marginally behind Chrétien's at 5.0. McDonough and Duceppe were tied at 4.4, ahead of Clark at 3.8. However, a closer analysis reveals that Day's comparative good positioning had little to do with his personal appeal, but was rather the result of a decline in the overall impression of the Prime Minister.

Comparing the 2000 data with those at a similar point in the 1997 electoral cycle, we see that Chrétien's impression ratings were down significantly from 5.8 in 1997 to 5.0 in 2000. (See Table 1) At 4.8, Day's impression ratings were only marginally better than those of Preston Manning (4.7). McDonough (up from 4.0 in 1997 to 4.4 in 2000) and Duceppe (up from 3.9 in 1997 to 4.4 in 2000) were performing marginally better, while Clark (at 3.8) fared much worse than his predecessor at the helm of the federal PC Party, Jean Charest (at 5.3).

Table 1
Leaders' Evaluation at the Starting Gate

	National	
	1997 (a)	2000 (b)
Chrétien	5.8	5.0
Day		4.8
Manning	4.7	
McDonough	4.0	4.4
Duceppe (c)	3.9	4.4
Clark		3.8
Charest	5.3	

Sources: (a) Feedback Research Corporation, April 1997, (N=2500)
(b) Pollara's Perspectives Canada Survey, August 2000, (N=1668)
(c) Québec only.

We find the same pattern when looking at the evaluation of leaders from a regional perspective (Table 2).[18] Overall impressions of the Prime Minister were on the decline in three of Canada's five regions. In specific terms, impressions of Chrétien deteriorated in British Columbia (down from 5.6 in 1997 to 5.0 in 2000), the Prairies (down from 5.5 to 4.9), and Ontario (down from 6.1 to 5.6), while remaining stable in Atlantic Canada (up marginally from 5.3 in 1997 to 5.4 in 2000). Chrétien's image had improved in his native Québec (up from 3.0 in 1997 to 3.8 in 2000).

Table 2
Regional Leaders' Evaluation at the Starting Gate

	B.C		Prairies		Ontario		Quebec		Atlantic	
	'97 (a)	'00 (b)	'97	'00	'97	'00	'97	'00	'97	'00
Chrétien	5.6	5.0	5.5	4.9	6.1	5.6	3.0	3.8	5.3	5.4
Day		5.3		5.2		4.8		4.1		4.8
Manning	4.9		5.0		4.8		4.0		4.4	
McDonough	3.5	4.1	4.0	4.3	3.8	4.7	3.2	3.6	5.3	5.3
Clark		3.6		3.9		3.9		3.5		4.2
Charest	5.3		5.2		5.2		5.6		5.8	

Sources: (a) Feedback Research Corporation, April 1997, (N=2500)
(b) Pollara's Perspectives Canada Survey, August 2000, (N=1668)

As for Stockwell Day, he was performing only marginally better than his predecessor did in 1997. Impressions of Day in 2000 were slightly higher than Manning's in 1997 in British Columbia (5.3 for Day in 2000 compared to 4.9 for Manning in 1997), the Prairies (5.2 for Day in 2000 compared to 5.0 for Manning in 1997) and in Atlantic Canada (4.8 for Day in 2000 compared to 4.4 for Manning in 1997). More importantly for the Alliance, Stockwell Day was not doing better than Manning did in 1997 in Ontario (both at 4.8) and in the province of Québec (4.1 for Day in 2000 compared to 4.0 for Manning in 1997). Thus, prior to the beginning of the election campaign, there was little indication that the change in Alliance leadership was about to translate into the much sought after electoral breakthrough in the East.

The Impact of the Campaign

As discussed, the media focused on leadership and the campaign was difficult for the five party leaders, especially for Jean Chrétien and Stockwell Day. Jean Chrétien, who called a much-resented early election that bloomed into a nasty campaign, won his political gamble by gaining a third-straight majority government. However, this victory did not come without a personal price for the Prime Minister. Throughout the campaign, he was labeled as "arrogant," "out of touch" after seven years in government, and surrounded by a "Power Corp. elite" of aides who insulate him from ordinary people. Stockwell Day went even further when, on November 17, he called the Prime Minister a "criminal." Whether because of these attacks or not, the overall impression of Chrétien declined. Specifically, Chrétien's impression ratings went down from 5.0 before the start of the campaign to 4.8 immediately after. While this represents a small decline, it is important since it occurred despite the overall Liberal vote and seat gains in the election results. Thus, it appears that the negative personal attacks and accusations had a detrimental effect on the image of Jean Chrétien.

Table 3
The Impact of the Campaign on Leaders' Evaluation

| | National | |
	Pre-Campaign 2000 (a)	Post-Campaign 2000 (b)
Chrétien	5.0	4.8
Day	4.8	4.6
McDonough	4.4	4.6
Duceppe (c)	4.4	4.6
Clark	3.8	5.0

Source: (a) Pollara's Perspectives Canada Survey, August 2000, (N=1668) (b) Pollara's Perspectives Canada Survey, December 2000, (N=1692) (c) Québec only.

The election campaign proved even more difficult for Stockwell Day. The leader of the Alliance was put on the defensive from the start of the campaign, and Day often suffered from self-inflicted wounds. Day opened the campaign trying to draw an analogy between the flow of Lake Erie and the brain drain. He suggested that "just as Lake Erie drains from north to south, there is an ongoing drain in terms of our young people."[19] Unbeknownst to Day, Lake Erie drains from south to north. Then, Day had to defend his party policies supporting a two-tier health care system in Canada, and the 17% flat-tax. More importantly, he constantly had to defend his personal views on abortion, gay rights, and the potential impact of his religious beliefs on his ability to govern an increasingly secular Canadian polity. He was repeatedly accused of harboring a "hidden agenda." At one point, Day even defended the literal interpretation of creationism that suggests that the earth is about 6 000 years old, and dinosaurs roamed the earth with humans. When asked to comment on creationism, Day suggested that "there is scientific evidence supporting the creationist view."[20]

On election day, Stockwell Day's Alliance, which was supposed to have transformed the Reform Party of the West into a new party capable of penetrating seat-rich Ontario, failed for the third consecutive time to make an electoral breakthrough in the East, winning only two rural Ontario seats. The Alliance nevertheless increased its seat share from 60 in 1997 to 66. Notwithstanding the Alliance gains, overall impressions of Stockwell Day worsened as a result of the campaign. While Day's impression rating stood at 4.8 at the start of the campaign, it deteriorated to 4.6 in its aftermath.

On a regional basis, Day's impression ratings declined in British Columbia (from 5.3 to 4.8), Ontario (from 4.8 to 4.6) and in Atlantic Canada (from 4.8 to 4.5), while remaining stable in Quebec (at 4.1) and increasing in the Prairies (from 5.2 to 5.4). (Table 4) Moreover, in Ontario, the gap between the evaluations of Day and Chrétien became wider than it was prior to the beginning of the election campaign. Not only did Day fail to make an electoral breakthrough in Ontario, he came out of the 2000 election comparatively worse off than the waning Chrétien.

With so much attention devoted to the two frontrunners, the other leaders fared comparatively well. Both McDonough and Duceppe made marginal gains in overall impression, while Joe Clark appeared to have redeemed himself, making impressive gains during the campaign (up from 3.8 to 5.0). In fact, Clark emerged from the election as the best-regarded leader in Canada. Unfortunately for him, the Tories lost seats in the 2000 election, and 41% of Canadians think Clark should step down as Tory leader.[21] It is therefore doubtful that Clark could sustain this new-found popularity until the next federal election.

Table 4
The Regional Impact of the Campaign

	B.C	Prairies	Ontario	Quebec	Atlantic
Chrétien					
Pre-Campaign (a)	5.0	4.9	5.6	3.8	5.4
Post-Campaign (b)	4.6	4.3	5.6	4.0	5.1
Day					
Pre-Campaign	5.3	5.2	4.8	4.1	4.8
Post-Campaign	4.8	5.4	4.6	4.1	4.5
McDonough					
Pre-Campaign	4.1	4.3	4.7	3.6	5.3
Post-Campaign	4.4	4.6	4.8	3.9	5.4
Clark					
Pre-Campaign	3.6	3.9	3.9	3.5	4.2
Post-Campaign	4.8	5.1	5.3	4.4	5.1

Source: (a) Pollara's Perspectives Canada Survey, August 2000, (N=1668)(b) Pollara's Perspectives Canada Survey, December 2000, (N=1692)

Aside from transforming Reform into a party capable of winning seats in the East, the Alliance was also formed to attract supporters of all parties in order to build an alternative to the governing Liberals (see Chapter Two of this volume). Preston Manning was perceived as a barrier to attracting supporters from other parties and Stockwell Day's leadership was aimed at overcoming this obstacle to growth. It is therefore important to look at the impact of the election campaign on leaders' evaluations among the different party supporters (Table 5).

Table 5
Leaders' Evaluation and Party Support

	Liberals	Alliance	PCs	NDP[22]
Chrétien				
Pre-Campaign (a)	6.2	3.8	4.8	4.9
Post-Campaign (b)	6.8	3.2	4.4	4.5
Day				
Pre-Campaign	4.5	6.8	4.4	3.7
Post-Campaign	4.4	6.9	4.3	3.6
Manning				
Post-Campaign	4.8	6.2	4.8	4.6
McDonough				
Pre-Campaign	4.8	3.5	4.4	5.6
Post-Campaign	5.7	4.6	5.0	6.5
Clark				
Pre-Campaign	4.0	3.0	5.0	3.9
Post-Campaign	5.4	4.4	6.4	5.6

Sources: (a) Pollara's Perspectives Canada Survey, August 2000, (N=1668)
(b) Pollara's Perspectives Canada Survey, December 2000, (N=1692)

First, every leader improved his or her impression ratings amongst their respective supporters. Clark made the biggest gains (from 5.0 among PC supporters before the campaign to 6.4 afterwards), followed by McDonough (from 5.6 to 6.5), and Chrétien (from 6.2 to 6.8). For his part, Day made only marginal gains amongst Alliance voters (from 6.8 to 6.9). More importantly for the Alliance, Day emerged from the election campaign as the worst regarded leader amongst Liberals, PCs, and NDP voters. In fact, Preston Manning is currently better regarded than Day by Liberals, PCs and NDP supporters. Accordingly, while Stockwell Day was able to solidify his appeal amongst Alliance supporters, he failed to meet the party's strategic objectives to build an alternative to the governing Liberals.

Conclusion: What the Future May Hold

Recent studies of leadership have suggested that in the modern political era, voters increasingly make their evaluations on the basis of media-reported individual performance. Voters focus on the personal qualities of a leader to gain important information about characteristics relevant to assessing how the individual will perform in office. Hence, voters would focus on a candidate's personal characteristics as a judgmental shortcut to assess his or her potential capabilities. However, this intense scrutiny comes with a price. Canadian studies have demonstrated that leaders' evaluations inevitably deteriorate as the electorate becomes more familiar with them. It has also been shown that, in Canada, there has been a steady erosion of public support for party leaders. The present analysis of the 2000 federal election tends to support this evidence. With the exception of Joe Clark, the 2000 federal election had a negative impact on the party leaders. Despite party gains in both vote and seats shares, the public's' evaluations of both Chrétien and Day have deteriorated as a result of the election campaign. While Clark, Duceppe, and McDonough have managed to maintain, and in the case of Clark improve, their ratings, collectively, impressions of the nation's political leaders are at their lowest point since such data have been collected. This tends to corroborate the general sense that Canada is experiencing a decline of leadership, a sentiment that was exacerbated by the passing of Pierre Trudeau in the fall of 2000.

Studies have also suggested that that every party leader since 1968 has declined in public esteem from the benchmark established from their first election as leader, no matter how popular or unpopular the leader was at that juncture. The 2000 federal election further supports this assertion. Chrétien has seen his image of "le p'tit gars de Shawinigan" seriously undermined during the campaign, and his impression ratings are the lowest ever recorded for a newly elected Prime Minister.[23] While Chrétien has been adept at bewildering experts throughout his career, it can be safely predicted that the Prime Minister will be replaced by a new Liberal Leader before the end of his mandate.

The impact of the campaign was even harsher for Stockwell Day. After winning the leadership of the Canadian Alliance, the expectations were high for him. It was believed that the appeal of the new leader would translate into an increase in party support and more seats for the Alliance, particularly in the East. But above all, Day had to complete the transformation of the Reform Party into an alliance able to attract supporters of all parties in order to build an alternative to the governing Liberals. Day failed to meet every objective. While the Alliance increased its seat share from 60 in 1997 to 66, we have seen that overall impressions of Stockwell Day worsened as a result of the campaign. While Day's impression rating stood at 4.8 at the start of the campaign, it deteriorated to 4.6 in its aftermath. On a regional basis, Day's impression ratings declined in British Columbia, Ontario, and in Atlantic Canada, while remaining stable in Quebec, and increasing in the Prairies. Moreover, in Ontario, the gap in leaders' evaluation between Day and Chrétien is now wider than it was prior to the beginning of the election campaign. Not only did Day fail to make an electoral breakthrough in Ontario, he comes out of the 2000 election comparatively worse off than the Prime Minister.

Among voters, every leader improved his or her impression ratings amongst their respective supporters, with Clark making the biggest gains. For his part, Day made only marginal gains amongst Alliance voters but more importantly, he is emerging from the election campaign as the worst regarded leader amongst Liberals, PCs, and NDP voters. Accordingly, while Stockwell Day was able to solidify his core support, he failed to meet the party's strategic objective to build an alternative to the governing Liberals.

Since he is a newcomer on the federal scene, it is difficult to ascertain what the future holds for Stockwell Day. He will have to face a leadership review within the next 18 months and it will be up to the Alliance members to decide if they want Day to remain as leader.

However, studies of leadership in Canada, and the result of the present analysis, suggest that Day is embarked on the same downward spiral of declining popularity that has been experienced by every recent political leader. His ratings are lower than Trudeau's and Mulroney's in their last election, and comparable to those of Stanfield and Turner at the end of their career.[24] Thus, regardless of what the future may hold, Day and Chrétien have now become the most recent "fallen heroes" of Canadian politics.

NOTES

1   The author would like to thank POLLARA's Chairman Michael Marzolini for the use of Perspectives Canada data in this chapter.

2   *Ottawa Citizen*, September 29, 2000

3   See Michael Marzolini, "The Regionalization of Canadian Electoral Politics" in Allan Frizzell and Jon H. Pammett eds., *The Canadian General Election of 1997*, (Toronto: Dundurn Press, 1997).

4   Michael Bliss, *Right Honourable Men*, (Toronto: HarperCollins Publishers Ltd), xvi.

5   Arthur H. Miller, Martin P. Wattenberg, and Oksana Malanchuk, "Schematic Assessments of Presidential Candidates," *American Political Science Review*, 80 (1986), 521-522.

6   Robert Elgie, *Political Leadership in Liberal Democracies*, (New York: St. Martin's Press, 1995), 23.

7   See Samuel Popkin, John W. Gorman, Charles Phillips, and Jeffrey A. Smith, "What Have You Done For Me Lately? Toward an Investment Theory of Voting," *American Political Science Review*, 70 (1976) and Goldie Shabad and Kristi Andersen, "Candidate Evaluations by Men and Women," *Public Opinion Quarterly*, 43 (1979).

8   Pamela J. Conover, "Political Cues and the Perception of Candidates," *American Politics Quarterly*, 9 (1981) and Donald R. Kinder, Mark D. Peters, Robert P. Abelson and Susan T. Fiske, "Presidential Prototypes," in Richard R. Lau and David O. Sears eds., *Political Cognition*, (Hillsdale, NJ: Lawrence Erlbaum Associates, 1985).

9   Lawrence LeDuc, "Leaders and Voters," in Maureen Mancuso, Richard G. Price, and Ronald Wagenberg, eds., *Leaders and Leadership in Canada*, (Toronto: Oxford University Press, 1994), 59.

10 Ibid., 62.

11 Steven D. Brown, Ronald D. Lambert, Barry J. Kay, and James E. Curtis, "In the Eye of the Beholder," *Canadian Journal of Political Science*, 21 (1988).

12 Ibid., 735.

13 Clarke et al., *Absent Mandate*, 2nd edition, (Toronto: Gage Educational Publishing Company, 1991), 107.

14 Ibid., 90.

15 Ibid.

16 Ibid., 90-91.

17 See Jon H. Pammett, "The Voters Decide" in Allan Frizzell and Jon H. Pammett eds., *The Canadian General Election of 1997*, (Toronto: Dundurn Press, 1997), 233-234, but also Harold Clarke, Jane Jenson, Lawrence LeDuc, and Jon H. Pammett, *Absent Mandate*, 3rd edition, (Toronto: Gage Educational Publishing Company, 1996).

18 We exclude Gilles Duceppe from this analysis since the Bloc Québécois did not run candidates outside of the province of Québec and impression ratings were not collected for the Bloc leader outside of Québec.

19 John Ward, "Liberals form majority government, hold Ontario, gain in Quebec and East," *Vancouver Sun*, 28 November, 2000.

20 See Ibid.

21 Pollara's Perspectives Canada, December 2000. The comparative figures for the other leaders are: Day (35%), McDonough (29%), and Duceppe (23%). No data was available for Chrétien.

22 The question asked was: "In the most recent election, which political party did you vote for?" Only those who voted were included in the analysis.

23 For comparative data, see Harold Clarke, Jane Jenson, Lawrence LeDuc, and Jon H. Pammett, *Absent Mandate*, 3rd edition, (Toronto: Gage Educational Publishing Company, 1996).

24 Ibid.

Chapter 13

The People's Verdict

by Jon H. Pammett

The similarities between the voting patterns and results of the 2000 Canadian General Election and its immediate predecessors of 1997 and 1993 are more prominent than the differences. Since the two main contenders, the Liberals and the Canadian Alliance, both improved their percentage of the national vote, the electoral arena may appear at first glance to be somewhat more polarized than before. The Liberals improved from 38.4% of the national vote to 40.8% (see Appendix for tables of results). The Alliance improved the showing of the old Reform party from 19.4% of the vote in the 1997 election to 25.5% this time. In part, however, these vote gains by the two major parties came in areas of the country where they were already dominant, thereby reinforcing the regionalized nature of Canadian electoral politics rather than paving the way for increased competition between these forces.

The Liberal vote increased two percentage points (to 51.5%) in Ontario, a region where they were already dominant and where they had obtained virtually all of the seats. The major gain for the Liberals was in Quebec, where they increased from 36.7% to 44.2% and picked up 11 seats in Parliament. In Quebec, however, the main battle is between the Liberals and the Bloc Québécois, and the latter party also increased its vote in the province, by two percentage points. Both of these results were occasioned in large part by the collapse of the Progressive Conservative strength in Quebec; that party went from 22.2% of the Quebec vote in 1997 to 5.6% in 2000, and lost four of its five seats. The competitive situation in the province was little changed from the past.

Most observers of the 2000 election were particularly interested in the extent to which the Canadian Alliance accomplished its goal of broadening its support base from that associated with the Reform Party. This was most noticeable in two areas of the country. The first was the West, already the party's region of strength. The increase in its Saskatchewan vote from 36% to 47.7%, for example, was enough to give the Alliance three extra seats, but did not affect the overall competitive situation in the West. The improvement in the Alberta vote for the Alliance (from 54.7% to 58.9%) was actually accompanied by a net loss in seats in that province. In British Columbia and Manitoba, the result was a moderate increase in both votes and seats. The results of increasing its support in the West, however, may have been a mixed blessing for the Alliance. On the one hand, evidence of increasing support anywhere can give a party momentum. On the other, however, it has the potential of being counterproductive if potential Ontario supporters are made nervous by its increasing association with Western representation.

The second area of growth of Alliance support, in absolute terms, came in the central provinces of Ontario and Quebec. The new party gained 6% of the Quebec vote this time, in a sense a dramatic improvement over the minuscule number of votes achieved by its predecessor. However, the starting point was so low that no observer expects the Alliance to be in a competitive position in the province in even the medium term, let alone the short term. The party's vote gain in Ontario (from 19.1% to 23.6%), while very much in line with the party's strategic goals, achieved only a limited improvement in the competitive position of the party in battles with the Liberals. Two Alliance members were elected, but the party had great difficulty being considered a major force in the province.

As for the Progressive Conservatives and the New Democratic Party, the 2000 election mostly brought bad news, as the parties dropped votes and seats, and appeared further marginalized once the results were tabulated. For the Conservatives, their losses in Ontario and Quebec undermined their claim to be the "national opposition party" to the Liberals. Most discouraging of all was the result given the widespread praise for the campaign performance of Joe Clark, the party's leader (see Chapter 3 of this volume and the later part of this chapter). The New Democrats declined in support in all regions of the country, even in the Atlantic region where they had enjoyed success in previous elections, and in Manitoba, Saskatchewan and British Columbia, where the party formed provincial governments.

The Patterns of Voting

Table 1

VOTE STABILITY & CHANGE 1997 - 2000

1997 Behaviour

		Non Voters	Liberals	PC	NDP	Reform	BQ	Others
2000 Behaviour	Did Not Vote	61%	9%	10%	12%	5%	15%	—
	Liberals	11	64	15	10	5	4	8
	PC	3	9	44	4	5	4	8
	NDP	6	4	2	56	2	1	33
	Alliance	13	12	26	13	80	5	8
	BQ	4	1	1	1	—	67	8
	Others	1	1	1	4	2	2	33
	N=	166	337	87	78	94	92	12

Source: POLLARA Post-Election Survey.

NOTE: Percentages sum to 100% in columns.

Table 2

SOURCES OF PARTY SUPPORT, 2000

1997 Behaviour

2000 Parties	Did Not Vote	Liberals	PC	NDP	Reform	BQ	Other	N
Liberals	7%	81	5	3	2	2	*	267
PC	6%	34	45	4	6	5	1	85
NDP	13%	17	3	58	3	1	5	76
Alliance	12%	23	13	6	42	3	1	177
BQ	8%	4	1	1	—	84	1	74
Other	12%	18	6	18	12	12	24	17

Source: POLLARA Post-Election Survey.

NOTE: Percentages sum to 100% across rows.

As in 1997, the basic building block of the Liberal victory was its ability to retain a substantial proportion (just under two-thirds) of its previous vote. The Liberal retention percentage was considerably better than that posted by the Progressive Conservatives (44%) and the New Democratic party (56%) (Table 1). The Canadian Alliance, the heir to the old Reform Party, received the votes of 80% of the people who had voted for Reform in 1997. Any questions, therefore, about whether Reform voters would accept the creation of the new party, with its somewhat broadened areas of appeal, appears to be answered in the affirmative. Furthermore, Table 1 shows that Reform/Alliance voters were far less likely to abstain from voting in 2000 than those who had previously supported any other major party. The Bloc Québécois, normally a party which depends on retention of its past voters, was again strong in this regard, but suffered from the decisions of a relatively high proportion of its previous voters not to go to the polls in 2000.

The patterns of vote-switching from 1997-2000 were substantially in favour of the Alliance, providing the boost which allowed them to increase their overall popular vote in the election to 26% from the 19% achieved by the Reform Party in 1997. While this did not result in the breakthrough in seats that the party strategists had hoped for (see Chapter 2) it was a more impressive performance than that registered by any other party in the 2000 election. Table 1 shows that the Alliance received the votes of one-quarter of previous Progressive Conservative voters, and one-eighth of those who had supported the NDP last time. More important in sheer numbers were the 12% of 1997 Liberal voters who decided to switch to the Alliance. Half of this group of vote-switchers came from the province of Ontario, and contributed to whatever inroads the Alliance was able to make in that key province. Of those who report switching from a 1997 Progressive Conservative vote to a 2000 Alliance vote, however, only one-third were from Ontario. Coupled with the fact that this was a rather small group to begin with, the "unite the Right" strategy which was supposed to boost the Alliance in Ontario had very limited success.

Table 2 uses the same data as Table 1, but provides a way for us to look at how important retention and conversion were in the composition of party support in the 2000 election. For the Liberals and the Bloc Québécois, much of their support (81% and 84% respectively) came from people who had been supporters of the party in the election immediately prior to the current one. For the Conservatives, however, less than half of their 2000 supporters had been with the party in 1997, with the remainder having to be recruited from others. The Alliance was even more heavily renovated, in that only 42% of its 2000 voters had voted Reform in 1997. The implications of these two situations are completely different however, as the Conservatives were losing votes overall and striving to retain past support, while the Alliance was gaining, and adding to its existing strength. Tables 1 and 2 in combination show that the Alliance retained much (80%) of the Reform vote from 1997, but that this group of former Reformers comprised less than half of Alliance voters in 2000. Looked at in this manner, the Alliance can claim some success in broadening the scope of the new party beyond its previous base. If it were to continue its high retention rate in the next election and continue to attract converts, its prospects for success, at least in English Canada, would be enhanced.

Factors in the Vote Decision

For the past two and one-half decades, election studies have been asking representative samples of Canadians an identical series of questions about their reasons for voting. The question format asked in the first instance whether party leaders, local candidates "here in this constituency," or parties as a whole were most important in deciding which way to vote. A follow-up question then asked whether the choice of leader or candidate was motivated by issues or by the personal qualities of the individuals, or in the case of parties whether it was the party's "general approach" or issues which was important. Thus we can look behind the leader, candidate or party factors in voting choice to determine whether or not there was an issue basis for it (while avoiding suggesting at the beginning that issues should be compared with the other three factors directly).

Table 3
MOST IMPORTANT FACTORS IN VOTING, 1974–2000
(Percent citing issue basis in parentheses)

Election	Party Leaders	Local Candidates	Party as a Whole
2000	22% (60)	21 (58)	58 (46)
1997	20% (71)	22 (59)	58 (57)
1993	22% (62)	21 (52)	57 (54)
1988	20% (71)	27 (57)	53 (57)
1984	30% (56)	21 (46)	49 (37)
1980	36% (53)	20 (40)	44 (43)
1979	37% (54)	23 (43)	40 (45)
1974	33% (58)	27 (48)	40 (43)

Sources: 1974-84 Canadian National Election Studies. 1988 re-interview of 1984 CNES. 1993 Insight Canada Research post-election survey. 1997 & 2000 POLLARA Post-Election Surveys
NOTE:Percentages sum to 100% across rows.

Table 3 shows the pattern of choice of the most important factors in the voting decision from the federal elections of 1974 to 2000. In the last three elections, the percentages of voters choosing leaders, candidates or parties as the most important factor have been almost identical. In 2000, just over one fifth (22% and 21%) felt that leaders or candidates were most important, while a substantial majority (58%) picked parties. The table shows a different picture at the end of the sequence of elections from the one that is evident at the beginning. During the years when the Canadian political stage was dominated by Pierre Trudeau, leaders were considerably more important than they have been in motivating voting behaviour. The decline of the leader factor took place in two distinct stages. The first began in 1984, when the percentage saying that leader was most important to them dropped from 36% to 30%; John Turner and Brian Mulroney, though new and putatively attractive leaders, failed to capture the public imagination to the same degree as had Trudeau. The second and larger drop, from 30% to 20%, occurred in 1988. In that election, Mulroney and Turner were not so new, and had dropped in public estimation. In addition, the 1988 election was so dominated by the free trade issue that personalities were to some extent eclipsed. Despite a series of new leaders of all the parties, the "leader factor" has never recovered from these two drops in the 1980s. And a contest in 2000 between the "old warhorses" for the Liberals and Conservatives and the "young Turk" for the Alliance did not appear to set the public's pulse racing any faster than it had in the recent past. The public outpouring of affection at the time of Pierre Trudeau's funeral made a poignant contrast with the disdain in which the current crop of leaders is held (see Chapter 12 of this volume).

Table 3 indicates in a set of parentheses the proportion of the leader, candidate and party vote that was attributed by survey respondents to "issues" rather than personal qualities or the general approach of parties. Interestingly, the 2000 election appears to be a partial exception to the general trend of increasing importance for the issue component of these factors. Ever since the 1988 election, the majority of those choosing "party" as the most important factor in their voting decision have reported that "issues" the party stood for were really behind this choice. For example, in the 1997 election, 57% took this position. In 2000, this percentage dived to 46%, indicating a dramatic drop in the degree of issue importance in this election. The "leader" factor showed an identical drop in the percentage of people stating that there was an issue basis to their choice. Here we have initial indications of the public's inability to find as much issue content in the 2000 election campaign as they were used to having.

Table 4
MOST IMPORTANT ELECTION ISSUES, 1993–2000

ISSUE	1993	1997	2000
Unemployment, jobs	44%	24%	2%
Economy	8	4	3
Deficit, debt	18	10	6
Taxes	—	3	7
National unity, Quebec, regionalism	4	13	3
Resources, environment	—	1	2
Social issues	4	10	35
			(health=31)
Government, trust, parties, accountability, leaders	7	3	8
Other	4	3	5
None, don't know	10	29	29

(1993) Insight Canada Research Post election survey
1997 & 2000 POLLARA Post-election Surveys. N= 1200 in all three studies
NOTE: Percentages sum to 100% in columns.

To some extent, the lesser degree of public concentration on issues in the 2000 election can be related to the type of issue which dominated the discussion. Traditionally, Canadian federal elections have focused on economic issues. These have varied widely in content, from inflation in the 1974 election, to energy pricing in 1980, to unemployment in 1984. In the 1988 election, free trade policy was the issue, and once that was settled, unemployment once again dominated the issue agenda in 1993, along with the deficit and debt reduction. In the 1997 election, jobs were once again at the forefront (Table 4); however, the issue picture in that election was one of more diversity than normal. Perhaps not since 1979, when several economic issues were joined by questions of Quebec independence as subjects of a diverse political discourse, had the issue picture been so scattered. In 1997, regional issues and social issues edged their way onto the issue agenda, the former to reflect concerns about regional disparities (which themselves often have an economic basis) and the latter to reflect public concern about the consequences of budget cutting.

The 2000 Canadian election was very different in the composition of the issue agenda. As Table 4 shows, social issues dominated the response when the public was asked about the most important election issue. Over a third of the electorate designated social issues as most important, with the bulk of these answers referring to the health system. To some extent, this attention given to health reflected the strategy of the parties in emphasizing concerns with medicare. The Liberal Party in particular saw an opportunity to portray the Alliance as a party which might "privatize" health care, or at least allow the creation of a parallel private health system alongside the state-run system. The Conservatives and the NDP were delighted to join these attacks on the Alliance, seeing the health issue as an opportunity to portray themselves as moderate and supportive of better public health care. The Alliance itself, though reluctant to engage in public debate on bringing fundamental change to health care, was able to criticize the "hypocrisy" of the Liberals in posing as champions of health care after cutting massive amounts of funding from this sector in recent years in the form of grants to the provinces to deliver health services.

Economic issues were not absent from the 2000 election campaign, although they were overshadowed by social issues. The Alliance, for example, proposed a tax cut plan, and the Liberals had already delivered a budget just before the election which announced a series of tax cuts. Cutting the government debt was still a point of concern to some, and once again the parties promised to continue (the Liberals) or accelerate (the Alliance) the pace of this reduction. But the question of jobs and the unemployment rate practically dropped off the issue agenda in 2000. Past experience with the unemployment issue in Canadian elections has been that it is relatively sensitive to the rise or fall of the unemployment rate rather than related to the absolute level of unemployment.[1] The unemployment rate at the time of the 2000 election was 6.9%, not low in absolute terms, but lower than it had been in recent years, and considerably lower than the 9.1% rate at the time of the 1997 election, and the 11.1% in 1993.[2] Were the unemployment rate to rise before the next election, we might predict a reappearance of this issue on the electoral agenda, even if it does not reach the level of 1993 or even 1997.

The question asking Canadians about the most important issue in the election campaign found 29% who stated that there was no issue, or that they did not know of one. This result, which was similar to that obtained in the relatively lacklustre 1997 campaign, was a considerable change from elections held since 1988 in which relatively few people were unable to identify an important issue. The 1988 agenda was dominated by the free trade issue, and the 1993 election featured the Liberal "Red Book" which delineated a series of plans that they promised to implement if elected. The 1997 and (especially) the 2000 versions of the Liberal "Red Book" were, however, pale imitations of that issued in 1993 (see Chapter One of this volume). The Liberals did not even have the "policy manifesto" completed at the beginning of the campaign, and seemed at a loss to explain to the public what policy or issue reason they had for calling the election at an unexpectedly early date. Canadian federal campaigns now seem to be settling into a pattern familiar from the politics of the Trudeau era, when campaign discussion was more about style than substance. Another indication of this phenomenon from Table 4 is the larger number of people (8%, up from 3% in 1997) who cited general ratings of parties or leaders as "issues," or told the interviewer that it was "time for a change" or that the main issue was "to keep the Alliance out of power."

An analysis of Prime Minister Jean Chrétien's speeches during the 2000 election campaign may help to explain the limited public engagement with the issue agenda.[3] Mr. Chrétien gave 54 speeches during the campaign, and referred to health care issues in about half of them. However, in only three of these speeches was there any reference to a specific commitment to increase public spending on health or to introduce any other change to the medical care system.[4] Thus, there was a lot of talk about the state of the health care system during the campaign, charges of past or planned misdeeds by opponents, pledges of continued support by all the contestants, but very little in the way of concrete discussion about actual changes which might be made. Nor was Mr. Chrétien very specific about any other issue either. The analysis of his speeches shows that only two specific pledges made appearances in a large number of speeches; a promise to have every community in Canada connected to the Internet by 2004, and a promise to set up a "registered individual learning account" for employment retraining.[5]

Table 5

PARTY CLOSEST ON MOST IMPORTANT ISSUE, 1993 –2000

	Liberals	PC	NDP	Ref/All	Bloc	Oth	None
Unemployment/jobs							
2000	18%	14	1	29	21	—	21
1997	33%	14	22	11	1	1	18
1993	61%	7	4	7	5	—	16
Taxes							
2000	25%	4	1	50	1	1	18
1997	22%	27	6	30	—	1	14
1993	46%	18	18	9	—	—	9
The deficit/debt							
2000	32%	13	1	29	7	4	14
1997	62%	8	2	19	3	1	6
1993	24%	21	4	29	4	1	17
Constitutional Issues							
2000	37%	16	3	11	13	—	21
1997	27%	19	7	29	8	—	11
1993	41%	6	2	16	16	4	14
Social Issues							
2000	33%	10	20	15	3	1	19
1997	31%	10	25	17	—	1	17
1993	40%	8	21	9	4	4	15
All Issues							
2000	31%	10	13	23	4	2	18
1997	35%	14	14	20	2	2	14
1993	48%	9	4	13	6	2	18

Source: (1993) Insight Canada Research post-election survey. 1997 & 2000 POLLARA Post-Election Surveys. NOTE: percentages sum to 100% across rows.

The predominance of social issues, primarily health, as election issues in 2000 had the potential to affect the results if these issues were differentially associated with a particular party. Table 5 shows that the Liberals benefited most from being identified as the party closest to people's own positions on social issues (33% choosing that party, whereas only 15% thought the Alliance was the closest party to them on those issues). The Alliance did much better on economic issues, where 50% of people stating taxes to be the most important election issue chose that party as the closest to their own position and 29% of those concerned with jobs or the debt chose the Alliance. This situation with the deficit/debt issue represents a departure from 1997, when most people (62%) citing deficit cutting as the major issue chose the Liberals as closest to them. It more closely resembles the 1993 election, when Preston Manning's Reform Party successfully appealed to the segment of the public that wanted a rapid pace of budget reduction. In the period between 1993 and 1997, Finance Minister Paul Martin made such a priority of budget cutting that it became a Liberal issue. In 2000, attention had shifted from the deficit (now that budgets were in surplus) to reducing the accumulated debt; the Liberals' "balanced" approach to debt reduction and spending appealed to just about the same proportion of the electorate as the Alliance's emphasis on further reductions.

Table 6

EFFECTS OF SELECTED ISSUES, 2000

	2000 VOTE					
Most Important Issue	Liberals	PC	NDP	Alliance	BQ	Other
Social Issues						
Switch to	2.3	2.6	2.2	3.7	0.1	2.6
Remain	11.1	2.3	3.7	2.9	1.8	0.3
	13.4	4.9	5.9	6.6	1.9	2.9

Most Important Issue	Liberals	PC	NDP	Alliance	BQ	Other
Taxes						
Switch to	0.4	0.7	—	2.2	—	.1
Remain	1.5	—	.1	1.8	.1	—
	1.9	1.7	.1	4.0	.1	.1
Debt						
Switch to	0.4	.3	—	1.4	—	.1
Remain	1.7	.6	.1	1.0	.8	.1
	2.1	.9	.1	2.4	.8	.2

Source: POLLARA Post-Election Survey

Table 6 shows the extent to which the issues just mentioned affected the voting in 2000. Moderate amounts of vote-switching toward the Alliance, Liberals, PCs and NDP were motivated by social issues, predominately health. The table shows that 3.7% of the electorate switched to the Alliance and cited this category of issue as most important, while 2.3% switched to the Liberals. So, some vote switchers were indeed attracted to the Alliance by their promises to re-think the health care delivery system in Canada. Health, however, was cited by 11.1% of the electorate as a reason for remaining Liberal, a much larger percentage than accrued to any of the other parties. So the Liberal campaign tactic of raising the supposed "hidden agenda" of the Alliance to implement a "two tier" health care system paid off for the party by keeping many of its faithful on board for another election. Similarly, the NDP was able to appeal to concerns over health care funding to keep an appreciable number of votes for the party. Table 6 also documents a lead for the Alliance among those voters acting on the basis of the economic issues, primarily tax reductions. But it was the Liberal ability to turn social issues to their advantage that ultimately won the issue battle in the 2000 election.

The Effect of the Campaign

Despite all the time, effort and money political parties put into running their campaigns, relatively little voter decision-making occurs during most of the campaign period, according to voters themselves. Table 7 reports the times at which the 2000 respondents made up their minds which way to vote. This table shows generally similar results to that of 1997, and many previous Canadian elections. Before the campaign even began, 60% of the electorate had made up their minds which way to vote, either because they had decided before the election was called, or at the time it was called. Only 16% report making their voting decision during the four weeks of the campaign. The remaining 24%, who report deciding their vote during the final days before the election date or on election day itself, may of course have been influenced by the campaigns of the parties, but it is equally likely that they only turned their attention to their prospective vote under the stimulus of election day itself.

Table 7
2000 VOTE, BY TIME OF VOTE DECISION

	Before Election Called (47%)	When Called (13%)	During Campaign (16%)	Final Days (24%)
2000 Vote				
Liberal	40%	39%	30%	35%
Progressive Conservative	8	9	21	18
New Democrat	9	11	12	12
Alliance	28	30	31	22
Bloc Quebecois	14	10	3	8
Other	1	2	3	5
N =	376	103	127	189

Source: POLLARA Post-Election Survey
NOTE: Percentages sum to 100% in columns.

When contemplating what effects the election campaign might have had other than to reinforce voting decisions which had already been arrived at, we can examine Table 7 for patterns of later deciders which might differ from those who had already made up their minds. The Liberal vote was generally stronger among those people who knew all along which party they were going to support. Conversely, the campaign effort put on by the Progressive Conservatives seems to have produced some results. Largely as a result, it may be speculated, of the performance of Tory leader Joe Clark in the leaders' debate and the subsequent renewed media attention this sparked, the PCs gained double the vote share of late deciders over those who had their minds made up all along. In fact, the percentage of voters who decided at the last minute to vote Tory (18%) was not far away from the percentage that opted for the Alliance (22%).

There is in fact some evidence that voter decision making at the tail end of the campaign reflected fear of the Alliance, as that party did significantly worse among people making up their minds at the last minute than those who decided their votes at any other time. Among those deciding in the campaign's final days, the Liberal vote picked up (35% as opposed to 30% of mid-campaign decision makers) as did that for the Bloc Québécois (8% instead of 3%) and that for the smaller parties (5%). The Conservative and NDP votes among last minute vote deciders remained at or near the rates of those choosing these parties during the campaign. Only the Alliance suffered a substantial dip at the end of the election campaign. On the one hand, the party might interpret this positively, by arguing that their campaign made its mark early; on the other, any campaign which tails off badly at the end can hardly be called a success.

The debate between the party leaders, which in this campaign took place on November 8 and 9, with the French language debate occurring first, has been noted in several of the preceding chapters of this volume. The leaders debate of 2000 was the seventh held at the federal level in Canada, and presented further proof of the institutionalized nature of this heavily-anticipated mid-campaign event.[6] Since all the other party leaders were more-or-less "known quantities," many eyes were on Alliance leader Stockwell Day, to see how he might fare in the rather unruly atmosphere of a debate where the leaders had considerable freedom to attack each other directly. As the events unfolded, Mr. Day's presence was barely noticeable in the French language debate, and he was not widely perceived as delivering a winning performance in the English one.

Table 8

2000 VOTE, BY PERCEIVED DEBATE WINNER

	Jean Chrétien (18%)	Joe Clark (51%)	Alexa McDonough (5%)	Stockwell Day (17%)	Gilles Duceppe (9%)
2000 Vote					
Liberal	75%	33%	17%	16%	16%
Progressive Conservative	7	20	13	3	13
New Democrat	5	12	44	1	3
Alliance	5	26	17	74	24
Bloc Quebecois	8	9	4	3	40
Other		1	4	3	5
N=	77	215	23	73	38

Source: POLLARA Post-Election Survey
NOTE: Percentages sum to 100% in columns.

Table 8 presents the answers of that percentage of the survey sample (53%) who reported seeing some part of one of the leadership debates. The proportion reporting that Stockwell Day gave the best performance in the debates was 17%, better than Alexa McDonough of the NDP (5%) or Gilles Duceppe of the BQ (9%), and virtually the same as Prime Minister Jean Chrétien (18%). For most respondents, however, the winner of the debates was Joe Clark of the Conservatives, who, with his party on the ropes and feeling he had nothing to lose, mounted assertive and well-researched attacks on the policies, values and records of both the Liberals and the Alliance. Mr. Clark, who had also appeared in the debate of 1979, was able to take advantage of Mr. Chrétien's defensiveness and Mr. Day's inexperience, positioning himself as the main challenger to both the Government and the Opposition.

We saw above in Table 7 some evidence that Mr. Clark's debate performance appears to have had some impact in raising the Conservative vote totals among those deciding during the campaign or in the final days. However, Table 8 shows us that Mr. Clark's ability to snare votes for the Tories was limited. Of those who felt that Joe Clark gave the best performance in the debates, only 20% ended up voting Conservative, fewer than supported the Liberals (33%) or the Alliance (26%). Mr. Clark's debate performance, though widely recognized and praised even by those who supported other parties, shows the limited impact that the debate can have when the other aspects of the party's campaign fall short (see Chapter three of this volume). This situation was not unlike the one which befell the Conservatives in the previous election. The generally acknowledged winner of the 1997 leadership debate was then-PC leader Jean Charest, but this victory had a very limited payoff when it came to the results.[7]

It is often said that leadership debates are more about reinforcement of voter intentions than about conversion. That is, the goal of leaders when they engage in these events is to avoid the kind of major mistakes which might shake the faith of voters who are otherwise favourable to their party. We can see evidence of such reinforcement in Table 8, as three-quarters of those who thought Jean Chrétien or Stockwell Day gave the best performance in the debates ended up voting for those parties. Though these two leaders may have converted relatively few wavering voters during the debates, they did well enough not to lose the support they already had.

The Declining Turnout Rate

The official turnout rate in Canada's thirty-seventh General Election, held on November 27, 2000, was 61.18% of registered voters, the lowest in Canadian history by a considerable margin.[8] The 2000 election saw an actual decline in the number of people voting from the previous election of 1997, despite the increase in population and in the number of voters registered.[9] The 12,993,855 voters who cast ballots in 2000 was 177,773 fewer than had voted in 1997, as well as 869,280 fewer votes than 1993, and 287,336 fewer than in 1988.[10] There were more actual voters in the 1988 election out of 17.6 million registered voters than there were in 2000 out of 21.2 million registered voters.

The decline in voting turnout despite an increase in registered voters of over one and one half million between the 1997 election and 2000 suggests that we must look beyond the registration process for explanations of the decline. Nevertheless, Elections Canada experienced significant problems in switching from the traditional system of house-to-house enumeration before the election to the new Permanent Register of Electors, which was based on updates of the final enumeration, held in 1997. Over one million voters had to register at the polling stations on election day itself, as they had not been included on the list and had not availed themselves of opportunities to get themselves added to the list during the campaign period, despite considerable advertising by Elections Canada exhorting them to do so.[11] A particular problem arises from the fact that newly eligible voters, qualifying either by virtue of age or citizenship, need to take the initiative to add themselves to the list, rather than being automatically entered.[12]

Table 9
REASONS FOR NON VOTING 1974–2000

	1974	1980	1984	2000
Uninterested, uninformed	37%	40%	39%	41%
Illness	13	13	9	8
Out of town, away	38	39	23	15
Too busy, working	10	2	19	21
Unenumerated/not on list	2	6	11	14
N =	437	182	483	211

Source: 1974, 1980 & 1984 Canadian National Election Studies; 2000 POLLARA Post-Election Study
NOTE: Percentages sum to 100% in columns.

It is also true that, in a series of national surveys asking those who abstained from voting their reasons for doing so, an increasing percentage reported not voting for reasons of "administrative disenfranchisement" (Table 9). Earlier studies, such as one done for the *Royal Commission on Electoral Reform and Party Financing* in 1991, identified fairly small but significant groups of nonvoters who might be persuaded to turn out to the polls if doing so was logistically easier.[13] Table 9 presents these findings from previous National Election Studies, and adds to it the results of a question on the 2000 POLLARA post-election survey on the same subject. In 1984, 11% of nonvoters claimed that they had not been enumerated. Most of these people lived in urban areas, and at that time eligible voters could not be added to the voters list on election day in those areas, as they could be in rural areas.[14] With the changes in the *Canada Elections Act* brought in as a result of recommendations of the *Royal Commission*, such election day registration was subsequently allowed in urban areas. Thus, there is no technical reason why the 14% of nonvoters who state in Table 9 that they did not vote in the 2000 election because they were not on the voter's list could not have added themselves to the list on election day along with the million Canadians in the same boat who did so. Still, it is interesting that being omitted from the Register apparently provided a psychological deterrent to voting for a substantial number of Canadians.

The reasons given for nonvoting have not changed dramatically over the years, as shown by Table 9. However, there are two trends of interest. The first is the decline in the number of people who did not cast a ballot because they were sick, or because they were "out of town" (away from their place of residence) on election day. In both of these areas, administrative changes have been implemented during the last decade to make it easier for those who are ill in hospital or are nursing homes to vote (primarily mobile polls) as well as for those who are going to be away from home (special ballots, more advertising for advance polls, and possible arrangements for proxy voting). It is reasonable to consider that some of these developments may have aided in providing voting arrangements for those otherwise prevented by force of circumstances from reaching their polling station on election day.

The second trend to be noted from Table 9 is the gradual increase in reasons related to disinterest in the election. The percentage of nonvoters who declared themselves to be disinterested in the process, or disappointed in all the parties or candidates, or not informed enough about the subject, reached 41% in 2000. Added to that number is the 21% of nonvoters who declared that their reason was related to lack of time, because they were "too busy," or were "working." Even though employers are obligated by law to give employees three consecutive hours off to vote, this rule may not have been followed in some cases. Moreover, some employees for whom the election was of marginal interest may not have taken advantage of the opportunity when it was offered. Finally, for the self-employed, the decision not to take time away from work to vote would have been tantamount to declaring that they were not interested in the election. Close to two-thirds of nonvoters in 2000, then, simply did not feel motivated to take part.

As is to be expected given past research,[15] turnout in the 2000 election varied by age. In the POLLARA post-election survey we have been using in this chapter, the reported turnout among 18-24 year olds was 59%, while over 90% of those over 55 years of age report voting (Cramer's V=.27 p<.001). Other demographic variables relate to voting turnout as well. University educated respondents were more likely to report voting than those with only a High School education (V=.14 p<.001). And income also relates to turnout, as higher income respondents were more likely to vote (V=.14 p<.01). These three groups, lower income, lower educated and younger citizens, were all more likely to cite reasons relating to lack of interest in the election to explain their decisions not to vote. They were also more likely to report problems with being registered on the voter's list. The highest income Canadians in the survey (those over $75,000 per year) were more likely to say they were working, or too busy to vote!

Turnout in 2000 also varied by province. Most noticeable is the fact that, for the third election in a row, Ontario had a lower turnout than the average. In Ontario, barely 58% of registered voters cast ballots in the election; this was a full 3 percentage points lower than the previous low turnout in the province (1896). And once again Ontario returned practically a full slate of Liberal members to the House of Commons. The electoral strategy of turning the Reform Party into the Alliance was primarily designed to create an electoral breakthrough in Ontario. Not only did this not happen, but the existence of the Alliance as an opponent for the Liberals appears to have generated even less interest among Ontario voters than did the Reform Party. The low turnout rate was particularly marked in ridings in and around Toronto. Some results there were: York West, 47.8%; Scarborough-Rouge River, 50.5%; Scarborough Centre, 54%; Mississauga Centre, 51.3%; Don Valley East, 54.8%; Davenport, 51.1%; Bramalea-Gore-Malton-Springdale, 49.5%.[16] These areas, particularly those in the suburbs around Toronto, were places where the Alliance originally felt they had an opportunity for a breakthrough. But turnout was low, and those who did vote re-elected the Liberals.

Table 10

MOST IMPORTANT ISSUES DISCUSSED AND NOT DISCUSSED, 2000
(those mentioning issues only)

Issues	Important in Campaign	Not Discussed but should have been
Economy General	4%	3%
Taxes	10	4
Debt	8	5
Unemployment	3	3
Constitutional	4	3
Resources, development	2	4
Environment	1	13
Health	43	8
Education	4	11
Other Social	3	8
Moral	2	.4
Crime	1	2
Other	4	35

Source: POLLARA Post-Election Survey
NOTE: Percentages sum to 100% in columns.

One indication of the sources of the discontent which seemed to permeate the election campaign comes from Table 10, which reports the results of a question asking about which issues should have been discussed during the campaign but were not. For comparison, the results of the identification of the most important issues in the campaign is repeated as well. Despite the focus of the campaign on the health care issue, exemplifying the attention given to social issues, Table 10 shows that many of the important issues which were not discussed fall into the social issue category. This includes 8% citing health (perhaps meaning some aspect of the issue which received short shrift), 11% mentioning education, and 8% citing other social issues ranging from child care to pensions. In addition, 13% of the public, the largest single group, felt that the environment did not get the attention it deserved from the politicians in the campaign of 2000. And finally, a whole host of "other issues," some highly idiosyncratic, indicate that the public finds the issue discussion as initiated and orchestrated by the media and political parties unsatisfactory in representing the multi-dimensionality of their concerns. Only if the voters become re-engaged with the official agenda, perhaps with the emergence of new economic problems, will interest likely revive in electoral politics.

Conclusion

The patterns one can discern in Canadian electoral politics at the beginning of the twenty-first century bear some similarities to, but contain some differences with, the situation which prevailed a century earlier. Canada's lowest-turnout elections are central to the periods concerned. The election of 1896 was fought in many parts of the country on the issue of the provision of a publicly-funded separate school system in Manitoba, and was less concerned than its predecessors with fundamental questions of economic policy, namely protectionism (the Tories' National Policy) versus free(er) trade (the traditional Liberal policy). Politics was highly regionalized in 1896, with Protestant Ontario electing a majority of Tories, and Catholic Quebec opting for Laurier, despite the Liberal position of upholding the right of the Manitoba provincial government to do away with support for the Catholic Schools. The West was concerned with its own issues in 1896, but a residue of bitterness toward the previous Liberal administration (in this case dating back to 1874-8) blunted the party's ability to make significant gains in an election in which they were in the ascendant elsewhere.

The 2000 election shows that at the present time, electoral politics in Canada are fractured and regionalized, a factor that has solidified during the past three elections and shows no signs of abatement. The West has its own agenda, and the bitterness with the Liberal Party seems to be on the increase. As in 1896, major economic issues shared the political stage with other important questions; not only, as one hundred years ago, by racial and ethnic ones, but also by questions of social welfare and the proper role of government. Perhaps social issues are not capable of generating as much public heat and agitation as economic issues. Some might look to the benefits of these quiescent political times, where the opposition looks even less likely to threaten the Liberal hegemony than it did during the Mackenzie King-St. Laurent years. But others will point to the unhealthy state of democracy when the public turns away from the exercise of the franchise, feels that important policy matters are ignored at election time, and feels frustrated at their inability to identify a meaningful choice between reasonable alternatives.

NOTES

1   Harold D. Clarke, Jane Jenson, Lawrence LeDuc and Jon H. Pammett, *Absent Mandate: Canadian Electoral Politics in an Era of Restructuring,* (Toronto: Gage, 1996) p 41.

2   Source: *Canadian Economic Observer* (Statistics Canada) various issues.

3   Lisa Van Buren, and Erika-Kirsten Paubst, *Analysis of Speeches Delivered by Prime Minister Jean Chrétien During the 2000 Electoral Campaign* (Ottawa, Public Policy Forum, 2001).

4   *Ibid.*, page 8.

5   *Ibid.*, page 9.

6   Background to the Canadian debates, and material on previous debates, can be found in Lawrence LeDuc, "The Leaders' Debates ... And the Winner Is," in Alan Frizzell and Jon H. Pammett, eds., *The Canadian General Election of 1997,* (Toronto, Dundurn, 1997) Chapter 11.

7   *Ibid.*

8   Only two previous Federal Elections have registered turnout rates below 65%. These were the elections of 1891 (64.4%), the last election won by John A. Macdonald, and 1896 (62.9%), when the Liberals came to power under Wilfrid Laurier. In the latter election, dominated by the issue of the Manitoba Schools, turnout in Quebec and the Eastern provinces held up at normal rates, but Ontario dipped to 61%, Manitoba was at 50% and British Columbia at 40%. See Elections Canada, *A History of the Vote in Canada* (Ottawa: Ministry of Public Works and Government Services, 1997) pp. 102-3.

9   Turnout figures for 2000 can be found on the Internet at: www.elections.ca these, totals include all ballots cast, including rejected ballots.

10 *A History of the Vote in Canada, cited above,* p 102-3.

11 *The Ottawa Citizen*, December 19, 2000, p A6.

12 Jerome H. Black, "The National Register of Electors: Raising Questions about the New Approach to Voter Registration in Canada," *Policy Matters,* December, 2000, Vol. 1, No. 10, Institute for Research on Public Policy.

13 Jon H. Pammett, "Voting Turnout in Canada," in Herman Bakvis, ed., *Voter Turnout in Canada* (Toronto: Dundurn, 1991) pp 33-60.

14 *Ibid.,* p 38.

15 *Ibid.,* p. 41.

16 A complete list of turnout rates in all Canadian constituencies can be found on the Internet at: www.elections.ca

Appendix

Key

ACTION	Canadian Action Party
Alliance	Canadian Reform Conservative Alliance
B.Q.	Bloc Québécois
G.P.	Green Party of Canada
Ind.	Independent
Lib.	Liberal Party of Canada
M-L	Marxist-Leninist Party of Canada
N.D.P.	New Democratic Party
N.L.P.	Natural Law Party
NIL	No Affiliation
P.C.	Progressive Conservative Party of Canada

Valid votes and seats received, by political affiliation and province or territory – 37th general election 2000

Province or territory	Alliance Valid votes (%)	Alliance Seats (%)	B.Q. Valid votes (%)	B.Q. Seats (%)	Lib. Valid votes (%)	Lib. Seats (%)	N.D.P. Valid votes (%)	N.D.P. Seats (%)	P.C. Valid votes (%)	P.C. Seats (%)	Other* Valid votes (%)	Other* Seats (%)	Total Valid votes (%)	Total Seats (%)
Nfld.	8 837 (3.9)	0 (0.0)	0 (0.0)	0 (0.0)	103 103 (44.9)	5 (71.4)	29 993 (13.1)	0 (0.0)	79 157 (34.5)	2 (28.6)	8 408 (3.6)	0 (0.0)	229 498 (100.0)	7 (100.0)
P.E.I.	3 719 (5.0)	0 (0.0)	0 (0.0)	0 (0.0)	35 021 (47.0)	4 (100.0)	6 714 (9.0)	0 (0.0)	28 610 (38.4)	0 (0.0)	400 (0.5)	0 (0.0)	74 464 (100.0)	4 (100.0)
N.S.	41 752 (9.6)	0 (0.0)	0 (0.0)	0 (0.0)	158 870 (36.5)	4 (36.4)	104 277 (24.0)	3 (27.3)	126 657 (29.1)	4 (36.4)	3 813 (0.8)	0 (0.0)	435 269 (100.0)	11 (100.0)
N.B.	60 277 (15.7)	0 (0.0)	0 (0.0)	0 (0.0)	159 803 (41.7)	6 (60.0)	44 778 (11.7)	1 (10.0)	116 980 (30.5)	3 (30.0)	1 174 (0.3)	0 (0.0)	383 012 (100.0)	10 (100.0)
Que.	212 874 (6.2)	0 (0.0)	1 377 727 (39.9)	38 (50.7)	1 529 642 (44.2)	36 (48.0)	63 611 (1.8)	0 (0.0)	192 153 (5.6)	1 (1.3)	80 891 (2.4)	0 (0.0)	3 456 898 (100.0)	75 (100.0)
Ont.	1 051 209 (23.6)	2 (1.9)	0 (0.0)	0 (0.0)	2 292 075 (51.5)	100 (97.1)	368 709 (8.3)	1 (1.0)	642 438 (14.4)	0 (0.0)	98 174 (2.3)	0 (0.0)	4 452 605 (100.0)	103 (100.0)
Man.	148 293 (30.4)	4 (28.6)	0 (0.0)	0 (0.0)	158 713 (32.5)	5 (35.7)	101 741 (20.9)	4 (28.6)	70 635 (14.5)	1 (7.1)	8 450 (1.8)	0 (0.0)	487 832 (100.0)	14 (100.0)
Sask.	207 004 (47.7)	10 (71.4)	0 (0.0)	0 (0.0)	89 697 (20.7)	2 (14.3)	113 626 (26.2)	2 (14.3)	20 855 (4.8)	0 (0.0)	2 515 (0.6)	0 (0.0)	433 697 (100.0)	14 (100.0)
Alta.	739 514 (58.9)	23 (88.5)	0 (0.0)	0 (0.0)	263 008 (20.9)	2 (7.7)	68 363 (5.4)	0 (0.0)	169 093 (13.5)	1 (3.8)	16 021 (1.2)	0 (0.0)	1 255 999 (100.0)	26 (100.0)
B.C.	797 518 (49.4)	27 (79.4)	0 (0.0)	0 (0.0)	446 624 (27.7)	5 (14.7)	182 993 (11.3)	2 (5.9)	117 614 (7.3)	0 (0.0)	69 972 (4.3)	0 (0.0)	1 614 721 (100.0)	34 (100.0)
Y.T.	3 659 (27.7)	0 (0.0)	0 (0.0)	0 (0.0)	4 293 (32.5)	1 (100.0)	4 223 (31.9)	0 (0.0)	991 (7.5)	0 (0.0)	53 (0.4)	0 (0.0)	13 219 (100.0)	1 (100.0)
N.W.T.	2 273 (17.7)	0 (0.0)	0 (0.0)	0 (0.0)	5 865 (45.6)	1 (100.0)	3 490 (26.7)	0 (0.0)	1 282 (10.0)	0 (0.0)	0 (0.0)	0 (0.0)	12 840 (100.0)	1 (100.0)
Nun.	0 (0.0)	0 (0.0)	0 (0.0)	0 (0.0)	5 327 (69.0)	1 (100.0)	1 410 (18.3)	0 (0.0)	633 (8.2)	0 (0.0)	349 (4.5)	0 (0.0)	7 719 (100.0)	1 (100.0)
Total	3 276 929 (25.5)	66 (21.9)	1 377 727 (10.7)	38 (12.6)	5 252 031 (40.8)	172 (57.1)	1 093 868 (8.5)	13 (4.3)	1 566 998 (12.2)	12 (4.0)	290 220 (2.2)	0 (0.0)	12 857 773 (100.0)	301 (100.0)

Note: Totals may not add to 100% due to rounding.

Percentage of Votes Received by Constituency

NEWFOUNDLAND

Bonavista—Trinity—Conception
Lib.	54.38
P.C.	27.10
N.D.P.	15.93
Alliance	2.59

Burin—St. George's
Lib.	47.52
NIL	25.68
P.C.	18.87
Alliance	4.92
N.D.P.	3.01

Gander—Grand Falls
Lib.	55.02
P.C.	28.39
N.D.P.	9.97
Alliance	6.63

Humber—St. Barbe—Baie Verte
Lib.	48.53
N.D.P.	26.14
P.C.	19.97
Alliance	5.36

Labrador
Lib.	68.99
N.D.P.	12.38
P.C.	12.09
Alliance	6.53

St. John's East
P.C.	53.22
Lib.	31.19
N.D.P.	12.16
Alliance	2.58
Ind.	0.57
N.L.P.	0.28

St. John's West
P.C.	53.62
Lib.	33.01
N.D.P.	11.08
Alliance	1.96
N.L.P.	0.33

PRINCE EDWARD ISLAND

Cardigan
Lib.	48.06
P.C.	46.51
Alliance	2.81
N.D.P.	2.62

Egmont
Lib.	50.05
P.C.	38.60
N.D.P.	6.18
Alliance	5.16

Hillsborough
Lib.	41.81
P.C.	30.50
N.D.P.	21.86
Alliance	5.08
N.L.P.	0.46
NIL	0.29

Malpeque
Lib.	48.62
P.C.	38.94
Alliance	6.84
N.D.P.	4.24
G.P.	1.35

NOVA SCOTIA

Bras d'Or—Cape Breton
Lib.	54.85

P.C.	21.38
N.D.P.	19.86
Alliance	3.91

Cumberland—Colchester

P.C.	48.49
Lib.	26.61
Alliance	12.91
N.D.P.	11.99

Dartmouth

N.D.P.	36.28
Lib.	33.14
P.C.	21.59
Alliance	8.76
M.-L.	0.23

Halifax

N.D.P.	40.36
Lib.	32.99
P.C.	17.68
Alliance	5.72
M.P.	1.53
G.P.	1.44
M.-L.	0.28

Halifax West

Lib.	39.21
N.D.P.	29.99
P.C.	20.76
Alliance	9.70
M.-L.	0.34

Kings—Hants

P.C.	40.29
Lib.	30.23
N.D.P.	16.57
Alliance	10.56
M.P.	1.53
Ind.	0.32
N.L.P.	0.30
Comm.	0.19

Pictou—Antigonish—Guysborough

P.C.	48.41

Lib.	31.57
N.D.P.	11.28
Alliance	7.35
Ind.	1.38

Sackville—Musquodoboit Valley—Eastern Shore

N.D.P.	34.48
Lib.	32.56
P.C.	19.21
Alliance	12.08
M.P.	1.67

South Shore

P.C.	39.69
Lib.	35.12
Alliance	13.01
N.D.P.	12.17

Sydney—Victoria

Lib.	49.83
N.D.P.	36.53
P.C.	9.71
Alliance	3.93

West Nova

Lib.	36.09
P.C.	34.11
Alliance	18.58
N.D.P.	11.23

Acadie—Bathurst

N.D.P.	46.61
Lib.	40.27
P.C.	8.55
Alliance	4.58

NEW BRUNSWICK

Beausejour—Petitcodiac

Lib.	47.10
P.C.	32.11
Alliance	13.73
N.D.P.	7.06

Fredericton

Lib.	38.60
P.C.	29.73
Alliance	24.00
N.D.P.	7.04
N.L.P.	0.63

Fundy—Royal

P.C.	40.51
Lib.	30.28
Alliance	22.25
N.D.P.	6.97

Madawaska—Restigouche

Lib.	52.27
P.C.	37.84
Alliance	5.14
N.D.P.	4.75

Miramichi

Lib.	51.44
P.C.	25.17
Alliance	15.99
N.D.P.	7.40

Moncton—Riverview—Dieppe

Lib.	58.74
Alliance	17.99
P.C.	15.67
N.D.P.	6.95
N.L.P.	0.66

New Brunswick Southwest

P.C.	47.25
Lib.	27.53
Alliance	21.40
N.D.P.	3.83

Saint John

P.C.	50.92
Lib.	28.98
N.D.P.	9.09
Alliance	9.06
M.P.	1.40
G.P.	0.40

N.L.P.	0.16

Tobique—Mactaquac

Lib .	33.60
P.C.	33.14
Alliance	29.51
N.D.P.	3.75

QUEBEC

Abitibi—Baie-James—Nunavik

Lib.	49.99
B.Q.	42.76
Alliance	3.56
P.C.	2.22
N.D.P.	1.47

Ahuntsic

Lib.	53.89
B.Q.	32.23
P.C.	5.68
Alliance	3.42
G.P.	2.11
N.D.P.	1.88
Comm.	0.49
M.-L.	0.30

Anjou—Rivière-des-Prairies

Lib.	57.86
B.Q	30.35
P.C.	4.18
Alliance	4.12
M.P.	1.89
N.D.P.	1.28
M.-L.	0.31

Argenteuil—Papineau—Mirabel

B.Q.	43.20
Lib.	42.12
Alliance	5.76
P.C.	3.68
M.P.	1.86
G.P.	1.44
N.D.P.	1.09

N.L.P. 0.51
NIL 0.33

Bas-Richelieu—Nicolet—Becancour
B.Q. 56.92
Lib. 31.04
Alliance 4.68
P.C. 4.38
M.P. 2.03
N.D.P. 0.95

Beauce
Lib. 56.01
B.Q. 26.51
Alliance 11.73
P.C. 3.50
N.L.P. 1.31
N.D.P. 0.94

Beauharnois—Salaberry
Lib. 48.26
B.Q. 42.39
P.C. 4.32
Alliance 3.61
N.D.P. 1.42

Beauport—Montmorency—Côte-de-
Beaupré—Île-d'Orléans
B.Q. 41.55
Lib. 36.43
Alliance 11.44
P.C. 5.68
M.P. 2.66
N.D.P. 1.69
M.-L. 0.55

Bellechasse—Etchemins—
Montmagny—L'Islet
Lib. 47.91
B.Q.3 7.44
Alliance 10.56
P.C. 4.09

Berthier—Montcalm
B.Q. 57.06
Lib. 30.05
Alliance 5.14
P.C. 3.63
M.P. 2.64
N.D.P. 1.48

Bonaventure—Gaspé—Îles-de-la-
Madeleine—Pabok
Lib. 53.19
B.Q. 43.00
Alliance 2.12
N.D.P. 1.70

Bourassa
Lib. 62.22
B.Q . 28.07
Alliance 3.51
P.C. 3.25
N.D.P. 1.80
M.-L. 0.81
Comm. 0.34

Brome—Missisquoi
Lib. 50.26
B.Q. 31.17
P.C. 12.84
Alliance 4.61
N.D.P. 1.12

Brossard—La Prairie
Lib. 52.69
B.Q. 32.94
Alliance 5.84
P.C. 5.47
N.D.P. 1.67
N.L.P. 1.04
M.-L. 0.34

Chambly
B.Q. 49.94
Lib. 33.31
P.C. 6.60
Alliance 5.32

M.P.	3.35
N.D.P.	1.47

Champlain

B.Q .	45.26
Lib.	45.23
Alliance	5.76
M.P.	2.26
N.D.P.	1.49

Charlesbourg—Jacques-Cartier

B.Q.	38.29
Lib.	36.85
Alliance	15.41
P.C.	5.70
G.P.	1.99
N.D.P.	1.75

Charlevoix

B.Q.	61.44
Lib.	27.93
Alliance	5.72
P.C.	3.46
N.D.P.	1.45

Châteauguay

B.Q .	47.12
Lib.	41.18
Alliance	5.59
P.C.	3.66
N.L.P.	1.33
N.D.P.	1.12

Chicoutimi—Le Fjord

Lib.	48.24
B.Q.	36.17
Ind.	9.11
Alliance	4.80
N.D.P.	1.67

Compton—Stanstead

Lib.	46.56
B.Q.	38.89
P.C.	6.36
Alliance	5.41

N.D.P.	1.52
N.L.P.	1.25

Drummond

B.Q.	45.27
Lib.	34.21
P.C.	15.65
Alliance	3.87
N.D.P.	1.01

Frontenac—Mégantic

Lib.	45.95
B.Q.	42.27
Alliance	4.71
P.C.	4.03
M.P.	1.88
N.D.P.	1.15

Gatineau

Lib.	51.45
B.Q.	25.40
Alliance	10.05
P.C.	7.17
N.D.P.	3.49
N.L.P.	0.94
Ind.	0.77
NIL	0.45
M.-L.	0.28

Hochelaga—Maisonneuve

B.Q.	49.20
Lib.	37.38
P.C.	4.05
Alliance	3.48
M.P.	2.84
N.D.P.	1.78
M.-L.	0.64
Comm.	0.63

Hull—Aylmer

Lib.	51.40
B.Q.	23.08
P.C.	9.60
Alliance	8.36
N.D.P.	3.49

M.P.	2.05
N.L.P.	0.98
NIL	0.42
Action	0.38
M.-L.	0.24

Joliette

B.Q .	52.20
Lib.	32.76
P.C.	6.03
Alliance	5.38
N.D.P.	2.40
Comm.	1.24

Jonquière

B.Q.	50.07
Lib.	35.80
Alliance	10.60
N.D.P.	3.52

Kamouraska—Rivière-du-Loup—Témiscouata—Les Basques

B.Q.	59.99
Lib.	30.34
P.C.	3.56
Alliance	3.53
N.D.P.	2.15
M.-L.	0.44

Lac-Saint-Jean—Saguenay

B.Q.	66.17
Lib.	23.31
Alliance	4.75
Ind.	2.82
P.C.	1.65
N.D.P.	1.29

Lac-Saint-Louis

Lib.	74.16
P.C.	7.52
Alliance	7.20
B.Q.	6.67
N.D.P.	2.50
M.P.	1.76
M.-L.	0.20

LaSalle—Émard

Lib.	65.75
B.Q.	24.20
Alliance	3.70
P.C.	2.28
N.D.P.	1.72
M.P.	1.57
N.L.P.	0.56
Comm.	0.22

Laurentides

B.Q.	49.90
Lib.	38.85
P.C.	5.09
Alliance	3.73
N.L.P.	1.25
N.D.P.	1.18

Laurier—Sainte-Marie

B.Q.	52.79
Lib.	25.75
G.P.	4.88
M.P.	4.85
N.D.P.	4.75
P.C.	4.23
Alliance	2.16
M.-L.	0.60

Laval Centre

B.Q.	43.35
Lib.	43.27
P.C.	5.07
Alliance	4.45
G.P.	2.35
N.D.P.	1.52

Laval East

Lib.	44.77
B.Q.	42.55
P.C.	4.23
Alliance	4.05
M.P.	1.53
G.P.	1.14
N.D.P.	0.99
Ind.	0.44

M.-L.   0.31

Laval West
Lib.   51.30
B.Q.   32.27
Alliance   7.48
P.C.   5.84
G.P.   1.59
N.D.P.   1.23
M.-L.   0.29

Lévis-et-Chutes-de-la-Chaudiere
B.Q.   41.85
Lib.   34.12
Alliance   14.51
P.C.   6.69
N.D.P.   2.24
Comm.   0.59

Longueuil
B.Q.   52.25
Lib.   32.53
P.C.   5.53
Alliance   5.17
M.P.   2.42
N.D.P.   1.64
M.-L.   0.46

Lotbinière-L'Érable
B.Q.   45.64
Lib.   37.35
Alliance   8.40
P.C.   7.01
N.D.P.   1.60
Lib.   41.14

Louis-Hebert
B.Q.   36.88
Alliance   10.22
P.C.   9.01
N.D.P.   2.08
M.-L.   0.66

Manicouagan
B.Q.   53.24

Lib.   35.68
Alliance   5.50
P.C.   3.81
N.D.P.   1.77

Matapédia—Matane
B.Q.   46.64
Lib.   45.76
P.C.   4.63
N.D.P.   2.97

Mercier
B.Q.   52.87
Lib.   32.93
G.P.   3.87
Alliance   3.60
P.C.   3.48
M.P.   2.00
N.D.P.   1.03
M.-L.   0.22

Mount Royal
Lib.   81.24
P.C.   6.11
B.Q.   4.27
Alliance   3.54
N.D.P.   2.54
G.P.   1.67
Comm.   0.34
N.L.P.   0.30

Notre-Dame-de-Grâce—Lachine
Lib.   60.72
B.Q.   18.11
P.C.   7.19
N.D.P.   4.73
Alliance   4.33
G.P.   2.21
M.P.   1.92
N.L.P.   0.44
M.-L.   0.34

Outremont
Lib.   47.68
B.Q.   28.29

P.C.	8.09
N.D.P.	5.58
G.P.	3.75
Alliance	3.25
M.P.	2.57
M.-L.	0.49
Comm.	0.30

Papineau—Saint-Denis

Lib.	54.10
B.Q.	26.60
Alliance	4.77
N.D.P.	4.48
P.C.	2.74
G.P.	2.55
M.P.	2.00
Ind.	1.67
M.-L.	1.09

Pierrefonds—Dollard

Lib.	72.85
B.Q.	10.99
Alliance	6.44
P.C.	5.54
M.P.	2.13
N.D.P.	2.05

Pontiac—Gatineau—Labelle

Lib.	45.36
B.Q.	32.06
Alliance	14.51
P.C.	3.95
N.D.P.	1.85
G.P.	1.44
N.L.P.	0.41
NIL	0.22
M.-L.	0.20

Portneuf

Lib.	40.78
B.Q.	35.23
Alliance	15.28
P.C.	8.71

Québec

B.Q.	43.43
Lib.	35.48
Alliance	7.58
P.C.	6.04
N.D.P.	3.25
M.P.	2.82
N.L.P.	0.92
M.-L.	0.49

Québec East

Lib.	38.61
B.Q.	37.47
Alliance	15.21
P.C.	6.60
N.D.P.	2.11

Repentigny

B.Q.	57.80
Lib.	26.88
P.C.	5.37
Alliance	5.09
M.P.	3.43
N.D.P.	1.43

Richmond—Arthabaska

P.C.	37.20
B.Q.	36.47
Lib.	21.03
Alliance	3.90
N.L.P.	0.76
N.D.P.	0.64

Rimouski-Neigette-et-la Mitis

B.Q.	59.55
Lib.	29.52
Alliance	3.86
P.C.	3.47
N.L.P.	2.03
N.D.P.	1.58

Rivière-des-Mille-Œles

B.Q.	49.41
Lib.	34.40
Alliance	6.85

P.C.   5.47
G.P.   2.48
N.D.P.   1.38

Roberval
B.Q.   55.06
Lib.   34.74
Alliance   5.95
P.C.   2.83
N.D.P.   1.42

Rosemont—Petite-Patrie
B.Q.   49.13
Lib.   33.83
P.C.   4.23
M.P.   3.13
G.P.   3.11
N.D.P.   2.99
Alliance   2.85
Comm.   0.49
NIL   0.24

Saint-Bruno—Saint-Hubert
B.Q.   43.98
Lib.   39.08
Alliance   6.54
P.C.   5.29
M.P.   3.06
N.D.P.   2.04

Saint-Hyacinthe—Bagot
B.Q.   55.41
Lib.   34.77
Alliance   4.62
P.C.   4.13
N.D.P.   1.07

Saint-Jean
B.Q.   47.44
Lib.   36.09
Alliance   6.63
P.C.   5.78
M.P.   2.61
N.D.P.   1.46

Saint-Lambert
Lib.   45.40
B.Q.   38.11
Alliance   7.07
P.C.   6.24
M.P.   3.18

Saint-Laurent—Cartierville
Lib.   73.58
B.Q.   13.07
P.C.   5.17
Alliance   4.27
N.D.P.   2.40
M.-L.   0.52
Action   0.52
Comm.   0.46

Saint-Léonard—Saint-Michel
Lib.   76.66
B.Q .   14.47
Alliance   3.79
P.C.   2.29
M.P.   1.38
N.D.P.   1.14
M.-L.   0.28

Saint-Maurice
Lib.   54.07
B.Q.   38.96
Alliance   3.38
P.C.   2.24
N.D.P.   0.83
Comm.   0.52

Shefford
Lib.   45.93
B.Q.   43.95
Alliance   4.14
P.C.   3.32
M.P.   1.82
N.D.P.   0.84

Sherbrooke
B.Q.   46.53
Lib.   41.84

Alliance	4.51
P.C.	3.86
N.D.P.	1.34
N.L.P.	0.98
Ind.	0.58
M.-L.	0.37

Témiscamingue

B.Q.	50.14
Lib.	42.75
Alliance	3.65
P.C.	2.14
N.D.P.	1.31

Terrebonne—Blainville

B.Q.	51.91
Lib.	31.70
Alliance	6.71
P.C.	5.54
N.L.P.	2.14
N.D.P.	1.99

Trois-Rivières

B.Q.	46.67
Lib.	42.92
Alliance	4.50
P.C.	3.33
N.L.P.	1.12
N.D.P.	1.07
M.-L.	0.38

Vaudreuil—Soulanges

Lib.	51.56
B.Q.	34.49
Alliance	8.21
P.C.	3.96
N.D.P.	1.77

Verchères—Les-Patriotes

B.Q.	52.29
Lib.	30.50
P.C.	7.03
Alliance	5.23
M.P.	2.99
N.D.P.	1.96

Verdun—Saint-Henri—Saint-Paul—Pointe Saint-Charles

Lib.	51.27
B.Q.	29.37
P.C.	6.55
Alliance	5.15
N.D.P.	2.46
G.P.	2.29
M.P.	2.27
Comm.	0.36
NIL	0.29

Westmount—Ville-Marie

Lib.	60.19
P.C.	11.98
B.Q.	10.71
N.D.P.	5.19
Alliance	4.42
G.P.	3.25
NIL	1.81
M.P.	1.80
M.-L.	0.39
N.L.P.	0.25

ONTARIO

Algoma—Manitoulin

Lib.	48.36
Alliance	28.99
N.D.P.	13.95
P.C.	7.32
G.P.	1.38

Ancaster—Dundas—Flamborough—Aldershot

Lib.	41.16
Alliance	31.55
P.C.	19.53
N.D.P.	7.76

Barrie—Simcoe—Bradford

Lib.	48.27
Alliance	32.29
P.C.	13.92

N.D.P.   4.38
Action   0.71
NIL   0.43

Beaches—East York
Lib.   52.74
N.D.P.   20.93
P.C.   13.51
Alliance   8.99
M.P.   1.60
G.P.   1.40
Action   0.30
N.L.P.   0.21
Comm.   0.19
M.-L.   0.12

Bramalea—Gore—Malton—Springdale
Lib.   57.05
Alliance   18.78
P.C.   15.67
N.D.P.   4.85
Ind.   2.04
Comm.   0.91
M.-L.   0.70

Brampton Centre
Lib.   50.64
P.C.   25.45
Alliance   17.23
N.D.P.   4.95
G.P.   1.73

Brampton West—Mississauga
Lib.   66.38
Alliance   16.39
P.C.   12.74
N.D.P.   3.35
G.P.   1.13

Brant
Lib.   56.42
Alliance   25.68
P.C.   8.39
N.D.P.   7.33

G.P.   1.13
Action   1.05

Bruce—Grey—Owen Sound
Lib.   44.22
Alliance   35.61
P.C.   15.33
N.D.P.   4.83

Burlington
Lib.   46.77
Alliance   24.26
P.C.   23.71
N.D.P.   3.63
G.P.   1.63

Cambridge
Lib.   46.60
Alliance   31.38
P.C.   12.60
N.D.P.   8.65
N.L.P.   0.44
NIL   0.34

Chatham—Kent Essex
Lib.   49.71
Alliance   32.07
P.C.   10.29
N.D.P.   5.47
G.P.   1.77
Action   0.53
NIL   0.18

Davenport
Lib.   66.72
N.D.P.   13.56
Alliance   7.93
P.C.   5.98
G.P.   2.52
M.P.   1.88
Action   1.13
N.L.P.   0.29

Don Valley East
Lib.   66.60

P.C.	14.51
Alliance	12.17
N.D.P.	5.78
NIL	0.54
M.-L.	0.39

Don Valley West

Lib.	55.37
P.C.	23.14
Alliance	15.83
N.D.P.	4.42
M.P.	1.03
M.-L.	0.21

Dufferin—Peel—Wellington—Grey

Lib.	45.57
Alliance	31.59
P.C.	16.66
N.D.P.	3.10
G.P.	3.08

Durham

Lib.	45.20
Alliance	30.15
P.C.	18.36
N.D.P.	5.58
NIL	0.72

Eglinton—Lawrence

Lib.	60.68
P.C.	17.26
Alliance	13.26
N.D.P.	6.42
G.P.	1.66
M.-L.	0.40
N.L.P.	0.32

Elgin—Middlesex—London

Lib.	41.02
Alliance	36.95
P.C.	14.50
N.D.P.	5.53
G.P.	1.03
NIL	0.97

Erie—Lincoln

Lib.	42.21
Alliance	37.11
P.C.	12.81
N.D.P.	6.00
NIL	1.18
N.L.P.	0.35
Action	0.34

Essex

Lib.	44.33
Alliance	34.60
N.D.P.	13.89
P.C.	6.86
M.-L.	0.33

Etobicoke Centre

Lib.	56.37
Alliance	22.30
P.C.	16.35
N.D.P.	4.59
M.-L.	0.39

Etobicoke—Lakeshore

Lib.	51.78
Alliance	21.11
P.C.	19.48
N.D.P.	6.53
N.L.P.	0.56
M.-L.	0.27
Comm.	0.26

Etobicoke North

Lib.	72.54
Alliance	19.51
N.D.P.	6.87
Comm.	1.08

Glengarry—Prescott—Russell

Lib.	67.96
Alliance	18.70
P.C.	8.54
N.D.P.	4.07
N.L.P.	0.74

Guelph—Wellington
Lib.   48.19
Alliance   20.12
P.C.   18.57
N.D.P.   10.36
G.P.   1.76
NIL   0.50
Action   0.38
M.-L.   0.12

Haldimand—Norfolk—Brant
Lib.   46.82
Alliance   34.59
P.C.   12.93
N.D.P.   4.77
Action   0.89

Haliburton—Victoria—Brock
Lib.   33.95
Alliance   31.68
P.C.   29.48
N.D.P.   4.89

Halton
Lib.   47.27
Alliance   26.27
P.C.   20.33
N.D.P.   4.42
G.P.   1.71

Hamilton East
Lib.   52.85
Alliance   19.42
N.D.P.   13.22
P.C.   10.68
M.P.   1.85
Ind.   0.87
Comm.   0.46
M.-L.   0.34
N.L.P.   0.31

Hamilton Mountain
Lib.   50.91
Alliance   21.73
P.C.   16.87

N.D.P.   9.91
M.-L.   0.59

Hamilton West
Lib.   52.72
Alliance   18.08
N.D.P.   13.13
P.C.   12.45
G.P.   1.53
M.P.   1.08
NIL   0.40
N.L.P.   0.23
Comm.   0.23
M.-L.   0.15

Hastings—Frontenac—Lennox and Addington
Lib.   39.00
Alliance   30.35
P.C.   23.48
N.D.P.   5.05
G.P.   1.18
Ind.   0.48
Action   0.36
NIL   0.10

Huron—Bruce
Lib.   49.91
Alliance   23.96
P.C.   18.85
N.D.P.   6.18
NIL   0.58
Action   0.52

Kenora—Rainy River
Lib.   45.21
Alliance   28.62
N.D.P.   21.54
P.C.   4.63

Kingston and the Islands
Lib.   51.69
P.C.   18.02
Alliance   15.44
N.D.P.   9.67

G.P.   5.18

Kitchener Centre
Lib.   52.84
Alliance   26.08
P.C.   13.85
N.D.P.   6.87
Comm.   0.36

Kitchener—Waterloo
Lib.   50.34
Alliance   23.01
P.C.   15.99
N.D.P.   8.15
G.P.   1.50
Action   0.51
M.-L.   0.30
NIL   0.19

Lambton—Kent—Middlesex
Lib.   48.95
Alliance   30.83
P.C.   13.71
N.D.P.   4.34
NIL   0.85
G.P.   0.79
Action   0.54

Lanark—Carleton
Alliance   38.93
Lib.   35.99
P.C.   19.61
N.D.P.   3.07
G.P.   1.37
Action   0.61
Ind.   0.24
N.L.P.   0.17

Leeds—Grenville
Lib.   39.51
Alliance   39.39
P.C.   16.87
N.D.P.   2.10
G.P.   1.73
Action   0.38

London—Fanshawe
Lib.   54.81
Alliance   22.28
P.C.   11.47
N.D.P.   11.44

London North Centre
Lib.   51.46
Alliance   20.46
P.C.   16.49
N.D.P.   8.89
G.P.   1.54
M.P.   1.02
M.-L.   0.15

London West
Lib.   49.37
Alliance   21.09
P.C.   20.31
N.D.P.   7.46
G.P.   1.27
Action   0.33
M.-L.   0.17

Markham
Lib.   66.64
Alliance   18.71
P.C.   10.55
N.D.P.   2.34
G.P.   1.02
Ind.   0.46
Action   0.27

Mississauga Centre
Lib.   64.13
Alliance   17.47
P.C.   13.35
N.D.P.   3.69
M.P.   1.02
M.-L.   0.33

Mississauga East
Lib.   64.50
Alliance   15.64
P.C.   14.97

N.D.P.	4.22
M.-L.	0.66

Mississauga South

Lib.	51.77
Alliance	25.39
P.C.	17.28
N.D.P.	4.10
G.P.	1.29
M.-L.	0.17

Mississauga West

Lib.	63.20
Alliance	21.40
P.C.	10.67
N.D.P.	3.10
G.P.	1.64

Nepean—Carleton

Lib.	41.16
Alliance	37.37
P.C.	15.98
N.D.P.	3.72
G.P.	1.35
Action	0.22
N.L.P.	0.20

Niagara Centre

Lib.	45.74
Alliance	28.14
N.D.P.	14.86
P.C.	10.34
Action	0.61
M.-L.	0.31

Niagara Falls

Lib.	45.92
Alliance	30.77
P.C.	15.58
N.D.P.	6.04
G.P.	1.28
N.L.P.	0.40

Nickel Belt

Lib.	55.57

N.D.P.	21.16
Alliance	18.45
P.C.	4.82

Nipissing

Lib.	57.04
Alliance	22.53
P.C.	12.66
N.D.P.	7.77

Northumberland

Lib.	45.90
Alliance	26.05
P.C.	20.02
N.D.P.	4.89
G.P.	2.52
Action	0.63

Oak Ridges

Lib.	59.41
Alliance	21.05
P.C.	15.11
N.D.P.	2.92
G.P.	1.21
N.L.P.	0.31

Oakville

Lib.	47.74
Alliance	28.02
P.C.	19.84
N.D.P.	2.76
G.P.	1.63

Oshawa

Lib.	42.92
Alliance	28.82
P.C.	15.05
N.D.P.	11.15
M.P.	1.80
M.-L.	0.26

Ottawa Centre

Lib.	40.01
N.D.P.	23.81
Alliance	17.91

P.C.	13.22
G.P.	2.70
M.P.	1.43
Action	0.37
Comm.	0.24
N.L.P.	0.20
M.-L.	0.12

Ottawa—Orléans

Lib.	51.01
Alliance	25.50
P.C.	16.73
N.D.P.	4.15
G.P.	1.07
M.P.	1.02
N.L.P.	0.22
Action	0.21
M.-L.	0.08

Ottawa South

Lib.	51.33
Alliance	24.48
P.C.	15.63
N.D.P.	6.69
M.P.	1.31
N.L.P.	0.27
M.-L.	0.15
Comm.	0.13

Ottawa—Vanier

Lib.	55.56
Alliance	15.79
P.C.	15.37
N.D.P.	8.71
G.P.	2.25
M.P.	1.51
N.L.P.	0.39
Action	0.26
M.-L.	0.15

Ottawa West—Nepean

Lib.	43.32
Alliance	28.27
P.C.	20.13
N.D.P.	5.21

G.P.	1.12
M.P.	0.81
Action	0.72
Ind.	0.17
Comm.	0.13
N.L.P.	0.11

Oxford

Lib.	35.55
P.C.	30.56
Alliance	26.82
N.D.P.	5.28
NIL	1.26
Action	0.53

Parkdale—High Park

Lib.	49.41
N.D.P.	18.99
P.C.	13.58
Alliance	11.67
G.P.	2.77
M.P.	1.85
Action	0.76
Comm.	0.37
NIL	0.32
M.-L.	0.29

Parry Sound—Muskoka

Lib.	47.52
Alliance	25.39
P.C.	18.72
N.D.P.	4.42
G.P.	3.97

Perth—Middlesex

Lib.	40.37
P.C.	27.44
Alliance	23.26
N.D.P.	6.65
G.P.	1.64
NIL	0.34
Action	0.30

Peterborough

Lib.	48.41

Alliance	28.54
P.C.	13.45
N.D.P.	7.59
G.P.	1.73
Ind.	0.28

Pickering—Ajax—Uxbridge

Lib.	57.44
Alliance	23.79
P.C.	13.71
N.D.P.	3.03
G.P.	2.02

Prince Edward—Hastings

Lib.	50.46
Alliance	24.43
P.C.	20.34
N.D.P.	4.77

Renfrew—Nipissing—Pembroke

Alliance	44.18
Lib.	39.00
P.C.	11.32
N.D.P.	3.44
M.P.	1.63
NIL	0.26
N.L.P.	0.17

Sarnia—Lambton

Lib.	50.97
Alliance	29.56
P.C.	8.76
N.D.P.	7.21
G.P.	1.36
NIL	0.94
Ind.	0.50
Action	0.38
N.L.P.	0.24
M.-L.	0.08

Sault Ste. Marie

Lib.	50.79
N.D.P.	24.77
Alliance	18.86
P.C.	3.14

G.P.	2.09
Action	0.34

Scarborough—Agincourt

Lib.	70.89
Alliance	13.40
P.C.	10.59
N.D.P.	3.94
Action	0.90
M.-L.	0.29

Scarborough Centre

Lib.	67.51
Alliance	22.15
N.D.P.	7.94
M.P.	2.40

Scarborough East

Lib.	59.82
Alliance	18.83
P.C.	15.65
N.D.P.	4.69
Action	0.73
M.-L.	0.28

Scarborough—Rouge River

Lib.	79.05
Alliance	8.93
P.C.	7.08
N.D.P.	4.94

Scarborough Southwest

Lib.	60.01
P.C.	14.68
Alliance	13.73
N.D.P.	10.17
Action	0.94
Comm.	0.46

Simcoe—Grey

Lib.	44.77
Alliance	32.46
P.C.	17.44
N.D.P.	3.32
Action	1.51

NIL	0.50

Simcoe North

Lib.	50.76
Alliance	29.58
P.C.	14.32
N.D.P.	4.71
NIL	0.63

St. Catharines

Lib.	44.93
Alliance	33.97
P.C.	13.96
N.D.P.	6.16
N.L.P.	0.43
NIL	0.36
M.-L.	0.20

St. Paul's

Lib.	54.01
P.C.	21.51
Alliance	11.62
N.D.P.	9.48
G.P.	1.64
M.P.	1.09
Action	0.27
M.-L.	0.19
N.L.P.	0.18

Stoney Creek

Lib.	51.08
Alliance	28.25
P.C.	12.91
N.D.P.	6.52
Action	0.95
M.-L.	0.29

Stormont—Dundas—Charlottenburgh

Lib.	46.69
Alliance	39.45
P.C.	8.88
N.D.P.	4.14
N.L.P.	0.52
Action	0.31

Sudbury

Lib.	58.52
Alliance	18.90
N.D.P.	12.60
P.C.	7.62
G.P.	1.45
Action	0.62
Comm.	0.28

Thornhill

Lib.	64.59
Alliance	15.80
P.C.	15.08
N.D.P.	3.93
Action	0.60

Thunder Bay—Atikokan

Lib.	36.98
Alliance	29.29
N.D.P.	19.45
P.C.	11.80
G.P.	2.48

Thunder Bay—Superior North

Lib.	48.12
Alliance	19.82
N.D.P.	19.48
P.C.	8.69
G.P.	2.05
M.P.	1.83

Timiskaming—Cochrane

Lib.	62.40
Alliance	18.78
P.C.	8.37
N.D.P.	7.91
G.P.	2.54

Timmins—James Bay

Lib.	54.22
N.D.P.	31.15
Alliance	11.14
P.C.	3.49

Toronto Centre—Rosedale

Lib.	55.33
P.C.	17.21
N.D.P.	11.19
Alliance	10.68
Action	3.10
M.P.	1.52
N.L.P.	0.47
Comm.	0.26
M.-L.	0.24

Toronto—Danforth

Lib.	51.90
N.D.P.	27.65
P.C.	8.01
Alliance	7.71
G.P.	1.96
M.P.	1.31
Action	0.52
N.L.P.	0.39
Comm.	0.33
M.-L.	0.21

Trinity—Spadina

Lib.	47.56
N.D.P.	37.99
P.C.	5.48
Alliance	5.34
M.P.	1.60
G.P.	1.33
M.-L.	0.24
N.L.P.	0.23
Comm.	0.21

Vaughan—King—Aurora

Lib.	67.22
Alliance	17.17
P.C.	11.53
N.D.P.	3.41
NIL	0.68

Waterloo—Wellington

Lib.	43.66
Alliance	32.93
P.C.	17.80

N.D.P.	4.11
G.P.	0.96
NIL	0.55

Whitby—Ajax

Lib.	52.68
Alliance	26.98
P.C.	15.51
N.D.P.	4.84

Willowdale

Lib.	61.27
Alliance	16.79
P.C.	16.17
N.D.P.	5.45
M.-L.	0.33

Windsor—St. Clair

N.D.P.	40.84
Lib.	39.87
Alliance	13.55
P.C.	4.58
G.P.	0.94
M.-L.	0.23

Windsor West

Lib.	54.21
Alliance	22.96
N.D.P.	15.90
P.C.	5.53
Ind.	0.80
M.-L.	0.60

York Centre

Lib.	71.09
Alliance	13.24
P.C.	7.22
N.D.P.	6.05
G.P.	1.53
Comm.	0.47
M.-L.	0.41

York North

Lib.	46.50
Alliance	24.59

P.C.	24.39
N.D.P.	3.48
NIL	1.04

York South—Weston

Lib.	45.60
NIL	41.29
Alliance	5.05
N.D.P.	3.71
P.C.	2.84
G.P.	0.84
Comm.	0.37
M.-L.	0.29

York West

Lib.	77.28
Alliance	10.69
N.D.P.	9.25
M.P.	2.11
M.-L.	0.68

MANITOBA

Brandon—Souris

P.C.	37.41
Alliance	31.87
Lib.	17.86
N.D.P.	12.33
Comm.	0.28
NIL	0.26

Charleswood St. James—Assiniboia

Lib.	36.21
Alliance	30.14
P.C.	26.03
N.D.P.	7.26
Comm.	0.36

Churchill

N.D.P.	44.94
Lib.	32.23
Alliance	17.70
P.C.	5.14

Dauphin—Swan River

Alliance	47.66
Lib.	21.32
N.D.P.	17.47
P.C.	11.86
Action	1.12
NIL	0.57

Portage—Lisgar

Alliance	50.31
Lib.	17.82
P.C.	15.51
Ind.	10.34
N.D.P.	6.02

Provencher

Alliance	52.76
Lib.	35.62
P.C.	6.73
N.D.P.	4.89

Saint Boniface

Lib.	52.17
Alliance	23.18
N.D.P.	13.00
P.C.	11.65

Selkirk—Interlake

Alliance	43.82
Lib.	23.59
N.D.P.	19.91
P.C.	12.25
NIL	0.44

Winnipeg Centre

N.D.P.	41.26
Lib.	34.11
Alliance	14.56
P.C.	7.02
G.P.	2.56
Comm.	0.49

Winnipeg North Centre

N.D.P.	58.39
Lib.	27.47

P.C.   12.00
Comm.   2.14

Winnipeg North—St. Paul
Lib.   38.78
Alliance   30.40
N.D.P.   21.13
P.C.   7.88
G.P.   0.62
Action   0.55
NIL   0.34
Comm.   0.29

Winnipeg South
Lib.   50.94
Alliance   30.04
N.D.P.   10.04
P.C.   8.55
Ind.   0.43

Winnipeg South Centre
Lib.   40.46
P.C.   28.36
N.D.P.   19.93
Alliance   8.53
M.P.   1.70
Action   0.54
Comm.   0.48

Winnipeg—Transcona
N.D.P.   47.85
Alliance   25.44
Lib.   18.43
P.C.   6.51
G.P.   0.70
NIL   0.45
Ind.   0.36
Comm.   0.27

SASKATCHEWAN

Battlefords—Lloydminster
Alliance   60.23
N.D.P.   17.39

Lib.   17.36
P.C.   5.02

Blackstrap
Alliance   44.24
N.D.P.   26.36
Lib.   22.65
P.C.   5.32
G.P.   1.43

Churchill River
Lib.   41.81
Alliance   32.57
N.D.P.   21.81
P.C.   3.20
Action   0.61

Cypress Hills—Grasslands
Alliance   61.65
N.D.P.   16.91
Lib.   12.57
P.C.   8.87

Palliser
N.D.P.   38.16
Alliance   37.50
Lib.   20.41
P.C.   3.92

Prince Albert
Alliance   45.59
Lib.   20.77
N.D.P.   20.53
P.C.   12.13
G.P.   0.97

Regina—Lumsden—Lake Centre
Alliance   42.94
N.D.P.   42.40
Lib.   14.66

Regina—Qu'Appelle
N.D.P.   41.30
Alliance   40.72
Lib.   17.98

Saskatoon—Humboldt

Alliance	44.28
N.D.P.	26.43
Lib.	21.72
P.C.	5.51
G.P.	1.37
Action	0.69

Saskatoon—Rosetown—Biggar

Alliance	41.66
N.D.P.	41.41
Lib.	11.27
P.C.	5.66

Saskatoon—Wanuskewin

Alliance	52.57
N.D.P.	24.23
Lib.	16.82
P.C.	5.16
G.P.	1.21

Souris—Moose Mountain

Alliance	63.28
N.D.P.	15.61
Lib.	14.35
P.C.	6.76

Wascana

Lib.	41.19
Alliance	36.12
N.D.P.	21.53
Action	1.16

Yorkton—Melville

Alliance	62.98
Lib.	16.24
N.D.P.	15.78
P.C.	4.99

ALBERTA

Athabasca

Alliance	54.46
Lib.	28.40

P.C.	12.25
N.D.P.	2.53
M.P.	1.36
G.P.	1.00

Calgary Centre

P.C.	46.05
Alliance	38.53
Lib.	9.84
N.D.P.	2.80
G.P .	2.04
Ind.	0.51
M.-L.	0.23

Calgary East

Alliance	54.26
Lib.	20.47
P.C.	16.48
N.D.P.	4.32
M.P.	3.65
Comm.	0.45
N.L.P.	0.37

Calgary Northeast

Alliance	62.54
Lib.	21.79
P.C.	11.56
N.D.P.	4.10

Calgary—Nose Hill

Alliance	60.13
Lib.	19.43
P.C.	14.56
N.D.P.	3.73
G.P.	1.83
Action	0.32

Calgary Southeast

Alliance	63.25
P.C.	20.82
Lib.	12.19
N.D.P.	2.04
G.P .	1.71

Calgary Southwest

Alliance	64.81
P.C.	16.29
Lib.	14.93
N.D.P.	3.97

Calgary West

Alliance	54.05
P.C.	21.57
Lib.	18.19
N.D.P.	3.82
G.P.	2.37

Crowfoot

Alliance	70.56
P.C.	14.16
Lib.	6.19
NIL	5.57
N.D.P.	3.04
NIL	0.47

Edmonton Centre-East

Alliance	42.44
Lib.	34.21
N.D.P.	17.44
P.C.	5.38
Comm.	0.53

Edmonton North

Alliance	51.22
Lib.	34.33
N.D.P.	7.47
P.C.	6.99

Edmonton Southeast

Lib.	50.87
Alliance	39.51
P.C.	5.47
N.D.P.	3.10
N.L.P.	0.45
Action	0.37
Comm.	0.23

Edmonton Southwest

Alliance	48.85

Lib.	33.98
P.C.	10.82
N.D.P.	5.12
G.P.	0.86
N.L.P.	0.36

Edmonton—Strathcona

Alliance	42.00
Lib.	31.89
N.D.P.	14.78
P.C.	9.04
M.P.	1.46
Action	0.54
M.-L.	0.29

Edmonton West

Lib.	44.24
Alliance	42.77
P.C.	6.06
N.D.P.	5.83
Action	0.71
M.-L.	0.39

Elk Island

Alliance	64.23
Lib.	17.69
P.C.	11.76
N.D.P.	6.31

Lakeland

Alliance	65.45
Lib.	20.18
P.C.	9.75
N.D.P.	4.61

Lethbridge

Alliance	66.02
Lib.	16.94
P.C.	8.83
N.D.P.	5.75
G.P.	1.88
Action	0.57

Macleod

Alliance	70.05

P.C.	13.83
Lib.	9.41
N.D.P.	6.70

Medicine Hat

Alliance	74.28
Lib.	10.48
P.C.	10.11
N.D.P.	5.14

Peace River

Alliance	65.59
Lib.	15.49
P.C.	11.97
N.D.P.	6.95

Red Deer

Alliance	72.61
Lib.	12.82
P.C.	9.95
N.D.P.	4.61

St. Albert

Alliance	59.50
Lib.	24.78
P.C.	10.33
N.D.P.	5.39

Wetaskiwin

Alliance	69.50
Lib.	17.17
P.C.	9.11
N.D.P.	4.22

Wild Rose

Alliance	70.36
P.C.	12.90
Lib.	11.09
N.D.P.	4.06
Ind.	1.59

Yellowhead

Alliance	66.08
Lib.	15.64
P.C.	12.66

N.D.P.	4.71
NIL	0.91

BRITISH COLUMBIA

Burnaby—Douglas

N.D.P.	37.39
Alliance	33.08
Lib.	23.67
P.C.	5.44
Comm.	0.42

Cariboo—Chilcotin

Alliance	59.63
Lib.	20.34
N.D.P.	9.05
P.C.	8.76
Ind.	1.83
M.-L.	0.38

Delta—South Richmond

Alliance	56.79
Lib.	29.16
P.C.	7.06
N.D.P.	5.63
Action	0.95
NIL	0.41

Dewdney—Alouette

Alliance	58.42
Lib.	18.07
P.C.	12.03
N.D.P.	11.47

Esquimalt—Juan de Fuca

Alliance	49.73
Lib.	23.92
N.D.P.	13.41
P.C.	8.00
G.P.	4.26
N.L.P.	0.67

Fraser Valley

Alliance	69.97

Lib.	16.29
N.D.P.	5.79
P.C.	4.23
M.P.	1.47
G.P.	0.96
Action	0.77
NIL	0.39
Comm.	0.13

Kamloops, Thompson and Highland Valleys

Alliance	48.59
N.D.P.	28.03
Lib.	15.63
P.C.	6.63
Action	1.12

Kelowna

Alliance	59.47
Lib.	23.86
P.C.	8.28
N.D.P.	6.28
Action	2.11

Kootenay—Boundary—Okanagan

Alliance	46.70
Lib.	27.36
N.D.P.	9.85
G.P.	6.48
P.C.	5.17
M.P.	2.14
Action	1.84
N.L.P.	0.46

Kootenay—Columbia

Alliance	67.78
Lib.	14.74
N.D.P.	8.71
P.C.	5.72
G.P.	3.06

Langley—Abbotsford

Alliance	70.11
Lib.	17.26
P.C.	7.62

N.D.P.	4.25
NIL	0.76

Nanaimo—Alberni

Alliance	50.45
Lib.	20.70
N.D.P.	14.53
P.C.	10.16
M.P.	2.14
Ind.	1.58
N.L.P.	0.45

Nanaimo—Cowichan

Alliance	46.63
Lib.	21.42
N.D.P.	16.96
P.C.	7.18
Action	2.96
M.P.	2.49
G.P.	2.36

New Westminster—Coquitlam—Burnaby

Alliance	43.97
Lib.	30.97
N.D.P.	15.03
P.C.	7.42
G.P.	2.18
Comm.	0.23
M.-L.	0.20

North Vancouver

Alliance	49.88
Lib.	32.77
P.C.	7.10
N.D.P.	4.93
M.P.	1.80
Action	1.57
Ind.	1.36
Ind.	0.45
M.-L.	0.14

Okanagan—Coquihalla

Alliance	59.37
Lib.	20.46

N.D.P.	8.45
P.C.	6.06
G.P.	2.29
M.P.	1.69
Action	0.95
N.L.P.	0.34
M.-L.	0.20
NIL	0.20

Okanagan—Shuswap

Alliance	61.30
Lib.	20.59
N.D.P.	8.48
P.C.	6.47
Action	1.51
NIL	0.93
Comm.	0.72

Port Moody—Coquitlam—Port Coquitlam

Alliance	49.69
Lib.	29.39
N.D.P.	9.27
P.C.	7.82
G.P.	1.46
M.P.	1.42
Action	0.78
Comm.	0.17

Prince George—Bulkley Valley

Alliance	58.84
Lib.	23.43
P.C.	6.99
N.D.P.	5.80
G.P.	2.27
Action	2.00
NIL	0.43
M.-L.	0.24

Prince George—Peace River

Alliance	69.62
Lib.	15.53
P.C.	6.14
N.D.P.	4.66
G.P.	2.17

Action	1.64
M.-L.	0.23

Richmond

Alliance	44.41
Lib.	42.04
N.D.P.	5.68
P.C.	5.44
G.P.	1.89
N.L.P.	0.35
M.-L.	0.20

Saanich—Gulf Islands

Alliance	43.16
Lib.	32.30
P.C.	10.28
N.D.P.	8.02
G.P.	5.51
N.L.P.	0.37
NIL	0.21
Comm.	0.15

Skeena

Alliance	42.73
Lib.	29.12
N.D.P.	20.96
P.C.	3.22
G.P.	2.30
NIL	1.21
N.L.P.	0.47

South Surrey—White Rock—Langley

Alliance	59.95
Lib.	21.26
P.C.	10.00
N.D.P.	5.66
G.P.	1.76
M.P.	1.17
N.L.P.	0.21

Surrey Central

Alliance	51.61
Lib.	33.78
P.C.	6.82

N.D.P.	5.56
G.P.	2.03
Comm.	0.20

Surrey North

Alliance	56.10
Lib.	28.87
N.D.P.	7.36
P.C.	4.81
G.P.	1.56
NIL	0.80
Comm.	0.49

Vancouver Centre

Lib.	42.30
Alliance	26.15
N.D.P.	12.05
P.C.	11.76
G.P.	3.94
M.P.	1.92
Action	1.28
N.L.P.	0.30
Comm.	0.17
M.-L.	0.13

Vancouver East

N.D.P.	42.28
Lib.	33.74
Alliance	13.92
P.C.	3.62
G.P.	2.45
M.P.	1.82
Action	1.09
NIL	0.49
NIL	0.36
N.L.P.	0.24

Vancouver Island North

Alliance	51.04
Lib.	24.84
N.D.P.	11.71
P.C.	6.16
G.P.	5.20
NIL	0.44
N.L.P.	0.42

M.-L.	0.19

Vancouver Kingsway

Lib.	43.07
Alliance	29.60
N.D.P.	15.82
P.C.	4.82
Action	3.21
G.P.	2.70
Comm.	0.45
M.-L.	0.34

Vancouver Quadra

Lib.	44.84
Alliance	37.50
P.C.	8.28
N.D.P.	5.23
G.P.	2.89
Action	0.79
N.L.P.	0.25
M.-L.	0.22

Vancouver South—Burnaby

Lib.	42.70
Alliance	37.10
N.D.P.	9.28
P.C.	6.39
G.P.	1.56
NIL	1.12
Action	1.04
Ind.	0.38
M.-L.	0.24
N.L.P.	0.20

Victoria

Lib.	42.65
Alliance	29.66
N.D.P.	13.02
P.C.	6.52
G.P.	5.87
M.P.	1.55
N.L.P.	0.25
Ind.	0.18
Comm.	0.17
NIL	0.13

West Vancouver—Sunshine Coast

Alliance	47.97
Lib.	26.60
P.C.	9.38
N.D.P.	6.29
G.P.	4.89
M.P.	3.04
Action	1.83

YUKON TERRITORY

Yukon

Lib.	32.48
N.D.P.	31.95
Alliance	27.68
P.C.	7.50
NIL	0.40

NORTHWEST TERRITORIES

Western Arctic

Lib.	45.60
N.D.P.	26.71
Alliance	17.70
P.C.	9.98

NUNAVUT

Nunavut

Lib.	69.01
N.D.P.	18.27
P.C.	8.20
G.P.	4.52

Contributors

Paul Attallah

Paul Attallah is associate director of the School of Journalism and Communication at Carleton University. He is the author of two books, in French, on communication theory and of numerous other chapters and articles on television and contemporary culture. He is currently president of the Canadian Communication Association and co-editor of a major textbook on communication in Canada.

André Bernard

André Bernard is a longtime member of the Department of Political Science at the University of Quebec in Montreal. He is author of several books on Quebec politics, including *La vie politique au Quebec et au Canada, What Does Quebec Want?* and *Les institutions politiques au Quebec et au Canada.* Professor Bernard is a Fellow of the Royal Society of Canada.

Angela Burton

Angela Burton is the Editor of PoliticsWatch.com — Canada's Political Portal and a communications consultant in Ottawa. She has a Master of Journalism from Carleton University. Her graduate work focused on the impact of the Internet on political communication in Canada.

Stephen Clarkson

Stephen Clarkson has written the chapter on the Liberal Party of Canada for every federal election book since the 1974 election, when the series began. He professes political economy at the University of Toronto where he has long taught a course on Canadian political parties. He is currently finishing a book on the impact of globalization and neoliberalism on the Canadian state.

Christopher Dornan

Christopher Dornan is the director of the School of Journalism and

Communication at Carleton University. His account of the 1993 federal election — "The Rise and Fall of Canada's Kim Campbell: The Media and the Unmaking of a Prime Minister" — appeared in *Media Information Australia*. He contributed the chapter "The Television Coverage: A History of the Election in 65 Seconds" to *The Canadian General Election of 1997*.

Faron Ellis

Faron Ellis teaches political science at Lethbridge Community College, specializing in Canadian government, public opinion, parties, and elections. His research on these topics appears in numerous books, journals, and newspapers, and at www.telusplanet.net/public/fellis.

Edward Greenspon

Edward Greenspon is political editor of *The Globe and Mail*. A graduate of Carleton University and the London School of Economics, he has specialized in his reporting career on business and the economy, European and Soviet bloc affairs, and national Canadian politics.

Mary McGuire

Mary McGuire is an Associate Professor of Journalism at Carleton University who teaches courses in online reporting and broadcast journalism. She is the co-author of *The Internet Handbook for Writers, Researchers and Journalists*.

Michael Marzolini

Michael Marzolini is Chairman and Chief Executive Officer of POLLARA Strategic Public Opinion and Market Research, the largest Canadian-owned market research company. He has served as the Chief Pollster to the Liberal Party of Canada since 1992, and has provided strategic direction to the Liberals in each of their last three majority election victories.

Janice Neil

Janice Neil was Ottawa Bureau Chief for TVOntario, a television and radio journalist before joining the faculty of Journalism and Communication at Carleton University to teach television news and current affairs.